THE AMERICAN FACE OF

Edgar Allan Poe

Edited by Shawn Rosenheim and Stephen Rachman

THE JOHNS HOPKINS UNIVERSITY PRESS   BALTIMORE AND LONDON

© 1995 The Johns Hopkins University Press
All rights reserved. Published 1995
Printed in the United States of America on acid-free paper

04 03 02 01 00 99 98 97 96 95   5 4 3 2 1

The Johns Hopkins University Press
2715 North Charles Street
Baltimore, Maryland 21218-4319
The Johns Hopkins Press Ltd., London

LIBRARY OF CONGRESS CATALOGING-IN-PUBLICATION DATA

The American face of Edgar Allen Poe / edited by Shawn Rosenheim and Stephen
Rachman.

     p.   cm.
  Includes bibliographical references and index.
  ISBN 0-8018-5024-x (cl). — ISBN 0-8018-5025-8 (pbk.)
  1. Poe, Edgar Allan, 1809–1849–Criticism and interpretation.   2. National
characteristics, American, in literature.   3. Literature, Comparative—American
and foreign.   4. Literature, Comparative—Foreign and American.
I. Rosenheim, Shawn.   II. Rachman, Stephen.
PS2638.A55   1995
818'.309—dc20   95-10302

A catalog record for this book is available from the British Library.

Contents

Acknowledgments

This volume has been a long time in coming, and there are many people to thank for that. Be that as it may, we are deeply grateful to those who aided and inspired this project. In particular we would like to single out Michael Bell, Cassandra Cleghorn, Rachel Howe, John Irwin, and John Kleiner. Several institutions have supported us during our labors, including Michigan State University, Williams College, and Yale University. We would also like to extend our thanks to the library staff at those institutions and especially to Jean-Bernard Bucky at the Williams Center for the Humanities and Social Sciences. Finally, this book is dedicated to our teachers Dick Brodhead and Bryan Wolf, who long ago first and fatally stimulated our interest in Edgar Allan Poe.

Stanley Cavell's essay is reprinted from *Reconstructing Individualism: Autonomy, Individuality, and the Self in Western Thought*, edited by Thomas C. Heller, Morton Sosna, and David E. Wellbery (Stanford University Press, 1986). Eva Cherniavsky's selection is drawn from her book *That Pale Mother Rising: Sentimental Discourses and the Imitation of Motherhood in Nineteenth-Century America* (Indiana University Press, 1994). Jonathan Elmer's piece is a shorter version of a chapter in his book *Reading at the Social Limit: Affect, Mass Culture, and Edgar Allan Poe* (Stanford University Press, 1995). John Irwin's essay originally appeared in *Raritan* 10, no. 4 (Spring 1991): 40–57. Barbara Johnson's selection is from her book *A World of Difference* (Johns Hopkins University Press, 1987). All are used here by permission.

Introduction

Beyond "The Problem of Poe"

SHAWN ROSENHEIM AND STEPHEN RACHMAN

Like so many of the faces sketched in his fiction, Edgar Allan Poe's literary profile presents the critic with a mixed physiognomic message, at once stereotypically familiar and strangely shadowed or absent. In Europe, in South and Latin America, and even in Japan, Poe has served as a crucial and much celebrated literary model for generations of writers and readers. In the country of his birth, however, Poe can hardly be said to be at home. The occasional formidable critic like William Carlos Williams could claim that "in him American literature is anchored, in him alone, on solid ground" (Williams 1956, 226), but Poe has far more often been left out of synthetic interpretations of American literary culture. "The problem of Poe, fascinating as it is," wrote Vernon Parrington in 1927, "lies quite outside the main current of American thought" (Parrington 1927, 58). F. O. Matthiessen tacitly concurred; Poe is barely present amid the Mount Rushmore–like profiles of Emerson, Hawthorne, Whitman, Melville, and Thoreau presented in his seminal *American Renaissance* (1941). This critical dismissal of Poe has followed from Poe's own seeming disengagement with American culture, as if Poe and his critics had silently agreed to turn their backs on one another.

Interest in Poe's writing is once more on the rise. But this newfound success is primarily due to his status as a sophisticated émigré, one who speaks a distinctly accented brand of English, and so this recent prominence seems merely to confirm Parrington's claim. Certainly, suspicions about Poe's relation to "the main current of American thought" remain: in a recent article in *American Quarterly* Terence Whalen notes that "to explore the relation between literary production and what has been thought of as production in general" we "must first confront an accumulated mass of Poe lore celebrating the isolation of art from 'external' social pressures." Which naturally leads Whalen to the query: "If Poe isn't in step with his time where is he?" (Whalen 1992, 381–83).

Where indeed? That Poe could appear at once "out of step" with his own day and culture and yet intimately bound to it is evident even from writings of his own period. In his famous *Fable for Critics*, for instance, James Russell Lowell wrote:

> There comes Poe, with his Raven, like Barnaby Rudge,
> Three fifths of him genius and two fifths sheer fudge,
> Who talks like a book of iambs and pentameters,
> In a way to make people of common sense damn metres,
> Who has written some things quite the best of their kind,
> But the heart somehow seems all squeezed out by the mind.
> (Lowell 1898, 141–42)

Like other antithetical characterizations of Poe—as aesthete or hack, votary or pervert, arch-Romantic or cynical parodist—Lowell's couplet suggests the compulsively polarized nature of Poe's writing, which generates antitheses, divides readers, and forces critics into hyperbolic evaluations of his work. "No poet," Shoshana Felman observes, "has been as highly acclaimed and, at the same time, as violently disclaimed as Edgar Allan Poe" (Felman 1988, 133). These bifurcations, which structure Poe's stance toward the self, gender, race, authenticity, mechanical reproduction, commodification, sensation, and "literariness" itself, provide the basis for a reconsideration of Poe that illuminates American writing and culture from the 1840s until today. *The American Face of Edgar Allan Poe* aims first of all to expose and to make sense of the apparent jumble of Poe's cultural physiognomy.

With few exceptions, everyone now writing on Poe is indebted to the work of Jacques Lacan, Jacques Derrida, and other Continental critics, who, by testing or contesting their theories in the crucible of Poe's prose, alchemically transformed his familiar stories and poems into something rich and strange. Many of the essays relevant to this transformation were collected in 1988 in *The Purloined Poe*, an anthology that marked both the consolidation of a certain psychoanalytic approach to reading and the high-water mark of its influence. This theoretical appropriation is only the most recent stage in a French tradition of reading Poe that began with Baudelaire, which is recorded in Patrick Quinn's study *The French Face of Edgar Poe* (1957). Yet despite their extraordinary critical fertility, the essays compiled in *The Purloined Poe* failed to give Poe's writing a local habitation. They failed, that is, to recognize that Poe's most extravagant literary maneuvers were usually based in the specific cultural and political climate of antebellum America. Although dozens of critics still proceed down largely psychoanalytic paths, there is a growing impulse to resist Poe's wholesale assimilation to the realm of psycholinguistic universals, and to restore his writings to the cultural milieu from which they appear to have been wrenched.

Yet although *The American Face of Edgar Allan Poe* is deeply concerned with historical issues, it represents no simple injunction to "historicize!"; nor is it an attempt to reclaim a Poe ostensibly purloined by French theorists. Rather, it is an effort to use Poe as an instrument with which to explore recurring questions in American literary culture. To address the renewed interest in Poe's work and also account for the nature of that interest, we must recognize that, like it or not, the main current of American thought has changed. When the best case for classic American literature was made through discussions of its binding and illusory myths (myths neatly conveyed in the titles of its leading studies, Perry Miller's *Errand into the Wilderness*, R. W. B. Lewis's *American Adam*, Henry Nash Smith's *Virgin Land*, and Matthiessen's *American Renaissance*), then Poe's Gothic, ratiocinative, and hoaxing works did not fit readily into these mythic models. But for some time now, other models of American culture have been advanced that downplay the common myths of our literature in favor of its varied rhetorics, its competing modes of articulation and representation.

This collection of essays, then, neither embraces nor disavows what scholarship has most commonly made of Poe. It remains easy enough to imagine how Poe's work has come to represent "timeless" psychoanalytic themes. In what century has the "Imp of the Perverse" held no sway? In what epoch has the heart failed to tell its tale? When have our purloined letters not failed to arrive at their phallogocentric destinations? Yet if one thinks of other tales, such as "The Mystery of Marie Rogêt" or "The Man That Was Used Up," the cultural side of Poe's writing becomes more conspicuous. Walter Benjamin's famous essay on "The *Flâneur*," one remembers, contains several pages on "The Man of the Crowd"; by virtue of this tale alone, Poe has insinuated himself into places one would not expect—an influential anthology of essays on American realism, another on ideology in American literature; even, obliquely, into an essay on Dreiser.[1] Robert Byer and Dana Brand have also produced stimulating discussions by using "The Man of the Crowd" to launch more extensive social analyses of antebellum culture.

This second group of sociologically inclined stories stands in evident tension with the critical tradition granting Poe's work almost complete autonomy from any social mooring. Anyone who would locate Poe's writing within a cultural context must confront the way his work tends to advertise itself as ethereal and otherworldly, or avowedly timeless, or preoccupied with aesthetic, cognitive, and linguistic categories or psychopathological conditions. Yet as Lowell's ditty points out, an author can be fairly representative of an era and also choose to write in such a willfully abstract mode that it makes people of common sense damn metres. Romanticism was, after all, the ethos in which Poe's writings declared their otherworldliness, and to see Poe's creative output as timeless is also to see it as being in step with his time. As Raymond Williams long ago pointed out, the Romantic tradition sought to distinguish literary culture, or "culture as art," from society, or "culture as a whole way of life" (Williams 1958, 30, 48); when critics assert the isolation of Poe's art from social pressures they are often doing little more than reiterating Poe's own aesthetic credo.

Poe, Charles Baudelaire noted in a letter to Sainte-Beuve, "is American only insofar as he is a *charlatan*" (Baudelaire 1972, 84). Though Baudelaire meant his comment to distinguish Poe from the vulgarity of a commercial American culture, Poe carried his charlatanism to such a pitch that it becomes hard to separate it from his literary force and originality; hard, that is, to tell his "genius" from his "fudge." Far from being a mere witticism, then, Lowell's cartoon of Poe offers a useful insight into a literary identity and career shaped by the pressures of a nascent mass culture. Many of the essays gathered here focus on the literary valence of Poe's charlatanism: on his phony claims to aristocratic erudition and leisure, on the self-suborning voices of his narrators, on his manipulative invention of his own biography, or on his self-appointed place in American letters. The effect of such hoaxes is not merely to create the kind of undecidability favored by teachers of freshman English, but to vex the categories by which we claim to know something about literature, the world, and the difference between them. For Stanley Cavell, Poe's unnerving first-person narrations trouble the constitutive suppositions of analytical philosophy to such a degree that they provide one of the founding voices of American skepticism. For Stephen Rachman, Poe's plagiarism needs to be understood as a form of Promethean self-creation that radically transfigures antebellum assumptions about the propriety—both legal and social—of any authorial claim to originality. For many of the authors collected here, it is precisely Poe's syncopated relation to American culture, at once both in and out of step, that gives his writing its unique power to clarify the American tradition. As these essays show, Poe's work invites the reader into a dialectical process of identification and differentiation that is one of his fundamental accomplishments.

The American Face of Edgar Allan Poe is divided into four sections: "Literary Relations," "Generic Logic," "Imagining Gender," and "Reading Culture," and in a general sense the book moves from a consideration of Poe in primarily literary terms to an evaluation of his broader imbrication in political, social, and economic contexts. As the reader will soon realize, however, Poe's writing blurs many of the boundaries that separate literary from cultural issues. These categories interpenetrate, forming dynamic and unstable connections that express many of the crucial themes of Poe's culture: the paranoiac mind-set of Jacksonian political culture; the reciprocal construction of white femininity and black masculinity; and the highly gendered and class-specific social functions of Poe's genres. Poe's construction of gender, for instance, sheds light not only on his essentialist notions of race, but on his literary pose as a southern aristocrat in a burgeoning industrial culture, and on the way in which the "mysteries" of the detective story are predicated on the previous occultation of the female body and voice.

We begin this collection with "Literary Relations" as a way of worrying the question of Poe's proper literary affiliations. Stanley Cavell confronts head-on the Anglo-American disregard for the intellectual claims of Poe's writing, and Barbara Johnson uses "The Philosophy of Composition" as an antidote to the sorts of highly expressive theories of poetic composition epitomized by Wordsworth's "Preface to *Lyrical Ballads*." In "Being Odd, Getting Even (Descartes, Emerson, Poe)," Cavell argues that "Poe's peculiar brilliance is to have discovered a sound, or the condition, of intelligence in which neither the reader nor the writer knows whether he or she is philosophizing, is thinking to some end." Through comparison of thematically and tonally related first-person passages by the three writers named in his title, Cavell suggests the difficulty of distinguishing with any certainty the literary from the philosophical. "The sound of Poe's prose, of its incessant and perverse brilliance," Cavell explains, "is uncannily like the sound of philosophy as established in Descartes, as if Poe's prose were a parody of philosophy's"—a parody that leads Cavell to the remarkable claim that in their writing Poe and Emerson seem "to be discovering or rediscovering the origin of modern philosophy, as sketched in Descartes's *Meditations*, as if literature in America were forgiving philosophy, not without punishing it, for having thought that it could live only in the banishing of literature."

For Barbara Johnson, the reiterative construction of "The Raven" points to something automatic, even robotic, at the very origin of poetic language. In "Strange Fits: Poe and Wordsworth on the Nature of Poetic Language," Johnson argues that their symmetrically inverse stories about the nature of poetic language complicate both Wordsworth's valorization of spontaneity and Poe's formalist account of poetic composition. Despite Wordsworth's attempt to prevent the poetic figure from losing its natural passion, from repeating itself as an empty stylistic device, the formula for recollection in tranquillity involves just such blind repetition of the lost language. Poe writes a poem packed with clichés in order to show that those clichés cannot succeed in remaining empty, that there is also a natural passion involved in repetition, that the mechanical is of a piece with profound feeling. Yet the poem's very success in embodying its message entails its failure to make it true; according to Johnson, this confirms "The Raven" as a metaphor for the nature of all poetic language.

Finally, in " 'Es Lässt Sich Nicht Schreiben': Plagiarism and 'The Man of the Crowd,' " Stephen Rachman identifies plagiarism as a key site for Poe's authorial identity-formation, through which he attempts "to unravel the problematics of originality and authority." Written into Poe's tales "in a deflected or tacit (but not unconscious) manner," plagiarism forms part of a theory of authorship in which true "originality" is determined not by temporal priority but by the theatrical literary and critical uses to which the plagiarized elements are put in new texts. Further, Poe's mania with plagiarized style concisely frames the paradox of artists who, to survive, must mass-market their style, the precise quality that makes them unique. By scrutinizing the way "The Man of the Crowd" is itself plagiarized from Dickens's *Sketches by Boz*, Rachman's essay presents Poe's obsession with plagiarism—with unearthing it in others, and with practicing it himself—as part of a strategic response to the problematic status of writers in antebellum culture.

The next section, "Generic Logic," considers Poe's complicated innovations in detective and horror fiction. Jonathan Elmer's "Terminate or Liquidate? Poe, Sensationalism, and the Sentimental Tradition" analyzes the social function of Poe's mesmeric tales in the context of a culture devoted to sentimental novels. Elmer reads death scenes in "Mesmeric Revelation" and "The Facts in the Case of M. Valdemar"—moments of corporal deliquescence in all their contaminating, unbounded fluidity—against the sentimental liquefaction into tears produced by Little Eva's demise in *Uncle Tom's Cabin*. Noting that the reader's social identity depends on the spectacle of the death of a more or less innocent protagonist, Elmer argues for the obligatory reappropriation of that death by the didactic discourse of the novel. Although the reader must "melt with sympathy" at the hero's death, he or she must thereafter sublimate this "passion" into the properly discursive realms of justice. By exploring the relation between sensation and sentiment, Elmer delineates the "viral" relation between Poe's particular vein of Gothic fictions and the broader sentimental literary culture in which they take place.

As a companion to "Terminate or Liquidate?" Eva Cherniavsky's "Revivification and Utopian Time: Poe versus Stowe" explores Lady Ligeia's relation to sentimental authority figured in Stowe's slave Cassy. For Cherniavsky, however, haunting rather than deliquescence is the operative term, specifically the way maternal authority haunts the masculine symbolic order. Where Elmer sees the Gothic as viral imitation of the sentimental, Cherniavsky explores how the sentimental exacts its revenge on the Gothic in its revenant and ghostly mothers. Identifying both Poe's Ligeia and Stowe's Cassy as versions of the sentimental mother, Cherniavsky contends that such mothers serve as a focus for antebellum discourse on the nature of the subject and the social order. But while Ligeia represents Poe's flirtation with the termination of the masculine subjectivity on which bourgeois patriarchy depends, Cassy, masquerading as the injured white mother's "authentic ghost," effects an irrecoverable disruption of masculine authority. Taken together, the essays delineate as never before the intimate relations between Poe's Gothic fictions and the sentimental writing from which they are traditionally dissociated.

Detective fiction is the generic terrain of John T. Irwin's "A Clew to a Clue: Locked Rooms and Labyrinths in Poe and Borges" and Shawn Rosenheim's "Detective Fiction, Psychoanalysis, and the Analytic Sublime." Describing Borges's three detective stories—"The Garden of the Forking Paths," "Death and the Compass," and "Ibn Hakkan al-Bokhari, Dead in His Labyrinth"—as antithetical doubles of Poe's three detective tales, in "A Clew to a Clue," John Irwin argues that Borges's rewriting of the Dupin stories registers not only the resemblance between the mystery of the locked room and the puzzle of the labyrinth, but also the resemblance between these two structures and the purloined letter. Pitting the logic of the locked-room mystery against the logic of the labyrinthine mystery, Irwin describes how the genre's alpha and omega, laid out by Poe, are reimagined by Borges. Through Borges, Irwin helps us see how "The Purloined Letter" engages the logical limits of detective fiction, deploying both the inevitable traces of entrance or exit in the locked-room mystery and the likely possibility of entrance without exit in the labyrinth. The peculiar force of hidden-object and locked-room detective stories is that they seem to present us with a physical embodiment, a concrete spatialization, of the very mechanism of logical inclusion/exclusion on which rational analysis is based, while apparently confounding just that analysis. By following a line that relates locked rooms, labyrinths, and clues, Irwin traces the concept of the clue back to the "clew," Ariadne's ball of thread with which Theseus escapes the labyrinth, articulating a figurative logic of the detective story.

Returning to that primal scene of detection, the bedchamber of the Mesdames L'Espanaye, Rosenheim uses cryptography and the distinctive pressures of "analysis" as master tropes for the linguistic logic germane to Freud's "Wolf Man," Lacan's *Écrits*, and Poe's "Murders in the Rue Morgue," illuminating the generic territory held in common by Dupin's analytic method and Freud's own "detective fiction" in the case histories. "If detective fiction is notoriously susceptible to psychoanalytic interpretation," Rosenheim explains, "this is only because psychoanalysis, too, has often seemed to presume the separation of its analytical procedures from the materiality of its objects—a separation between language and the body that 'Rue Morgue' both constructs and, finally, destroys." The process of deciphering the clues and symptoms associated with the crime or trauma entangles the analyst's (or reader's) own body in a series of somatic responses that offer unexpected proof of Poe's claim that analysis may be best known only by its effects.

There is probably no better example of the mixture of cultural abstraction and specificity than the problem of gender in Poe's psychic economy. "Imagining Gender" affords the opportunity to redress this long-neglected but troubling question. Because Poe's representations of women are so patently obsessive and repetitive, they have availed themselves of psychoanalytic interpretation to the point of obscuring their cultural valences. In "Amorous Bondage: Poe, Ladies, and Slaves," Joan Dayan meditates on the spectralization of Poe: what must be excluded from the legend to make him a proper icon for those who "serve" him. Dayan engages these issues through the lens of her own experience—a talk she gave before the Poe Society in Baltimore in 1989. In the preservationist atmosphere of the Poe Society, Dayan felt a hint of the cultural forces that seek to preserve the "idealized" gender relations of Poe's "ladies." "It is perhaps not surprising," Dayan writes, "that some Poe critics—the founding fathers of the Poe Society, for example—sound rather like the proslavery ideologues who promoted the ideals of the lady, elegant, white, and delicate. Poe's ladies, those dream-dimmed, ethereal living dead of his poems, have been taken straight as exemplars of what Poe called 'supernal Beauty'—an entitlement that he would degrade again and again." Since Allen Tate's "Our Cousin, Mr. Poe," critics have sought to put Poe's legacy in the South into proper context, but "Amorous Bondage" articulates a crucial distinction between what Poe does to his ladies and what a particular "southern" element of Poe's legacy, an element different from Tate's ironic voice, does to Poe's ladies. It is more like the transformation of Poe that occurred when Poe's first great southern imitator, Dr. Thomas Holly Chivers, created "Eulalie" out of "The Raven," unambiguously rendering the grotesque and arabesque elements of Poe's ladies as conventional aspects of supernal, lily-white, "southern" beauty; or the mentality Katherine Anne Porter represents in "Old Mortality" when, in a discussion of southern womanhood, her narrator's father refers to Poe as "our finest poet," where the pronoun means "southern" (Porter 1964, 12). By powerfully contextualizing these abstractions of femininity, Dayan suggests how "Poe's 'ladies,' once returned to their home in the South, urge us to think about the way rituals of purity depend on reminders of dirt."

Alongside "Amorous Bondage," David Leverenz's "Poe and Gentry Virginia" offers a thick description of Poe's manipulation of the real and fictional aspects of "the cult of true manhood" known as the southern gentleman. "For Poe and the gentry," Leverenz explains, "aristocracy signifies an idealized realm dislocated from specific social contexts . . . used to elevate high culture above history. If the romance of the gentleman displaces a yearning for high metropolitan status, its theatricality signals self-consciousness about social conventions that were beginning to seem more alien than natural." In his baroque, almost Elizabethan narrations, Poe inflates and deforms the fiction that helped empower the Virginia gentry: an ideology of rationality, theatrical display, honor, and shame, within which a shameless trickster apes and empties out its meanings. "Poe and Gentry Virginia" complements Joan Dayan's piece by helping clarify how the peculiar quality of Poe's hoaxing (that is, his fudge) is not only a token of his American birth, but an even more direct response to the gentry ideals of the Old Dominion. We recognize in his argument another facet of the process by which Poe's fictions simultaneously attempt to abstract themselves from and allude to the particulars of their cultural moment.

Laura Saltz's "'(Horrible to Relate!)': Recovering the Body of Marie Rogêt" resonates not only with Dayan's and Leverenz's work but with the essays in the "Generic Logic" section as well. For Saltz, the feminine body is a precondition of Poe's detective fictions, and yet—decentered, uninte-grated, and resistant to essentialist definition as it is—it remains the site of constant cultural and literary aporia. Saltz carefully explores how "The Mystery of Marie Rogêt" displaces the actual death of Mary Rogers, the beautiful New York "segar girl," who likely died under the knife of an abortionist. As Saltz explains, the text both is and is not about Marie: "The effacement of Marie's abortion signals Poe's need to contain and obscure questions about the public visibility of women and their participation in a market economy. . . . Oscillating between the suppression of Marie's abor-tion and the contemplation of his own authorship, Poe's story never quite comes to life. Marie remains a blank slate, inscribed by Poe with the contra-dictory plots of an antebellum woman in public." The detective narrative's solution/resolution becomes an insoluble question of reading the femi-nine—a project that involves the relations between displaced woman's bod-ies (found in the chimney, in the Seine, in somebody else's bed) and their replacement by, and in, male-generated texts, including newspaper stories, advertisements, and finally Poe's stories themselves. Saltz's essay explains hitherto unresolved aspects of Poe's ratiocination in terms of reimagining the feminine, especially as elements of antebellum culture sought to reduce the visibility of women in urban environments. In recovering the body of Marie Rogêt, Saltz also recovers Poe's attempts to realize textual autonomy by disguising or transforming just that evidence which most marks his writing as a product of its time.

The fourth section, "Reading Culture," most directly addresses Poe's con-frontation with his time, by locating the places where Poe can be seen most clearly stepping in and out of the main currents of American thought. Not surprisingly, one finds that determining Poe's place in American literary history first requires careful analysis of what it is we mean by "the literary." Poe's claims for the supremacy of his art were not only part and parcel of Romantic ideology, but often served his bread-and-butter interests in quite direct ways. As Meredith L. McGill observes in "Poe, Literary Nationalism, and Authorial Identity," when Poe moved to New York in 1843, his fierce critical judgments and oft-proclaimed independence from coteries made him seem just the man to advance the Young American cause of literary nationalism. As a result of the Young Americans' support, and of Lowell's biographical essay "Edgar Allan Poe," the period from March 1843 to late 1845 (climaxing in the debacle at the Boston Athenaeum) came to represent "a significant consolidation of Poe's identity as an author, and a milestone in the popularization of this identity." But such popularity was purchased at a price, for Poe's autonomy—the very quality for which Duyckinck and others valued him—was "jeopardized when the literary nationalists embraced *his* principles, invoking him as an idealized figure of independent judgment within their discourse. Poe did not abandon his critical ideals so much as he lost control over them as they were translated into the literary nationalist idiom." The process of mythifying Poe's autonomy undid that very independence, as, ironically enough, Poe's essentially commercial negotiations with literary nationalism led to "a crucial chapter in the history of the production of Poe as a subject who stands outside history."

For Louis A. Renza, on the other hand, Poe's political allegories and polemics themselves conceal a deeper fantasy of the absolutely private moment of literary creation. In "'Ut Pictura Poe': Literary Politics in 'The Island of the Fay' and 'Morning on the Wissahiccon,'" Renza argues that Poe's little-known "Plate" fantasies both encode and expose the ideological shibboleth about American exceptionalism as justified by an idealized or "picturesque" notion of American nature. At the same time, both pieces also suspend their apparent critical judgments about this (ideologically motivated) notion, expressing Poe's own writerly displacement of it. "It is as if," Renza writes,

Poe's text continues to wish itself free from its unavoidable sociopolitical—or indeed any of its possible public—appropriations or readings, so that these remain "in the vicinity," but do not determine his text's identity. In fact, both plate articles constitute perverse autobiographical revisions of their otherwise politically codifiable meanings. Poe ultimately uses the political codifications of his articles as pretexts for disclosing his own "intangible" autobiographical scene of writing: his reimagined spatial and temporal origins as a writer that occurred, as it were, before producing an "American literature" became for him subject to political or literary-political determinations.

Finally, in "The Poetics of Extinction" Gillian Brown reads the anticipatory mode of Poe's tales of terror as a peculiar nineteenth-century version of the *ars longa*. This same structure of obsessive acceleration and prefabrication of an inevitable fate can be traced in a reverse pattern in the tales of detection, where the processes through which the criminal plots have come about are revealed and recapitulated. Brown reads Poe's aesthetic project of matching anticipation with event—of inventing or experiencing a phenomenon before its natural eventuality—in light of a similar anticipatory impulse in nineteenth-century popular science: Lamarck's hypothesis of spontaneous generation. Both Poe and Lamarck participate in the enterprise of preempting natural progression by fashioning prefigurements of it. Reading Poe in the context of Lamarck roots Poe's abstractions of horror and detection in a popular concern with asserting control over developments and modes of growth that appeared increasingly impervious to human will, and reveals "the terror of demise" in such texts as "The Fall of the House of Usher" as a strategy for "the perpetuation of consciousness. There is no ultimate extinction in Poe's tale, for the aesthetics of terror preserve and transmit signs of intelligence."

The essays gathered here suggest that many of the most celebrated, even postmodern features of Poe's writing—its generic instability, concern with simulation and pastiche, and fictive self-exposure—emerge from Poe's attempts to think through the mediating institutions of antebellum literature. In their individual arguments, but even more through their mutual amplification, the essays in *The American Face of Edgar Allan Poe* offer new insights into the complex and unavoidable relations between traditionally literary issues and broader aspects of a democratic mass culture. Instead of continuing to see Poe's contradictions as a problem, we can now face up to their constitutive role within his *oeuvre*. Poe's influence remains vast because many of the cultural vexations that animate his texts have become the full-blown preoccupations of our culture and our writing. His literary dilemmas, his irresolutions, speak to our own. Because he was always both in and out of his time, Poe can now stand, Janus-faced, in—and out—of ours as well.

NOTE

1. Benjamin 1973, 48–55; Trachtenberg 1974; Byer 1986, 221–46; Fisher 1985, 164.

PART ONE

LITERARY RELATIONS

Being Odd, Getting Even

(Descartes, Emerson, Poe)

STANLEY CAVELL

In the lobby of William James Hall at Harvard, across the story-tall expanse of concrete above the bank of elevators facing you as you enter, brass letters spell out the following pair of sentences, attributed by further such letters to William James:

THE COMMUNITY STAGNATES WITHOUT THE IMPULSE
OF THE INDIVIDUAL
THE IMPULSE DIES AWAY WITHOUT THE SYMPATHY
OF THE COMMUNITY

The message may be taken as empirically directed to whoever stands beneath and reads it, and thence either as a warning, or an exhortation, or a description of a state of current affairs—or else it may be taken as claiming a transcendental relation among the concepts of community and individual as they have so far shown themselves. Does this multiplicity produce what certain literary theorists now speak of as the undecidable? Or is the brass indifference of this writing on the wall an apt expression of our avoidance of decision, a refusal to apply our words to ourselves, to take them on?

This essay is a kind of progress report on my philosophical journey to locate an inheritance of Wittgenstein and Heidegger, and of Emerson and Thoreau before them, for all of whom there seems to be some question whether the individual or the community as yet, or any longer, exists. This question (or, you may say, this fantasy) gives ground equally for despair and for hope in the human as it now stands. It is also the question or fantasy in which I have been seeking instruction from certain Hollywood comedies of remarriage and, before them, from Shakespearean romance and tragedy. In this mood I do not wish to propose a solution to the riddle of whether society is the bane or the blessing of the individual, or to offer advice about whether a better state of the world must begin with a reformation of institutions and individuals and their modes of interpenetration. So I will pick up the twist in the story of the discovery of the individual where Descartes placed it in his *Meditations*—before, so to speak, either individual or institutional differences come into play. This twist is Descartes's discovery that my existence requires, hence permits, proof (you might say authentication)—more particularly, requires that if I am to exist I must name my existence, acknowledge it. This imperative entails that I am a thing with two focuses, or in Emerson's image, two magnetic poles—say a positive and a negative, or an active and a passive.

Such a depiction may not seem to you right off to capture Descartes's cogito argument. But that something like it does capture that argument is what I understand the drift of Emerson's perhaps inaudibly familiar words in "Self-Reliance" to claim. My first task here will be to establish this about Emerson's essay; my second will be to say why I think Emerson is right, as right in his interpretation and inheritance of Descartes as any other philosophical descendant I know of. Following that, as a third principal task, I will take up a pair of tales by Edgar Allan Poe, primarily "The Imp of the Perverse" and subordinately "The Black Cat." These stories, I find, engage with the same imperative of human existence: that it must prove or declare itself. And since Poe's "The Imp of the Perverse" alludes more than once to *Hamlet*, it will bring us to my title, the idea of thinking about individuality (or the loss of it) under the spell of revenge, of getting even for oddness.

Emerson's incorporation of Descartes into "Self-Reliance" is anything but veiled. At the center of the essay is a paragraph that begins: "Man is timid and apologetic; he is no longer upright; he dares not say 'I think,' 'I am,' but quotes some saint or sage" (Emerson 1960, 157). It is my impression that readers of Emerson have not been impressed by this allusion, or repetition, perhaps because they have fallen into an old habit of condescending to Emerson (as if to pay for a love of his writing by conceding that he was hardly capable of consecutive thought, let alone capable of taking on Descartes), perhaps because they remember or assume the cogito always to be expressed in words that translate as "I think, *therefore* I am." But in Descartes's Second Meditation, where I suppose it is most often actually encountered, the insight is expressed: "*I am, I exist,* is necessarily true every time that I pronounce it or conceive it in my mind" (Descartes 1958, 183). Emerson's emphasis on the *saying* of "I" is precisely faithful to this expression of Descartes's insight.

It is this feature of the cogito that is emphasized in some of the most productive thinking about Descartes in recent analytical philosophy, where the issue, associated with the names of Jaakko Hintikka and Bernard Williams, is phrased as the question whether the certainty of existence required and claimed by the cogito results from taking the claim "I think" as the basis (i.e., premise) for an inference, or as the expression of some kind of performance. Williams does not quite rest with saying, with Hintikka, that the cogito just is not an inference, and just is a performance of some kind, but Williams does insist that it is not an ordinary, or syllogistic, inference, as he insists, at the end of his intricate discussion, that the performance in play is no less peculiar of its kind, demanding further reflection. The cogito's peculiarity can be summarized as follows, according to Williams. On the one hand, the force of the first person pronoun is that it cannot fail to refer to the one using it, hence one who says "I exist" must exist; or, put negatively, "I exist" is undeniable, which is to say, "I do not exist" cannot coherently be said. On the other hand, to be said sensibly, "I" must distinguish the one saying it, to whom it cannot fail to refer, from others to whom it does not, at that saying, refer. But Descartes's use of it arises exactly in a context in which there are no others to distinguish himself (so to speak) from. So the force of the pronoun is in apparent conflict with its sense.

Compared to such considerations, Emerson's remark about our not daring to say "I think," "I am," seems somewhat literary. But why? Emerson is picking up a question, or a side of the question, that succeeds the inferential or performance aspect of the cogito—namely, the question of what happens if I do *not* say (and of course do not say the negation of) "I am, I exist" or "conceive it in my mind." An analytical philosopher will hardly take much interest in this side of the question, since it will hardly seem worth arguing for or against the inference that if I do not say or perform the words "I am" or their equivalent (aloud or silently), therefore I perhaps do not exist. Surely the saying or thinking of some words may be taken to bear on whether the sayer or thinker of them exists at most in the sense of determining whether he or she *knows* of his or her existence, but surely not in the sense that the saying or thinking may create that existence.

But this assurance seems contrary to Descartes's findings. He speculates a few paragraphs after announcing the cogito: "I am, I exist—that is certain; but for how long do I exist? For as long as I think; for it might perhaps happen, if I totally ceased thinking, that I would at the same time completely cease to be" (ibid., 185). This does not quite say that my ceasing to think would cause, or would be, my ceasing to exist. It may amount to saying so if I must think of myself as having a creator (hence, according to Descartes, a preserver) and if all candidates for this role other than myself dropped out. These assumptions seem faithful to Descartes's text, so I am prepared to take it that the cogito is only half the battle concerning the relation of my thinking to my existing, or perhaps "I think, therefore I am" expresses only half the battle of the cogito: Descartes establishes to his satisfaction that I exist only while, or if *and only if,* I think. It is this, it seems, that leads him to claim that the mind always thinks, an idea Nietzsche and Freud would put to further use.

Emerson goes the whole way with Descartes's insight—that I exist only if I think—but he thereupon denies that I (mostly) do think, that the "I" mostly gets into my thinking, as it were. From this it follows that the skeptical possibility is realized—that I do not exist, that I as it were haunt the world, a realization perhaps expressed by saying that the life I live is the life of skepticism. Just before the end of the Second Meditation, Descartes observes that "if I judge that [anything, say the external world] exists because I see it, certainly it follows much more evidently that I exist myself because I see it" (ibid., 190). Since the existence of the world is more doubtful than my own existence, if I do not know that I exist, I even more evidently do not know that the things of the world exist. If, accordingly, Emerson is to be understood as describing the life left to me under skepticism—implying that I do not exist among the things of the world, that I haunt the world—and if for this reason he is to be called literary and not philosophical, we might well conclude, So much the worse for philosophy. Philosophy shrinks before a description of the very possibility it undertakes to refute, so it can never know of itself whether it has turned its nemesis aside.

But it seems to me that one can see how Emerson arrives at his conclusion by a continuing faithfulness to Descartes's own procedures, to the fact, as one might put it, that Descartes's procedures are themselves as essentially literary as they are philosophical and that it may even have become essential to philosophy to show as much. After arriving at the cogito, Descartes immediately raises the question of his metaphysical identity: "But I do not yet know sufficiently clearly what I am, I who am sure that I exist" (ibid., 183). He raises this question six or seven times over the ensuing seven or eight paragraphs, rejecting along the way such answers as that he is a rational animal, or that he is a body, or that his soul is "something very rarefied and subtle, such as a wind, a flame, or a very much expanded air . . . infused throughout my grosser components," before he settles on the answer that he is essentially a thing that thinks. There is nothing in these considerations to call argument or inference; indeed, the most obvious description of these passages is to say that they constitute an autobiographical narrative of some kind. If Descartes is philosophizing, and if these passages are essential to his philosophizing, it follows that philosophy is not exhausted in argumentation. And if the power of these passages is literary, then the literary is essential to the power of philosophy; at some stage the philosophical becomes, or turns into, the literary.

I think one can describe Emerson's progress as his having posed Descartes's question for himself and provided a fresh line of answer, one you might call a grammatical answer: I am a being who to exist must say I exist, or must acknowledge my existence—claim it, stake it, enact it.

The beauty of the answer lies in its weakness (you may say its emptiness)—indeed, in two weaknesses. First, it does not prejudge what the I or self or mind or soul may turn out to be, but only specifies a condition that whatever it is must meet. Second, the proof only works in the moment of its giving, for what I prove is the existence only of a creature who *can* enact its existence, as exemplified in actually giving the proof, not one who at all times does in fact enact it. The transience of the existence it proves and the transience of its manner of proof seem in the spirit of the *Meditations,* including Descartes's proofs for God; this transience would be the moral of Descartes's insistence on the presence of clear and distinct ideas as essential to, let me say, philosophical knowledge. Only in the vanishing presence of such ideas does proof take effect—as if there were nothing to rely on but reliance itself. This is perhaps why Emerson will say, "To talk of reliance is a poor external way of speaking" (Emerson 1960, 158).

That what I am is one who to exist enacts his existence is an answer Descartes might almost have given himself, since it is scarcely more than a literal transcript of what I set up as the further half of the cogito's battle. It is a way of envisioning roughly the view of so-called human existence taken by Heidegger in *Being and Time:* that *Dasein's* being is such that its being is an issue for it (Heidegger 1962, 68). But for Descartes to have given such an answer would have threatened the first declared purpose of his *Meditations,* which was to offer proof of God's existence. If I am one who can enact my existence, God's role in the enactment is compromised. Descartes's word for what I call "enacting"—or "claiming" or "staking" or "acknowledging"—is "authoring." In the Third Meditation:

I wish to pass on now to consider whether I myself, who have the idea of God, could exist if there had been no God. And I ask, from what source would I have derived my existence? Possibly from myself, or from my parents . . . . But if I were . . . the author of my own being, I would doubt nothing, I would experience no desires, and finally I would lack no perfection . . . I would be God (himself) . . . . Even if I could suppose that possibly I have always been as I am now . . . it would not follow that no author of my existence need then be sought and I would still have to recognize that it is necessary that God is the author of my existence. (Descartes 1958, 207)

Apparently it is the very sense of my need for a human proof of my human existence—some authentication—that is the source of the idea that I need an author. ("Need for proof" will be what becomes of my intuition of my transience, or dependence, or incompleteness, or unfinishedness, or unsponsoredness—of the intuition that I am unauthorized.)

But surely the idea of self-authorizing is merely metaphorical, the merest exploitation of the coincidence that the Latin word for author is also the word for creating, nothing more than the by now fully discredited romantic picture of the author or artist as incomprehensibly original, as a world-creating and self-creating genius. It is true that the problematics of enacting one's existence skirt the edge of metaphysical nonsense. They ask us, in effect, to move from the consideration that we may sensibly disclaim certain actions as ours (ones done, as we may say, against our wills), and hence from the consideration that we may disclaim certain of our thoughts as ours (ones, it may be, we would not dream of acting on, though the terrain here gets philosophically and psychologically more dangerous), to the possibility that none of my actions and thoughts is mine—as if, I am not a ghost, I am, I would like to say, *worked,* from inside or outside. This move to the metaphysical is like saying that since it makes sense to suppose that I might lack any or all of my limbs I might lack a body altogether, or that since I never see all of any object and hence may not know that a given object exists I may not know that the external world as such exists. Ordinary language philosophy, most notably in the teaching of Austin and of Wittgenstein, has discredited such moves to the metaphysical, as a way of discrediting the conclusions of skepticism. But in my interpretation of Wittgenstein, what is discredited is not the appeal or the threat of skepticism as such, but only skepticism's own pictures of its accomplishments. Similarly, what is discredited in the romantic's knowledge about self-authoring is only a partial picture of authoring and of creation, a picture of human creation as a literalized anthropomorphism of God's creation—as if to create myself I were required to begin with the dust of the ground and magic breath, rather than with, say, an uncreated human being and the power of thinking.

That human clay and the human capacity for thought are enough to inspire the authoring of myself is, at any rate, what I take Emerson's "Self-Reliance," as a reading of Descartes's cogito argument, to claim. I take his underlying turning of Descartes to be something like this: there is a sense of being the author of oneself that does not require me to imagine myself God (that may just be the name of the particular picture of the self as a self-present substance), a sense in which the absence of doubt and desire of which Descartes speaks in proving that God, not he, is the author of himself is a continuing task, not a property, a task in which the goal, or the product of the process, is not a state of being but a moment of change, say of becoming—a transience of being, a being of transience. (Emerson notes: "This one fact the world hates; that the soul *becomes*" [Emerson 1960, 158].) To make sense of this turn, Emerson needs a view of the world, a perspective on its fallenness, in which the *uncreatedness* of the individual manifests itself, in which human life appears as the individual's failure at self-creation, as a continuous loss of individual possibility in the face of some overpowering competitor. If my gloss of Emerson's reading of Descartes is right, the cogito's need arises at particular historical moments in the life of the individual and in the life of the culture.

Emerson calls the mode of uncreated life "conformity." But each of the modern prophets seems to have been driven to find some way of characterizing the threat to individual existence, to individuation, posed by the life to which their society is bringing itself. John Stuart Mill (in *On Liberty*) called it the despotism of opinion, and he characterized being human in his period in terms of deformity; he speaks of us as withered and starved, and as dwarfs (58–59). Nietzsche called the threat: the world of the last man ("Zarathustra's Prologue," §5), the world of the murderers of God (*Gay Science*, §125). Marx thinks of it rather as the preexistence of the human. Freud's discovery of the uncomprehended meaningfulness of human expression belongs in the line of such prophecy. Emerson's philosophical distinction here lies in his diagnosis of this moment and in his recommended therapy.

It is as a diagnosis of this state of the world that Emerson announces that Descartes's proof of self-existence (the foundation, Descartes named it, of the edifice of his former opinions, the fixed and immovable fulcrum on which to reposition the earth) cannot, or can no longer, be given, thus asking us to conclude (such is the nature of this peculiar proof) that man, the human, does not, or does no longer, exist. Here is Emerson's sentence again, together with the sentence and a half following it: "Man is timid and apologetic; he is no longer upright; he dares not say 'I think,' 'I am,' but quotes some saint or sage. He is ashamed before the blade of grass or the blowing rose . . . they are for what they are; they exist with God today" (Emerson 1960, 157). We can locate Emerson's proposed therapy in this vision of so-called man's loss of existence if we take the successive notations of this vision in apposition, as interpretations of one another: being apologetic; being no longer upright; daring not to say, but only quoting; being ashamed, as if for not existing today. There are, as Wittgenstein is once moved to express himself (§525), a multitude of familiar paths leading off from these words in all directions. Let us take, or at least point down, two or three such paths.

To begin with, the idea that something about our mode of existence removes us from nature, and that this has to do with being ashamed, alludes to the romantic problematics of self-consciousness (or the post-Kantian interpretation of that problematic), a particular interpretation of the Fall of Man. But put Emerson's invocation of shame in apposition to his invocation of our loss of uprightness, and he may be taken as challenging, not passing on, the romantic interpretation of the Fall as self-consciousness, refusing to regard our shame as a metaphysically irrecoverable loss of innocence but seeing it instead as an unnecessary acquiescence (or necessary only as history is necessary) in, let me say, poor posture, a posture he calls timidity and apologeticness. I will simply claim, without citing textual evidence (preeminently the contexts in which the word "shame" and its inflections are deployed throughout Emerson's essay), that the proposed therapy is to become ashamed of our shame, to find our ashamed posture more shameful than anything it could be reacting to. One might say that he calls for more, not less, self-consciousness; but it would be better to say that he shows self-consciousness not to be the issue it seems. It, or our view of it, is itself a function of poor posture.

But really everything so far said about existence, preexistence, and so forth may be some function of poor posture—including our view of what poor posture may be. Bad posture Emerson variously names, in one passage, as peeping or stealing or skulking up and down "with the air of a charity-boy, a bastard, or an interloper in the world which exists for him"; in another, he finds men behaving as if their acts were fines they paid "in expiation of daily non-appearance on parade," done "as an apology or extenuation of their living in the world—as invalids and the insane pay a high board. Their virtues are penances" (Emerson 1960, 158). This vision of human beings as in postures of perpetual penance or self-mortification will remind readers of *Walden* of that book's opening pages (not to mention Nietzsche's *Genealogy of Morals*).

Good posture has two principal names or modes in "Self-Reliance": standing and sitting. The idea behind both modes is that of finding and taking and staying in a place. What is good in these postures is whatever makes them necessary to the acknowledgment, or the assumption, of individual existence, to the capacity to say "I." That this takes daring is what standing (up) pictures; that it takes claiming what belongs to you and disclaiming what does not belong to you is what sitting pictures. Sitting is thus the posture of being at home in the world (not peeping, stealing, skulking, or, as he also says, leaning), of owning or taking possession. This portrayal of the posture of sitting is, again, drawn out in *Walden,* at the opening of the second chapter ("Where I Lived, and What I Lived For") where what Thoreau calls acquiring property is what most people would consider passing it by. Resisting the temptation to follow the turnings of these paths, I put them at once in apposition to the notation that in not daring to say something what we do instead is to quote.

There is a gag here that especially appeals to contemporary sensibilities. Emerson writes, "Man dares not say . . . but quotes." But since at that moment he quotes Descartes, is he not confessing that he too cannot say but can only quote? Then should we conclude that he is taking back or dismantling (or something) the entire guiding idea of "Self-Reliance"? Or is he rather suggesting that we are to overcome the binary opposition between saying and quoting, recognizing that each is always both, or that the difference is undecidable? That difference seems to me roughly the difference between what Thoreau calls the mother tongue and the father tongue, hence perhaps makes the difference between language and literariness. And since I am taking the difference between saying and quoting as one of posture, the proposal of undecidability strikes me as the taking of a posture, and a poor one. I imagine being told that the difference in posture partakes of the same undecidability. My reply is that you can decide to say so. My decision is otherwise. (It is helped by my intuition that a guiding remark of Freud's is conceivable this way: Where thought takes place in me, there shall I take myself.)

Emerson's gag, suggesting that saying is quoting, condenses a number of ideas. First, language is an inheritance. Words are before I am; they are common. Second, the question whether I am saying them or quoting them—saying them firsthand or secondhand, as it were—which means whether I am thinking or imitating, is the same as the question whether I do or do not exist as a human being and is a matter demanding proof. Third, the writing, of which the gag is part, is an expression of the proof of saying "I," hence of the claim that writing is a matter, say the decision, of life and death, and that what this comes to is the inheriting of language, an owning of words, which does not remove them from circulation but rather returns them, as to life.

That the claim to existence requires returning words to language, as if making them common to us, is suggested by the fourth sentence of "Self-Reliance": "To believe your own thought, to believe that what is true for you in your private heart is true for all men,—that is genius" (Emerson 1960, 148). (One path from these words leads to the transformation of the romantics' idea of genius: Genius is not a special endowment, like virtuosity, but a stance toward whatever endowment you discover is yours, as if life itself were a gift, and remarkable.) Genius is accordingly the name of the promise that the private and the social will be achieved together, hence of the perception that our lives now take place in the absence of either.

So Emerson is dedicating his writing to that promise when he says: "I shun father and mother and wife and brother when my genius calls me. I would write on the lintels of the door-post, *Whim*" (ibid., 150). (I will not repeat what I have said elsewhere concerning Emerson's marking of Whim in the place of God and thus staking his writing as a whole as having the power to turn aside the angel of death.) The point I emphasize here is only that the life-giving power of words, of saying "I," is your readiness to subject your desire to words (call it Whim), to become intelligible, with no assurance that you will be taken up. ("I hope it may be better than Whim at last, but we cannot spend the day in explanation.") Emerson's dedication is a fantasy of finding your own voice, so that others, among them mothers and fathers, may shun you. This dedication enacts a posture toward, or response to, language as such, as if most people's words as a whole cried out for redemption: "Conformity makes them not false in a few particulars, authors of a few lies, but false in all particulars . . . so that every word they say chagrins us and we know not where to begin to set them right" (ibid.).

Citing authorship as the office of all users of language, a thing as commonly distributed as genius, is the plainest justification for seeing the enactment or acknowledgment of one's existence as the authoring of it and in particular for what we may take as Emerson's dominating claims for his writing: first, that it proves his human existence (i.e., establishes his right to say "I," to tell himself from and to others); second, that what he has proven on his behalf, others are capable of proving on theirs.

These claims come together in such a statement as "I will stand for humanity," which we will recognize as marking a number of paths: that Emerson's writing is in an upright posture; that what is says represents the human, meaning both that his portrait of himself is accurate only insofar as it portrays his fellows and that he is writing on their behalf (both as they stand, and as they stand for the eventual, what humanity may become); that he will for the time being stand humanity, bear it, as it is; and that he will stand up for it, protect it, guard it, presumably against itself. But to protect and guard someone by writing to and for that same one means to provide them instruction, or tuition.

The path I am not taking at this point leads from Emerson's speaking of "primary wisdom as Intuition," to which he adds, "All later teachings are tuitions" (ibid.). I note this path to commemorate my annoyance at having to stand the repeated, conforming description of Emerson as a philosopher of intuition, a description that uniformly fails to add that he is simultaneously the teacher of tuition, as though his speaking of all later teachings as tuitions were a devaluing of the teachings rather than a direction for deriving their necessary value. Take the calling of his genius as a name for intuition. Marking *Whim* on his doorpost was intuition's tuition; an enactment of the obligation to remark the calling, or access, of genius; to run the risk (or, as Thoreau puts it, to sit the risk) of noting what happens to you, of making this happenstance notable, remarkable, thinkable—of subjecting yourself, as said, to intelligibility.

How could we test the claim Emerson's writing makes to be such enactment, its claim to enact or acknowledge itself, to take on its existence, or, in Nietzsche's words, or rather Zarathustra's (which I imagine are more or less quoting Emerson's), to show that Emerson "does not say 'I' but performs 'I' " ("On the Despisers of the Body," 34)? (The mere complication of self-reference, the stock in trade of certain modernizers, may amount to nothing more than the rumor of my existence.) How else but by letting the writing teach us how to test it, word by word?

"Self-Reliance" as a whole presents a theory—I wish we knew how to call it an aesthetics—of reading. Its opening words are "I read the other day," and four paragraphs before Emerson cites the cogito he remarks, "Our reading is mendicant and sycophantic" (Emerson 1960, 158), which is to say that he finds us reading the way he finds us doing everything else. How can we read his theory of reading in order to learn how to read him? We would already have to understand it in order to understand it. I have elsewhere called this the (apparent) paradox of reading; it might just as well be called the paradox of writing, since of writing meant with such ambitions we can say that only after it has done its work of creating a writer (which may amount to sloughing or shaking off voices) can one know what it is to write. But you never know. I mean, you never know when someone will learn the posture for themselves that will make sense of a field of movement, it may be writing, or dancing, or passing a ball, or sitting at a keyboard, or free-associating. So the sense of paradox expresses our not understanding how such learning happens. What we wish to learn here is nothing less than whether Emerson exists, hence could exist for us; whether, to begin with, his writing performs the cogito he preaches.

He explicitly claims that it does, as he must. But before noting that, let me pause a little longer before this new major path, or branching of paths: the essay's theory of reading, hence of writing or speaking, hence of seeing and hearing. The theory, not surprisingly, is a theory of communication, hence of expression, hence of character—character conceived, as Emerson always conceives it, as naming at once, as faces of one another, the human individual and human language. The writing side of the theory is epitomized in the remark: "Character teaches above our wills. Men imagine that they communicate their virtue or vice only by overt actions, and do not see that virtue or vice emit a breath every moment." The reading side of the theory is epitomized in: "To talk of reliance is a poor external way of speaking. Who has more obedience than I masters me, though he should not raise his finger."

On the reading side, the idea of mastering Emerson is not that of controlling him, exactly (though it will be related to monitoring him), but rather that of coming into command of him, as of a difficult text, or instrument, or practice. That this mastery happens by obedience, which is to say, by a mode of listening, relates the process to his dedicating of his writing as heeding the call of his genius, which to begin with he is able to note as Whim. It follows that mastering his text is a matter of discerning the whim from which at each word it follows. On the writing side, the idea of communicating as emitting a breath every moment (as if a natural risk of writing were transmitting disease) means that with every word you utter you say more than you know you say (here genteel Emerson's idea is that you cannot smell your own breath), which means in part that you do not know in the moment the extent to which your saying is quoting.

(Let me attract attention to another untaken path here, on which one becomes exquisitely sensible of the causes of Nietzsche's love of Emerson's writing. I am thinking now of Nietzsche's *Ecce Homo*, a book about writing that bears the subtitle *How One Becomes What One Is*. Its preface opens with the declaration that the author finds it indispensable to say who he is because in his conversations with the educated he becomes convinced that he is not alive; the preface continues by claiming or warning that to read him is to breathe a strong air. That book's opening part, "Why I Am So Wise," closes by saying that one of its author's traits that causes difficulty in his contacts with others is the uncanny sensitivity of his instinct for cleanliness: the innermost parts, the entrails, of every soul are *smelled* by him [233–34].)

So the question Emerson's theory of reading and writing is designed to answer is not "What does a text mean?" (and one may accordingly not wish to call it a theory of interpretation) but rather "How is it that a text we care about in a certain way (expressed perhaps as our being drawn to read it with the obedience that masters) invariably says more than its writer knows, so that writers and readers write and read beyond themselves?" This might be summarized as "What does a text know?" or, in Emerson's phrase, "What is the genius of the text?" (Emerson 1960, 160).

Here I note what strikes me as a congenial and fruitful conjunction with what I feel I have understood so far of the practices of Derrida and of Lacan. Others may find my conjunction with these practices uncongenial if, for example, they take it to imply that what I termed the genius of the text, perhaps I should say its engendering, is fatal to or incompatible with the idea of an author and of an author's intention. This incompatibility ought to seem unlikely since both genius and intending have to do with inclination, hence with caring about something and with posture. Austin, in a seminar discussion at Harvard in 1955, once compared the role of intending with the role of headlights (on a miner's helmet? on an automobile?). (This material is published under the title "Three Ways of Spilling Ink.") An implication he may have had in mind is that driving somewhere (getting something done intentionally) does not on the whole happen by hanging a pair of headlights from your shoulders, sitting in an armchair, picking up an unattached steering wheel, and imagining a destination. (Though this is not unlike situations in which W. C. Fields found himself.) Much else has to be in place—further mechanisms and systems (transmission, fuel, electrical), roads, the industries that produce and are produced by each, and so on—in order for headlights and a steering mechanism to do their work, even to be what they are. Even if some theorists speak as though intention were everything there is to meaning, is that a sensible reason for opposite theorists to assert that intention is nothing, counts for nothing in meaning? Is W. C. Fields our only alternative to Humpty Dumpty?[1]

But I was about to locate Emerson's explicit statement, or performance, of his cogito. In his eighth paragraph he writes: "Few and mean as my gifts may be, I actually am, and do not need for my own assurance or the assurance of my fellows any secondary testimony." Earlier in the paragraph he had said: "My life is for itself and not for a spectacle . . . . I ask primary evidence that you are a man, and refuse this appeal from the man to his actions." And two paragraphs later he will promise: "But do your work, and I shall know you" (Emerson 1960, 157).

In refusing the evidence of actions, or behavior, Emerson is refusing, as it were before the fact, the thrashing of empiricist philosophy to prove the existence of other minds by analogy with one's own case, which essentially involves an appeal to others' behavior (and its similarity to our own) as all we can know of them with certainty. But how does Emerson evade and counter the picture on which such a philosophical drift repeatedly comes to grief, namely the picture according to which we cannot literally or directly have the experiences of others, cannot have what it is he apparently calls "primary evidence" of their existence? Emerson's counter is contained in the idea of what I called his promise: "But do your work, and I shall know you" (ibid., 156). Your work, what is yours to do, is exemplified, when you are confronted with Emerson's words, by reading those words—which means mastering them, obeying and hence following them, subjecting yourself to them as the writer has by undertaking to enact his existence in saying them. The test of following them is, according to Emerson's promise, that you will find yourself known by them, that you will take yourself on in them. It is what Thoreau calls conviction, calls being convicted by his words, read by them, sentenced. To acknowledge that I am known by what this text knows does not amount to agreeing with it, in the sense of believing it, as if it were a bunch of assertions or as if it contained a doctrine. To be known by it is to find thinking in it that confronts you. That would prove that a human existence is authored in it. But how will you prove thinking? How will you show your conviction?

One possibility Emerson presents as follows: "The virtue in most request is conformity. Self-reliance is its aversion" (ibid., 149). This almost says, and nearly means, that you find your existence in conversion, by converting to it, that thinking is a kind of turning oneself around. But what it directly says is that the world of conformity must turn from what Emerson says as he must turn from it and that since the process is never over while we live— since, that is, we are never finally free of one another—his reader's life with him will be a turning from, and returning from, his words, a moving on

from them, by them. In "Fate," Emerson would call this aversion "antagonism": "Man is a stupendous antagonism," he says there (ibid., 334). I can
testify that when you stop struggling with Emerson's words they become
insupportable.

But why does self-reliance insist that it will know its other, even create its
other, meaning authorize the other's self-authorization, or auto-creation?
Because it turns out that to gain the assurance, as Descartes had put it, that I
am not alone in the world has turned out to require that I allow myself to be
known. (I have called this requirement subjecting myself to intelligibility,
or, say, legibility.) But doesn't this beg the question whether there *are* others
there to do this knowing?

I would say rather that it orders the question. The fantasy of aloneness in
the world may be read as saying that the step out of aloneness, or self-
absorption, has to come without the assurance of others. (Not, perhaps,
without their help.) "No one comes" is a tragedy for a child. For a grownup
it means the time has come to be the one who goes first (to offer oneself,
allow oneself, to be, let us say, known). To this way of thinking, politics
ought to have provided conditions for companionship, or fraternity; but
the price of companionship has been the suppression, not the affirmation,
of otherness, of difference and sameness, or liberty and equality. A mission
of Emerson's thinking is never to let politics forget this.

In declaring that his life is not for a spectacle but for itself, Emerson is not
denying that it is a spectacle, and he thus inflects and recrosses his running
themes of being seen, of shame, and of consciousness. A last citation on this
subject will join "Self-Reliance" with Poe's "Imp of the Perverse."

In his fifth paragraph, Emerson says: "The man is as it were clapped into
jail by his consciousness. As soon as he has once acted or spoken with éclat
he is a committed person, watched by the sympathy or the hatred of hun-
dreds, whose affections must now enter into his account. There is no Lethe
for this" (ibid., 150). The idea is that we have become permanently and
unforgettably visible to one another, in a state of perpetual theater. To turn
aside consciousness, supposing that were possible, would accordingly only
serve to distract us from this fact of our mutual confinement under one
another's guard. The solution must then be to alter what it is we show,
which requires turning even more watchfully to what it is we are conscious
of and altering our posture toward it.

For example: "A man should learn to detect and watch that gleam of light
which flashes across his mind from within, more than the lustre of the
firmament of bards and sages. Yet he dismisses without notice his own

thought, because it is his. In every work of genius we recognize our own rejected thoughts; they come back to us with a certain alienated majesty" (ibid., 151). Here I find a specification of finding myself known in this text; in it certain rejected thoughts of mine do seem to come back with what I am prepared to call alienated majesty (including the thought itself of my rejected thoughts). Then presumably this writer has managed not to dismiss his own thoughts but to call them together, to keep them on parade, at attention. ("Tuition" speaks differently of being guarded, and unguarded.)

Yet he speaks from the condition of being a grownup within the circumstances of civil (or uncivil) obedience he describes, so he says all he says clapped into jail by his consciousness—a decade before Thoreau was clapped into jail, and for the same reason, for obeying rejected things. How is he released? If, going on with Emerson's words, there were Lethe for our bondage to the attention of others, to their sympathy or hatred, we would utter opinions that would be "seen to be not private but necessary, would sink like darts into the ear of men and put them in fear" (ibid., 153)—that is, my visibility would then frighten my watchers, not the other way around, and my privacy would no longer present confinement but instead the conditions necessary for freedom. But as long as these conditions are not known to be achieved, the writer cannot know that I am known in his utterances, hence that he and I have each assumed our separate existences. So he cannot know but that in taking assurance from the promise of knowing my existence he is only assuming my existence and his role in its affirmation, hence perhaps shifting the burden of proof from himself and still awaiting me to release him from his jail of consciousness, the consciousness of the consciousness of others. When is writing *done?*

That "self-reliance" may accordingly be understood to show writing as a message from prison forms its inner connection with Poe's "Imp of the Perverse." (The thought of such a message forms other connections as well—for example, with Rousseau's *Social Contract,* whose early line "Man is born free and everywhere he is in chains" names a condition from which the writer cannot be exempting his writing, especially if his interpretation of his writing's enchainment is to afford a step toward the freedom it is compelled, by its intuition of chains, to imagine.) I can hardly do more here than give some directions for how I think Poe's tale should, or anyway can, be read. This is just as well, because the validation of the reading requires from first to last that one take the time to try the claims on oneself. The claims have generally to do with the sound of Poe's prose, with what Emerson and Nietzsche would call its air or its smell. Poe's tale is essentially about the breath it gives off.

The sound of Poe's prose, of its incessant and perverse brilliance, is uncannily like the sound of philosophy as established in Descartes, as if Poe's prose were a parody of philosophy's. It strikes me that in Poe's tales the thought is being worked out that, now anyway, philosophy exists only as a parody of philosophy, or rather as something indistinguishable from the perversion of philosophy, as if to overthrow the reign of reason, the reason that philosophy was born to establish, is not alone the task of, let us say, poetry but is now openly the genius or mission of philosophy itself. As if the task of disestablishing reason were the task of reconceiving it, of exacting a transformation or reversal of what we think of as thinking and so of what we think of as establishing the reign of thinking. A natural effect of reading such writing is to be unsure whether the writer is perfectly serious. I dare say that the writer may himself or herself be unsure, and that this may be a good sign that the writing is doing its work, taking its course. Then Poe's peculiar brilliance is to have discovered a sound, or the condition, of intelligence in which neither the reader nor the writer knows whether he or she is philosophizing, is thinking to some end. This is an insight, a philosophical insight, about philosophy: namely, that it is as difficult to stop philosophizing as it is to start. (As difficult, in Wittgenstein's words, as to bring philosophy peace [§133]. Most people I know who care about philosophy either do not see this as a philosophical problem or do not believe that it has a solution.)

A convenient way of establishing the sound of Poe's tales is to juxtapose the opening sentences of "The Black Cat" with some early sentences from Descartes's *Meditations*. Here is Descartes:

There is no novelty to me in the reflection that, from my earliest years, I have accepted many false opinions as true, and that what I have concluded from such badly assured premises could not but be highly doubtful and uncertain. . . . I have found a serene retreat in peaceful solitude. I will therefore make a serious and unimpeded effort to destroy generally all my former opinions. . . . Everything which I have thus far accepted as entirely true and assured has been acquired from the senses or by means of the senses. But I have learned by experience that these senses sometimes mislead me, and it is prudent never to trust wholly those things which have once deceived us. . . . But it is possible that, even though the senses occasionally deceive us . . . there are many other things which we cannot reasonably doubt . . . —as, for example, that I am here, seated by the fire, wearing a winter dressing gown, holding this paper in my hands, and other things of this nature. And how could I deny that these hands and this body are mine, unless I am to compare myself with certain lunatics . . . [who] imagine that their head is made of clay, or that they are gourds, or that their body is glass? . . . Nevertheless, I must remember that I am a man, and that consequently I am accustomed to sleep and in my dreams to imagine the same things that lunatics imagine when awake. . . . I realize so clearly that there are no conclusive indications by which waking life can be distinguished from sleep that I am quite astonished, and my bewilderment is such that it is almost able to convince me that I am sleeping. (Descartes 1958, 178)

Now listen to Poe:

For the most wild, yet almost homely narrative which I am about to pen, I neither expect nor solicit belief. Mad indeed would I be to expect it, in a case where my very senses reject their own evidence. Yet, mad am I not—and very surely do I not dream. But to-morrow I die, and today I would unburthen my soul. My immediate purpose is to place before the world, plainly, succinctly, and without comment, a series of mere household events. In their consequences, these events have terrified—have tortured—have destroyed me. Yet I will not attempt to expound them. (Poe 1969–78, 3:849)

The juxtaposition works both ways: to bring out at once Poe's brilliance (and what is more, his argumentative soundness) and Descartes's creepy, perverse calm (given the subjects his light of reason rakes across), his air of a mad diarist.

Moreover, the *Meditations* appear within the content of "The Imp of the Perverse," as indelibly, to my mind, as in "Self-Reliance." Before noting how, let me briefly describe this lesser-known tale. It is divided into two parts, each more or less eight paragraphs in length. The first half is, as Poe says about certain of Hawthorne's tales, not a tale at all but an essay. The essay argues for the existence of perverseness as a radical, primitive, irreducible faculty or sentiment of the soul, the propensity to do wrong for the wrong's sake, promptings to act for the reason that we should not—something it finds overlooked by phrenologists, moralists, and in great measure "all metaphysicianism," through "the pure arrogance of the reason." This phrase "the pure arrogance of the reason," to my ear, signals that Poe is writing a *critique* of the arrogance of pure reason—as if the task, even after Kant, were essentially incomplete, even unbegun. (This characterization is not incompatible with the appreciation of Poe as a psychologist, but only with a certain idea of what psychology may be). The second half of "The Imp of the Perverse," which tells the tale proper, begins:

I have said thus much, that in some measure I may answer your question—that I may explain to you why I am here—that I may assign to you something that shall have at least the faint aspect of a cause for my wearing these fetters, and for my tenanting this cell of the condemned. Had I not been thus prolix, you might either have misunderstood me altogether, or, with the rabble, have fancied me mad. As it is, you will easily perceive that I am one of the many uncounted victims of the Imp of the Perverse. (Ibid., 3: 1223–24)

Since we have not been depicted as asking, or having, a question, the narrator's explanation insinuates that we ought to have one about his presence; thus it raises more questions than it formulates.

The tale turns out to be a Poe-ish matter about the deliberately wrought murder of someone for the apparent motive of inheriting his estate, a deed that goes undetected until some years later the writer perversely gives himself away. As for the means of the murder: "I knew my victim's habit of reading in bed. . . . I substituted, in his bed-room candlestand, a [poisoned] wax-light of my own making, for the one which I there found" (ibid., 1229). The self-betrayal comes about when, as he puts it, "I arrested myself in the act" (ibid., 1225). That act is murmuring, half-aloud, "I am safe," and then adding, "yes, if I be not fool enough to make open confession." But "I felt a maddening desire to shriek aloud. . . . Alas! I well, too well understand that, to *think*, in my situation, was to be lost. . . . I bounded like a madman through the crowded thoroughfare. At length, the populace took the alarm, and pursued me" (ibid., 1225–26).

To the first of my directions for reading "The Imp" I expect nowadays little resistance: both the fiction of the writer's arresting himself and wearing fetters and tenanting the cell of the condemned and the fiction of providing a poisonous wax light for reading are descriptions or fantasies of writing, modeled by the writing before us. There is, or at least we need imagine, no actual imprisoning and no crime but the act of the writing itself. What does it mean to fantasize that words are fetters and cells and that to read them, to be awake to their meaning, or effect, is to be poisoned? Are we being told that writer and reader are one another's victims? Or is the suggestion that to arrive at the truth something in the reader as well as something in the writer must die? Does writing ward off or invite in the angel of death?

I expect more resistance to, or puzzlement at, the further proposal that the fiction of words that are in themselves unremarkable ("I am safe"), but whose saying annihilates the sayer, specifies the claim that "I well, too well understand that, to *think*, in my situation, was to be lost"—which is a kind of negation or perversion of the cogito. Rather than proving and preserving me, as in Descartes, thinking precipitates my destruction. A little earlier

Poe's narrator makes this even clearer: "There is no passion in nature so demoniacally impatient, as that of him, who shuddering on the edge of a precipice, thus meditates a plunge. To indulge for a moment, in any attempt at *thought*, is to be inevitably lost; for reflection but urges us to forbear, and *therefore* it is, I say, that we *cannot* . . . we plunge, and are destroyed" (ibid., 1223). If the Whim drawing on Emerson's "Self-Reliance" is to say "I do not think, therefore I do not exist," that of Poe's Imp is to say, "I think, therefore I am destroyed." This connection is reinforced, in this brief passage, by the words "meditates" and "demoniacally." Poe's undetected, poisoned wax light may even substitute for, or allude to, Descartes's most famous example (of materiality) in the *Meditations,* the piece of melting wax whose identity cannot be determined empirically, but only by an innate conception in the understanding. (That in Poe's tale the act of thinking destroys by alarming the populace and turning them against the thinker and that perverseness is noted as the confessing of a crime, not the committing of it—as if the confessing and the committing were figurations of one another—mark paths of parody and perverseness I cannot trace here. That thinking will out, that it inherently betrays the thinker—[th]inker—is a grounding theme of *Walden.* Its writer declares in the opening chapter, "Economy," that what he prints must in each character "thus unblushingly publish my guilt." He says this upon listing the costs of what he ate for the year. It is as if his guilt consists exactly in keeping himself alive ["getting a living," he says] in his existing, as he exists, and his preserving himself, for example, by writing.)

My third suggestion for reading Poe's tale is that the presiding image collecting the ideas I have cited and setting them in play is given in its title. The title names and illustrates a common fact about language, even invokes what one might think of as an Emersonian theory of language: the possession of language as the subjection of oneself to the intelligible. The fact of language it illustrates is registered in the series of imp words that pop up throughout the sixteen paragraphs of the tale: *impulse* (several times), *impels* (several times), *impatient* (twice), *important, impertinent, imperceptible, impossible, unimpressive, imprisoned,* and, of course, *Imp.* Moreover, *imp.* is an abbreviation in English for *imperative, imperfect, imperial, import, imprimatur, impersonal, implement, improper,* and *improvement.* And *Imp.* is an abbreviation for *emperor* and *empress.* Now if to speak of the imp of the perverse is to name the imp in English, namely as the initial sounds of a number of characteristically Poe-ish terms, then to speak of something called the perverse as containing this imp is to speak of language itself, specifically of English, as the perverse. But what is it about the imp of

English that is perverse, hence presumably helps to produce, as users of language, us imps?

It may well be the prefix *im-* that is initially felt to be perverse, since, like the prefix *in-*, it has opposite meanings. With adjectives it is a negation or privative, as in *immediate, immaculate, imperfect, imprecise, improper, implacable, impious, impecunious;* with verbs it is an affirmation of intensive, as in *imprison, impinge, imbue, implant, impulse, implicate, impersonate.* (It is not impossible that *per-verse,* applied to language, should be followed out as meaning poetic through and through.) In plain air we keep the privative and the intensive well enough apart, but in certain circumstances (say in dreams, in which, according to Freud, logical operations like negation cannot be registered or pictured but must be supplied later by the dreamer's interpretation) we might grow confused about whether, for example, *immuring* means putting something into a wall or letting something out of one, or whether *impotence* means powerlessness or a special power directed to something special, or whether *implanting* is the giving or the removing of life, or whether *impersonate* means putting on another personality or being without personhood.

But the fact or idea of imp words is not a function of just that sequence of three letters. "Word imps" could name any of the recurrent combinations of letters of which the words of a language are composed. They are part of the way words have their familiar looks and sounds, and their familiarity depends on our mostly not noticing the particles (or cells) and their laws, which constitute words and their imps—on our not noticing their necessary recurrences, which is perhaps only to say that recurrence constitutes familiarity. This necessity, the most familiar property of language there could be—that if there is to be language, words and their cells must recur, as if fettered in their orbits, that language is grammatical (to say the least)—ensures the self-referentiality of language. When we do note these cells or molecules, these little moles of language (perhaps in thinking, perhaps in derangement), what we discover are word imps—the initial, or it may be medial or final, movements, the implanted origins or constituents of words, leading lives of their own, staring back at us, calling on one another, giving us away, alarming—because to note them is to see that they live in front of our eyes, within earshot, at every moment.

But the perverseness of language, working without, even against, our thought and its autonomy, is a function not just of necessarily recurring imps of words but of the necessity for us speakers of language (us authors of it, or imps, or emperors and empresses of it) to mean something in and by our words, to desire to say something, certain things rather than others, in certain ways rather than in others, or else to work to avoid meaning them. Call these necessities the impulses and the implications of the saying of our words. There is—as in saying "I am safe," which destroys safety and defeats what is said—a question whether in speaking one is affirming something or negating it. In particular, in such writing as Poe's has the impulse to self-destruction, to giving oneself away or betraying oneself, become the only way of preserving the individual? And does it succeed? Is authoring the obliteration or the apotheosis of the writer?

In the passage I cited earlier from "The Black Cat," the writer does not speak of being in fetters and in a cell, but he does name his activity as penning; since the activity at hand is autobiography, he is penning himself. Is this release or incarceration? He enforces the question by going on to say that he will not expound—that is, will not remove something (presumably himself) from a pound, or pen. But this may mean that he awaits expounding by the reader. Would this be shifting the burden of his existence onto some other? And who might we be to bear such a burden? Must we not also seek to shift it? Granted that we need one another's acknowledgment, is there not in this very necessity a mutual victimization, one that our powers of mutual redemption cannot overcome? Is this undecidable? Or is deciding this question exactly as urgent as deciding to exist?

I will draw to a close by forming three questions invited by the texts I have put together.

First, what does it betoken about the relation of philosophy and literature that a piece of writing can be seen to consist of what is for all the world a philosophical essay preceding, even turning into, a fictional tale—as it happens, a fictional confession from a prison cell? To answer this would require a meditation on the paragraph, cited earlier, in which Poe pivots from the essay to the tale, insinuating that we are failing to ask a question about the origin of the writing and claiming that without the philosophical preface—which means without the hinging of essay and tale, philosophy and fiction—the reader might, "with the rabble, have fancied me mad," not perceiving that he is "one of the many uncounted victims of the Imp of the Perverse." The meditation would thus enter, or center, on the idea of counting, and it is one I have in fact undertaken, under somewhat different circumstances, as part 1 of The Claim of Reason.

There I interpret Wittgenstein's Philosophical Investigations, or its guiding idea of a criterion, hence of grammar, as providing in its responsiveness to skepticism the means by which the concepts of our language are *of* anything, as showing what it means to have concepts, how it is that we are able to word the world together. The idea of a criterion I emphasize is that of a way of counting something as something, and I put this together with accounting and recounting, hence projecting a connection between telling as numbering or computing and telling as relating or narrating. Poe's (or, if you insist, Poe's narrator's) speaking pivotally of being an uncounted victim accordingly suggests to me that philosophy and literature have come together (for him, but who is he?) at the need for recounting, for counting again, and first at counting the human beings there are, for reconceiving them—a recounting beginning from the circumstances that it is I, some I or other, who counts, who is able to do the thing of counting, of conceiving a world, that it is I who, taking others into account, establish criteria for what is worth saying, hence for the intelligible. But this is only on the condition that I count, that I matter, that it matters that I count in my agreement or attunement with those with whom I maintain my language, from whom this inheritance—language as the condition of counting—comes, so that it matters not only what some I or other says but that it is some particular I who desires in some specific place to say it. If my counting fails to matter, I am mad. It is being uncounted—being left out, as if my story were untellable—that makes what I say (seem) perverse, that makes me odd. The surmise that we have become unable to count one another, to count for one another, is philosophically a surmise that we have lost the capacity to think, that we are stupefied.[2] I call this condition living our skepticism.

Second, what does it betoken about fact and fiction that Poe's writing of the Imp simultaneously tells two tales of imprisonment—in one of which he is absent, in the other present—as if they are fables of one another? Can we know whether one is the more fundamental? Here is the relevance I see in Poe's tale's invoking the situation of Hamlet, the figure of our culture who most famously enacts a question of undecidability, in particular, an undecidability over the question whether to believe a tale of poisoning. (By the way, Hamlet at the end, like his father's ghost at the beginning, claims to have a tale that is untellable—it is what makes both of them ghosts.) In Poe's tale, the invocation of *Hamlet* is heard, for example, in the two appearances of a ghost, who the first time disappears upon the crowing of a cock. And it is fully marked in the second of the three philosophical examples of perversity that Poe's narrator offers in order to convince any reader, in his words, "who trustingly consults and thoroughly questions his own soul" of "the entire radicalness of the propensity in question" (Poe 1969–78, 3:1221):

The most important crisis of our life calls, trumpet-tongued, for immediate energy and action. We glow, we are consumed with eagerness to commence the work. . . . It must, it shall be undertaken today, and yet we put it off until to-morrow; and why? There is no answer, except that we feel *perverse*, using the word with no comprehension of the principle. To-morrow arrives, and with it a more impatient anxiety to do our duty, but with this very increase of anxiety arrives, also, a nameless, a positively fearful because unfathomable, craving for delay. (Ibid., 1222)

These words invoke Hamlet along lines suspiciously like those in which I have recently been thinking about what I call Hamlet's burden of proof—but no more suspiciously, surely, than my beginning to study Poe while thinking about Hamlet.

Hamlet studies the impulse to take revenge, usurping thought as a response to being asked to assume the burden of another's existence, as if that were the burden, or price, of assuming one's own, a burden that denies one's own. Hamlet is asked to make a father's life work out successfully, to come out even, by taking his revenge for him. The emphasis in the question "to be or not" seems not on whether to die but on whether to be born, on whether to affirm or deny the fact of natality, as a way of enacting, or not, one's existence. To accept birth is to participate in a world of revenge, of mutual victimization, of shifting and substitution. But to refuse to partake in it is to poison everyone who touches you, as if taking your own revenge. This is why if the choice is unacceptable the cause is not metaphysics but history—a posture toward the discovery that there is no getting even for the oddity of being born, hence of being and becoming the one poor creature it is given to you to be. The alternative to affirming this condition is, as Descartes's *Meditations* shows, world-consuming doubt, which is hence a standing threat to, or condition of, human existence. (I imagine that the appearance of the cogito at its historical moment is a sign that some conditions were becoming ones for which getting even, or anyway overcoming, was coming to seem in order: for example, the belief in God and the rule of kings.) That there is something like a choice or decision about our natality is what I take Freud's idea of the diphasic structure of human sexual development (in "Three Essays") to show—a provision of, so to speak, the condition of the possibility of such a decision (Freud 1953–, 12:147). The condition is that of adolescence, considered as the period in which, in preparation for becoming an adult, one recapitulates, as if suffering rebirth, one's knowledge of satisfactions. This is why, it seems to me, one speculates about Hamlet's age but thinks of him as adolescent. These matters are represented in political thought under the heading of consent, about which, understandably, there has from the outset been a question of proof.

Finally, what does it betoken about American philosophy that Emerson and Poe may be seen as taking upon themselves the problematics of the cogito (Emerson by denying or negating them, Poe by perverting or sub-verting them) and as sharing the perception that authoring—philosophical writing, anyway, writing as thinking—is such that to exist it must assume, or acknowledge, the proof of its own existence? I have in effect said that to my mind this betokens their claim to be discovering or rediscovering the origin of modern philosophy, as sketched in Descartes's *Meditations,* as if literature in America were forgiving philosophy, not without punishing it, for having thought that it could live only in the banishing of literature. What does it mean that such apparent opposites as Emerson and Poe enter such a claim within half a dozen years of one another?

Let us ask what the connection is between Emerson's ecstasies (together with Thoreau's) and Poe's horrors (together with those of Hawthorne). The connection must be some function of Poe's and Hawthorne's worlds, or houses and rooms, having other people in them, typically in marriages, and typically showing these people's violent shunning, whereas Emerson's and Thoreau's worlds begin with or after the shunning of others ("I shun father and mother and wife and brother when my genius calls me") and typically depict the "I" just beside itself. The interest of the connection is that all undertake to imagine domestication, or inhabitation—as well, being Amer-icans, they might. For Emerson and Thoreau you must learn to sit at home or to sit still in some attractive spot in the woods, as if to marry the world, before, if ever, you take on the burden of others; for Poe and Hawthorne even America came too late, or perhaps too close, for that priority.

A more particular interest I have in the connection among these Ameri-can writers is a function of taking their concepts or portrayals of domestica-tion and inhabitation (with their air of ecstasy and of horror turned just out of sight) to be developments called for by the concepts of the ordinary and the everyday as these enter into the ordinary language philosopher's under-taking to turn aside skepticism, in the pains Austin and Wittgenstein take to lay out what it is that skepticism threatens. In the work of these philoso-phers, in their stubborn, accurate superficiality, perhaps for the first time in recognizable philosophy this threat of world-consuming doubt is inter-preted in all its uncanny homeliness, not merely in isolated examples but, in Poe's words, as "a series of mere household events."

I end with the following prospect. If some image of marriage, as an interpretation of domestication, in these writers is the fictional equivalent of what these philosophers understand to be the ordinary, or the everyday, then the threat to the ordinary named skepticism should show up in fiction's favorite threat to forms of marriage, namely, in forms of melodrama. Accordingly, melodrama may be seen as an interpretation of Descartes's cogito, and, contrariwise, the cogito can be seen as an interpretation of the advent of melodrama—of the moment (private and public) at which the theatricalization of the self becomes the sole proof of its freedom and its existence. This is said on tiptoe.

Postscript: Poe's Perversity and the Imp(ulse) of Skepticism

Looking back at Robert Penn Warren's essay on *The Ancient Mariner,* I see I had forgotten that he adduces the following paragraph from Poe's "The Black Cat."

In the meantime the cat slowly recovered. The socket of the lost eye presented, it is true, a frightful appearance, but he no longer appeared to suffer any pain. He went about the house as usual, but, as might be expected, fled in extreme terror at my approach. I had so much of my old heart left, as to be at first grieved by the evident dislike on the part of a creature which had once so loved me. But this feeling soon gave place to irritation. And then came, as if to my final and irrevocable overthrow, the spirit of Perverseness. Of this spirit philosophy takes no account. Yet I am not more sure that my soul lives, than I am that perverseness is one of the primitive impulses of the human heart—one of the indivisible primary faculties, or sentiments, which give direction to the character of Man. Who has not, a hundred times, found himself committing a vile or a silly action, for no other reason than because he knows he should *not?* Have we not a perpetual inclination, in the teeth of our best judgment, to violate that which is *Law,* merely because we understand it to be such? This spirit of perverseness, I say, came to my final overthrow. It was the unfathomable longing of the soul *to vex itself*—to offer violence to its own nature—to do wrong for the wrong's sake only—that urged me to continue and finally to consummate the injury I had inflicted upon the unoffending brute. One morning, in cold blood, I slipped a noose about its neck and hung it to the limb of a tree;—hung it with the tears streaming from my eyes, and with the bitterest remorse at my heart;—hung it *because* I knew that in so doing I was committing a sin—a deadly sin that would so jeopardize my immortal soul as to place it—if such a thing were possible—even beyond the reach of the infinite mercy of the Most Merciful and Most Terrible God. (Poe 1969–78, 3:851–52)

Some of this can indeed sound similar, and should, to the view I have taken of the Mariner's killing of the bird. Poe's view and mine both assert some relation between the wish to be loved and the fear of it, and between this conflict and the sense that one's existence lies under some metaphysical suspicion. The views also seem opposite, since mine takes the moral to demand that one accept the claim of others as the price of knowing or having one's existence, whereas Poe—rather, Poe's narrator—asserts the denial or annihilation of the other as that price. I might try to fix the distance between these views by noting my having said (in the closing pages of *The Claim of Reason*) that Othello kills Desdemona not because she is faithless and disperses love but on the contrary because she is faithful, because the very reciprocity of the thing he has elicited from her is what makes him feel sullied. Poe's words are, "hung it because I knew that it *had loved* me" (my emphasis), which, if this means that the love has now been withdrawn, however understandable the cause, would be a reasonably understandable case of rage and vengefulness.

But then again, are these views so different? Poe's (narrator's) revenge would still be taken because he was loved, perhaps because he feels the love was too little, or because love is too little. Whereas to murder or abandon as Othello does, because the love of you persists, is hardly an acceptable return of love, perhaps feeling that the love was too much, or because love is too much. The views seem closer and more distant than this makes out.

I have claimed that skepticism is our philosophical access to the human wish to deny the conditions of humanity, relating this, as well as to Kant's vision, both to Christianity's and to Nietzsche's hopes for the human to be overcome. Along this line we might understand Poe as asserting that skepticism itself is the best assurance of existence, as if skepticism's very will to emptiness should draw us to it. This apparently perverse account of skepticism (turning its effect into its cause) bears to familiar philosophical accounts of skepticism something like the relation Poe's paragraph from "The Black Cat," in its arrangement of sin and law and the Most Merciful and Most Terrible God, bears to St. Paul's account of such things. As if it reads Paul's saying that there were no sin but for the law, and reads it to advise, Break the law. One may take this as an insight into Christianity or as a parody of it.

What I am calling Poe's perverse account of skepticism does, I think, capture an essential perverseness in skepticism, at once granting an insight into skepticism and enacting a parody of it. The insight is that skepticism, the thing I mean by skepticism, is, or becomes, necessarily paradoxical, the apparent denial of what is for all the world undeniable. I take skepticism not as the moral of a cautious science laboring to bring light into a super-stitious, fanatical world, but as the recoil of a demonic reason, irrationally thinking to dominate the earth. I take it to begin as a wish not to reject the world but rather to establish it. The parody is to deny this, to conceal the longing for assurance under an allegedly more original wish for self-vexa-tion. This concealment is revealed at the end of the confessional stories, when the walls (inner or outer) are broken open and the repressed returns. But if the murder of the world (or the soul) will out, in these stories the end is as perverse as the beginning, or rather the perversity is still unmoved, still original, and tragedy and its recognition are still deflected into inscrutably multiplied ironies. (G. R. Thompson, in introducing his selection of Poe's short works, speaks of Poe's writing "as the work of one of the greatest ironists of world literature.")

Poe's view, so characterized, is a materialization, no doubt ironic, of the most familiar understanding I used to hear of philosophical skepticism in school, and one that I believe retains a certain currency yet. It is the view, roughly, that skepticism's repudiation of knowledge is merely a function of having set the sights of knowledge too high: *of course* if you impose the idea of absolute certainty on knowledge, you will not find that we know any-thing (except perhaps mathematics, together with what, if anything, is given to the senses); *of course* if you try to turn induction into deduction, induc-tion will seem wanting; *of course* if you demand that in order to see an object you have to see *all* of the object, then we can never really or directly or immediately *see* an object. (I give other examples of this pattern, espe-cially with respect to the question whether a critical paraphrase, say of a metaphor, is really a paraphrase, in "Aesthetic Problems of Modern Philos-ophy," 76–77.) So skepticism is just the cause of the disappointments of which it complains. People have said this about philosophy as a whole. And earlier I alluded to a similar understanding of romanticism, as wanting in its disappointments (say, in melancholy or withdrawal) exactly what cannot exist.

I had not understood how a philosopher could claim to be satisfied with such an understanding of skepticism in the absence of an understanding of how, and by what, a human being, call him or her a philosopher, would be drawn to "set the sights" so, drawn to just *this* form of self-defeat. Now, however, as a version of Poe's discrimination of perversity, it begins to make sense to me. What I am to conceive is that the self-defeat of skepticism is precisely the point of it. But does this finally make sense to me? Or is its *not* exactly making sense something I should further regard as precisely its point?

I do not, as I said, object to the idea of perversity as a description of the skeptic's outcome; I accept it as a kind of translation of the paradoxicality that is an essential feature of the skepticism I mean. It is, as elsewhere, the attitude that rings false to me, or forced. (But does attitude much matter where what is at stake is the truth?) As I do not take the owner of Pluto—for that was the cat's name—to feel about the wife into whose head he buried an axe just the way Othello feels about the wife he suffocated, so I do not take the narrator committing and confessing his denials to be the Cartesian or the Humean or the Kantian thinker bringing himself or herself back from, or giving himself or herself up for, deeds of doubt, back to the brink of the common world.

The attitude I am pointing to is one typically presented upon the promulgation of a paradox. When Pythagoras proved what has been called the incommensurability of the long side of a right triangle with the other (equal) sides, also called its measurement by an irrational number, some were frightened, some tried to keep the secret confined to an institution of intellectuals, some, I dare say right at the beginning, took it as a cosmic joke on humankind. Something similar happened in this century when Gödel's proof of formally undecidable propositions became known. So some seem to find these attitudes appropriate toward the discovery that there are no marks or features by which to distinguish dreams from waking life, fiction from fact, literature from life, as though this kind of indistinguishability made them identical—as though literature and life were known to be familiar objects and the issue remaining were to decide whether they are to be counted as one or as two. Well, if not a sense of absurdity, or of ironic pleasure or pain, at the dashable hopes of humankind, what attitude would you recommend? None.

I might describe the attitude I find myself resisting, the posture I would alter toward the events of horror in Poe's stories, as one in which the narrator is "acting out" a fantasy or an unconscious impulse, as opposed (as Freud does typically oppose "acting out," thus partially defining it) to re-membering something, an opposite way of bringing the past into the present, a way that brings the promise of a freedom from the violence and the alienatedness of the impulsion to repeat.[3]

Since remembering is the organ of that way of philosophizing to which I am drawn, naturally I am distrustful of what would oppose it. Sometimes you could call this the merely literary, or impulsive playfulness, which may sometimes take the form of a technical and seemingly rigorous discourse. Far be it from me either to take it for granted that psychoanalysis has made sufficiently clear Freud's distinction between repeating and remembering (in "Remembering, Repeating, and Working Through," Freud 1953–), or to take Poe the writer as sufficiently like his narrator to be indistinguishable intellectually from him. But whether Poe is sufficiently unlike his narrator to draw on our (of course I mean my) philosophical interest is a function of how interesting and convincing an account his discourse provides by way of grounding the notion of perversity; of, that is to say, accounting for the human temptation to deny the conditions of humanity, or in other words, the will to be monstrous.

The question as to the existence of myself, or creation of myself, is modeled by Poe as the existence of a writer, who exists simultaneously with the writing, only as it is being written, uttered. Users of language, humans are creatures of language and exist only from it, as equally it exists only from us. If one is perverse so is the other. If we cannot speak (if, e.g., we have something so terrible to say that it either cannot be said or cannot be believed) we are inhuman. If the responsibility for speech is suffocating, you might think of enacting a deed so horrible that speech seems impossible; you might choose to become a monster. (Here it may be worth comparing Wittgenstein's speculation concerning what a private language would be.)

When the narrator of "The Imp of the Perverse" asks us to question our own soul in order to find undeniably "the entire radicalness of the propensity [viz., perverseness] in question," the example he thereupon appeals to is the torment "by an earnest desire to tantalize a listener by circumlocution," which is to say, the torment of the desire to tell stories, even (as this tale manifests) the torment of the desire to write a certain kind of philosophy— thus using himself (whom else would a skeptic invoke?) as the image or scapegoat of humankind. I mention one further region of the unsayable in Poe's tale, a region that is not a function of the imps in language but of ourselves as its imp and image: our power of affirmation (without which there is no assertion), hence of denial.

Years after the narrator committed a perfect crime, impossible to detect, the narrator's imp presented itself and made detection possible. "I would perpetually catch myself pondering upon my security, and repeating, in a low undertone, the phrase, 'I am safe.' One day, whilst sauntering along the streets, I arrested myself in the act of murmuring, half aloud, these customary syllables. In a fit of petulance, I remodelled them thus:—I am safe—I am safe—yes—if I be not fool enough to make open confession!" (Poe 1969–78, 3:1225). That is, "I am safe" is true as long as it is not said; saying refutes it. More famous sayings whose saying refutes them are "This statement is not true" and "I do not exist." (It may thereupon occur to you that [therefore] "I exist" is necessarily true, or undeniably true each time it is said.) But you equally cannot safely say, in Poe's depicted circumstances, "I am not safe." (Hence this example is unlike other unsayables, like "I am not here" and "I am asleep." These are pleasantries, and their negations are, in certain circumstances, informative.) One's safety, or lack of it, is unknowable. What can be known is the fact of one's existence, and whatever follows from that. Philosophers such as Descartes and Kant and Heidegger and Wittgenstein may agree on this point, and vary completely in what it is they find to follow. One may further try out the thought that the knowledge philosophers such as Marx and Kierkegaard and Nietzsche (and you may say Freud) begin from is that we do *not* exist, and vary in what they find follows from that.

It seems reasonably clear that Poe's (narrator's) search for a proof of his (her?) existence (in the confessional tales I was citing) is for a proof that he breathes—that is, that he is alive. "I am not more certain that I breathe, than that the assurance of the wrong or error of any action is often the one unconquerable *force* which impels us, and alone impels us, to its prosecution." Assume that he is betraying here an uncertainty that he breathes; and then turn around his comparison of certainties. The imp of himself here apparently gives him to think that he is not *less* certain that he breathes than that there is the impulsion in question. So his certainty of breathing becomes dependent on his impulse to wrongdoing. In Descartes the capacity for "the wrong or error of any action" is the proof of the possession of free will. For Descartes it follows that we are responsible for our error because we are free not to refrain from it (in particular, free to judge beyond the knowable). For Poe we are responsible metaphysically for our errors exactly because we are not morally responsible for them. I *am* the one who cannot refrain. Some moralists are of the view that when I do what I am impelled to do, the action is not exactly mine. Poe's view seems to be that in such case the responsibility is never discharged—it sticks to me forever. Of course not all actions are of such a kind but only ones that show what I have been calling the inhuman in the human, the monstrousness of it, ones that, I would like to say, come before and after morality: an example Poe gives of the former is the desire to tantalize in telling a good tale; examples of the latter are the more baroque Poe-behaviors, gouging out the eye of the cat, axing your wife, almost without provocation. The implication is that morality is stumped at certain points in judging human nature, a fact that should illuminate both those points "before" and those "after" morality. If there is a target of satire here, it is those who say they believe in determinism, who do not appreciate how free we are (capable of things it is hard to imagine) and how far from free (incapable of resisting this imagination).

"The Imp of the Perverse" opens with an explanation for our having overlooked perversity as a *primum mobile* of the human soul—all of us, the "phrenologists" and "all the moralists who have preceded them." The explanation is: "We saw no *need* for the impulse—for the propensity. We could not perceive its necessity. We could not understand, that is to say, we could not have understood, had the notion of this *primum mobile* ever obtruded itself;—we could not have understood in what manner it might be made to further the objects of humanity" (ibid., 1219). And a little further on:

It will be said, I am aware, that when we persist in acts because we feel we should *not* persist in them, our conduct springs from the *combativeness* of phrenologists. But combativeness is our safeguard against injury. Its principle regards our well-being. . . . It follows, that the desire to be well must be excited simultaneously with any principle which shall be a modification of combativeness, but in the case of that something which I term *perverseness,* the desire to be well is not only not aroused, but a strongly antagonistical sentiment exists. (Ibid., 1221)

Is this antagonistical sentiment a sentiment to be ill, which here must mean a desire to be injured? Say if you like (G. R. Thompson says it in the introduction to his edition of Poe cited earlier) that "the 'The Imp of the Perverse' clearly spells out Poe's fundamental conception that it is man's fate to act against his own best interests." But I see no original desire for self-injury in the tale, however much self-injury results from the events. True, the imp may have to forfeit perverseness as a "safeguard against injury"; that is not the kind of need that the evolution of perverseness can be understood to serve. But perhaps it is a safeguard against something else, something more original, even humanly more needful—a safeguard against annihilation, the loss of (the proof of) identity or existence altogether. (I am perhaps cagily masking the question as to what the proof of human life would primarily be directed to, to its existence or to its identity. To say both are in question is easy, if doubtless true. The question is about priorities.) God's existence has been said to follow from God's identity. Human existence no more follows from its identity that the existence of a stone is assured from a description of a stone. But unlike a stone, a human identity is not assured, as certain existentialists used to like to say, from the fact that a human being exists. Romantics are brave in noting the possibility of life-in-death and of what you might call death-in-life. My favorite romantics are the ones (I think the bravest ones) who do not attempt to escape these conditions by taking revenge on existence. But this means willing to continue to be born, to be natal, hence mortal.

One has to distinguish *what* it is that proofs of my existence are supposed to, or do, prove; what question it is one has to answer. Descartes's proof proves my existence as mind, it answers the question "Am I a mind or a body?" Psychoanalysis has distinguished the question "Am I a woman or am I a man?" from the question "Am I alive or dead?"—the former as the hysterical question, the latter as the obsessional. Obviously I am taking the latter as Poe's question. But I earlier complicated what this will mean by in effect also giving him the question "Am I a human being or a monster?" (I have said a few words about these questions in "On Makavejev On Bergman," in relation to *The Claim of Reason*.)

The desire to be well is preceded by the desire to be. And against annihilation, ceasing to exist as the one I am, there is no safeguard, none suppliable by the individual, not even God's hand in our creation; its safeguard is the recognition of and by others. (So saying "I am safe" may in a sense save you after all.) If at the same time this recognition of and by others strikes you as threatening your life, you will be perplexed. I think we all more or less know of this perplexity. But to struggle with it by impulsively or obsessionally proposing that to gain proof you have to create (to be the author of) what there is to confess, as though there is nothing to acknowledge but in such confession, is comparatively trivial. It is trivial in comparison with the effort to acknowledge your unauthorized life as it is, taking an interest in it. Some will, I think, wish to say that there is no way one's life is; to me this betokens a refusal to try putting it into (provisional) words (a refusal to struggle for its authorship).

Poe's Perverseness may be seen as a parody of the vulnerability, the dropping of safeguard, in the placing of interest, in Poe's cases, the investment of love, the inevitable risks in its improbabilities. The truth of the parody is its measure of the pain these risks run, of how far our lives take on and maintain their forms by their need to ward off abandonment.[4]

NOTES

1. In linking W. C. Fields's suffering of convention with Humpty Dumpty's claim to be master, by his very wishes, of what words shall mean (and thinking of his fate), I find I

have not forgotten a passage during the discussions of "Must We Mean What We Say?" the day I delivered it in 1957 (at Stanford, as it happens). Against a certain claim in my paper, one philosopher cited Humpty Dumpty's view of meaning (by name) as obviously, in all solemnity, the correct one. This was, I think, the first time I realized the possibility that parody is no longer a distinguishable intellectual tone, since nothing can any longer be counted on to strike us in common as outrageous.

2. I find it hard not to imagine that this surmise has to do with the history of the frantic collection of statistical tables cited in Ian Hacking's "Making Up People" and "Prussian Statistics." Emerson's essay "Fate" self-consciously invokes the new science of statistics as a new image of human fate—a new way in which others are finding us captured by knowledge, and which Emerson finds a further occasion for ignorance.

3. See the entry under "Acting-out" in Laplanche and Pontalis 1974.

4. The philosophical address of Cavell's original essay (first given as part of a 1984 conference at Stanford called "Reconstructing Individualism") was somewhat wider than the scope of this volume. We have, in consequence, chosen not to reprint two additional postscripts to "Being Odd, Getting Even." Anyone wishing to encounter the full text can find it in Cavell 1988. [Eds.]

Strange Fits

Poe and Wordsworth on the Nature of Poetic Language

BARBARA JOHNSON

No two discussions of poetry could at first sight appear more different than Wordsworth's "Preface to *Lyrical Ballads*" and Poe's "Philosophy of Composition."[1] The first has been read as an important Romantic manifesto, sometimes inconsistent, sometimes dated, but always to be taken seriously. The second has been read as a theoretical spoof that, because it cannot be taken at face value, cannot be taken seriously at all. Both, however, can be read as complex texts in their own right—as texts whose very complexities tell us a great deal about the nature of poetic language. I would like to suggest here some directions for such a reading, first by examining the rhetorical slipperiness of each theoretical text, then by invoking for each a poem—Wordsworth's "Strange Fits of Passion" and Poe's "Raven"—that both exemplifies and undermines the neatness of the explicit theory.

Despite their differences, Poe and Wordsworth do in fact agree on one thing—that the object of poetry is to produce pleasure:

Wordsworth:

The first Volume of these Poems has already been submitted to general perusal. It was published, as an experiment, which, I hoped, might be of some use to ascertain, how far, by fitting to metrical arrangement a selection of the real language of men in a state of vivid sensation, that sort of pleasure and that quantity of pleasure may be imparted, which a Poet may rationally endeavour to impart. (69)

Poe:

Beauty is the sole legitimate province of the poem. . . . That pleasure which is at once the most intense, the most elevating, and the most pure, is, I believe, found in the contemplation of the beautiful. (1082)

The nature of the pleasure in question, however, is, in both cases, pushed to the edge of trauma: dead women, mad mothers, idiot boys, lugubrious birds—the poems are populated with images that are clearly situated beyond any simple notion of a pleasure principle. Poe indeed goes so far as to make his poem aim for the utmost "luxury of sorrow" to be obtained by "the human thirst for self-torture" (1088). What is at stake in both cases would seem to have something to do with the beyond of pleasure, which for Freud was associated with two highly problematic and highly interesting notions: the repetition compulsion and the death instinct. Questions of repetition and death will indeed be central to my discussion both of Wordsworth and of Poe.

I will begin by outlining, somewhat reductively, the broadest possible differences between the two theoretical texts. Many of the differences are, of course, historical, and can be derived from the type of fashionable poetry each poet is writing *against*. Poe designs his poetics in opposition to the American tradition of long, sentimental, or didactic poetry associated with such figures as Longfellow or Bryant. Wordsworth is writing against the eighteenth-century British tradition of witty, polished, mock-heroic or rhetorically ornate verse associated with such names as Johnson, Pope, and Gray. But the poetic boundary lines each poet attempts to draw are perhaps of broader applicability, and their attempts can be read as exemplary versions of tensions inherent in the modern Western poetic project as such.

What, then, are the salient differences between these two theories of poetic language? In a well-known passage from the preface, Wordsworth states that "poetry is the spontaneous overflow of powerful feelings: it takes its origin from emotion recollected in tranquillity" (85). Poe, on the other hand, writes of his method of composing "The Raven" that it was written backward, beginning with a consideration of the desired *effect*. "It is my design to render it manifest that no one point in its composition is referrible either to accident or intuition—that the work proceeded, step by step, to its completion with the precise and rigid consequence of a mathematical problem" (1081). Poe's poetic calculus leads him to choose an optimal length of about one hundred lines; then, after consideration of the desired effect and tone (beauty and sadness), he decides that the poem should be structured around a refrain ending in the most sonorous of letters, *o* and *r*. The syllable -*or* is thus the first element of the text of the poem to be written. "The sound of the *refrain* being thus determined," Poe goes on, "it became necessary to select a word embodying this sound, and at the same time in the fullest possible keeping with that melancholy which I had pre-determined as the tone of the poem. In such a search it would have been absolutely impossible to overlook the word 'Nevermore.' In fact, it was the very first which presented itself" (1083–84).

Spontaneous overflow versus calculation, emotion versus rigid consequence, feelings versus letters of the alphabet: a first comparison would lead us to see Wordsworth's poetry as granting primacy to the *signified* while Poe's grants primacy to the *signifier*. This distinction is borne out by the fact that while Wordsworth claims that the language of poetry should be indistinguishable from that of good prose, Poe aims to maximize the difference between prose and poetry, excluding for that reason the long poem from the canon of true poetry. But neither text presents its case as simply as it might appear.

For all his emphasis on emotion, Wordsworth is of course acutely conscious of the centrality of form to the poetic project. He describes the use of verse as a kind of contract made between form and expectation. Form itself constitutes a promise which Wordsworth then claims to have broken:

It is supposed, that by the act of writing in verse an Author makes a formal engagement that he will gratify certain known habits of association; that he not only apprizes the Reader that certain classes of ideas and expressions will be found in his book, but that others will be carefully excluded. I will not take upon me to determine the exact import of the promise which by the act of writing in verse an Author, in the present day, makes to his reader; but I am certain, it will appear to many persons that I have not fulfilled the terms of an engagement thus voluntarily contracted. (70)

Verse, then, is a contract made by form, a formal promise to include and to exclude certain classes of ideas. Wordsworth's violation of that contract comprises both inclusions and exclusions. He warns the reader that these shifts in boundary lines may produce "feelings of strangeness and awkwardness." Feelings of strangeness are, of course, often the subjects of the poems, as is the case with the poem to which we will later turn, "Strange Fits of Passion." That poem may well tell us something about the nature of strangeness of Wordsworth's poetics, but strangeness is not the only metapoetic expression glossed by the poem. Wordsworth's first description of his experiment, in the opening paragraph of the preface, speaks of the poems as "*fitting* to metrical arrangement a selection of the real language of men in a state of vivid sensation." The word "fit," which occurs several times in the preface,[2] thus in the poem takes on the double meaning of both uncontrolled overflow and formal containment. Interestingly, the word "fytt" is also a term for a medieval stanza form. As I will try to show, Wordsworth's entire preface can be read as an attempt to fit all the senses of the word "fit" together.

What does Wordsworth mean by "the real language of men"? In the 1798 "Advertisement to *Lyrical Ballads,*" Wordsworth had spoken of "the language of conversation in the middle and lower classes of society." These, then, are the "classes of ideas" that poetry had previously excluded. But Wordsworth includes them only to exclude them again; the substitution of the expression "the real language of men" for the "conversation in the middle and lower classes" acts out an erasure of "class," a gesture of de-historicization and universalization. Poetic inclusions and exclusions clearly operate on more than one level at a time. Others are more qualified than I am to comment on Wordsworth's tendency to pastoralize away the historical reality of the rural along with the urban and the industrial, grounding "*human* nature" instead in a state of congruence with "the beautiful and permanent forms" of *external* nature. Let it suffice here to suggest that, in the discussion that follows, the complex fate of the word "mechanical" may not be unconnected to a set of attitudes toward the industrial revolution.

There is one type of exclusion about which Wordsworth's preface is very clear—or at least it tries to be. The crucial exclusion for Wordsworth would seem to be the exclusion of personification.

The reader will find that personifications of abstract ideas rarely occur in these volumes; and, I hope, are utterly rejected as an ordinary device to elevate the style, and raise it above prose. I have proposed to myself to imitate, and, as far as possible, to adopt the very language of men; and assuredly such personifications do not make any natural or regular part of that language. They are, indeed, a figure of speech occasionally prompted by passion, and I have made use of them as such; but I have endeavoured utterly to reject them as a mechanical device of style. (74)

The operative opposition here is the opposition between the "natural" and the "mechanical." Personifications, says Wordsworth, are not "natural," but rather "a mechanical device of style." But already there is an exception: they are sometimes naturally prompted by passion. If poetry is located at a point of vivid sensation, if it is defined as always being in some sense a strange fit of passion, then where does Wordsworth draw the line? Are personifications natural or mechanical? How natural is the natural language of passion?

Look further at Wordsworth's attempts to distinguish between the natural and the mechanical. Since his whole sense of value and originality seems to depend on his making that distinction clear, one would expect him to clarify it in the essay. One of the ways in which Wordsworth works the distinction over is by telling it as a story. He tells it twice, once as a story of degradation, and once as a story of recollection. The first is a history of abuse; the second, a history of recovery. What I will do is look closely at the rhetorical terms in which the two stories are told. They are both, of course, stories *of* rhetoric, but what I will analyze will be the rhetoric of the stories.

First, from the "Appendix on Poetic Diction," the history of abuse:

The earliest Poets of all nations generally wrote from passion excited by real events; they wrote *naturally,* and as men: feeling powerfully as they did, their language was daring, and figurative. In succeeding times, Poets, and men ambitious of the fame of Poets, perceiving the influence of such language, and desirous of producing the same effect, without having the same animating passion, set themselves to a *mechanical* adoption of those figures of speech, and made use of them, sometimes with propriety, but much more frequently applied them to feelings and ideas with which they had *no natural connection* whatsoever. A language was thus insensibly produced, differing materially from the real language of men in *any situation* [emphasis in original]. The Reader or Hearer of this *distorted language* found himself in a perturbed and unusual state of mind: when affected by the genuine language of passion he had been in a perturbed and unusual state of mind also: in both cases he was willing that his common judgment and understanding should be laid asleep, and he had no instinctive and infallible perception of the true to make him reject the false. . . . This *distorted language* was received with admiration; and Poets, it is probable, who had before contented themselves for the most part with *misapplying* only expressions which at first had been dictated by real passion, *carried the abuse still further,* and introduced phrases composed apparently in the spirit of the original figurative language of passion, yet altogether of their own invention, and distinguished by various degrees of *wanton deviation* from good sense and *nature.* . . . In process of time metre became a symbol or promise of this unusual language, and whoever took upon him to write in metre, according as he possessed more or less of true poetic genius, introduced less or more of this *adulterated phraseology* into his compositions, and the true and false became so inseparably interwoven that the taste of men was gradually *perverted;* and this language was received as a *natural* language; and at length, by the influence of books upon men, did to a certain degree really become so. (90–91; emphasis added unless otherwise indicated)

In this history of abuse, the natural and the mechanical, the true and the false, become utterly indistinguishable. It becomes all the more necessary— but all the more difficult—to restore the boundary line. Each time Wordsworth attempts to do so, however, the distinction breaks down. The natural becomes unnatural, life imitates art, and mechanical inventions are mistaken for the natural language of passion.

Wordworth's other developmental narrative is one that leads not to degradation but to amelioration. This time the story takes place in a temporality of the self, the temporality expressed by the juxtaposition of the two clauses: "Poetry is the spontaneous overflow of powerful feelings," and "it takes its origin from emotion recollected in tranquillity." For Wordsworth, in other words, the poet is a man who attempts to write in obedience to the classic example of the double bind: "be spontaneous." In an early paragraph in the preface, Wordsworth makes the double bind into a developmental narrative, in which the acrobatics of grammar—the sustained avoidance of any grammatical break—mimes the desire for seamless continuity. If the whole story can be told in one breath, Wordsworth implies, then nothing will be lost, the recuperation of the spontaneous will be complete.

For all good poetry is the spontaneous overflow of powerful feelings: but though this be true, Poems to which any value can be attached, were never produced on any variety of subjects but by a man, who being possessed of more than usual organic sensibility, had also thought long and deeply. For our continued influxes of feeling are modified and directed by our thoughts, which are indeed the representatives of all our past feelings; and, as by contemplating the relation of these general representatives to each other we discover what is really important to men, so, by the repetition and continuance of this act, our feelings will be connected with important subjects, till at length, if we be originally possessed of much sensibility, such habits of mind will be produced, that, by obeying blindly and mechanically the impulses of those habits, we shall describe objects, and utter sentiments, of such a nature and in such connection with each other, that the understanding of the being to whom we address ourselves, if he be in a healthful state of association, must necessarily be in some degree enlightened, and his affections ameliorated. (72)

The astonishing thing about this story is that it uses the word "mechanical"—which has been the name of a negative value everywhere else in the preface—as the height of poetic activity. "Obeying blindly and mechanically the impulses of . . . habits" was exactly what produced abuse and corruption in the other story, but here it produces health, enlightenment, and amelioration. What can be said about the relation between the two stories?

Both stories are designed to define and judge the relation between an original moment of feeling and utterance and its later repetition. Wordsworth's task is to distinguish between good repetition and degraded, hollow repetition. In describing his own creative process, he speaks of the art of developing habits that will lead to a "blind, mechanical" reproduction of the original emotion. In describing the poetic degradations he wants to condemn, he again speaks of a "mechanical" adoption of figures of speech. For Wordsworth's theory to stand, it is urgent for him to be able to distinguish between good and bad repetition. Yet the good and the bad are narrated in almost the same terms. Wordsworth again and again repeats the story of repetition, but is never able to draw a reliable dividing line. He can *affirm* good repetition, but he cannot tell a story that will sufficiently distinguish it from bad. What Wordsworth's essay shows is that talking about poetry involves one in an urgent and impossible search for that distinction, for a recipe for reliable blindness. This is not an inability to get it right, but rather the acting out of an insight into the nature of poetry and the poetic process. For what, indeed, is the problem in any modern theory of poetic language, if not the problem of articulating authenticity with conventionality, originality, and continuity, freshness with what is recognizably "fit" to be called poetic?

While Wordsworth is thus attempting to instate the naturalness of "genuine" repetition, Poe would seem to be doing just the opposite: mechanical repetition is clearly in some sense what "The Raven" is all about. In turning to Poe, one can therefore expect some sort of inversely symmetrical plea for the poetic quality of the mechanical, the empty, and the hollow. It is as though a talking bird were the perfect figure for the poetic parroting of personification that Wordsworth would like to leave behind. But before moving on to Poe, look at Wordsworth's "Strange Fits of Passion" as another inscription of the theories expounded by the preface.

It has already become clear that the phrase "Strange Fits of Passion" can be read in at least two ways as a summary of Wordsworth's poetic project: poetry is a fit, an outburst, an overflow, of feeling;[3] and poetry is an attempt to fit, to arrange, feeling into form. The poem would seem to be about an example of an experience fit to be made into poetry:

Strange fits of passion have I known:
And I will dare to tell,
But in the Lover's ear alone,
What once to me befell.

When she I loved looked every day
Fresh as a rose in June,
I to her cottage bent my way,
Beneath an evening-moon.

Upon the moon I fixed my eye,
All over the wide lea;
With quickening pace my horse drew nigh
Those paths so dear to me.

And now we reached the orchard-plot;
And, as we climbed the hill,
The sinking moon to Lucy's cot
Came near, and nearer still.

In one of those sweet dreams I slept,
Kind Nature's gentlest boon!
And all the while my eyes I kept
On the descending moon.

My horse moved on; hoof after hoof
He raised, and never stopped:
When down behind the cottage roof,
At once, the bright moon dropped.

What fond and wayward thoughts will slide
Into a lover's head!
"O mercy!" to myself I cried,
"If Lucy should be dead!"

The lover's alarm at his wayward thought indicates that he does not know what put it into his head, that he sees no connection between that thought and any part of his waking or dreaming life. The obvious connection the poem invites us to make is between the moon dropping and Lucy dying. But in the poem, that connection is elided, replaced by a mere discontinuity. That connection can in fact be made only in a world that admits the possibility of personification. The moon must be seeable as a correlative, a personification of Lucy.[4] And the hiatus marks the spot where that possibility is denied. The strange fit depicted in the poem can in some sense be read, therefore, as the revenge of personification, the return of a poetic principle that Wordsworth had attempted to exclude. The strangeness of the passion arises from the poem's uncanny encounter with what the theory that produced it had repressed.[5] Indeed, this is perhaps why the *Lyrical Ballads* are so full of ghosts and haunting presences. It is as though poetry could not do without the figures of half-aliveness that the use of personification provides. Or perhaps it is the other way around: that personification gives us conventionalized access to the boundary between life and death that Wordsworth, by repressing explicit personification, uncovers in a more disquieting way.[6]

It is doubtless no accident that a by-product of this fit is the death of a woman. In speaking to the lover's ear alone, Wordsworth is profoundly, as he says in the preface, "a man speaking to men." Even when Wordsworth speaks of or as a woman, the woman tends to be abused, mad, or dead. If Wordsworth's aim in these poems is to undo the abuse of dead poetic figures and recover a more natural language, he seems to have transferred the abuse from personifications to persons.

Poe makes the connection between poetry and dead women even more explicit when he writes, "the death, then, of a beautiful woman is, unquestionably, the most poetical topic in the world—and equally is it beyond doubt that the lips best suited for such topic are those of a bereaved lover" (1084). The work of poetry may well be the work of mourning, or of murder—the mourning and murder necessitated by language's hovering on the threshold between life and death, between pleasure and its beyond, between restorative and abusive repetition. But why, in Poe's case, does the male mourner require a talking bird to make his grief into a poem?

The raven, as Poe explains it in "The Philosophy of Composition," is chosen as a plausible vehicle for the repetition of the refrain—the word "nevermore." The bird is thus a figure for mechanical poetic repetition. The purveyor of the burden has to be a bird: the intentional relation to a signified is denied through the nonhuman repetition of a pure signifier. The word "nevermore," offered here as the most poetical of words, in fact crops up uncannily in Wordsworth's essay too as a distinguishing poetic mark. In differentiating between admirable and contemptible uses of "real language," Wordsworth juxtaposes two short stanzas, one by Dr. Johnson, the other from "Babes in the Wood." Johnson's contemptible stanza goes:

> I put my hat upon my head,
> And walked into the Strand,
> And there I met another man
> Whose hat was in his hand.

The admirable stanza reads:

> These pretty Babes with hand in hand
> Went wandering up and down;
> But never more they saw the Man
> Approaching from the Town.

It is hard to see what Wordsworth considers the key distinction between the two if it is *not* the expression "nevermore." In choosing to have the raven repeat the single word "nevermore," Poe may well have put his finger on something fundamental about the poetic function as a correlative, precisely, of loss.

If the word "nevermore" stands in Poe as a figure for poetic language as such, a number of theoretical implications can be drawn. Since the bird is not human, the word is proffered as a pure signifier, empty of human intentionality, a pure poetic cliché. The empty repetition of the word therefore dramatizes the theoretical priority of the signifier over the signified that Poe claimed when he said that he began the text of the poem with the letters *o* and *r*. The plot of "The Raven" can be read as the story of what happens when the signifier encounters a reader. For the narrator of the poem first introduces himself as a reader, not a lover—a reader of "quaint and curious . . . forgotten lore." Poe's claim, in "The Philosophy of Composition," that the poem was written backward (commencing with its *effect*) applies both to the poem and to the essay about it: both are depictions not of the writing but of the *reading* of "The Raven."

The poem's status as mechanical repetition is signified in another way as well. It would be hard to find a poem (except perhaps "Strange Fits of Passion") that is packed with more clichés than "The Raven": ember, remember, December, midnight, darkness, marble busts—all the bric-a-brac of poetic language is set out in jangling, alliterative trochees to hammer out a kind of ur-background of the gothic encounter. And the conversation begins in pure politeness: "Tell me what thy lordly name is," asks the speaker of the bird, and the bird says, "Nevermore."

The poem within the poem—the single word "nevermore"—has at this point finally been spoken and the reader sets out to interpret it. He begins by finding it obscure:

> Much I marvelled this ungainly fowl to hear discourse so plainly,
> Though its answer little meaning—little relevancy bore.

Then he tries a little biographical criticism:

> "Doubtless," said I, "what it utters is its only stock and store
> Caught from some unhappy master whom unmerciful Disaster
> Followed fast and followed faster. . . . "

Sinking onto a velvet couch, the reader then turns to free association—"linking fancy unto fancy"—until the air grows denser and the reader sees the bird as a messenger of forgetfulness (psychoanalytic criticism), to which the Raven's "nevermore" comes as a contradiction. It is at this point that the reader begins to ask questions to which the expected "nevermore" comes as a ferociously desired and feared answer. The reader cannot leave the signifier alone. Reader-response criticism has set in. In this way, he writes his *own* story around the signifier, letting it seal the letter of his fate until, finally, it utterly incorporates him:

> And my soul from out that shadow that lies floating on the floor
> Shall be lifted—nevermore.

Sense has been made through the absorption of the subject by the signifier. The poem has sealed, without healing, the trauma of loss. What began as a signifier empty of subjectivity has become a container for the whole of the reader's soul. A poetry of the pure signifier is just as impossible to maintain as a poetry of the pure signified. Repetition engenders its own compulsion-to-sense. Poetry works *because* the signifier cannot remain empty—because, not in spite, of the mechanical nature of its artifice.

Paradoxically, then, Poe is writing a highly artificial poem that describes the signifier as an artifice that somehow captures the genuine. Yet generations of American readers have responded to it backward: rejecting it for the artifice its own genuineness is demystifying. It cannot communicate its insight about how poems work if it does not work as a poem. Yet if the poem worked better, it would not carry the insight it carries.

Wordsworth and Poe are thus telling symmetrically inverse stories about the nature of poetic language. Wordsworth attempts to prevent the poetic figure from losing its natural passion, from repeating itself as an empty, mechanical device of style. But the formula for recollection in tranquillity involves just such a blind, mechanical repetition of the lost language. Poe writes a poem packed with clichés in order to show that those clichés cannot succeed in remaining empty, that there is also a natural passion involved in repetition, that the mechanical is of a piece with the profoundest pain. Yet the poem's very success in embodying its message entails its failure to make it true. If it were possible to differentiate clearly between the mechanical and the passionate, between the empty and the full, between the fit and the fit, between "real" language and "adulterated phraseology," there would probably be no need for extensive treatises on the nature of poetic language. But there would also, no doubt, be no need for poetry.

NOTES

1. Citations are from the 1805 version of the preface, as printed in Wordsworth 1974. "The Philosophy of Composition" appears in Poe 1983 (1079–89).

2. For example: "I hope that there is in these Poems little falsehood of description, and that my ideas are expressed in language *fitted* to their respective importance" (75); "If the

Poet's subject be judiciously chosen, it will naturally, and upon *fit* occasion, lead him to passions the language of which, if selected truly and judiciously, must necessarily be dignified and variegated, and live with metaphors and figures" (77); "As it is impossible for the Poet to produce upon all occasions language as exquisitely *fitted for the passion* as that which the real passion suggests, it is proper that he should consider himself as in the situation of a translator" (79). The question then becomes, "Is every fit that fits fit?"

3. In addition to its meaning of "outburst," *fit* can also refer to an arrest, a stroke, a hiatus. Silas Marner's strange fits, for example, freeze him in stop-action stillness while the rest of life continues around him. That the notion of "fits" carries with it a suggestion of the supernatural or the mysterious is indicated by George Eliot's report of folk belief: "Some said that Marner must have been in a 'fit,' a word which seemed to explain things otherwise incredible." Eliot 1984, 55.

4. Cf. Geoffrey Hartman: "To take the moon's drop as the direct cause of the thought assumes that the lover has identified his beloved with the moon." Hartman 1964, 23. The imputation of a suppressed personification here implies that Lucy herself is a person. But is she? The longstanding and unresolved debate over the identity of Wordsworth's Lucy would suggest that Lucy is already not a person but a personification. For a fascinating conceptualization of the question of rhetorically mediated, "naturalized" personifications (that is, those that are made to seem real, "found" rather than allegorically made) and their relation to eighteenth-century allegory, see Knapp 1985. At one point, Knapp essentially uses the notion of a "strange fit" to refer to the Wordsworthian sublime: "Sometimes—and most strikingly in episodes of naturalized personification—the gap between two moments is replaced by a *curious lack of fit* between two ways of perceiving a single object" (108).

5. It might be objected that this is not the type of personification Wordsworth had in mind, that what he wished to avoid was personifications of abstract ideas, not celestial bodies. Yet the example of bad personification Wordsworth cites in the preface *does* in fact involve celestial bodies, not abstract ideas. In the sonnet by Gray in which Wordsworth italicizes only the parts he considers valuable, it is the personification of the sun and of the natural world ("reddening Phoebes lifts his golden fire," etc.) that Wordsworth does *not* italicize.

6. A suggestive gloss on what is unsettling in Wordsworth's rejection of personification is given by Frances Ferguson: "The insistence of the cottage girl in 'We are Seven' that she and her dead siblings are not separated from one another by death involves a kind of personification, but it is personification pushed to such an extreme that it becomes a virtual anti-type to personification. This girl personifies *persons*, and the radically disquieting element in her remarks is the growing consciousness in the poem that persons should need to be personified, should need to be reclaimed from death by the imagination. Her version of personification revolves around death as the essential abstract idea behind personification. Persons and personifications become united members in the community of the living and the dead." Ferguson 1977, 26–27.

"Es lässt sich nicht schreiben"

Plagiarism and "The Man of the Crowd"

STEPHEN RACHMAN

Pap always said it warn't no harm to borrow things, if you was meaning to pay them back, sometime; but the widow said it warn't anything but a soft name for stealing, and no decent body would do it. Jim said he reckoned the widow was partly right and pap was partly right; so the best way would be for us to pick out two or three things from the list and say we wouldn't borrow them anymore—then he reckoned it wouldn't be no harm to borrow the others. —Mark Twain, *Huckleberry Finn*

In other words, everyone will decode it into an admission of plagiarism. But one must not say the "p" word. —Thomas Mallon, *Stolen Words*

At the time of his death in 1849, Edgar Allan Poe left behind an unfinished manuscript of an article earmarked for *Graham's Magazine* entitled "A Reviewer Reviewed." Under the pseudonym Walter G. Bowen, Poe insists that given his literary career as a niggling, fractious critic it is only fair that he "should have the bitter chalice of criticism returned to his own lip," and in a further act of doubling he delivers his criticisms, as he says, in imitation of Poe's "own apparently frank mode of reviewing." Bowen/Poe proceeds in his "apparently frank" way to damn and grudgingly praise himself, to reveal a specious reference to Archimedes in his "Descent into the Maelstrom," and to accuse himself of "the great *point* which Mr. Poe has become notorious for making . . . that of *plagiarism*." This is followed by a series of relatively trivial examples: a line from "Eulalie" is likened to a line from Tom Moore's "Last Rose of Summer"; a phrase from "Al Aaraaf" sounds like a phrase from some anonymous poet; "The City in the Sea" has a line close to one from Mrs. Sigourney's "Musing Thoughts"; and at the point where Bowen/Poe promises to expose the more egregious examples of *"wilful and deliberate literary theft"* in his tale "Hans Pfaall," the manuscript, like its forebears—Poe's other fictionalized, incomplete narratives "MS. Found in a Bottle" and "The Narrative of A. Gordon Pym"—breaks off (Poe 1969–78, 3:1377–87).

Poe, like the Widow Douglas, does not use "soft name[s] for stealing"; unlike Thomas Mallon's academics, he likes to use the "p" word, especially when using it against a fellow scribbler. But when exposing himself, his resolve wavers, his logic falters, his examples fail to persuade. Truth be told, the accusations of "Walter G. Bowen" have merit. Poe is a plagiarist; but if he does not make his claims palpable to us it is because even in death, Poe has managed to imitate his art. "A Reviewer Reviewed" is at once a fictional and a critical act, and as such it calls attention to the way Poe characteristically conflated these literary modes. As a ruse that tends to betray itself in its impossibly intimate scrutiny of Poe's *oeuvre*, it displays his uneasy attitude toward his literary reputation and his criticism as a strategy for enhancing (or destroying) it. But most central to this investigation is the way these concerns converge in Poe's inevitable obsession with plagiarism as the final act of literary self-exposure, and in that convergence the article seems to promise what John Irwin has called "an area of ultimate knowledge," a zone found in Romantic voyage literature where all is revealed, a place like the strange polar sea at the end of A. Gordon Pym's narrative. Typically, when we are cast adrift in these sites of "ultimate knowledge" the moment of revelation is denied us as the narrative is interrupted or the narrator (and in this final instance Poe himself) dies (Irwin 1980, 66). Instead of revelation we get questions about Poe's literary origins and an undermining of the credibility of this act of self-exposure. Essentially, "A Reviewer Reviewed" holds out the promise of resolution; every claim Bowen/Poe makes will be "accompanied *by the proof*," we are informed; but the proof remains as inconclusive as the narrator is unreliable. The questions surrounding Poe's literary origins go unanswered and are displaced by a series of histrionic critical postures, because for Poe (and for us) plagiarism is "an area of ultimate knowledge" and we are denied access to it.

One can understand the fascination plagiarism held for Poe in terms of its potential for ultimate revelation and exposure, as a quest into the dark sources of his own creativity, as a terrain for self-exploration that is central to his and our understanding of his literature. If, as John Irwin suggests, Poe's narrative enterprise seeks to decipher the hieroglyphic code of the self as it grows out of "a question of the development of writing from its origins, and thus the origin of language," then Poe's preoccupation with plagiarism functions as a question of the origins of *his* language and a problem with his own "originality" (ibid., 66, 69). Thus, it is not only in a polar sea that Poe leaves off his narratives but in an inconclusive sea of accusations of plagiarism and parallel texts with an unfulfilled promise of condemnation, confession, and "some never-to-be-imparted secret."

"A Reviewer Reviewed" gives a somewhat extravagant indication of Poe's lifelong obsession with "detecting" plagiarisms, but it is representative of most of his writing about the subject in its preoccupation with the theatrics of making the charge, the inconclusive quality of his "evidence," and the way the trajectories of his arguments inevitably redirect themselves toward investigations into the nature of creativity and defenses or apologies for literary plagiarism. Poe scholars have demonstrated that he accused many authors, some justly, some unjustly, of plagiarism, typically claiming himself as the victim. For example, in a well-known review essay of 1842 in *Graham's Magazine*, where Poe first lays out his concept of effect in the short story, he unjustly and absurdly accuses Hawthorne of plagiarizing from his tale "William Wilson"—paradoxically, after praising the author of "Twice-Told Tales" for his originality.[1] The critical contemplation of Hawthorne's originality occasions both Poe's articulation of his nascent theory of literary effect and a minor charge of plagiarism. It is as if the critical appropriation of Hawthorne, an appropriation Poe would make wholly his own in "The Philosophy of Composition," is insufficient and requires a further act of deep (mis)appropriation. The language and tenor of Poe's criticism display a proprietary need to make Hawthorne's virtues his own (witnessed by his ability to recognize them), a need to boost both his reputation and Hawthorne's, and a need to find in Hawthorne's originality a fragment of his own text—a further, phoenixlike source in which he sees himself.

Poe could easily have numbered himself among the justly accused in his proposed work on plagiarism, *Chapters on American Cribbage*. (Ironically, he could have claimed himself in some cases as the perpetrator and the victim of a kind of autoplagiarism, which speaks volumes about the pseudocritical pose of "A Reviewer Reviewed.") This knowledge is the source of much of his anxiety. Many critics have remarked on Poe's "mania for plagiarism," and virtually none of the major studies of Poe fails to give it some treatment (Hoffman 1972, 100–102). Nevertheless, while scholars are beginning to understand the extent of Poe's "purloinings," there remains a critical uneasiness about and reluctance to recognize the centrality of plagiary to Poe's *modus scribendi*: not simply his methods of constructing his text but the peculiar social construction of his literary style (critical and fictional) and its implications for modern authorship.

To be sure, the reasons behind this attitude toward plagiarism owe much to its scandalous, and perhaps scandalmongering, aspects, not to mention the pedagogical anxieties that render plagiarism inappropriate as a central topos of "respectable" academic literary investigation and analysis (Hertz 1982). Literary plagiarism is a social transgression, policed communally. As a consequence, the topic has enjoyed a marginal, offbeat status as a "curiosity of literature," a dark alley in the psychopathology of literary practice, which is a result of the practical difficulties of defining literary plagiarism. Bowen/Poe defined it as "wilful and deliberate literary theft," but the examples he cites do not convey the force of his formulation. The *Oxford English Dictionary* also puts it directly: "The wrongful appropriation or purloining, and publication as one's own, of the ideas, or the expression of the ideas (literary, artistic, musical, mechanical, etc.) of another," and at Peter Shaw's insistence one should add that the criterion that distinguishes plagiarism from its more benign cousins—intertextuality, imitation, and the oxymoronic "inadvertent plagiarism"—is "an intent to deceive" (Shaw 1982, 334). But plagiarism has its root in *plagiarus*, Latin for "a kidnapper, a seducer," as well as a literary thief. Hence, "plagiarism," Christopher Miller has observed, "is kidnapping, a false fatherhood" (Miller 1985, 220).[2]

In the face of these older meanings, plagiarism as the authorial strategy of Edgar Allan Poe, the rebellious foster son of John Allan, whose literary career was predicated on defying his own "false father," has an obviously uncanny and ironic resonance. Literary authorship, being both a kind of parenthood and a form of artifice, contains within its meanings a fundamental "intent to deceive," and when we take into account the way the modern literary climate privileges so-called originality with this "intent to deceive" it becomes possible to see the attraction (especially for Poe) of a "creative plagiarism," a willfully ambiguous literary surrogation, as a theme and device—one that has an imaginative thrust dependent in part on another text, but by no means circumscribed by that text. I am suggesting a species of literary plagiarism where texts are lifted but put to different ends, ends that are paradoxically creative and "original," which call into question our concepts of literary property and proprietorship. In a culture that on the one hand celebrates originality and its poor relation, novelty, and on the other hand dismisses originality as overrated, plagiarism can become a subversive, quasi-justifiable literary strategy to devalue, revalue, or realign our ambivalence toward "originality" in literature.

This explains in part Poe's suggestion, "When a plagiarism is detected it generally happens that the public sympathy is with the plagiarist" (Shaw 1982, 332). It also explains William Dean Howells's puzzling conclusion:

Plagiarism is not the simple "crime" or "theft" the lexicographers would have us believe. It argues a strange and peculiar courage on the part of those who commit it or indulge it, since they are sure of having it brought home to them, for they seem to dread exposure, though it involves no punishment outside of themselves. Why do they do it, or having done it, why do they mind it, since the public does not? Their temerity and their timidity are things almost irreconcilable, and the whole position leaves one quite puzzled as to what one should do if one's own plagiarisms were found out. (Howells 1902, 277)

Sympathy arises out of complicity, the near-confessional quality of Howells's final sentence would seem to suggest. The discourse of plagiarism deeply invests itself in imagining authorial thought processes or "authorial intention." When fantasy is wed to sympathy, an uneasy logic emerges. The "intent to deceive," to pass another's work off as one's own, becomes its opposite, to "undeceive," to expose oneself. Howells understands plagiarism to be a fundamentally masochistic act in a world where plagiarisms are ultimately revealed and mysteriously treated with indifference by all except the plagiarist, who is deeply mortified by his or her exposure but otherwise goes unpunished. One aspect of the problem resides in the premise that all plagiarisms are "brought home" to their perpetrators, when clearly they are not. Like great spies of whom the world never learns because they have never been discovered, we could reply to Howells, how can we know about what has not been detected? And given this doubt, how can we fail to recognize that, in one critic's words, "it is always possible for profiteers of difference to take advantage of the distance between legitimate authors and the sheets of paper on which their words are registered and distributed" (Hertz 1982, 61)? To take it a step further: it is always possible for "legitimate authors" to take advantage of the distance between their own acts of greater or lesser creativity and the sources that inspired them.

To account for the possibility of a plagiarist going undetected, we must factor an uncertainty principle into Howells's conception, one that alters the quality of the "strange and peculiar courage" for which plagiarism argues. It bespeaks not a guaranteed masochism, but rather an intriguant's uneasy courage on the order of Minister D—— in Poe's "Purloined Letter," who must leave the letter in plain view in the hope (or cunning calculation) that it will go undetected (Poe 1969–78, 3:972–97). Because plagiarists cannot "fence" their goods, there is no statute of limitations on their actions. Thus literary plagiarism engages a peculiar hypocrisy wherein the plagiarist lives not with the weight of inevitable exposure, but with the perpetual burden of potential exposure; in this perpetual burden we find the impetus of Howells's final remark. But if, as in Howells's case, fantasy is wed to sympathy, plagiarism can argue equally for a different kind of marriage, one in which the fantasy of author as plagiarist elicits critical antipathy, and yet this position too exhibits its own uneasy rhetoric. Critics who are outraged by works they believe to be plagiarized also create a projection or fantasy of authorial intention, and from that, not an apology for the irreconcilable "timidity and temerity" of the plagiarist, but a rationale for the deception and an explanation of either the plagiarist's healthy but criminal craftiness, or of his or her pathological imagination. Unlike Howells, in understanding the plagiarist's motives the unsympathetic critic responds by asserting a moral and intellectual superiority rather than an acknowledgment of complicity, and yet this moral assertion invokes a rhetorical confidence greater than the limits of its knowledge.

Specifically, the unsympathetic critic often shares with the sympathetic critic the belief that all plagiarisms are eventually detected. This, as I have suggested above, is clearly unknowable, but what should be kept in mind is that once plagiarism is suspected, the inevitability of its detection is read back into the imagined reconstruction of the author's act of creation. "But one certainty that should be urged upon the aspirant plagiarist," writes Lord Goodman in a *Times Literary Supplement* symposium, "is of early detection. No one can believe into what nooks and crannies readers will penetrate. . . . Therefore, dear plagiarist, hesitate long before you make a deliberate use of a piece of someone else's intellectual property" (Goodman 1982). In a more complex analysis, Peter Shaw insists that

plagiarism remains what it is no matter how inexplicable the manner in which it may have been carried out. As it develops, giving the game away proves to be the rule rather than the exception among plagiarists. Both in the commission of the original act and in the fantastic excuses that follow it, plagiarism is often calculated above all to result in detection. . . . And here the common excuse that the act was unconscious, it seems evident, was not the plagiaristic act itself, the deceptions surrounding which testify to a plentiful awareness of what was being done, but rather the desire to be caught. (Shaw 1982, 330)

While Lord Goodman seeks to deter plagiarists with the fantasy of a reading public composed of literary Mounties and bloodhounds who always get their plagiarist, Peter Shaw relies on the unconscious desire of plagiarists to expose themselves, but both insist on the certainty of discovery. What is more, the attendant moral superiority in their tone would cast the literary plagiarist into the considerably less ambiguous role of the wayward student plagiarist. Goodman and Shaw embrace a "see here" attitude in the face of the labyrinthine motivations literary plagiarism presents. (Shaw's phrases "giving the game away" and "fantastic excuses" suggest an unproblematic, "schoolboy" understanding of "the intent to deceive.") They insist on the ultimate legibility and detectability of plagiarism.

Here again, the psychology found in Poe's "Purloined Letter" can be instructive. In many plagiarism cases, the arena of suspicion quickly makes guilt a matter of confirmation. Likewise, in the tale there is no question of Minister D——'s guilt, only the intellectual challenge and schadenfreude of watching Dupin "detect" the evidence and confirm the suspicion. The imagined nature and psychology of the "intent to deceive" are foregone conclusions. Richard Wilbur has observed how Dupin and Minister D—— are doubles, how Dupin seems to "know" Minister D——'s mind, and that Dupin's conjectures are by no means watertight (Wilbur 1967). Doubles have no need to confirm their intentions, and this sheds light on the pseudonymous Bowen/Poe exposing Poe of plagiarism in "A Reviewer Reviewed." Bowen/Poe has no immediate difficulty with his subjects' intent to deceive, because he is his subjects' double. The psychology and projection invoked in Poe's fashioning of a double to expose plagiarism is the same that led Dupin to expose his double in the purloining of the "letter."

Poe's detective stories promise the reader solutions, even the origin of all solutions, but the solutions they deliver invariably invite the reader to question the assumptions that underlie the process of detection itself. Nancy Harrowitz has demonstrated that Dupin's logic of detection is most typically not one of induction or deduction, but what the philosopher Charles S. Peirce termed abduction. "Abduction is the step in between a fact and its origin; the instinctive perceptual jump allows the subject to guess an origin which can be tested out to prove or disprove the hypothesis" (Harrowitz 1983, 181–82). Abduction is an "originary argument," a conjectural model that allows theorizing to take place, a kind of educated guessing. Through a happy coincidence of meaning "abduction" is also kidnapping, the root meaning of plagiarism. The point is that both forms of abduction recur in Poe's work as self-authorizing acts, ultimately inexplicable moments when logic and writing begin, but cannot be explained as beginnings.

It is not surprising, then, that the critical projections applied to plagiarism are similar to those invoked in Poe's detective or ratiocinative fictions, because they arouse the same suspicions and the same need to obviate the uncertainty of authorial intentions. Lord Goodman's "aspirant plagiarist" hesitating long with poised pen, Shaw's frustrated, reflexive comment "plagiarism remains what it is no matter how inexplicable the manner," and Poe's epigraph "Nil sapientiae odiosius acumine nimio" (Nothing is more hateful to wisdom than too much cunning) exhibit a characteristic tendency to collapse the distance between the act of creation and the act of detection, making the motives transparent, stabilizing the meanings of behavior that is by no means stable. Plagiarism poses a moral threat to the legibility as well as to the attributability of signs; this accounts for the wish of critics disturbed by literary plagiarisms to insist on its inevitable detection, whether, like Poe/Dupin in "The Purloined Letter" and Lord Goodman, they explain it through the superior intellectual and detective powers of others, or, like Peter Shaw, they attribute it to the aberrant psychology of perpetrators who kleptomaniacally "wish to be detected" and unconsciously leave a trail.

In a similar vein, Neil Hertz has observed that academic plagiarism cases are often the sites of professorial fantasies of detecting plagiarism in which the accused student is conflated with his or her work "as an object of interpretation." That interpretation, as in the above examples, focuses on the inevitability of detection and the legibility of plagiarism in the student. Hertz constructs a revealing scene that has implications for literary plagiarism: "There is, first, the moment of suspicion, reading along in a student's paper; then the verification of the hunch, the tracking down of the theft, most exhilarating when it involves a search through the library stacks, then the moment of 'confrontation' when the accusation is made and it is no longer the student's paper but this face we read for signs of guilt, moral anguish, contrition, whatever" (Hertz 1982, 62).[3]

It is striking how much this resembles a detective narrative, how it invokes the theatricality of detection, and in many ways it is a near-synopsis of Poe's "Man of the Crowd." In that story, which I will examine in greater detail below, the narrator sits at a table "reading" the faces of the passing throng when a face in the crowd arouses his interest. He then pursues the man for twenty-four hours through the mazelike streets of London, and ultimately confronts his quarry in front of the very coffeehouse from which he set out, only to declare that his face, like some books ("er lasst sich nicht Lesen"), does not permit itself to be read (Poe 1969–78, 2:505–18). "The Man of the Crowd" resembles, then, a version of Hertz's plagiarism scene, where the confirmation is thwarted because of an inability to read a face. Plagiarism is written into Poe's tales in a deflected or tacit (but not unconscious) manner, operating on a deeper level of narrative silence, attempting to unravel the problematics of originality and authority.

Typically, Poe entangles these problematics in the theater of unveiling. The *coup de théâtre* can be found in many Poe stories, such as "The Black Cat" or "The Tell-Tale Heart." Perhaps we know it best in the formulaic confession-on-the-stand conclusions to Perry Mason mysteries. But in every case, including that of the academic who rifles the library stacks, the intellectual confirmation of plagiarism seems to demand a further physical confirmation. The narrator of Poe's "Thou Art the Man" uses ventriloquism and a case of Château-Margaux rigged with the corpse to frighten "Old Charley" Goodfellow into confessing to the murder of Mr. Shuttleworthy and the framing of Shuttleworthy's dissipated nephew, Mr. Pennifeather (who is reflexively referred to as "Mr. P."). Without demonstrating all the overt and covert ways Poe has made this detective fiction an allegory of plagiarism, suffice it to say that "Thou Art the Man" resembles plagiarism cases in the way inevitably "circumstantial" evidence is used to inform public opinion. Poe explores the psychology of physiognomic "misreading" as the "Rattleburghers" and the court have misread both the faces and the names of Mr. P. and "Old Charley" Goodfellow; it is up to the narrator to engineer a "true confession," which is at once grotesque and comic. In Hertz's example and in Poe's tales, the comparison of texts (evidence) yields to a physiognomy, and in that moment of "confrontation" suspicion becomes fact, the unstable is stabilized, and what we had only suspected becomes what we had known all along.

We enjoy confession, when it is convincing, because it temporarily obviates the need to rely on the uncertain literary or legal systems we require to identify transgression or serve justice, and the suspicion of plagiarism provokes the need both to identify and to confirm the system that makes the identification possible. But keep in mind that Hertz's scene is set in academia, an arena whose immediate moral imperatives are greater than those of the literary world. It is easier to exact a confession from a quaking undergraduate or a broken colleague than from a well-counseled author of bestsellers. It is easier to get a confession across a seminar table than through a heated exchange of letters in a literary journal.

It can hardly be surprising, then, that in literary circles the cry of plagiarism typically elicits anything but a satisfying confession. Since the time of Poe, its potential for totemic or criminal retribution has been mired in the critical theatricality of thrust-and-parry controversy, downgrading plagiarism to something of a literary grievance. Shrill, self-righteous accusation is countered with vehement, indignant denial. Calmer finger pointing often meets with haughty pooh-poohing. On the sidelines, the grim head shaking of critics who bemoan the sorry, profligate times that allow plagiarism to go unpunished is answered by Ecclesiastes-like pronouncements of "nothing new under the sun" and ironic reminders that most so-called originality in literature is only a more successful strain of plagiarism.[4]

While they last, plagiarism cases make for good theater because at their scandalous hearts they destabilize, or rather point out the unstable nature of, the social practice of authorship and the making and unmaking of literary reputations. The instability raises the critical tenor to a histrionic level where high-minded posturing seeks to exaggerate the character of literary practice in order to stigmatize, to minimize, or to attribute this behavior to a postlapsarian *Zeitgeist*. In other words, cases of literary plagiarism set up the expectation of confession and judgment, but because there can be no Supreme Court of Letters, the furor tends to fizzle. "After an initial flurry of discussion," laments Peter Shaw, "most charges of plagiarism tend to disappear from public view" (Shaw 1982, 332).

This contributes to the belief shared by Howells, Shaw, and many other critics who have broached the subject that the general public is quite indifferent to the outcome of plagiarism cases, and its corollary, that the charge of plagiarism, even when successfully pursued, rarely succeeds in damaging the reputation of established authors (ibid., 333). While intuitively I agree with these suggestions, I wonder how we could fairly measure a literary reputation for damage. If established authors who have been accused of plagiarism, such as Alex Haley, Samuel Coleridge, Norman Mailer, or Edgar Poe seem to escape more or less unscathed, then perhaps the retraction, apology, or similar act of recantation that a serious plagiarism case demands can taint a literary reputation but not fully rescind the cultural imprimatur that undergirds that reputation. Literary apologies (in the cases where the author is deceased, the scholars who study them make the apologies) and academic debates are relatively private, quiet affairs, whereas important authors are heralded. So when the hue and cry of plagiarism fades to the whisper of a settlement, Lord Goodman's fantasy of the ever-vigilant public becomes its opposite: the indifferent public. Because the social need for confession so often goes unsatisfied in plagiarism cases, critics complain of a lack of public determination, or general moral laxity.

I find this critically interesting in the way it attacks and attaches itself to the fallen (or "belated," as Harold Bloom would put it) moral and literary state we associate with Romantic, modern, and postmodern thought. On the one hand, plagiarism provokes a moral criticism of the general public; on the other, it provokes a meditation on the psychological disturbances this behavior seems to embody, which also can be called a quality of the modern or postmodern age. We feel the conservative burden of the first position because it implies that, as a literary community, we have fallen from some previous standard of moral rectitude and that the reactionary imposition of some standard may ameliorate the situation. From the perspective of the second position, the general public's purported tolerance of plagiarism is symptomatic of the collective "unhingedness" of the postmodern condition. We have lost touch with our sources, immuring ourselves in a tomb of words, of signs without referents.

Both criticisms, with their Spenglerian sense of the historical decline of a reading public, have lingered at the margins of structuralist and poststructuralist efforts to characterize literary practice. While structuralist and poststructuralist investigations have typically emphasized "intertextuality" and the blurring of boundaries between one text and another, they have done so at the expense of authorial intention and agency (Rose 1988). By suggestively problematizing the concepts of author and originality, poststructuralist approaches tend to dehistoricize "intertextual moments" and neutralize the moral anxiety that surrounds acts of literary appropriation.

But as the issue of plagiarism upsets these concepts, it also insists on a more traditional agency. Recently, Mark Rose has traced the development of the idea of the modern author through the landmark copyright cases of eighteenth-century England and Scotland, and how the concept of the author as a proprietor emerged from that struggle. That proprietary concept allowed for works to be individuated by literary style, which came to mean "the objectification of a personality." But the eighteenth century reserved that objectification for writers and works that possessed "original genius." That is, the individuation of texts depended on the distinction between "an 'original genius' and a mere hack writer" (ibid., 74–75). In Poe we find an author who is both a "hack" and a "genius," two aspects of his literary identity that continually went to war in his prose.

In all the doubling, self-exposure, and mystification, we can see a Poe worrying the proprietary aspects of his critical and literary voices. Literary plagiarism in general, and specifically its role in the work of Poe, with the attendant concepts of intellectual property, copyright, literary reputation, cultural "indebtedness," and the "criminal" and social practices of authorship, offer an opportunity to unite the destabilized concepts of author and originality while historicizing the "intertextual moment."

II

"In getting my books," commences Poe's first installment of *Marginalia* in November 1844, "I have always been solicitous of an ample margin" (Poe 1981b, 1). How fitting in a discussion of Poe and plagiarism that we find him in his *Marginalia* at the margins of other texts. Coleridge, perhaps the greatest of the Romantic plagiarists (De Quincey runs a close second), whose "unpublished marginalia alone would fill several stout volumes," has a library of over six hundred well-marked volumes bearing witness to his predatory habits of reading and writing (Mallon 1989, 29; Fruman 1971). But Poe, in what remains one of the more singular enterprises in literary annals, *published* his marginalia, and he discussed plagiarism and plagiarized frequently in writing them, often reproducing or rehashing bits of his tales and criticism. Poe did not see his marginal scribbling into print merely out of a unconscious exhibitionism, as Peter Shaw might explain it, because he did not in practice mark up his books. "Poe really wrote almost no marginal notes in the books he owned," writes Thomas Ollive Mabbott, justifying his inclusion of the preface to *Marginalia* in his collection of Poe's *Tales and Sketches* (Poe 1969–78, 3:1112). This makes his published marginalia a more artificial order of literary predation than that of Coleridge. In the *Marginalia*, which preoccupied him for the rest of his career, Poe did not merely leave behind a direct record of literary appropriations, he fabricated an intense and fastidious fiction of intellectual activity, an intellectual life central to both Poe's *modus scribendi* and his creation of the detective narrative.

The hallmark of Poe's marginal persona is a fussy idiosyncrasy. "Where what I have to note is too much to be included within the narrow limits of a margin, I commit it to a slip of paper, and deposit it between the leaves; taking care to secure it by an imperceptible portion of gum tragacanth paste" (Poe 1981b, 1; Poe 1969–78, 3:1112).[5] The meticulous delicacy of this image tests our credulity, but in its theatricality and precision it contains an eccentric plausibility, and is representative of the persona readers of Poe cannot help accepting on some level. The marginalia are composed of "extracts and reviews and some articles" (Poe 1969–78, 3:1112); Poe attempts to "literalize" (by actually claiming to have written in the margins of his books) what is a metaphoric condition for his authorial voice. The absurdity of affixing his writings between the leaves of other texts renders the act of marginal writing literally an allegory for plagiarism—writing that exists between the leaves of foreign texts.

As literary practice, *Marginalia* can be seen as a paradigm for and commentary on Poe's conception of literary authorship in the ways he uses it to efface, displace, manipulate, and appropriate other works. By situating himself on the margins (however fictional), Poe creates a kind of writing that draws attention to its own idiosyncrasies while being "about" other texts. In the simplest terms, the marginalia are about sources, about appropriating other texts, about plagiarism and indebtedness, but also about the transfiguration and translation of those texts as a way of incorporating them into his literary identity. Compare the following piece, first published in the *Democratic Review* of July 1846, with its source—a passage from "Tour of a Prince," Sarah Austin's translation of "Die Briefe eines Verstörbenen" by the impossibly named Prince Pückler-Muskau.

POE'S MARGINALIA

"Gênes dans ce temps achetait tout le blé de l'Europe."

For an hour I have been endeavoring, without success, to make out the meaning of this passage—which I find in a French translation of Lady Morgan's "Letters on Italy." I could not conceive how or why all the corn of Europe should have been bought, or what corn, in any shape, had to do with the matter at issue. Procuring the original work, after some trouble, I read that "the Genoese, at this period, bought the *scorn* of all Europe by," etc., etc. Now, here the translator is by no means so much at fault as Lady Morgan, who is too prone to commit sin with the *verbum insolens*. I can see no force, here, in the unusuality of "bought" as applied to scorn—(although there are cases in which the expression would be very appropriate)—and cannot condemn the Frenchman for supposing the *s* a superfluity and a misprint. (Poe 1981b, 117; 1984a, 1397; Schreiber 1930, 2)

AUSTIN'S "TOUR OF A PRINCE"

In the evening Lady Morgan told me that the translations of her works, which were often so bad as to destroy the sense, were a source of great vexation to her. In her "Letters on Italy" for instance, where she says of the Genoese, "They bought the scorn of all Europe," the translator read for *scorn*, corn, and wrote, *"Gênes dans ce temps achetait tout le blé de l'Europe."* (Pückler-Muskau 1833, 430).[6]

Shawn Rosenheim has argued that the central problem of Poe's fiction is "the problem of the existence of other minds" (Rosenheim, 388). I would reformulate this as a problem with the existence of other texts. Other minds are, for Poe, other texts, and they require translation; plagiarism, therefore, as in the July 1846 note, is displaced by its own thematic, by a miniature fiction of translation, sleuthing, and textual comparison. The truly extravagant conceit of the note about the Genoese stockpiling corn is that of Poe at the margins of a French translation of Lady Morgan's "Letters on Italy." Even if we did not have the evidence of the Austin translation, available in the United States in the 1840s, it would be highly implausible that Poe would have possessed a French version of a book that could only be obtained "after some trouble" in the original English. The in situ deception is another "imperceptible portion of gum tragacanth paste." Plagiarism becomes an act not of displacing one text with another but of displacing one margin with another, pretending to be at the edge of Lady Morgan's book(s). It becomes a "marginal fiction" that takes as its subject the difficulties of translation.

And to what end? To niggle over Lady Morgan's "sin" of the *verbum insolens*—the indecent (read inappropriate) word. Poe plagiarizes for ulterior theatrical and self-aggrandizing purposes: petty theft is rendered as an act of petty ratiocination by an adept linguist, yet the uneasy way he corrects Lady Morgan's use of the word "bought" introduces a note of uncertainty. In the face of this shiftiness one should keep in mind that ulterior motives are not the only true motives. Poe, I think, uses the marginal framework as an investigation into his own phraseology; he is attracted to "bought the scorn of all Europe," or at least the idea behind it. When he writes that "there are cases in which the expression would be very appropriate," perhaps he is recalling William Wilson, "outcast of all outcasts most abandoned," "too much an object for the *scorn*—for the horror—for the detestation of [his] race" (Poe 1969–78, 2:426). He seems to buy the scorn of Europe. When Poe plagiarizes he does not so much leave smoking guns as take up the themes of plagiarism allotropically; he views them as an issue of *verbum insolens* and linguistic "sin," of scorn and detection, of translation and mistranslation.

Marginalia shares with plagiarism the common and slippery enterprise of translation, of removing a text to another space. In the handsel to *Marginalia* Poe half-explains:

The main difficulty [in making *Marginalia*] respected the mode of transferring the notes from the volumes—the context from the text—without detriment to that exceedingly frail fabric of intelligibility in which the context was imbedded. With all appliances to boot, with the printed pages at their back, the commentaries were too often like Dodona's oracles—or those of Lycophron Tenebrosus—or the essays of the pedant's pupils, in Quintillian, which were "necessarily excellent; since even he (the pedant) found it impossible to comprehend them:"—what then, would become of it—this context—if transferred?—if translated? Would it not rather be *traduit* (traduced) which is the French synonym, or *overzezet* (turned topsy-turvy) which is the Dutch one? (Poe 1981b, 3)[7]

Traduit and *overzezet:* whenever Poe reaches for his notoriously idiosyncratic foreign lexicon, the wary reader must sense Poe's recourse to a higher authority, and in that recourse a desire ostensibly to stabilize, but also, through theatricality, intonation, and deception, to destabilize (play, pun, invert, expose) its meanings (Campbell 1933, 7–9; Philips 1927; Schreiber 1930).[8] In this example, Poe has in effect traduced his translations, while authenticating with truth-fixing details the fictional (there are no notes!) act of transferring the notes. Most French dictionaries render traduce as *diffamer*, not *traduire*, which means to translate in the ordinary sense. Likewise, the senses of *overzetten* are to ferry over, or to translate; the Dutch equivalent of topsy-turvy is *onderstboven* or *op zijn kop.*[9]

Poe has not simply (unwittingly) mistranslated these words; he has evidently gone to some trouble to mistranslate them. Given the fictional quality of the whole description, one is struck by the attention he gives to his mistranslation. Apparently he needs to append these "synonyms" to his argument, an argument that is about translation—to clinch it, as it were. By phrasing his conclusions in the form of questions he alludes knowingly (without admission) to the darker, more transgressive aspects of translation. We hear in *traduit* and *overzezet* Poe's false cognates "traduce" and "overset," and recognize Poe on another level of clever inversion offering a homeopathic example of traducement. The false cognates become interesting not simply for the irony in their translational inaccuracy but for the mixture of negative and neutral English meanings embedded in them. As plagiarism and *plagiarus* have their roots in kidnapping and seduction, "traduce" enjoys the meanings "to translate, render, alter, convey"; "to produce as offspring"; "to falsify, misrepresent, pervert, turn into (something bad)"; and "to lead astray, mislead, seduce, betray." "Topsy-turvy" conveys the haphazard "in confusion or disorder" as well as the more intentional "inverted or upside-down."

In describing *Marginalia* as translation, Poe lays out the central issue of theatricality that surrounds plagiarism controversies. What is the intent of the author who appropriates or displaces other texts? Is the intertextual moment one of willful inversion or inadvertent disorder? Is it an act of cunning deception or unconscious exhibition or self-display? In many cases, mitigating explanations for plagiarism invoke misplaced quotation marks and garbled notebooks (Mallon 1989, 75, 111, 116; Miller 1985, 223–25; Shaw 1982, 332–50).[10] Because these are transgressive acts, one can feel the manipulative inflection in Poe's use of *traduit* and *overzezet*, conveying an aura of veiled meaning and knowingness, but also remaining deliberately inconclusive. Poe wants his *Marginalia* and other writings to enjoy every meaning of the terms *traduce* and *topsy-turvy*—terms at once neutral and duplicitous.

The problem of other minds and texts is a problem of a will to knowledge that occurs in Poe's plagiarisms and misrepresentations, as in the note about Lady Morgan, predictably in the form of boasts or expressions of vanity; these usually attempt to reflect a wealth of knowledge through a morsel of learning, the existence of a deep mind implied in a fragment of text. Nowhere is this tendency more obvious than in his use of foreign words and phrases. The hallmark of Poe's persona of the literary gentleman is his legerdemain with European and classical languages, and when Poe compulsively dots his narratives with foreign words and quotations one can recognize it as a mark of his ambivalent will to authority. Eighteenth- and nineteenth-century literary gentility was conveyed through a liberality of quotation bespeaking a classical education. *Le mot juste* for such authors as Byron, Isaac Disraeli, and Edward Bulwer-Lytton, to cite three English examples whose miscellaneous writings were models of genteel literary practice for Poe, consisted as often as not in finding an original application of a quotation rather than striving for an original formulation itself (Disraeli 1823, 85–95).

One can often sense in Poe's prose constructions, as in the July 1846 note, a tendency to build around quotations, a willful lack of economy in a willingness to swerve or veer to make some phrase applicable to his meaning. The embedding of text within text in order to create a "frail fabric of intelligibility" is the aligned work of the *Marginalia* and quotation or translation, and when Poe quotes or raises the issue of translation, plagiarism is never far away. Just as the contemplation of Hawthorne's originality leads to an imputation of plagiarism, so does the issue of translation of foreign phrases. In "Thou Art the Man" (1844), while discussing the motives for the murder, Poe digresses in marginal fashion about the misuse of a legal term.

And here, lest I be misunderstood, permit me to digress for one moment merely to observe that the exceedingly brief and simple Latin phrase which I have employed, is invariably mistranslated and misconceived. *"Cui bono,"* in all the crack novels and elsewhere,—in those of Mrs. Gore, for example, (the author of "Cecil,") a lady who quotes all tongues from the Chaldean to Chickasaw, and is helped to her learning, "as needed," upon a systematic plan, by Mr. Beckford,—in *all* the crack novels, I say, from those of Bulwer and Dickens to those of Turnapenny and Ainsworth, the two little Latin words *cui bono* are rendered "to what purpose," or, (as if *quo bono*) "to what good." Their true meaning, nevertheless, is "for whose advantage." (Poe 1969–78, 3:1051)

As Poe swerves to disabuse the "crack" novelists concerning their applica-tion of the term *cui bono,* he accuses Catherine Gore of cribbing from William Beckford, and with a peculiar emphasis on the word "all" he impli-cates Bulwer and Dickens in both matters.[11] The distinction in the Latin that Poe makes is also telling. It is as if Poe is pointing out a Freudian slip that suggests the pervasiveness of cribbing or plagiarism, not just a sole-cism. Poe's pedantic emphasis on the mistranslation of a phrase about profit and motivation indicates an obscurity of motive common to authors; this is reflected in Poe's prose as the detection of the crime digressively becomes the detection of literary theft. That "Thou Art the Man" is more about the theft of an inheritance and the extraction of a confession than murder is underscored by the *cui bono* discussion, linking translation with appropriation.

In his well-known reading of "The Purloined Letter," Jacques Derrida observes, "1. Everything begins 'in' a library: among books, writing, refer-ences. Hence nothing begins" (Derrida 1975, 101).[12] This holds equally true for plagiarized narrative. For Poe, perhaps more than for writers of a dif-ferent stamp, everything does indeed begin in the library. Many of Poe's fictions literally begin in libraries, in the gentleman's study, pondering "over many a quaint and curious volume of forgotten lore" such as Lady Morgan's "Letters on Italy." According to the fictional preface, the idea for *Marginalia* came to Poe from and in his library:

During a rainy afternoon not long ago, being in a mood too listless for continuous study, I sought relief from *ennui,* in dipping here and there, at random among the volumes of my library—no very large one, certainly, but sufficiently miscellaneous; and, I flatter myself, not a little *recherché.*

Perhaps it was what the Germans call the "brain-scattering" humor of the moment; but, while the picturesqueness of the numerous pencil-scratches arrested my attention, their helter-skelter-iness of commentary amused me. I found myself at length forming a wish that it had been some other hand than my own which had so bedevilled the books, and fancying that, in such case, I might have derived no inconsiderable pleasure from turning them over. (Poe 1981b, 2–3)

As a fable of origins, the problem of other minds becomes literalized as the problem of other texts, and the fabricated story of the origins of his marginalia makes an argument for the literary value of a kind of writing so closely allied to reading that it explicitly relies on other texts. The whole discourse is inflected with a connoisseurship: the "miscellaneous" and "recherché" taste that informs the library ("recherché" indeed, since the volumes with marginal notes do not exist in an ordinary sense) informs the author's ability to perceive his marginalia as valuable literature. The point of the fiction is that Poe has to invent his authorship as both marginal and valuable; in a single act thoroughly to conflate his twin careers of critic and author: to be both the creator and the arbiter of his literary value. When he offers the raison d'être for his *Marginalia* he is in effect offering a raison d'être for his literary practice as a whole. Thus, with a blush of modesty, he concludes "that there might be something even in *my* scribbling."

The library, the quotations, the translations, the tidbits of erudition that, for Poe, compose his literary identity and the stuff of which plagiarisms are made contribute in some measure to his literary pedigree. At the same time the preposterously obscure allusions, the knowingness, the gum tragacanth paste, if you will, seem a pose. Poe allows us to see him posing; he "ex-poses" himself. By allegorizing plagiarism in the very act of plagiarizing, he "converses with himself," invoking the dialectic of credibility on which all genteel authorship rests (Irwin 1980, 118).[13] He reneges on his claim to that pedigree of literary gentility by calling it into question as he calls it forth. In short, he plagiarizes in order at once to pose and to dispose of a claim to genteel authorship, and thereby create and control his literary value. Talking only to himself, Poe engages in a full spectrum of genteel literary postures that parallel the theatricality of plagiarism introduced in the first part of this essay.

The process registers a moment of self-forgetting, an unselfconscious moment in which a truer self is taken to be represented. It is akin to scenes of absorption or "the state or condition of rapt attention, of being completely occupied or engrossed . . . in what he or she is doing, hearing, thinking, feeling" that Michael Fried has associated with eighteenth- and nineteenth-century French painting and aesthetic thought (Fried 1980, 10). Poe's narratives frequently begin in moments of absorption, but typically

Poe emphasizes the theatricality of absorption—not a genuine lack of self-consciousness, but a carefully constructed one, designed to figure the impossibility of representing a truly absorbed moment. "The Man of the Crowd" provides striking examples of Poe's use of states of absorption, and analogously so do the marginalia: "because the mind of the reader wishes to unburthen his *thought* [emphasis in original]. . . . we talk only to ourselves; we therefore talk freshly—boldly—originally—with *abandonnement*—without conceit."

Poe claims his scholia as an act of pure reader-response and a style of writing valued for its extemporaneous, almost automatic qualities. The marginal note promises the candor and spontaneity of impromptu, unpremeditated thought, the possibility of witnessing a man thinking, a glimpse of the mind in a germinal stage of association, and a mind under the economizing pressure of limited space compelled to "unburthen" itself. If we did not know that Poe invented it, we might give credence to his abandon. Talking only to oneself increases an author's candor, and so Poe, an author hardly associated with frank simplicity—hardly "without conceit"—ostensibly champions his *Marginalia* for its lack of self-consciousness. But we know that the marginalia are in fact rethinkings, reshapings, and carefully crafted reconstitutions of his purportedly random, spontaneous musings on literature.

Whether or not the marginalia have the abandon Poe suggests they do is debatable, but his claim is important, especially given that his writing grew steadily less arabesque as his career went on (Poe 1969–78, 2:xvii). Fried suggests that "the pursuit of absorption . . . demand[s] that the artist bring about a paradoxical relationship between painting and beholder—specifically, that he find a way to neutralize or negate the beholder's presence, to establish the fiction that no one is standing before the canvas. (The paradox is that only if this is done can the beholder be stopped and held precisely there)" (Fried 1980, 108). If we liken this to writing, authors create the illusion of writing for themselves in order, paradoxically, to transfix their readers with something like a voyeuristic pleasure. It is essentially a confessional mode, or a fictive-confessional mode, which by negating the reader's presence would announce itself as untheatrical. In states of absorption we write "originally," says Poe, but because the absorption is a fiction, so too is the originality a fiction. This effect is in part what Poe attempts in the theme of plagiarism—"the fiction of originality," or what Roland Barthes has called the creation of "believable neologisms" (believable in their newness) (Barthes 1973, 16). Poe's theatricality suggests that claims to a state of absorption are inauthentic, and, by extension, that the originality of anything composed in that alleged state is suspect. The attraction of plagiarism as a practice and a theme lies in the way it allows Poe, as author and critic, to be both painter and beholder, both writer and reader, both creator and arbiter of its literary value.

In what came to be known as Poe's "Little Longfellow War," in which he accused the Boston poet of plagiarism, Poe makes the connection between plagiarism and absorption explicit. Responding to "Outis" (Nobody) in the *Broadway Journal* of April 1845, Poe, in typical fashion, ends up defending plagiarism:

the poetic sentiment . . . implies a peculiarly, perhaps an abnormally keen appreciation of the beautiful, with a longing for its assimilation, or absorption, into the poetic identity. What the poet intensely admires, becomes thus, in fact only partially, a portion of his own intellect. . . . he thoroughly feels it as *his own*—and this feeling is counteracted only by the sensible presence of its true, palpable origin in the volume from which he has derived it—an origin which, in the long lapse of years it is almost impossible *not* to forget. . . . Now from what I have said it will be evident that the liability to accidents of this character is in the direct ratio of the poetic sentiment—of the susceptibility to the poetic impression; and in fact all literary history demonstrates that, for the most frequent and palpable plagiarisms, we must search the works of the most eminent poets (Poe 1984a, 757–58).[14]

The deeply textual character of Poe's apologia should be underscored. Poetic identity is shaped most tellingly solely by one's reading. The greater one's sensibility, the greater one's capacity to absorb, the greater one's susceptibility to plagiarism. Writing is merely a deferred form of reading.

"For an hour I have been endeavoring" is the way Poe characterizes his contemplation of Lady Morgan's corny phrase. The present perfect tense of his logical analysis of the puzzling text not only lends a sense of drama to his solution, but reinforces the illusion of temporal abundance and leisure. Absorption is a prerequisite of genteel scholarship and literary detection, and we recognize the aristocratic class inflection that states of absorption demand. The figure of a gentleman-scholar pondering minutiae in foreign languages for extraordinary amounts of time implies an intense desire for a virtually eternal leisure. The plagiarism in which this fiction is grounded is a way of stealing time, as it were, in order to "forge" space for a narrative of detection that is predicated on a certain amount of leisure for absorption. But once again the theatricality of this gentlemanly pose seeks to undermine the rapt concentration. After all, marginal notes are *brief;* so are most of his tales. Poe writes like a man with little time using a shorthand that seeks to give the impression that he has all the time in the world.

The pose as pose cues the reader of *Marginalia* to the painter as beholder; the artist in the midst of creating his work seeks to ward off criticism by being its critic, by anticipating the challenges of other theories of value. "All this [*Marginalia*] may be whim; it may be not only a very hackneyed, but a very idle practice—yet I persist in it still; and it affords me pleasure; which is profit, in despite of Mr. Bentham with Mr. Mill on his back" (Poe 1981b, 1). Pleasure is profit, says Poe, thumbing his nose at the utilitarians and their unliterary concepts of value.[15] He writes "for the mere sake of scribbling" (Poe 1981b, 3). But one can nevertheless recognize a proprietary anxiety behind the antiutilitarian barb that sidesteps the question of originality. Pleasure may be personally profitable, but does it have any literary value? Can any deep literary value exist in a kind of writing so dependent on other texts for its significance?

The answer is yes; their value lies precisely in their dependence, but Poe can only arrive at this through a dramatization of a circular dynamic. In the library of Poe's marginalia, a pattern emerges. Ennui leads Poe to his re-cherché volumes, establishing (too theatrically) his genteel literary status. Then Poe has a "brain-scattering" moment of absorption. He is transfixed, his attention is "arrested," by the marginalia that were written in a state of absorption, without regard to his beholder/reader ("we talk only to our-selves"). The fiction of his transfixion reinforces the prior fiction of his absorption. Yet even the moment of transfixion betrays its theatrical quality. The "amusement" he expresses seems to belie the intensity of the defamiliar-izing, uncanny experience of confronting the helter-skelter nature of his literary practice. Then coming out of his absorbed state, Poe writes, "I found myself at length forming a wish that it had been some other hand than my own which had so bedevilled the books." In order to be author and beholder he "literally" creates a double, and in that double he finds value in his marginal comments. Through absorption Poe dramatizes an "aboriginal moment" when, at the point of creation and identity formation, the acts of absorbing and being absorbed coexist and are temporarily and temporally resolved by the formation of a wish for a double or "some other hand."

The doubling fiction, one of the most salient features of Poe's *oeuvre*, parallels the will to create the fiction of ratiocination, tracking down the meaning of "[buying] the corn of Europe" (when he knows the answer and has no copy of Lady Morgan). The plagiarism of the Austin text is displaced by the doubling fiction of possessing both French and English versions of Lady Morgan's text. Like the doubling of M. Dupin and Minister D—— in "The Purloined Letter," and the narrator and his quarry in "The Man of the Crowd," this suggests that the mechanism of Poe's literary authority and value relies on a bifurcation and alienation of personality in order to compensate for the presence of other minds and texts created by the plagiarized source.

Yet at the moment of establishing his literary value, he seeks to expose and undermine that posture. Looking at the final words of "The Purloined Letter"—"They are to be found in Crébillon's 'Atrée' "—Derrida observes that "Dupin is obliged to quote this last word in quotation marks, to recount his signature: that is what I wrote to him and how I signed it. What is a signature within quotation marks?" (Derrida 1973, 112–13). It is the sign of a plagiarist, I would respond, but not that of an unconscious plagiarist, a clockwork plagiarist. It is a sign of one who quite consciously purloins and transfigures, and makes themes of those very transfigurations, forging a chain of ambiguous literary parentage that, like the purloined letter, because it cannot do otherwise, remains in plain view. It is a way of both asserting and canceling his literary authority, and in some measure controlling it.

III

"At the outset of Poe's story, we find the narrator seated next to the window of a London coffeehouse on one of the city's busiest streets as evening settles in," writes Robert H. Byer, describing the setting of "The Man of the Crowd" (1840) (Byer 1986, 222). But this is somewhat misleading; "at the outset," the story begins not with the coffeehouse but with its own ending, a quotation, or, more precisely, a misquotation. The tale itself, with its wisp of a plot—from the London coffeehouse, through the teeming city streets, through the narrator's twenty-four-hour pursuit of the old man, "the man of the crowd," and back to the selfsame coffeehouse—is bounded on both ends, parenthetically circumscribed, by Poe's obscure and problematic German phrase: "er lasst [sic] sich nicht lesen." Therefore we begin Uroborus-like, at a point of origin (which is no origin at all) akin to those found in Poe's detective fictions. We are again in Derrida's library, as it were: "among books, writing, references." Imposed on this rigorously circular tale is a further doubling in which the conclusion mirrors not only the opening but the title and epigraph.

Beginning

THE MAN OF THE CROWD

Ce grand malheur, de ne pouvoir être seul.
La Bruyère

It was well said of a certain German book that *"er lasst sich nicht lesen"*—it does not permit itself to be read. There are some secrets which do not permit themselves to be told. Men die nightly in their beds . . . on account of the hideousness of mysteries which will not *suffer themselves* to be revealed. . . . And thus the essence of all crime is undivulged. (Poe 1969–78, 2:506)[16]

Conclusion

"This old man," I said at length, "is the type and genius of deep crime. He refuses to be alone. *He is the man of the crowd.* It will be in vain to follow; for I shall learn no more of him nor of his deeds. The worst heart of the world is a grosser book than the *'Hortulus Animae'** and perhaps it is but one of the great mercies of God that *'er lasst sich nicht lesen.'"* (Poe 1969–78, 2:515)

*The "Hortulus Animae cum Oratiunculis Aliquibus Superadditus" of Grünninger.

What is quoted in the beginning is doubly quoted in the end. "The Man of the Crowd" presents a permutation of Poe's tendency to construct around quotations; he has in effect sandwiched a narrative between two uses of the same quotation. It recalls Derrida's question at the end of his analysis of "The Purloined Letter": "What is a signature within quotation marks?" In that case, one might reply that it is a signet, a seal offered in lieu of a signature—a sign of displaced authorship. But in "The Man of the Crowd," the narrative logic of the closing recapitulates that of the opening in mirror-image fashion. By placing the German phrase and his earlier prose into the mouth of his narrator, incorporating the title and epigraph between those quotation marks, Poe's narrative frame suggests a pair of quotation marks: the inverse "close quote" to match the "open quote." And what is a narrative in quotation marks? A borrowed text, a plagiarism.

Poe evidently based his tale of urban portraiture on Charles Dickens's *Sketches by Boz* (1836), in the first instance using "The Drunkard's Death."

Poe

There are some secrets that do not permit themselves to be told. Men die nightly in their beds, wringing their hands of ghostly confessors, and looking them piteously in the eyes—die with despair of heart and convulsion of throat, on account of the hideousness of mysteries which will not *suffer themselves* to be revealed. Now and then,

Dickens

Such nights only watchers by the bed of sickness know. It chills the blood to hear the dearest secrets of the heart— the pent-up, hidden secrets of many years—poured forth by the unconscious helpless being before you; and to think how little the reserve and cunning of a whole life will avail, when fever and delirium tear off the mask at alas, the conscience of man takes up a burden so heavy in horror that it can be thrown down only into the grave. And thus the essence of all crime is un-divulged. (Poe 1969–78, 2:506–7)

last. Strange tales have been told in the wanderings of dying men; tales so full of guilt and crime, that those who stood by the sick person's couch have fled in horror and affright, lest they should be scared to madness by what they heard and saw; and many a wretch has died alone, raving of deeds the very name of which has driven the boldest man away. (Dickens 1865, 466)

While clearly indebted to Dickens, Poe stands Dickens's passage on its head. The horror of confession, in Dickens conjured from the depths of delirium tremens, Poe transfigures into the horror of aposiopesis. The "rav-ing of deeds the very name of which has driven the boldest man away" becomes secrets that "will not *suffer themselves* to be revealed"; "those who stood by the sick person's couch" become "ghostly confessors" (Byer 1986, 224). Dickens's description relies on a different version of the Romantic sublime[17]—Irwin's hieroglyphic terrain, "an area of ultimate knowledge where one learns 'some never-to-be-imparted secret, whose attainment is destruction'" (Irwin 1980, 69). But for Poe it is some never-to-be-imparted secret whose *revelation* is destruction. Heard crimes are ghastly, but those unheard are ghastlier. At the aposiopetic moment the horror of the crime is internalized, and it becomes a revelation of nonrevelation, compounded by a further passivity: the secrets themselves do not permit themselves to be revealed.

Dickens arrives at his rhetorical pitch through a socially contextualized portrait of alcoholic misery, Poe through an obscure, decontextualized quo-tation.[18] The opening paragraph of "The Man of the Crowd" rapidly moves from a witticism about an "illegible" book to the incongruously emotional and sensational rhetoric of "thus the essence of all crime is undivulged." Pointedly, Poe's tonal flux seems to spring from nowhere, justifying itself only in the tale that follows. Poe's text shadows Dickens, as the narrator shadows the man of the crowd, and Dickens haunts Poe's text in the way the old man occupies the psyche of Poe's narrator. Poe's plagiarism translates tonally into histrionic moral bruxism, altering borrowings so that the prior easily identifiable criminal meaning (drunkenness) is signified by the guilt of undisclosed crime (plagiarism). Moving from text to crime, Poe's alter-ations suggest a transference of the secret textual sin to the corporeal realm ("convulsion of the throat"); plagiarism is rendered in a theater of retribution, where repression administers its own bodily punishment. We recognize this uneasiness and theatricality as the rhetoric of plagiarism, as in Harold C. Martin's *The Logic and Rhetoric of Exposition*, which includes a "Definition of Plagiarism":

it is obvious that plagiarism is a particularly serious offense and the punishment for it is commensurately severe. What a penalized student suffers can never really be known by anyone but himself; what the student who plagiarizes and "gets away with it" suffers is less public and probably less acute, but the corruptness of his act, the disloyalty and baseness it entails, must inevitably leave an ineradicable mark upon him as well as on the institution of which he is privileged to be a member. (Hertz 1982, 60–62)

The plagiarist is ineradicably marked, even if he or she "gets away with it" or, as Poe put it, "er lasst sich nicht lesen."

"*Er lasst* sich nicht lesen?" Should that not read "*es lässt* sich nicht lesen," after all, since the neuter *Das Buch* calls for *es*?[19] Although Poe would not start publishing the *Marginalia* series until 1844, one hears clearly his "marginal" voice as he reaches for his telltale *Wörterbuch*. Regardless of Poe's limited knowledge of German, the mistakes seem too obvious not to be considered as the intentional traducement of his meanings. One cannot too hastily dismiss this as a simple error because "The Man of the Crowd" takes as its theme the act of equating a man (*er*) with a thing, a book, the crowd (*es*). When the phrase appears at the end Poe does not translate it, but leaves it so one may read it either as he translated it at the beginning or as the German suggests, "he does not permit himself to be read." The "German book" is, in the end, likened to the man of the crowd in their mutual illegibility and therefore it (or he) does not permit itself (or himself) to be read.

The "misapplication of quotations is clever, and has a capital effect when well done," Poe observes elsewhere in the *Marginalia* (Poe 1981b, 46). The parallel constructions, at once passive and reflexive ("does not permit itself"), suggest a link between the permissibility of reading, balked confession, and the borrowed Dickensian text. Unreadable books double as unspeakable secrets, as a confession of the unconfessable stands in for plagiarism. Thus, the first paragraph of "The Man of the Crowd," in an act of mistranslation or misapplied quotation, functions as an act of doubling. John Irwin recognized the way Poe's relationship to Pym "suggests the constitutive opposition between the writing self and the written self, the problematic doubling of the writer and his book" (Irwin 1980, 120). But what happens when we learn, as in cases of plagiarism, that the "written self" is composed of other written selves? Authorship becomes an opposition between the written self and the read self: the doubling of the writer and the reading. Thus, "The Man of the Crowd," the title of the story, doubles as "the man of the crowd," the narrator's orphic "text." As in Poe's *Marginalia*, reading is equated with writing, and it follows that what does not permit itself to be read does not permit itself to be written. "Er lasst sich nicht lesen" becomes "es lässt sich nicht schreiben."

One can begin to explain Poe's translation "It does not permit itself to be read" for "er lasst sich nicht lesen." Poe has effectively not "written" what he has read. The latent theme of plagiarism offers a homeopathic example of how the man, the book, and ultimately the story "The Man of the Crowd" do and do not permit themselves to be read; or rather permit themselves to be read, like *Marginalia*, only as "translations" (traductions); they permit themselves to be read only in quotation marks, which is to say as "borrowed" text. In the tale's conclusion, the ambiguous sentences enjoy both a parataxic and a subordinated relation to each other. Should we read: "This old man is the type and genius of deep crime [because] he refuses to be alone, [and therefore] is the man of the crowd," or read it as three separate, noncausal statements? If subordinated, the man of the crowd's criminality is deemed unreadable by virtue of his unwillingness to be alone, but if the "man of the crowd" is anything he is alone in the crowd.[20] "He refuses to be alone" seems ultimately not to follow from the previous sentence; rather, it sits emblematically like the story's epigraph from La Bruyère, "Ce grand malheur, de ne pouvoir être seul" (That great evil, to be unable to be alone) (Poe 1969–78, 2:506), referring us back to the epigraphical (quotable) space between the title and the tale.

La Bruyère's general and passive "ne pouvoir être" becomes Poe's demonic and active "he refuses." The "aloneness" applies to both "the man of the crowd" (the old man) and "The Man of the Crowd" (the tale). He is the "type" (model, foreshadowing, sign) of deep crime, which in the mirror logic of the tale refers to the undivulged secret, the deep crime of type, of signs (Byer 1986, 224). He is objectified, conflated with a text, and becomes the text itself—"The Man of the Crowd." The text then refuses to be "alone"; it suffers from a problem of textual autonomy. It is a composite text, plagiarized and permeated with other texts; it is the text of the crowd.[21]

Poe reviewed Dickens's *Sketches by Boz* in the *Southern Literary Messenger* of June 1836, and found them "all exceedingly well managed," singling out "The Black Veil" and "The Pawnbroker's Shop" while reprinting the "The

Gin-Shops" (Poe 1984a, 205–7).[22] As in the case of Hawthorne, Poe's critical appreciation coincided with a need to plagiarize. Apparently Poe's "abnormally keen appreciation" allowed for the "absorption" of Dickens's words "into his poetic identity." Poe wrote in his *Marginalia* in November 1844, "The serious (minor) compositions of Dickens have been lost in the blaze of his comic reputation. One of the most forcible things ever written, is a short story of his, called 'The Black Veil;' a strangely pathetic and richly imaginative production, replete with the loftiest tragic power" (Poe 1981b, 11). It is no accident that of all Poe's tales this one alone takes the city of London for its backdrop, for we find that, as he did with the foreign citations he culled from English sources, Poe borrowed details from Dickens to pretend to the same kind of intimate knowledge of the city.

Poe	*Dickens*
It was the most noisome quarter of London, where every thing wore the worst impress of the most deplorable poverty, and of the most desperate crime. By the dim light of an accidental lamp, tall, antique, worm-eaten, wooden tenements were seen tottering to their fall. . . . Suddenly a corner was turned, a blaze of light burst upon our sight, and we stood before one of the huge suburban temples of Intemperance—one of the palaces of the fiend, Gin.	The filthy and miserable appearance of this part of London can hardly be imagined by those (and there are many such) who have not witnessed it. Wretched houses with broken windows patched with rags and paper. . . . You turn the corner. What a change! All is light and brilliancy. The hum of many voices issues from that splendid gin-shop. . . . It is growing late, and the throng of men, women, and children who have been constantly going in and out, dwindles down to two or three occasional stragglers—cold, wretched-looking creatures. (Dickens 1865, 171–73)
It was now nearly daybreak; but a number of wretched inebriates still pressed in and out of the flaunting entrance. (Poe 1969–78, 2:514–15)	

Despite the brevity of "The Man of the Crowd," these thinly veiled borrowings from *Sketches by Boz* are not isolated incidents. Many of Poe's details can be found in similar phrasing in other sketches by Dickens: the recurrent descriptions of incandescent lamps in fog and wetness, and of a theater letting out ("The Streets—Night"); a description of a prostitute ("The Pawnbroker's Shop" and "The Prisoner's Van"); a man who wanders in circles aimlessly ("Thoughts about People"); and a depiction of being "once haunted by a shabby-genteel man; he was bodily present to our senses all day, and he was in our mind's eye all night. The man of whom Sir Walter Scott speaks in his Demonology did not suffer half the persecution from his imaginary gentleman-usher in black velvet, that we sustained from our friend in quondam black cloth" ("Shabby-Genteel People," in Dickens 1865, 24).

"The Man of the Crowd" condenses and decontextualizes the ambiance of *Sketches by Boz* into a single continuous foray. While unabashedly relying on Dickens for the details of his London picture, and at times even for his turns of phrase, Poe transmogrifies the socially intelligible world of Dickens into a diabolical parade of types, of urban hieroglyphics ostensibly significant to the narrator only in their potential decipherability. Poe's narrator maintains a disparaging contempt for the types and classes he identifies. As he peers into the mob he recognizes "the loathsome and utterly lost leper in rags—the wrinkled, bejeweled, and paint-begrimed beldame, making a last effort at youth . . . drunkards innumerable and indescribable" (Poe 1969–78, 2:510). The essentials of this description are extracted from Dickens's sketch "The Pawnbroker's Shop" (Dickens 1865, 188–95), but they achieve their exoticism as commodities of interpretation (Poe 1969–78, 2:516). The intrigue they hold for the narrator derives from the "concealment of the social relations that produced it" (Byer 1986, 227). But the mystery is also one of concealed textual relations. The mystification of the city relies on Poe's transfiguration of Dickens's text and the effacement of London's social relations. Dickens assembled his motley cast of characters in the pawnbroker's shop in order to illustrate the ties between the institution and the wretched poverty of its patrons. Dickens draws his characters with sympathy. Poe erases the intimate moral relationship between people and the places they inhabit by subsuming these establishments under the guise of the crowd. His parade of the impoverished evokes no context other than the suspicions of the street.

To clarify this distinction, recall the "Gin-Shops" passages above and, granting the obvious similarity in form and description, note how Poe alters his Dickensian model. Poe makes sensational the filth in his description. The splendid light of the gin shop becomes eerie. The scene resembles a form of devil worship or black mass in a "temple of Intemperance," rather than a foible of the economically depressed. Dickens, while offering a more detailed and charitably comic portrait, asserts quite a different message: "Gin-drinking is a great vice in England, but wretchedness and dirt are a greater; and until you improve the homes of the poor, or persuade a half-famished wretch not to seek relief in the temporary oblivion of his own misery, . . . gin-shops will increase in number and splendour" (Dickens 1865, 173–74). Poe's description relishes the gin shop's "otherness"; the contrast of dark and "a blaze of light" serves only to dazzle. Dickens's contrast of the dark and the splendid does not relish sublime urban landscapes, but points to dire socioeconomic causes he deems responsible for such obvious contrasts. Whereas Dickens grounds his description in Christian, sentimental moral realism, Poe insinuates both the melodramatic and the uncanny. Dickens's voyeuristic curiosity never exists for its own sake, but weds itself to civic and moral issues such as poverty and the degradation it causes, and the gin shops and pawnbrokers' shops and Newgate Prisons amid which it thrives.

The Dickensian mode of authorship maintains a definite sense of Dickens's relationship to his audience. His editorial "we," as in "We will endeavour to sketch the bar of a large gin-shop, and its ordinary customers, for the edification of such of our readers as may not have had opportunities of observing such scenes" (Dickens 1865, 171), conveys his purpose as edifying agent and member of the community he observes. Dickens's authorial voice contains a civic propriety that makes comprehensible the city's divergent behavior—the otherness, or alien qualities—under a rubric of idiosyncratic character (what we have come to recognize as Dickensian tics or mannerisms). Dickens's moral appeal is directed at the better-off, potentially hostile, segment of his community that he feels has blinded itself to the human reality of the impoverished undercultures of London, and rests on the firm belief that all men are basically "good"—unthreatening to the dominant class—and their drastic socioeconomic circumstances are the source of their misery, and ultimately, their otherness.

Poe's mode of authorship is much less assured of its audience ("We talk only to ourselves") and of its authority. Walter Benjamin, in his essay "The Flâneur," recognized in Poe's old man a dark version of the flâneurs—the strolling, loafing sidewalk superintendents, the "botanists on asphalt"—who loitered about the arcades of all the world cities during the first half of the nineteenth century (Benjamin 1973, 48–55). More recently, Dana Brand has suggested that Poe's *narrator* is the real *flâneur*, with his attention to physiognomy; the old man and the narrator are both *flâneurs* of a sort in their un-Dickensian lack of compunction or justification for their idle, voyeuristic gazes (Brand 1985, 36–37, 38).[23] But in their efforts to extend the metaphoric act of reading the public, what Robert Byer calls "the social production of the 'uncanny,' " critics have tended to overlook the literal acts of reading that inform Poe's narrative (Byer 1986, 221; Brand 1985, 37). Poe is a textual *flâneur*, and if Poe's *flâneur*-like narrator is observing anything it is Dickens's text, not the streets of London, Paris, or New York. Poe explores two kinds of public "reading," the latent one being about textual doubling, fusing physiognomic reading with not only social control but textual doubling—that is, plagiarism.

Earlier, I suggested that plagiarism represents itself in Poe's work through a metaphor of absorption. The absorbed gaze incorporates texts into its own text, and corresponds to the mode in which Poe plagiarizes, incorporating bits of other texts into his prose. But I have also suggested that Poe undermines his claim to that state of absorption by leaving some detail, some excessive transfiguration (for example, gum tragacanth paste), that exposes the theatricality of moments of intertextual appropriation. Poe leaves vestiges (traces, signs) of crime that call into question his authority.

I take this to be the central metaphor of "The Man of the Crowd." On several levels, Poe equates absorption with a predatory, appropriative style of reading. The latent level, absorption as *modus scribendi,* in which Poe plagiarizes, reading and absorbing other texts into his work, shadows the telescopic representations of absorption in the text. Poe's London is a veritable chamber of absorption, of concentric levels of rapt attention that reach their *ne plus ultra* in the old man. The narrator is absorbed in watching a crowd of people absorbed in their tasks, until he is thoroughly absorbed in watching an old man who is thoroughly absorbed in watching the crowd, which is absorbed, or at least unaware of being watched.

At the beginning, the narrator identifies gazing and reading with craving and appetite when, in a mood "of the keenest appetency," he amuses himself in the coffeehouse "now in poring over advertisements, now in observing the promiscuous company of the room, and now in peering through the smoky panes into the street." Increasingly rapt, he draws us into his narrative with demonstrations of his own deepening focus. "I gave up, at length, all care of things within the hotel, and became absorbed in contemplation of the scene without" (Poe 1969–78, 2:507). As the narrator turns his gaze away in absorption, setting off a chain of states of absorption, we recognize Poe writing out a prescription for transfixing the reader. Poe wants us to give him the same scrutiny, wants us, finally, to be absorbed in his text.

It reads like a variation of the fable of origins recalled in Poe's preface to *Marginalia.* Analogous to Poe's behavior in his miscellaneous and recherché library of marginal notes, an omnivorous browsing, as a prelude to fixation, occurs in the coffeehouse. Libraries and coffeehouses are both traditional sites of literary confluence. But unlike its eighteenth-century London counterparts, Poe's coffeehouse is more like a library in that it is not a place of public literary discourse but one of private exchanges in public. No conversation takes place at all; in fact, with the exception of a clock striking the hour, Poe's London is largely a silent city.[24] In both *Marginalia* and "The Man of the Crowd," the act of writing is represented by an act of reading that is predicated on a state of absorption. The coffeehouse window that borders on the thronged thoroughfare inhabits essentially the same fictional margin from which Poe writes his scholia. Not only does Poe take much of his description of the crowd from Dickens's text, but as Robert Byer observes, "his descriptions of the crowd often seem mysteriously to offer the precise words by which we might want to describe his own act of storytelling" (Byer 1986, 223).

Men are described as "feeble and ghastly invalids, upon whom death had placed a sure hand, and who sidled and tottered through the mob, looking every one beseechingly in the face, as if in search of some chance consolation, some lost hope" (Poe 1969–78, 2:509–10). This description echoes Poe's prefatory description of men who die "wringing the hands of ghostly confessors," which in turn echoes Dickens's "wanderings of dying men . . . raving of deeds." The plagiarism gets written into the tale as something witnessed but whose content is mute; like books that do not permit themselves to be read, verbal wanderings in Dickens ("strange tales have been told in the wanderings of dying men") become, in Poe, pantomime acts of physical wandering. Through the mirrorlike windowpane the narrator seems to gaze on a representation of Poe's reflexive mode of authorship, which like the *Marginalia* is a public forum in which we talk to ourselves.

But if the windowpane is a mirror, it is also a canvas. It frames the narrator's urban portrait. Absorbed gazing is rendered both as portraiture (painting in a window) and self-portraiture (painting in a mirror). The narrator beholds as he paints, intrigued by his own tableau of the crowd moving from "an abstract and generalizing turn . . . descend[ing] to details." Absorption deepens, offering the narrator enhanced powers. "In my peculiar mental state," he claims, "I could frequently read, even in that brief interval of a glance, the history of long years." Then, at the moment of deepest absorption ("with my brow to the glass"), the narrator arrives at the "brain-scattering" moment of recognition: "a countenance which at once arrested and absorbed my whole attention, on account of the absolute idiosyncrasy of its expression." The old man's appearance disturbs the balance between portraiture and beholding by transfixing the narrator. Through increasingly deeper levels of absorption he enters, at first imaginatively, then literally, the painting, by pursuing the old man through the streets.

In its deepest moment, absorbed beholding is an obsessively allusive gesture; it always holds out the promise of a further text that may be appropriated. Upon glimpsing the old man the narrator wonders, "How wild a history . . . is written within that bosom!" Even the most idiosyncratic incarnations have textual precedents, and the narrator's desire and pursuit spring from the keenest appetency to possess that wild history, to tell it. The narrator's compulsion to compare the face before him with Friedrich Retzch's illustrations of the "fiend" recalls Poe's stunned reaction when he came upon his picturesque pencil scratchings in the margins of his books; his "wish that some other hand than my own had so bedevilled the books." "Brain-scattering" is the word Poe coined to describe that moment, and it applies aptly to "The Man of the Crowd." Brain-scattering connotes the alienation of an absorbed identity, one composed, like marginalia, of an agglomeration of fragments. Recovering from this dispersal, the temporarily scattered identity reconstitutes itself as a collection embodied in "some other hand" or the "man of the crowd."

The chief attraction for Poe of physiognomy and phrenology lay in their power to constitute personality in a composite fashion that corresponds to his techniques of plagiarized composition, his *modus scribendi*.[25] The old man's face, as the narrator reads it, is a composite of paradoxical attributes extracted from the phrenological cabinet of Dr. Caligari: "ideas of vast mental power, of caution, of penuriousness, of avarice, of coolness, of malice, of blood-thirstiness, of triumph, of merriment, of excessive terror, of intense—of supreme despair" (Poe 1969–78, 2:511). Mental power? Coolness? Merriment? Supreme despair? At the moment of descriptive drama, Poe resorts to a typological vocabulary ("The *type* and genius of deep crime") of such generality that, like the language of astrological prediction, it could mean anything. The sublime otherness of this figure arises less from a grisly detailing of physical horror than from the utterly artificial quality of this assemblage of characteristics. The old man is a purely phrenological man, an aggregation of physiognomic traits construed as whole, and this makes him uncanny or "scary." Phrenological vocabulary, because of its typological abstraction, voids itself of stabilized meaning, and does not as such permit itself to be read. But physiognomy and phrenology, like astrology, are forms of wish fulfillment, and when something does not permit itself to be read, when a text does not speak for itself, the reader determines its meaning; the reader speaks for it.

In "The Man of the Crowd" languages of wish fulfillment, like physiognomic/phrenological reading, complement absorption (and plagiarism) as expressions of desire for knowledge (and texts). In describing the narrator's attraction to the old man, Poe attempts to articulate the reasons for idiosyncratic interest, for one's predilections. This butts up against one of the limits of human knowledge. On some level, we need not (perhaps because we cannot) account for what fascinates us; as Poe said of his marginal scribbling, "pleasure is profit." Absorption and plagiarism are continually figured in Poe's *oeuvre* because they premise this inexplicable origin, the source of interest itself. Plagiarism argues not a peculiar courage but a peculiar attraction to some words or thoughts that one would try to possess as one's own. Absorption suggests a tropism, an unaccountable predisposition for intrigue and for temporal dilation, the desire to be fascinated. Intrigue and mystery occur when we cannot account for motive or behavior, and thus the purest form of mystery, Poe implies, lies in the mystery of our idiosyncrasies of interest, or our interest in idiosyncrasy.

Absorption, authorship, and plagiarism are linked in their idiopathy. In fact, it may be argued that absorption is a disease with unknown causes. The story is bounded by quotation; it is equally circumscribed by unspecified illness and death. The narrator of "The Man of the Crowd" informs us, "For some months I had been ill in health, but was now convalescent, and, with returning strength, found myself in one of those happy moods which are so precisely the converse of *ennui*" (Poe 1969–78, 2:507). And by the story's conclusion it appears that the narrator is going to require further convalescence: "I grew wearied unto death" (ibid., 515). Like the cortical excitement found in victims of tertiary-stage syphilis, absorption suggests a hiatal moment between phases of a disease, a manic high in which the patient enjoys a preternatural "appetency," "the film from the mental vision departs . . . and the intellect, electrified" (ibid., 507). Poe claims for writing, at least for his *modus scribendi,* a kind of pathological status.

Dickens writes of the "hidden secrets" and "strange tales" that are told "when fever and delirium tear off the mask at last." Illness occasions lurid storytelling. But in "The Man of the Crowd" the state of absorption stands in for the latent pathological one; absorption occasions the reading of the crowd (and Dickens's text). Absorption, not delirium and fever, becomes the agent that tears off of the narrator's mask in "The Man of the Crowd"; the narrator's telling of the strange tale is predicated by close reading, just as Poe's writing of the story is predicated by his "close reading" of Dickens.

For all this, there remains a deep incongruity about "The Man of the Crowd." The tonal effect of calling this apparition "the type and genius of deep crime" and the air of dismissal in "er lasst sich nicht lesen" as some kind of merciful truism has the effect of putting a moral bandage on a gaping wound. The preposterous allusion to the obscure "Hortulus Ani-mae" of Grünninger is lifted out of Isaac Disraeli's *Curiosities of Literature* (as if someone could possibly have this thought), once again cementing the link between his plagiarism and his willingness to undermine his authority with overtheatricality (Disraeli 1823, 364).[26] In this way "the man of the crowd" is linked to "The Man of the Crowd"; they are both composites couched in a language of wish fulfillment, where the wish is knowledge. Plagiarism is thus a will to knowledge. Perhaps "The Man of the Crowd" is a more vulnerable form of the detective narrative, in which we confirm our suspicions in spite of our uncertainty. It reminds me of Neil Hertz's sce-nario for catching a student plagiarist. We have "the moment of suspicion"; the "exhilarating search through the library stacks" (city streets); "then the moment of 'confrontation'"; but the moment of confrontation is no con-frontation; we talk only to ourselves. We expose only ourselves.

IV

How does Poe's brand of plagiarism inform our ideas of authorship? In "What Is an Author?" Michel Foucault made strange the lineaments of the cultural concept of the author, or "author function" as he called it. In this celebrated essay Foucault disabused us of our transparently held notions of the relations between authors and texts. Authors are not an inalienable property of texts, but part of an evolutionary development in the individua-tion of ideas. At some vaguely modern historical moment texts began to point in a more commodified way to their authors, to the "figures" that are ostensibly outside them and antecede them. In a moment of almost Martian defamiliarization, he suggests how the author function allows critics to make unities of textual disquietude:

The author is also the principle of a certain unity of writing. . . . [that] serves to neutralize the contradictions that may emerge in a series of texts: there must be at a certain level of his thought or desire, of his consciousness or unconscious—a point where contradictions are resolved, where incompatible elements are at last tied together or organized around a fundamental or originating contradiction. (Foucault 1984, 111)

If plagiarism can be rightly said to have any teleological purpose in Edgar Allan Poe's authorial strategy, then it seems to be to disturb the principle of unity to which Foucault refers. Our concept of plagiarism accords with this premise of authorial unity because it presumes a kind of textual consis-tency—if not consistency of style, then of effect.

Plagiarism takes on the status of an originating contradiction that explains textual inconsistencies. Typically, it is not authorship itself that is being called into question by plagiarism, but whose authorship. Poe uses plagiarism to question the very nature of authorship itself, not to "tie together" but to untie "originating contradictions." Poe takes the debate of plagiarism, which is organized around a dialogue between individual authorial voices, and turns its dialectical energies toward a more generalized debate with an inherited tradition of authority itself. Thus, Poe plagiarizes not simply to usurp another's authority, but to assert his own authority while questioning the tradition in which he asserts it.

Foucault suggests that "texts, books and discourses really began to have authors ... to the extent that authors became subject to punishment, that is, to the extent that discourses could be transgressive" (ibid., 108). Plagiarism offers Poe a special, inherently transgressive discourse regardless of content; like the "man of the crowd" it can only be read as crime. "It is as if the author, beginning with the moment at which he was placed in the system of property that characterizes our society, compensated for the status that he thus acquired by rediscovering the old bipolar field of discourse, systematically practicing transgression and thereby restoring danger to a writing which was now guaranteed the benefits of ownership" (ibid., 108–9). Poe finds his transgression in the literal; he seeks to expose his plagiarisms to make a perverse claim to authority and originality.

And it seems that the strategy has worked. No amount of scholarly effort or negative press, no accusations of plagiarism, can rescind the authorial status our culture has attributed to Poe. He is part of the cultural apparatus itself. Nevertheless, plagiarism is central to his *modus scribendi* and helps us make sense of many of his perplexities and conundrums, as well as pointing to the peculiarly textual preoccupations of the detective story, the literary form for which Poe makes his greatest claim to originality. An awareness of plagiarism sets in a new light the comment of Méryon, an associate of Baudelaire, who wondered about "the real existence of this Edgar Allan Poe." He attributed Poe's tales "to a group of highly skilled and most powerful men of letters, acutely aware of everything that was going on" (Derrida 1973, 103).

NOTES

1. Poe suggested that Hawthorne's "Howe's Masquerade" borrowed from "William Wilson." But Hawthorne had actually published his story in the *Democratic Review* in May 1838, whereas "William Wilson" was completed in 1839. But more striking and to the

point is the generic quality of the passage Poe cites as parallel. They are both about cloaks, capes, and men with swords; otherwise there is no literal resemblance (Regan 1970; Poe 1984a, 568–77). In his marginalia of December 1844, Poe maintains, in an otherwise unqualifiedly positive assessment of Hawthorne, that "he is not always original in his entire theme—(I am not quite sure, even, that he has not borrowed an idea or two from a gentleman whom I know very well, and who is honored in the loan)" (Poe 1981b, 47).

2. All definitions are taken from the *Oxford English Dictionary*. Miller (1985, 216–45) offers an important discussion of literary plagiarism in the European Africanist tradition. Miller discusses Ouologuem's plagiaristic literary strategy as a way of focusing on the literary tradition in which he is trying to operate. Ouologuem, an outsider trying to establish an African voice in a European tradition, Miller concludes, "refuses to be either 'original' or 'copy'" (238). Poe's situation is analogous to Ouologuem's if one thinks of him either as trying to fit into an Anglo-American tradition or as establishing a southern literary tradition in the face of the New England literary tradition.

3. For another example of the "confrontation," see Mallon 1989, where the teacher, Anna, uses a "dramatic Perry Mason approach." After lulling the student-suspect into a false sense of security, "quick as a flash, Anna pulled the desk drawer open, whipped out the book he had plagiarized from, and thrust it into his face. 'Did you get any of your ideas from *this?*' she asked, and the student all but collapsed" (96).

4. For an example of the typical theatrics the subject can provoke, see Goodman 1982, 413. Christopher Miller, who finds plagiarism so commonplace in the European Africanist tradition that "one begins to see theft as origin itself," writes: "Plagiarism as a problem in literary criticism tends to elicit two responses: either an accusation of criminality or a recuperation as originality" (1985, 219–20).

5. One wonders if Professor Mabbott checked the books extant in Poe's library for imperceptible traces of gum tragacanth residuum.

6. Poe evidently knew of this book through a pirated edition of 1833, which was reviewed during his tenure as editor of the *Southern Literary Messenger* (Schreiber 1930, 2). In looking through Morgan 1821, chiefly her chapters on Genoa (230–58), I could not find the line in question, which implies that her comments and Poe's were purely anecdotal.

7. For notes, see Poe 1969–78, 3:1112–18. The willfully obscure references to Lycophron Tenebrosus and Quintilian's obscurantists are found in Disraeli 1823 (72). Poe frequently relied on Disraeli for displays of obscure learning. Poe's obscurity in the face of worrying over the obscurity of his meaning is analogous to his strategy of plagiarizing a text about plagiarism.

8. The consensus is that his quotations from Latin, the language he seems to have known best, are frequently inaccurate. His French is, to use a favorite word of Poe's, "outré," and given to frequent idiomatic inaccuracy. His knowledge of German was limited. But the point is what Poe makes of these materials, as he was never one to let the unknown stop him from using it.

9. Mabbott suggests that "Poe's intentional confusion here is compounded by what is probably a printer's error—*z* for *g* in *overgezet*." While this suggests the false cognate "overset," I think that is equally conveyed in *overzezet*. Given Poe's emphasis on translation, *overzetten* is equally apropos.

10. Plagiarism cases raise quite directly the question of the author's method of construction, and inevitably authors who admit that they were influenced by another author claim that they had inadvertently transferred things from their notebooks into their work without being aware of the plagiarism. This is even more common in cases of scholarly plagiarism. "Sloppy note-taking" is frequently offered as an explanation for uncited or unconscious quotation. It is an admission of the use of another person's words without being an admission of "the intent to deceive."

11. Ironically, Poe borrows heavily from Bulwer and Dickens in "The Man of the Crowd." "Turnapenny," a name for one who writes for money, points to the proprietary anxiety behind this attack.

12. This is also a response to Rosenheim 1989 (380) and Johnson 1988 (235). The difference between Johnson's "source" for Dupin (in a book called *Sketches of Conspicuous Living Characters of France*) and the appropriations from Austin's translation lies in the way the latter compromises Poe's claim to a kind of intellectual activity (reading French, and hunting down sources), whereas finding the germ for Dupin in no way impugns the act of detection as an imaginative one. "The Murders in the Rue Morgue" and "William Wilson" begin in libraries, and "The Man of the Crowd" begins in a coffeehouse/library of sorts.

13. Irwin writes, "Poe is, of course, a master at creating narrators who in the attempt to establish the credibility of their narratives manage to unravel their own efforts. . . . They add a detail that arouses our distrust, usually a revelation of doubleness." Plagiarism differs in that it remains a doubleness of text, and operates at a level of relative narrative silence, though Poe and his personae arouse our distrust with peculiar details.

14. For a complete history of the Longfellow War, see Moss 1963, 132–89. Hovey 1987 places Poe's charges against Longfellow in the context of sectional bias, with Poe championing a southern, Byronic, dissolute pessimism and Longfellow a New England Wordsworthian (via Bryant) moral optimism. Ljungquist and Jones 1988 contradict the contention of Mabbott, Perry Miller, and G. R. Thompson that "Outis" was Poe. They claim that "Outis" was the editor of the New York *Rover*, Lawrence Labree, and that Labree was integral in forcing Poe to retract his charge. Poe did retract a charge of plagiarism against Longfellow, but always maintained that the author of *Hymn to the Night* was fundamentally epigonic and didactic. One should also bear in mind that Poe sought contributions from Longfellow at the time he was making his charges.

15. For a similar attack on Jeremy "Diddler" Bentham, see Poe's "Raising the Wind; or, Diddling Considered as One of the Exact Sciences" (Poe 1969–78, 3:869–82).

16. The title and epigraph are included to demonstrate the way the conclusion mirrors the introduction. For Poe's other uses of the phrase "er lasst sich nicht lesen" see his 1845 review of Cornelius Mathews's *Big Abel and Little Manhattan* (Poe 1984a, 837). For this I am indebted to the source hunting of Mabbott (Poe 1969–78, 2:518). So fond was Poe of this remark that he recycled it in an 1849 *Marginalia*-like piece entitled "Fifty Suggestions" (Poe 1984a, 1307).

46.

"It is not fair to review my book without reading it," says Mr. M—— [Mathews],
talking at the critics, and as usual, expecting impossibilities. The man who is
clever enough to *write* such a work, is clever enough to read it, no doubt; but we

should not look for so much talent in the world at large. Mr. M— will not imagine that I mean to blame *him*. The book alone is in fault, after all.

The fact is, that *"er lasst sich nicht lesen"*—it will not *permit* itself to be read. Being a hobby of Mr. M—'s, and brimful of spirit, it will let nobody mount it but Mr. M—.

17. If we take both authors' gestures seriously, not as a form of histrionics, they suggest a truly dark vision. In Dickens's case, what deathbed confession could be so horrifying that it would actually drive a listener away in fear for his sanity? For Poe, what crimes will not suffer themselves to be revealed? Poe fixes not on the tale of horror but on the effect of the information on the teller. For both writers the actual tale is beyond the pale of their imaginative frameworks, but for Dickens it is a fantasy of completely and totally alienating his audience. For Poe it is a fantasy of not being able physically ("convulsion of the throat") to tell what so desperately desires to be told.

18. Poe's revisions of "The Oval Portrait" (1842) (Poe 1969–78, 2:659–67) exhibit the same tendency to decontextualize or make unspecific the causes of strange visions. Poe excised large chunks of the story that dealt with administering opium and narcotic illusions, leaving only the state of absorption, in which "Long—long I read—and devoutly, devotedly I gazed."

19. Mabbott suggests that the *er* could refer to the word *hortulus,* in the title of the "German book" named when the phrase is repeated at the story's close, and he notes that "in 1837 Poe boarded with the learned bookseller William Gowans, who took an interest in incunabula, of which Grünninger's 'small octavo in Gothic type' is an example" (Poe 1969–78, 2:518).

20. This reads like an abductive syllogism (Harrowitz 1983, 182).

21. The line in *Les caractères* by La Bruyère reads, "Tout notre mal vient de ne pouvoir être seuls." This line was also used by Bulwer-Lytton in *Mortimer; or, Memoirs of a Gentleman* (1835). Poe relied on a chapter of Bulwer-Lytton's *Pelham; or, Adventures of a Gentleman* (1827) for his tale "Lionizing" (1835); see Benton 1968. The line from La Bruyère itself is recycled and cited by proxy in "Metzengerstein" (1832) (Poe 1969–78, 2:18); Poe evidently came across it in *Pelham* as the epigraph to chap. 42. Byer (1986, 224) finds another source for the story in Bulwer-Lytton's *Eugene Aram.*

22. For a history of the relationship between Poe and Dickens, particularly Poe's debt to Dickens, see Grubb 1950. It is well known that Poe's "Raven" has its roots in *Barnaby Rudge;* it is not so widely known that "The Black Cat" and "The Tell-Tale Heart" have their roots in a story from *The Old Curiosity Shop* entitled "Confessions Found in a Prison in the Time of Charles the Second," which Poe praised in a May 1841 *Graham's* review (Poe 1984a, 212). See also Krappe 1940.

23. Brand demonstrates that Poe's acquaintance with the *flâneur*-figure is found not in the French but in the English tradition of "Addison, Steele, Lamb, Hunt, the Dickens of the *Sketches by Boz.*" See also Trachtenberg (226).

24. The conspicuous absence of noise from "The Man of the Crowd" is another indicator of the story's origins in text rather than "life." Remarkably, for all its menacing aspects, the crowd never intrudes on the narrator, and Poe offers one of his implausible explanations for being able to pursue the old man in all this silence without being noticed. "Luckily," the narrator interjects at one point, "I wore a pair of caoutchouc

over-shoes, and could move about in perfect silence." More gum—or should I say "caoutchouc"?—tragacanth paste.

25. In a postscript to the marginal note about Dickens, Poe reflected: "P.S. Mr. Dickens' head must puzzle the phrenologists. The organs of ideality are small; and the conclusion of the 'Curiosity-Shop' is more truly ideal (in both phrenological senses) than any composition of equal length in the English language" (Poe 1981b, 11). Poe toys with the idea that the phrenological equation could work in reverse: from reading a person's work one could determine the lineaments of the writer's head.

26. There is no realistic possibility of Poe having ever seen this book, and his use of Disraeli's misspelling of the text reinforces this claim.

PART TWO

GENERIC LOGIC

Terminate or Liquidate?

Poe, Sensationalism, and the Sentimental Tradition

JONATHAN ELMER

There is a scene in Carl Theodore Dreyer's film *Vampyr* (1931) that exhibits clearly the way in which the sensational—the moment of shock, or horror, or revulsion—vampirizes the sentimental. One of a pair of sisters lies expiring on her deathbed: she is beautiful and wan, and Dreyer films her as if she were literally fading away before our eyes. She is watched over by the tender and anxious figures of her sister and a nun. Suddenly, the dying sister's eyes open; she picks up her head, fixes her sister with a gaze of vampiric lust, and slowly tracks her sister across the room with a chillingly unnatural smile. What is shocking here is the disruption of the sentimental scene, the way in which the object of our memorializing desire—for the sentimental, as I will argue, always works on the desire for an object that is disappearing—suddenly becomes horrifyingly revitalized by an unnatural, illicit desire *for us*. One aspect of the uncanniness of this moment is surely the odd self-recognition it induces, odd because what we are confronted with is something that looks like our own desire turned upside down, inverted—so that rather than the tender and pained grimace that marks the solicitude of the living for the dying, we see directed back at us the steely and lascivious grin of the dead desiring the living. Poe knew well the force of such alienated self-recognitions: Ligeia's struggle to take over Lady Rowena's dying body is the sign of what Poe calls her "gigantic volition," in which the narrator of the tale both does and does not see reflected his own perverse desire. And the modulation of a primed sentimental affect into excess and shock remains a favorite effect: for every sentimental deathbed scene in contemporary mass culture—Debra Winger's pallid farewells to her family in *Terms of Endearment*, say—we can find its corresponding mutation into the horrific. Thus Linda Blair's evilly smirking and foul-mouthed Regan in *The Exorcist* can be seen to depend for its effect on the fact that underneath the open wounds she is "simply" a little girl on her sickbed in a nightie—that is, a descendant of Little Eva.

I mention Stowe's child-hero because I want eventually to place the sickbeds of Little Eva and Poe's revolting M. Valdemar next to one another in order to demonstrate what a comparative diagnosis can turn up. It is in their methods of literary assassination, or more gently, their respective treatments of the spectacle of "the death of the other," that we can see how the sentimental and the sensational are complementary modes, dependent on each other for their own proper functioning. "The death of the other" represents a foundation and limit to our sociality, Hegel argued, in what has become one of the most reworked motifs in this Hegelian century: we can find this idea that the *socius* is inaugurated essentially, originally, and incessantly through the spectacle of the suppression (or death or murder) of the other in Freud's *Totem and Taboo*, Lacan's *Seminars*, Heidegger's *Being and Time*, and—the version most helpful for my immediate purposes—Walter Benjamin's well-known essay "The Storyteller." The encounter with the death of the other is an essentially dialectical affair in which the self invests and disinvests, alienates his or her identity and receives it back again. In playing across this dialectical space, in taking up their various stances toward it, the sentimental and the sensational communicate across a divide that is simultaneously encompassing and interior to each side, paradoxically both externally limiting and internally dividing. This divide is what I call the social limit, since it is the place of the encounter with an other, that place in which social identity—one's imagination of self as a *social* self—is negotiated with other figures who either do or do not return or confirm one's desire in recognizable forms. These figures can be the others in a book, or the other that is the book, or the other that is one's own self reading the book: the interactions of desire and identification at the social limit are also, in other words, inflected as scenes of reading and interpretation.

I take my cue here from Benjamin's essay, which describes the different social functions of the novel and the story in terms of their disposition of the dead. According to Benjamin, the novel's desire for strong closure—"that limit at which [the novelist] invites the reader to a divinatory realization of the meaning of life by writing 'Finis' "—finds its most powerful vehicle in the death of a character: "A man . . . who dies at the age of thirty-five. In other words, the statement that makes no sense for real life becomes indisputable for remembered life. The nature of a character in a novel cannot be presented any better than is done in this statement, which says that the 'meaning' of his life is revealed only in his death" (Benjamin 1969, 100). The novel thus provides its readers with what seems to be an external purchase on fate, a chance retroactively to fix and order a life in a way that we never can for our own lives, so that the figure appears to be at all points what he or she in fact only becomes at the point of termination.

What is most significant here is not, however, the particularities of the life that becomes so ordered, the content of the lesson, but the very commitment and engagement on the part of the reader to the ordering process itself: "The novel is significant, therefore, not because it presents someone else's fate to us, perhaps didactically, but because this stranger's fate by virtue of the flame which consumes it yields us the warmth which we never draw from our own fate. What draws the reader to the novel is the hope of warming his shivering life with a death he reads about" (ibid., 101). The novel's significance lies in the reader's relation to this "representation of [life's] fulness" (ibid., 87) as fixed by death; for the reader of a novel knows beforehand that he or she will be required to read all moments in the lives of the characters as defined by their death. It is as though Benjamin were intimating that the novel-reader stands in a zone of death toward which the characters are wending their way, and it is merely the promise of their arrival in that zone that animates the reader: "How do the characters make him understand that death is already waiting for them—a very definite death at a very definite time? That is the question which feeds the reader's consuming interest in the events of the novel" (ibid., 101). As Benjamin says, extrapolating from Lukács, the novel-reader operates in a temporality of remembrance, a constitutively elegiac time defined by the future perfect: every event he reads about *will have been* the act of someone who will die "a very definite death at a very definite time."

What seems to stick in everyone's mind from Benjamin's essay is that line about "warming his shivering life with a death he reads about." This is because we see an image of repose, even coziness—someone seated by a fire reading a book—while fluttering beneath it, or hazily floating over it, are elements of a scene of sacrifice, a ritual immolation: what remains so striking is the intimation of violence visible about the edges of a *scene of reading*. The story, too, in Benjamin's account, emerges from a scene of reading, in which we can make out the features of another conventional tableau—the collective witness around the deathbed: "Just as a sequence of images is set in motion inside a man as his life comes to an end—unfolding the views of himself under which he has encountered himself without being aware of it—suddenly in his expressions and looks the unforgettable emerges and imparts to everything that concerned him that authority that even the poorest wretch in dying possesses for the living around him. This authority is at the very source of the story. Death is the sanction of everything that the storyteller can tell" (ibid., 94). The storyteller, then, like the novelist, must also make use of the "authority" of death, but there are two features that serve to distinguish this use. If the novelist offers a sacrificial victim to the reader, the storyteller presents, rather, the aspect of a martyr giving himself over completely to the "gentle flame" in the cause of "counsel" (ibid., 86): "The storyteller: he is the man who could let the wick of his life be consumed completely by the gentle flame of his story" (ibid., 108–9). This self-positioning in the consuming fire of the reader's attention has a decisive consequence, for the limit presupposed and operated by the novelist, the limit of a symbolizing and exemplifying death, is here precisely held open, rendered visible, by the storyteller. The holding open of this limit, this tarrying in a moment of affective authority, is what makes the story constitutively open-ended; as Benjamin remarks, "there is no story for which the question as to how it continued would not be legitimate" (ibid., 100). As opposed to the closure of the novel, which accords with and reconfirms the individualism of its epoch, the story renders visible, rather than evanescent, the social and collective confrontation with death. The novel speaks of death; in the story, the dead speak.

Benjamin's remarks allow us to see that the varied solicitations and manipulations of readerly affect in the face of the representation of death correspond to two quite different social and ideological programs. I am not interested, as Benjamin evidently is, in nostalgically heroizing the story or the storyteller as "righteous" (ibid., 109), "rooted in the people" (ibid., 101), the last flashing vision of an epic consciousness. But Benjamin's historical argument does not suggest that the mode of the story continues to live on past its historical supersession by the form of the novel, almost as though the story is the undead of the novelistic age. In the eighteenth and nineteenth centuries the sentimental novel induced mourning as a social program, one serving a liberal ideology that, in provoking sympathetic distress, aims to affirm a prediscursive, prerational unity of human feeling. In Poe's hands,[1] the tale programmatically zeroes in on the distress itself and aims to restrict itself to that. Recall the two scenes I contrasted above: the solitary reader by the fire, the gathering of the survivors around the deathbed. As the history of the novel in the eighteenth and nineteenth centuries shows clearly, the novel needs that deathbed scene, needs to sublimate its affective energy so that it can be converted into fuel for the solitary reader's fire. But if the sentimental novel aims to make affective sympathy—which is, as it well knows, constitutively social, collective—safe for the bourgeois individual by his fire, the Poesque tale occasionally manages to make that latter image itself the site of horror, or anxiety, or revulsion. Before getting to Poe's sensationalizing of the sentimental, however, I need to sketch the complex mechanisms of identification at play in the sentimental novel, for it is against and within the conventions of the sentimental that Poe's horror emerges.

Lives Fit to Be Written

In his *Autobiography*, Benjamin Franklin gives an account of the initial motivation for the composition of his book as well as of the detour through which what ostensibly started as a private correspondence came to be overtly framed as a public and exemplary tale. Writing during a "Weeks uninterrupted leisure" in 1771, Franklin addressed his son in the belief that a description of the "conducing Means [he] made use of" in attaining a "State of Affluence & some Degree of Reputation in the World" would be of interest to his family, and that these "Means" would perhaps even prove "fit to be imitated" (Franklin 1987, 1307). While such an address may look like the typically paternal appeal to "follow in my footsteps," in fact Franklin goes out of his way to excuse in advance any potential reader: he will not be "troublesome to others who thro' respect to Age might think themselves oblig'd to give me a Hearing, since this may be read or not as any one pleases" (ibid.). The writing of his *Autobiography*, Franklin admits, is essentially a private affair of vanity, an attempt at "living [his] Life over again" in the form of a "second Edition" (ibid.). Franklin presents himself, in the printing metaphors here and throughout the *Autobiography*, as a book that can picked up or laid aside at the reader's pleasure.

Twelve years later, Benjamin Vaughan urged Franklin to continue his *Autobiography* and to make it available to the public: "If it encourages more writings of the same kind with your own, and induces more men to spend lives fit to be written; it will be worth all Plutarch's Lives put together" (ibid., 1377). In Vaughan's view, the advantage of striving to lead a life that, like Franklin's, is "fit to be written" is that it disposes the individual to conceive of his or her life as a whole, that is, as a work that, since it must finish in any case, might as well be a finished product: "Our sensations being very much fixed to the moment, we are apt to forget that more moments are to follow the first, and consequently that man should arrange his conduct so as to suit the *whole* of a life" (ibid., 1376). Vaughan's idea is that if a person can plot his or her own life, that person can rise above the flux and confusion of a series of "sensations . . . fixed to the moment." Instead of the book of his life that Franklin provides his son, Vaughan proposes that Franklin offer the life of a book as an object of imitation. It is less important, Vaughan implies, to follow in the footsteps of a great man, no matter how freely or selectively, than it is to follow the plot of your own self-written text: Franklin is exemplary not so much because he is an admirable character as because he is the successful author (of himself).

We have here a sketch of the structure of "the liberal example," by means of which a formalizing liberalism aims to ground politics in an aesthetic pedagogy. Three features need to be distinguished in this structure. First, the exemplary figure, in his or her commitment to individual freedom ("this may be read or not as any one pleases"), does not demand imitation of his or her life, but simply demands or solicits *imitation of his or her freedom*. Franklin here conforms exactly to what Kant in *The Critique of Judgment* calls the "exemplary originality" of the genius: what the genius offers others are not rules to follow, but an example that can be imitated *only in its exemplarity* (Kant 1951, 161). Second, this paradox of exemplary originality implies an ideal that is, as David Lloyd has persuasively argued, constitutively out of reach. Liberal pedagogy will thus demand a "free" conformity to an unrealizable ideal: we will all be examples together of the failure to reach the ideal, but we will each be exemplary in our own way, in accord with our individual freedom. This structure of necessary failure, and free conformity, leads to what Lloyd has memorably called the "inexpungible melancholy of the pedagogical scene" (Lloyd 1989, 39), a melancholy, I would add, marking the entire sentimental tradition in its enforcement of the liberal example. Third, the structure of Franklin's example requires individuals to view their lives from the "other" side, as though their stories were already finished. They have to attempt to live their lives as they would like them to be seen from the perspective of a reader of their lives. This double consciousness entails the suppression of "sensations . . . fixed to the moment," a transcendence of the affective that, as Lloyd remarks, occupies a crucial place in Kant's universalization of aesthetic judgment.[2] To summarize: Franklin's exemplary life, insofar as it displays the structure of the liberal example, solicits an impossible *identification* with an inimitable and unreachable ideal, an identification that depends on, if only in order to move beyond, the more immediate "sensations . . . of the moment." Moreover, this supersession of affect is imagined in terms of writing and written narrative, for in the transformation from an ostensibly private correspondence to a public work, the exemplary force of Franklin's *Autobiography* has modulated from an account of behavior "fit to be imitated" to one of a life "fit to be written."

Franklin's self-presentation to his son not as the father who is due the "respect to age" demanded by a patriarchal culture, but rather as the *book* of the father, suggests the extent to which the published word had already infiltrated the family structure, intervening between parent and child and powerfully modifying, through its own structures of exemplarity, the moral instruction of the young.[3] Jay Fliegelman has demonstrated the ways in which the massive influence of Locke's pedagogical theory, as outlined in *Some Thoughts concerning Education* (1693), found expression in the latter half of the eighteenth century in the extraordinary outburst of works designed to aid parents in the moral education of their children. While most of these "family instructors," to recall the title of Defoe's early example of the genre, were directed toward parents, the translation of this moral pedagogy into the forms of fiction, a translation effected most notably with the publication in 1740 of Richardson's *Pamela,* tended to result in the works' more overt address to the children themselves. It was not simply that children needed to be protected from the snares and temptations of the world beyond the family confine (although this remained the dominant moral lesson); parents themselves could well be responsible for their children's misery through various "infringements of filial liberty or independence," such as "denying a child a proper education, arranging a marriage for 'family aggrandizement,' unjustly denying a child an inheritance, or irrationally preferring one child to another" (Fliegelman 1982, 36). Richardson's preface to *Clarissa* (1747–48), for example, is marked by this double address: "the principal views of the publication," he writes, were "to caution parents against the undue exertion of their natural authority over their children in the great article of marriage: and children against preferring a man of pleasure to a man of probity, upon that dangerous but too commonly received notion, *that a reformed rake makes the best husband*" (Richardson 1985, 36). Richardson understands the publication of his novel as the insertion of a caution, a kind of pedagogical mediation of the relationship between parent and child, as well as that between the (female) child and the public world of men and courtship.

The preface to *Clarissa,* however, looks suspiciously like damage control, since it was, at least in part, the unprecedented popularity of Richardson's earlier *Pamela* that had caused the notion that "a reformed rake makes the best husband" to be "too commonly received." In setting up Pamela as an example of virtue rewarded, Richardson evidently could not prevent his young readers' powerful identification with the heroine from taking an improper turn. This turn, as always in liberal aesthetic pedagogy, is to take what was meant as an *example* as a *model* for an all-too-faithful imitation. In the United States, Timothy Dwight's alarm is typical: the reader of a novel—whom Dwight characteristically assumes to be a woman—"must one day act in the real world. What can she expect, after having resided so long in novels, but that fortunes, and villas and Edens, will spring up every where in her progress through life, to promote her enjoyment. She has read herself into a heroine, and is fairly entitled to all the appendages of this character" (Davidson 1986, 51). Dwight offers here a vision of an irredeemable absorption in the text and a consequent inability, on the part of the impressionable reader, to distinguish fiction from reality. The novel becomes a model for the world, rather than a more or less instructive example of real-life behavior. As a result, and according to the same error, the young reader "reads herself into a heroine," which means she takes as a model for a hopeful imitation everything about this female hero save her mere exemplarity. Dwight's language here is instructive, for to describe the reader's identification with the protagonist as a desire for "all the appendages" is to call up, behind the primary meaning of Dwight's term, an image of an improper attachment to the character's bodily "appendages."

Richardson wrote *Clarissa* in order to disrupt this tendency toward improper imitation: rather than the appealing example of Pamela, which might encourage imitative readers to entertain hopes of converting the local rake, Richardson offers Clarissa, who, because she is both warning and paragon, can remain exemplary only by provoking an ambivalent investment on the part of the reader. By having his hero both retain her spotless purity and suffer "seduction" and death, Richardson manages to keep Clarissa before his readers as a model of virtue, while at the same time preventing the attraction to this model from articulating itself narratively, as a desire for "all the appendages" of Clarissa's story. Part of what frustrates a sense of readerly identification with Clarissa is her impossible patience and perfection; as Richardson himself commented, Clarissa is set up as an exemplary figure in order that she might, like the unreachable ideal of the liberal example, all the more effectively "reproach" the reader. Comparing his novel to Fielding's *Tom Jones*, Richardson writes that with "illegitimate Tom, there is nothing that very Common Persons may not attain to . . .

while Clarissa's Character, as it might appear unattainable by them, might be supposed . . . a silent Reproach to themselves" (Moretti 1987, 190). But what differentiates the exemplary force of Clarissa from that of Pamela most significantly is not, I would argue, Clarissa's inimitable perfection, nor her seduction, but simply the fact of her death. If a young reader's identification with Pamela could be imagined to lead to disastrous attempts at imitation, what happens to that same reader's identification when the protagonist dies? It will be transferred from the body of Clarissa to the discourse that memorializes her as a paragon of virtue. Clarissa's life will no longer be seen so much as a life "fit to be imitated" as one "fit to be written."

One way to understand this transfer of affective energy is as a move from imaginary to symbolic identifications, as Slavoj Zizek has described this distinction in Lacan's thinking: "imaginary identification is identification with the image in which we appear likable to ourselves, with the image representing 'what we would like to be', and symbolic identification, identi-fication with the very place *from where* we are being observed, *from where* we look at ourselves so that we appear likable to ourselves, worthy of love" (Zizek 1989, 105). Imaginary identification has all the marks of an absorp-tion in an image (as indeed does the imaginary register as a whole in Lacan), and entails a kind of mirroring imitativeness. Symbolic identification, by contrast, is with a place ("*from where* we are being observed"), or we might say, with a prior set of discursive rules (the symbolic precedes and de-termines the imaginary), rules that dictate the attractiveness or appropri-ateness of images. The feared identification with Pamela would, on this account, be an instance of imaginary identification, while the reader's sym-bolic identification with the moral discourse underpinning Richardson's second novel would allow her to continue to celebrate Clarissa's perfections, only now from the safer locale of a memorializing gaze.

Pamela can be seen as the ancestor of an entire tradition of novels about women who endure a series of temptations and aggressions in order finally to be rewarded for their virtue by a romantically or economically satisfying marriage. Such novels—sometimes drained of the overt sexual aggression found in Richardson—flourished particularly in America for much of the nineteenth century; Nina Baym has dubbed the genre "woman's fiction."[4] They are novels of socialization, although the ideological and narrative emphasis, as Baym argues, is on the replacement of the traditional male social world by one modeled on and centered around the woman-controlled domestic household. But if *Pamela* offers the model for a certain kind of Bildungsroman, what kind of socialization can be said to take place in

Clarissa, or the host of "seduction novels" that reworked its basic narrative? Given that these novels inevitably describe the abandonment, social stigmatization, and death of their protagonists, we could understand them as telling the story of a woman's *de*socialization. Cathy Davidson argues that these novels, in the very starkness of their implacable exposition of sociosexual rules and (double) standards, constitute a mute protest against that repressive social world. As Davidson herself notes, however, seduction novels were clearly read by men as well as by women, and the value of such a mute protest for men, while not unimaginable, needs nevertheless to be shown.

It is here that the role of the sentimental seduction novel in liberal aesthetic politics becomes crucial. Insofar as these novels strive to bring about a symbolic identification with the moral discourse defining the death of the female hero (as just, as tragic but necessary, as beautiful, and so forth), they depend on the reader's ability to transcend the particularities—those "appendages" of character—that concretize and crystallize imaginary identification: "we could say that in imaginary identification we imitate the other at the level of resemblance—we identify ourselves with the image of the other inasmuch as we 'like him', while in symbolic identification we identify ourselves with the other precisely at a point at which he is inimitable, at the point which eludes resemblance" (Zizek 1989, 109). In leading a reader's identificatory energy toward the inimitable, the sentimental seduction novel provides training in the liberal self-abstraction by means of which gender divisions are ideologically (but not practically) subordinated to the affirmation of a unity of human feeling.

This ostensible bracketing of gender, however, is a ruse, for if the novels aim to induce, in both male and female readers, a flexibility with respect to the identificatory registers, the registers themselves remain strictly gender coded. Zizek reminds us that while the symbolic may seem secondary to the imaginary, in fact "it is the symbolic identification (the point from which we are observed) which dominates and determines the image, the imaginary form in which we appear to ourselves likable" (ibid., 108). It is from the vantage of the male symbolic that the imaginary is marked as feminine: this is why the sentimental seduction novel aims to disrupt a fantasized scene of woman-woman identificatory merger by not only erasing the female hero, but also by writing into the fabric of the tale the instruction of the female *reader.* The imitative reader, the one caught up in the lures of a too-affective imaginary identification, is always a woman, or rather, is always feminized. This doubled purging—of the female hero and of the feminized reader—implicates the sentimental seduction novel in a fundamentally ironic structure, since it must pose within its very structure the figure of a naive reader from which it strives to separate both itself and its actual readers. This ironic structure forms the essential duplicity of the sentimental novel.[5]

The Sacred Drop of Humanity

We can see the duplicity of this doubled purging at work in the conventional deathbed scene, in which the final moments of the doomed female hero are played for maximum affective response, only to be immediately contained by a didactic discourse. Grief and mourning, even if only their simulation in a fictional world, constitute extreme affective states resistant to the recuperative discourse of liberalism; for this very reason, that discourse would like both to contain and to redirect this seemingly recalcitrant intensity.[6] We could call this process, after Arnold Schwarzenegger and the argot of thuggery, the "termination" of the character, in that such scenes mark both the "finishing off" of the hero and the placement of her life and death in their proper *terms*. If we wish to find a sophisticated example of sentimental termination we can hardly do better than look at the death of Eva St. Clare in Stowe's *Uncle Tom's Cabin* (1852), surely the most widely consumed sentimental death in nineteenth-century America.

It would be a mistake to characterize Stowe's novel as sentimental *tout court*, but there are features in *Uncle Tom's Cabin* that reveal it to be continuous with the exemplary structure of *Clarissa*, most notably in that the novel's didactic force—and both novels commit themselves overtly to didacticism—is a function of the simultaneous triumph and victimization of the central character; in Stowe's novel, this victimization is distributed between two central characters, Little Eva and Uncle Tom. Like Clarissa, both Stowe's characters are simultaneously *examples to* and *examples of.* They are exemplary victims of the injustice of the slave system Stowe so relentlessly exposes: Tom is killed through a brutality both simple and systematic, while Eva is laid low through a more insidious kind of exposure to the unsought knowledge of evil, which the lack of an adequate domestic regimen renders her incapable of resisting. But while both characters are meant to warn us away, they are also meant to draw us toward them, for they are also both examples to the reader of the triumphant power of Christian faith in the face of death. This positive exemplarity has observable effects within the novel: it is through the force of Eva's example that Ophelia learns to recognize her Northern brand of unfeeling racism, its essential lack of sympathy, and finally becomes, in her changed attitude to Topsy, what Tom and others call her, "Miss Feely."

The death of Little Eva serves as the effective cause of this conversion of Ophelia, the coldly efficient homemaker, into "Miss Feely," the sympathetic guardian of Topsy; in this respect, Miss Feely can be seen as a figure for the proper reader of Stowe's novel, brought down from an abstract understanding of the evils of slavery to a personal recognition of the ameliorative efficacy of social sympathy. It is true that Ophelia's sympathetic engagement is so limited and selective that her nickname never ceases to strike the reader as more than a little grotesque. Nevertheless, it would be a mistake to see Stowe as endorsing such an equivocal stance toward Ophelia, since it is finally in the very limitation and control of her sympathy that the latter is exemplary, as she steers a middle course between an extreme sympathetic absorption and an inability to engage at all. This strategy of controlled sympathy is figurally linked to the duplicitous disposition of the body in sentimental termination. On the one hand, the body must be suppressed: hence the stoic, and of course Christian, indifference of Little Eva to her gradual dissolution; indeed, given the alarming transparency Eva's body assumes toward the end, we might see her as simply being erased. But the body must not be denied entirely, and it is for this reason that Little Eva engages in the dispersion of her corporality, with the parceling-out of her locks of hair coming to stand as the figure for each survivor's moment of connection, each lock a little morsel of sympathy, the circumscribed bit of affect simultaneously solicited and controlled.

The sophistication of Stowe's staging of the sentimental termination is due in large measure to the way in which she includes within her scene all its possible readings. Thus, it is not just the positive example of Miss Feely that we discern at Eva's bedside, but the two negative extremes she successfully avoids as well. On the one hand, there are the household slaves, extremely impressionable, almost blindly imitative. Their presence during Eva's deathbed sermon is marked by a kind of hypnotic assent to everything she says: " 'I know,' said Eva, 'you all love me.' 'Yes; oh, yes! Indeed we do! Lord bless her!' was the involuntary answer of all!" (Stowe 1982, 421). The "involuntary" aspect of the slaves' response to Eva is to be understood not simply as an incorrect reading, but fundamentally as an inability to read, as Eva herself makes plain with unwitting comedy: " 'If you want to be Christians, Jesus will help you. You must pray to him; you must read—' The child checked herself, looked piteously at them, and said, sorrowfully, 'O dear! You can't read—poor souls!' " (ibid., 418–19). But while the sentimental tradition will not fail to marginalize this kind of deep absorption as an excessive and blameworthy naiveté, Stowe condemns Eva's mother for the opposite reason. The calm resignation that marks the entire scene of Eva's termination is disrupted at only one weird moment, which is no less striking for being entirely unremarked by the text:

> Eva soon lay like a wearied dove in her father's arms; and he bending over her, soothed her by every tender word he could think of.
>
> Marie rose and threw herself out of the apartment into her own, when she fell into violent hysterics.
>
> "You didn't give me a curl, Eva," said her father, smiling sadly. (Ibid., 421)

Together with the slaves' absorption, Marie St. Clare's "violent hysterics" erupting within this scene of sentimental termination figures for Stowe the dangers of a sensationalized reading. For Stowe the moments represent simply the failure of reading, since sentimental reading can only properly take place in a disciplined act of superseding an affective reading, and not in either its complete acceptance or its violent rejection. But Stowe's control here is signaled by this very eruption, for the flare of hysteria, a hysteria of reading, which bursts forth in this exemplary termination is the sign of the power of affect subsisting beneath this controlled veneer.

Stowe's most complex mobilization of the duplicity of the sentimental novel is reserved for her treatment of Eva herself, who represents both figures sentimentalism poses in order to purge, both the feminine reader and the female who is read. Speaking of St. Clare's past history, Stowe writes, with the recognizable self-ironization of the sentimental: "Of course, in a novel, people's hearts break, and they die, and that is the end of it; and in a story this is very convenient. But in real life we do not die when all that makes life bright dies to us" (ibid., 241). The implication here is that Stowe's novel is not in fact a novel, or rather that it is not a novel of a certain sentimental kind, in which people die of broken hearts for the convenience of a story interested in maintaining its separation from something called "real life." Stowe is disingenuous, however, since it is manifestly the case that the central scene of the novel is precisely such a death as she ridicules: surely Little Eva dies of a broken heart as much as from consumption. She dies, in fact, as Philip Fisher has pointed out, through the consumption of other people's stories, which are themselves stories of broken hearts.

In this way, Eva herself is the supreme figure for the reader, a reader lauded as properly sympathetic (that is, naturally sympathetic, unlike Ophelia, who must be trained) and overcome by a too affective reading: it is thus the constitutive ambivalence of the sentimental novel toward its reader that requires that Eva be simultaneously celebrated and exorcised.[7] She is the figure of sentimental identification par excellence: as the focus of an ambivalent attraction, she is the very shape of sentimental reading, that movement by which the reader's body becomes first penetrated and then purged by sympathetic affect. Fading away before our eyes are both the feminized object of identification and the feminized subject of reading. In reading Eva's death, the reader sees "her" own reading overcome and superseded; in dropping a tear, "she" memorializes—from the vantage of a symbolic identification—a necessary but dangerous affective reading.

In its careful control of readerly affect, Stowe's novel is heir not simply to the Richardsonian model, but also to an extensive eighteenth-century discourse that linked "sympathy" to a fundamental and innate human sociability. By locating social affection in a realm of sensation, where it must exist in an "uneasy strong" relation to the entire range of suspect, even antisocial, "bodily appetites," Scottish moral philosophy bequeathed to American social thought at best a vexed compromise with—and at worst an exacerbation of—the epistemological difficulties engendered by Lockean sensationalist psychology.[8] How exactly was one to distinguish the laudable and public-minded "compassion and pity for the distressed" from a sensualistic indulgence in "passion" per se? In late-eighteenth-century America, the vogue for the novels of Laurence Sterne, and what was seen as a "cult of sensibility," provoked this question in a pointed way. As Herbert Ross Brown notes, "Critics immediately perceived the seductive nature of this new menace": "In the half-light of sensibility, benevolence seemed to blend with indulgence; even moralists found it a bit difficult to distinguish delicacy from looseness in the mysterious shades of the finer feelings" (Brown 1940, 75). Most accounts of the sentimental tradition in England or America describe the conflict between compassion and passion in terms of the vagaries of the sentimental vocabulary: while "sentiment" and "sentimental" continued to connote a Richardsonian emphasis on the instructive moralizing made available by strong feeling, the term "sensibility" came to designate, especially after Sterne, a more rapturous, involuntary, and finally, morally inefficacious indulgence in sensation for its own sake.[9] In the first letter of William Hill Brown's *Power of Sympathy* (1789), Harrington writes to his friend Worthy: "you call me, with some degree of truth, a strange medley of contradiction—the moralist and the amoroso—the sentiment and the sensibility—are interwoven in my constitution, so that nature and grace are at continual fisticuffs" (Brown 1969, 8). The alignments between moralism and sentimentality, and a suspect amorousness with sensibility, are clear enough here, but it is the "strange medley of contradiction," the sense of an inextricable relation between passion and morality, that is the emphasis of the passage, as it is of the entire novel.

The Power of Sympathy is an exemplary sentimental novel precisely because of its contradictory and ambivalent investment in the force its title designates—a force at once irresistible and dangerous, both "natural" (tokening suspect animality) and a sign of "grace" (indicating divine sanction). Brown's novel manages both to celebrate a humanizing and beneficent sensibility ("From thee! Author of Nature! from thee, thou inexhaustible spring of love supreme, floweth this tide of affection and SYMPATHY" [105]) and to detail the disastrous effects such sympathy can have. After all, Harrington's troubles arise from his peculiar susceptibility to the irresistible attraction that draws him unwittingly toward his illegitimate sister: he has, in short, "too much sensibility" (ibid., 169). Insofar as sensibility and sympathy signify an innate principle of sociality they must be honored and celebrated; to the extent that they evoke the involuntary submission (recall Stowe's distressed slaves) to an attraction so strong that it transgresses the divisions of class, gender, and family that safeguard social morality, such forces must be warned against and overcome. Sympathy and sensibility must be both invoked and suppressed in the sentimental novel.

The vocabulary that sustains liberalism's fundamental ambivalence toward its affective principle of sympathy figures this principle as liquid. Sensibility has its "source" in God or nature, "an inexhaustible spring of love supreme," to quote Brown again, from which "floweth this tide of affection and SYMPATHY." In the sentimental novel, what "floweth" most of all are tears. As the signs of a divinely implanted social sympathy, tears are universally valorized. Here is Susannah Rowson in *Charlotte Temple* (1791): "For ever honoured be the sacred drop of humanity; the angel of mercy shall record its source, and the soul from whence it sprang shall be immortal" (Brown 1940, 87). And although tears are coded as feminine, sentimentalism will celebrate this kind of "weakness" as the indication of social affections that do often lie too deep for gender divisions: when Charlotte's father "relieved his almost bursting heart by a friendly gush of tears," Rowson has this to say: "Should any one, presuming on his own philosophic temper, look with an eye of contempt on the man who could indulge a woman's weakness, let him remember that man was a father, and he will then pity the misery which wrung those drops from a noble, generous heart" (ibid., 52–53).

Rowson's confrontation here with the contemptuous "philosophic temper" indicates that, if tears signal a social affection that is understood as antecedent to gender distinction, they also claim precedence over systematic thought, and indeed over language itself. As Flaubert's Rodolphe Boulanger was well aware when he dribbled drinking water over his farewell epistle to Emma, a tear-stained letter communicates more fully than one in which every word is legible. Tears flow but they also blot out: thus Harriot, in *The Power of Sympathy,* exclaims when she has written the word "brother" against her will, "blot it out my tears!" This blotting out seems to promise a cleansing, something like a correction of the book of fate: "Ye eloquent *tears* of *beauty*! that add dignity to human nature by correcting its foibles—it was *these* that corrected my faults when recrimination would have failed of success—it was *these* that opened every avenue of contrition in my heart, when *words* would have dammed up every sluice of repentance" (Brown 1986, 120). While tears figure here a triumph of social affection over rigidifying language, it is a triumph notably in the service of the moralism of "repentance." Finally, tears are not enough: Harriot's tears cannot blot out the word "brother" from the text of her fate, and the seducer Harrington Senior, who speaks the paean to tears, will not be allowed a full and satisfying penitence until his heinous deed has been seen to result in the deaths of his two children.

Tears are not enough because they are too much, and threaten to open up the sluices too soon. They must be regulated and directed toward the proper objects, as Rowson unaffectedly makes clear in the following instructions to her readers: "Yes, my young friends, the tear of compassion shall fall for the fate of Charlotte, while the name of La Rue shall be detested and despised. For Charlotte, the soul melts with sympathy; for La Rue, it feels nothing but horror and contempt" (Rowson 1986, 99). Precisely because tears have this ability—both celebrated and feared—to overcome language, they must be subsumed by the duplicitous mechanisms of the sentimental novel. The negative counterparts of tears—the floods, streams, and other ruinous liquids—will thus be associated with the kind of reading sentimentalism hopes to contain through its didacticism. We can turn here to the sententious Reverend Holmes in *The Power of Sympathy:*

I would describe the human mind as an extensive plain, and knowledge as the river that should water it. If the course of the river be properly directed, the plain will be fertilized and cultivated to advantage; but if books, which are the sources that feed this river, rush into it from every quarter, it will overflow its banks, and the plain will become inundated: When, therefore, knowledge flows on in its proper channel, this extensive and valuable field, the mind, instead of being covered with stagnant waters, is cultivated to the utmost advantage . . . for a river properly restricted by high banks, is necessarily progressive. (Brown 1986, 30)

Holmes's concern about flooding echoes the general social fear to which the sentimental novel so successfully played, the fear that the rising tide of novels dispensed by the circulating libraries would circulate something more than moral instruction. This anxiety was not only an eighteenth-century affair: Nina Baym has noted that the "language of tide, flood, deluge, and inundation also suggests uneasiness" on the part of the cultured elite watching over antebellum literary culture.[10] The "stagnation" Holmes fears is a relatively mild version of the way books and reading can lead to the annulment of what should be a "progressive" moral instruction; more often than not, the images are of women and men "plunge[d] still deeper into the sea of dissipation" (Brown 1986, 130). These floods and streams represent the dark underside of the moment of sensibility, the readerly affect that sentimental novels invoke in order to control, social sympathy gone wild. The "sea of dissipation" is the social soul "melted in sympathy," the dissolution of the distinctions of gender, class, and morality, the dreadful realization of egalitarian liberal sociality per se, threatening at all times a universal imitativeness. The "sacred drop of humanity" becomes the terrible flood of humanity.

The fundamental boundary threatened by such an uncontrollable sensibility is that of the body itself, for the affect of tears, in this discourse, is nothing less than the registration in one's own body of the penetration of social sympathy. The sentimental narrative of seduction attempts to regulate this breaching of boundaries by containing the reader's experience through its representation. Thus, the seduction of the female hero becomes the sign of the fearful vulnerability of the body to invasion, and her death the necessary suppression of that body. In Stowe's nineteenth-century version, the body is vulnerable to a kind of sympathetic identification that, without proper precautions, can quite simply kill, as the case of Eva shows. In like manner, the reader must be affected, must "melt with sympathy," but must thereafter sublimate this "passion" into the properly discursive realm of justice and repentance. The genius of the sentimental novel's manipulation of readerly affect, the cleverness of its doubled purging, lies in the way the reading body and the represented are always out of sync, for it is precisely when the represented body is being erased, at the moment of death, that the reading body is opened up to tears. Opened up, but no longer to the danger of imitation, since the figure of identification is even now passing beyond the realm of imitation. While the earlier penetration of the hero (through "seduction" or through sympathy) prefigures and anticipates the penetration of the reader's body by the affect that tears make visible, those tears can now merely memorialize that body, and testify to its suppression. The social body: affirmed as it is suppressed, fulfilled in cancellation.

While the sentimental novel will always thus conclude in the regulation—to the point of death—of the body, it cannot afford to do so too soon. If there is a danger in allowing tears to turn into floods, there is perhaps a greater danger in suppressing tears altogether. In Rowson's later novel, *Sarah; or, The Exemplary Wife* (1813), the protagonist finds this out on her wedding day: "Tears rose to my eyes; I endeavoured to chase them back to my swelling heart; I succeeded, but the consequences were worse than had I suffered them to flow; for just as the clergyman pronounced us man and wife, my nose gushed out blood; my handkerchief and clothes were suffused with the crimson torrent" (Brown 1940, 87). There is, for me, something *right* about this eruption of blood at such a sentimental moment. It is the figure for a kind of pure sensationalism lodged in the heart of sentimentality, one that must be regulated because it cannot be disallowed. Stowe made use of a similarly sensational moment in her persecution of Simon Legree: when the lock of Eva's hair "comes alive" in Legree's hand we are meant to see the revenge simultaneously of the feminine and the affective on an individual whose brutishness is coincident with the denial and fear of such essentially humane traits.[11] I turn now to Poe's attempts to delimit and tap into this realm of sensation lying within sentimentalism. Poe's exploration will continue to play itself out in the social limit opened up by the death of the other, but will offer as an alternative to sentimental termination what one could now call, looking forward to M. Valdemar, liquidation.

Sentiment and Substance

"The death . . . of a beautiful woman is, unquestionably, the most poetical topic in the world" (Poe 1984a, 19). Poe took seriously his own critical dictum: all the Lenores, Ligeias, Morellas, Berenices, and Madeleine Ushers attest to his fascination with the more or less protracted dissolution of beloved women. In this fascination, however, Poe was by no means alone, for if, as Nina Baym has suggested, sentimental literature eschewed the narrative of seduction in the second quarter of the nineteenth century, it nevertheless manifested an increasing, even obsessional, interest in the spectacle of the death of innocent victims. And as Ann Douglas points out, "young women were especially popular subjects, both in biography and fiction, for the necrophiliac drama" (Douglas 1975, 59). This "drama" continued to be enacted around the deathbed, but with the rise during Poe's lifetime of a more frankly religious novelistic vocabulary, the central focus of such deathbed farewells switched from the guilt or forgiveness allotted to the this-worldly actors to an increasingly detailed vision of the world that was to come. As Douglas describes this shift, the writers of sentimental consolation literature "focused rather on the accessibility of the celestial kingdom to earthly intelligence and the similarities between the two which made communication possible. They depicted and emphasized heaven as a continuation and a glorification of the domestic sphere" (ibid., 55). It is thus not simply in the tales recounting the death of women that Poe's work evinces an affinity with the sentimental tradition; his very "otherworldliness," so often invoked to point up his anomalous position in the antebellum world of American letters, is continuous with sentimentalism's "necrophiliac drama," taking off from—and opening up—the liminal, visionary moment between life and death so insistently invoked and elided in sentimental deathbed scenes.

In saying that Poe opens up the limit of death I am suggesting that his tales are not finally so much about the death of their characters as about those characters' *inability to die*. All the live entombments, graverobbings, revenant wives, hopelessly mourning lovers, perversely confessional murderers, and communications from beyond annihilation—all these characteristic features of Poe's tales and poems bespeak less a fear of the irrevocable termination of life than the correlative anxiety before the interminable nature of death. Poe's own "necrophiliac dramas," so often enacted with stage sets and tableaux borrowed from the sentimental novel, can thus be seen to operate as viruses within sentimentalism: inhabiting the scene of death so crucial to the sentimental mechanism, the tales zero in on the moment of sensation, and the reader's registration of it as literary affect. Poe's tales thus assign themselves to a twilight region of ambivalence that the supersession of affect in sentimental termination is designed to manage. This ambivalence is played out in the tales themselves as the inability of the characters to assign the dead their proper terms—as either alive or dead—and is quite often registered by the reader as an uncertainty concerning such tales' literary value. In focusing on the moment of sensation, Poe's tales thus activate certain dangers that sentimentalism mobilizes but attempts to sublimate: the danger of a kind of absorptive identification, a dubiousness about truth-claims (with the concomitant suspension of moral certitude), and a heightened awareness on the part of the reader of the artificiality of discursive closure.

In "Mesmeric Revelation" (1844), Poe provides a clear instance of his sensationalizing of the sentimental. The formal trajectory of the tale is entirely sentimental. Mr. Vankirk is dying of the disease of choice in nineteenth-century sentimentalism—consumption, or what Poe, in his penchant for technical jargon, likes to call "phthisis." Having called the narrator to his bedside precisely at the point at which death is both certain and imminent, Vankirk delivers his last communications and visions of the world to come, after which, "with a bright smile irradiating all his features, he fell back upon his pillow and expired" (Poe 1969–78, 3:1040). Thus far, the dying character could be Charlotte Temple or Little Eva; but it is the content of Vankirk's "mesmeric revelation" that displays its viral relation to its host and model.

"I need not tell you how skeptical I have hitherto been on the topic of the soul's immortality," says Vankirk as soon as the narrator arrives at his bedside. As a result of his repeated submission to "mesmeric influence," however, Vankirk has become extraordinarily sensitive, and has registered a "certain deepening of the feeling [that the soul is immortal], until it has come so nearly to resemble the acquiescence of reason, that I find it difficult to distinguish between the two" (Poe 1969–78, 3:1031). This perception of the deepening fusion between feeling and reason—between affect and discourse—is the truth Vankirk is most intent on communicating. As it turns out, "there is no immateriality—it is a mere word. That which is not matter, is not at all" (ibid., 1033). The soul, or spirit, does indeed exist, but it exists as matter—infinitely rarefied, but matter nonetheless. Rather than a qualitative severance marking the limit between life and death, there is a continuum. And rather than a liberatory shedding of the earthly husk, the material refinement effected in death verges only toward increased density and absolute coalescence: "These gradations of matter increase in rarity or fineness, until we arrive at a matter *unparticled*—without particles—indivisible—*one;* and here the law of impulsion and permeation is modified. The ultimate, or unparticled matter, not only permeates all things but impels all things—and thus *is* all things within itself. This matter is God. What men attempt to embody in the word 'thought,' is this matter in motion" (ibid.).[12] Vankirk's vision is thus of a purely material "spiritual" world, in which thought is matter in motion, and which tends toward an "unparticled" identity that annuls not only the boundaries defining material entities, but those defining what we normally consider mental entities as well: the actively "impelling" matter thus becomes identified with the passively "permeating" matter. We are told that "substance" is in fact a "sentiment" (Poe 1969–78, 3:1039), and that, should we find this hard to understand, it is because "abstractions may amuse and exercise, but take no hold on the mind" (ibid., 1031)—unless the abstract "sentiments" are simultaneously a kind of materialized sensation, or unless, as with Vankirk's recognition of the soul's immortality, "feeling" deepens until it becomes indistinguishable from the "acquiescence of reason."

One reason that the "science" of mesmerism appealed to Poe was precisely its insistence, so weirdly exemplified in Vankirk's mesmerically induced communications, on speaking of the most abstract and spiritual matters in terms of material forces. In *Facts in Mesmerism, with Reasons for a Dispassionate Inquiry into It* (1841), which Poe praised in his marginalia of November 1846, the Reverend Chauncey Hare Townshend claimed that mesmeric experiments had finally made visible the "language of sensation."[13] From the start of his career, in such tales as "Loss of Breath," Poe is obsessed with this "language," its manipulation and its effects, but in mesmerism he found a particularly sophisticated vehicle for its analysis. The mesmeric trance, as Townshend and others stressed, was a kind of artificially induced death state. In the opening paragraph of "Mesmeric Revelation" the narrator observes, "man . . . can so impress his fellow, as to cast him into an abnormal condition, of which the phenomena resemble very closely those of *death*" (Poe 1969–78, 1030). As the story strikingly demonstrates, the "facts" of mesmerism allowed Poe to breach the limit of death, speak from beyond the grave, and describe what he found there—"substance" as "sentiment." Against sentimental termination, which insists that death is the overcoming of the body and its registration of affect, Poe's sensational deathbed scene in "Mesmeric Revelation" is intent on staying within this moment of transition, or rather, it denies the transition itself: as in the mesmeric trance, where the suspension of the external sense organs merely presages the heightening of internal and immediate sensitivity, the transition to death in Vankirk's vision is less the overcoming of substance and affect than the identification with substance, the metamorphosis into pure affect. If the sentimental tradition tries to channel its affect toward a disembodied discourse, Poe's mesmeric sensationalism here moves "sentiment" and affect back toward the body and the realm of sentient "substance."

It is hard to overlook the indications that Poe also aimed to induce a kind of mesmeric submission in his reader. When the narrator speaks of "man [who] can so impress his fellow, as to cast him into an abnormal condition, of which the phenomena resemble very closely those of *death*," we can also hear Poe's own megalomaniacal critical pronouncements, in which the requirement that the tale be read at a single sitting is simply the guarantee that "during the hour of perusal the soul of the reader is at the writer's control" (Poe 1984a, 572), much as a mesmeric patient's "soul" is at the complete and exclusive command of the mesmerist's for the length of that "sitting." Poe was hardly alone in seeing a strong connection between mesmerism and writing. I could adduce Hawthorne here, but in fact the mesmerists themselves were generally eager to concede that their discovery was not different in kind than other, entirely known, instances of mental control or influence—such as, for instance, the kind of "sympathy" aroused in oratorical persuasion: "But what is sympathy? It is the nervo-vital fluid thrown from a full, energetic brain, upon another of kindred feeling. That brain, being roused, affects another, and that still another, till the whole assembly are brought into magnetic sympathy with the speaker, and by him are moved as the soul of one man" (Dods 1886, 313).

This description of the way "sympathy" tends to condense a "whole assembly" into the unity of the "soul of one man" finds a striking reflection in Poe's well-known second review of Hawthorne. He is describing the best kind of originality for a writer to pursue: "It is clear, however, not only that it is the novelty of *effect* which alone is worth consideration, but that this effect is *best* wrought, for the end of all fictitious composition, pleasure, by shunning rather than seeking the absolute novelty of combination" (Poe 1984a, 580). This is because absolute originality "cannot fail to prove unpopular with the masses, who, seeking in this literature amusement, are positively offended by instruction" (ibid.). But while it is on grounds of mass appeal that Poe measures the effectiveness of this "true originality," paradoxically that appeal is also, in each instance, singular and exclusive. In the reader's perception of that true originality

his pleasure is doubled. He is filled with an intrinsic and extrinsic delight. He feels and intensely enjoys the seeming novelty of the thought, enjoys it as really novel, as absolutely original with the writer—*and* himself. They two, he fancies, have, alone of all men, thought thus. They two have, together, created this thing. Henceforward there is a bond of sympathy between them, a sympathy which irradiates every subsequent page of the book. (Ibid., 581)

Like the "sympathy" that draws the separate listeners into the unity of "the soul of one man," Poe's sympathy creates a unity, in this case a single reading public. In both cases, however, the elements making up the amassed unity all feel as though they maintained an exclusive relation with the source of sympathy—either the orator or the writer of "true originality." Mesmerism, too, worked through this kind of exclusive relation: as all accounts stressed, the mesmerized patient would be entirely oblivious to external influences— hair pulling or sticking with pins received no response—while remaining inordinately sensitive to the least movement of the mesmerist.[14] But if, from one perspective, mesmeric manipulation seemed to induce a kind of antiso- cial indifference in the patient, it was only in order to put that patient into direct contact with the very principle of sociality itself, namely, the "nervo- vital fluid" coursing through all animate and inanimate matter, the uni- versal medium. In the mesmeric trance, then, as in the "sympathetic" phenomena of oratory and reading, social unity is achieved through a simultaneous dissociation, a heightened communication through its ex- treme limitation, an increased sensitivity through its apparent extinction. It would seem, then, that mesmerism and Poe's aesthetics of the tale both reproduce, rather than oppose, the management of affective sympathy that characterizes sentimental termination, a management that in all cases re- sults in the reaffirmation of an individual integrity in the face of a recently encountered social fusion.[15]

But Poe's interest in the moment of affective merger is not finally directed by the same commitment to what I have called, in discussing sentimental deathbed scenes, symbolic identification. If Poe's sensationalism shares with sentimentalism the invocation of a moment of imaginary and absorp- tive merger, he does not aim to redirect this attachment to a social and symbolic discourse; rather, as I have suggested in discussing "Mesmeric Revelation," he seems concerned to "substantialize" this moment of con- nection itself. "They two have, together, created this thing," Poe imagines the mesmerized reader thinking. What is this "thing"? There seems to be a kind of objectification here of the intersubjective encounter entailed in the act of reading, what I call a substantialization of the very language-thing that sustains and constitutes the social limit. If in the dispersal of Eva's locks we have the apportionment of the affective moment of connection, one can, I think, see its loathsome substantialization in the "nearly liquid mass" of Valdemar's corpse. If sentimental termination modulates from imaginary to symbolic, one can see Poe's sensational liquidation as moving in an opposite direction, as transforming the imaginary into what one could call an instance of the Lacanian Real.[16]

The Oozy Tide-Mud of the Real

In *The Sublime Object of Ideology*, Zizek offers a rich and complex account of Lacan's notion of the Real. I will not attempt to summarize fully that account here, but will simply recall the motifs that seem strikingly relevant for an understanding of Poe's tale. (1) The Real emerges as the "leftover" of a constitutively incomplete symbolization: "the Real is . . . the product, remainder, leftover, scraps of this process of symbolization, the remnants, the excess which escapes symbolization and is as such produced by the symbolization itself" (Zizek 1989, 169). In my terms, I could say that whatever affective "bits and pieces" (such as Eva's locks) remain after the sentimental symbolization of the death of the other can take on the status of the Real. (2) This failure of symbolization that produces the Real attests to a lack in the big Other, by which term Zizek (if not always Lacan) means to indicate the ideological field. The Symbolic is unable to totalize, to close in on itself, and this failure is made manifest as the Real's embodiment of a lack in the Symbolic. The Symbolic cannot seal up the social limit (though it strives to do nothing else). In my terms, I could say that to the extent that the symbolization of the corporeal (the hero's body, the reader's affect) is an uncompleted or failed disembodiment, that failure will be present in the sentient substances we find in sensational literature. (3) The Real can be thought of as a "language-thing" to the extent that its embodiment of the failure of symbolization takes the form of an "impossible" metalanguage. Let me examine this last feature first.

In *Uncle Tom's Cabin*, at the same moment in which Stowe disparages novels in which "people's hearts break, and they die, and that is the end of it"—disparages, in other words, the novelistic representation of the death of the other she will not fail to put to use—she refers to what, conveniently enough, she calls the "real": "But the *real* remained—the *real*, like the flat, bare, oozy tide-mud, when the blue sparkling wave, with all its company of gliding boats and white-winged ships, its music of oars and chiming waters, has gone down, and there it lies, flat, slimy, bare,—exceedingly real" (Stowe 1982, 241). The real, for Stowe, is what gets left over when the imaginary identification of love—"the whole romance and ideal of life"—is dissipated through the loss of the other. One could say that Stowe's striking image of the oozy tide-mud of the real designates the resistant affective remains, the recalcitrant intensity that will not be quickly recuperated by a tidying symbolic discourse of gliding boats and white-winged ships. And yet there is, as I have already suggested, something disingenuous about this reference to what cannot be symbolized: in fact, the "real"—as what opposes the imaginary absorption of naive love—is here posed by the symbolic discourse of sentimentalism. Stowe's passage is a lure asking us to read it as actually standing outside its own array of discourses, as having successfully taken up an "objective" distance toward sentimental discourse, as being something like an ironic metalanguage. That is, we are meant to see this as designating and occupying an "outside" to the sentimental discourse, a certain irrecoverably nonlinguistic limit. But it is this limit that is precisely invoked in order to be suppressed in sentimental discourse. Stowe's description of the real functions here like the Freudian *Vorstellungsrepräsentanz:* "the representative, the substitute of some representation, the signifying element filling out the vacant place of the missing representation. . . . The field of representation [*Vorstellung*] is the field of what is positively depicted, but the problem is that everything cannot be depicted. Something must necessarily fall out . . . and the [*Vostellungsrepräsentanz*] takes the place of this void, of this missing, 'originally repressed' representation: its exclusion functions as a positive condition for the emergence of what is being depicted" (Zizek 1989, 159). Stowe's description of the real is of an object that precisely must *not* be in the picture for what *is* in the picture to be there. That is, Stowe's passage describes an object that is not there; in gesturing outside its own discourse, Stowe's cagey maneuver performatively excludes what it constatively designates.

It may be that Stowe's combination of sentimental and realist discourse requires such a maneuver, for insofar as both realism and sentimentalism strive to absorb within themselves their own discursive limits, they need to pretend to stand outside those limits, in some place that looks like pure unsignifying "reality," or the other side of death. This need to exclude while seeming to occupy what lies outside its discourse is linked to the political and ideological stakes of novelistic discourse, whether sentimental or realist. As Benjamin suggests, the novel's tie to bourgeois individualism commits it to a project of totalization and closure, to the notion that representation can cover, without lack or remainder, the whole field of the social and the individual. While there is certainly no reason to imagine that Poe had some *political* stake in questioning this program of closing off the social limit, his aesthetic fascination with the effects wrought by inhabiting that limit led to rather different results. If, as I extrapolate from Benjamin, the novel speaks of the dead, while in the tale the dead speak, I can find no better instance of this impossible speech than "The Facts in the Case of M. Valdemar."

"*I say to you that I am dead!*" (Poe 1969–78, 3:1242). While Stowe's novel speaks of the real, here is the strictly "impossible" metalanguage in which the Real speaks. Valdemar has been mesmerized at the point of death, with the result that what normally is a momentary passage has been grotesquely sustained for seven months. The limit of death that is so fascinatedly and prettily witnessed in the sentimental deathbed scene is here pried open and distended. The view we are given is recognizably a distortion of certain sentimental motifs. In what may be the most grotesque revision of sentimentalism in all of Poe's work, the tears that figure and confirm the precious moment of connection—those "sacred drops of humanity"—become here revoltingly opaque: "It was observed, as especially remarkable, that this lowering of the pupil was accompanied by the profuse out-flowing of a yellowish ichor (from beneath the lids) of a pungent and highly offensive odor" (ibid., 1242). Indeed, in keeping with the figuration of the mesmeric medium as liquid (recall the "nervo-vital fluid"), Poe indulges in an imaginative liquefaction of whatever he can: beneath Valdemar's apparent corporeal integrity, for example, lies a horrific wet mess: "The right [lung], in its upper portion, was also partially, if not thoroughly, ossified, while the lower region was merely a mass of purulent tubercles, running into one another" (ibid., 1235). Even his voice, that traditional figure for a disincarnated spirituality, is here uncannily material, striking the narrator in the same way that "gelatinous or glutinous matters impress the sense of touch" (ibid., 1240). Wherever the sentimental would look for transparency and disembodiment, we find a nauseating opacity (even Valdemar's tongue turns black), a liquid substantialization. This substantialization is finally that of the sustaining "communication" itself, the medium through which the limit of death has been breached. Poe underlines this—and ends his tale—by having Valdemar's final words and his dissolution coincide: "amid ejaculations of 'dead! dead!' absolutely *bursting* from the tongue and not from the lips of the sufferer, his whole frame at once—within the space of a single minute, or even less, shrunk—crumbled—absolutely *rotted* away beneath my hands. Upon the bed, before that whole company, there lay a nearly liquid mass of loathsome—of detestable putridity" (ibid., 1242–43).

This is, I think, one of the most powerfully effective moments in all of Poe, a moment of shock and disgust and uneasiness rolled into one. It is as though the story "itself" had become horribly corporealized before our very eyes. After Valdemar cries "*I say to you that I am dead*" the narrator writes: "I was thoroughly unnerved, and for an instant remained undecided what to do. At first I made an effort to re-compose the patient; but, failing in this through total abeyance of the will, I retraced my steps and as earnestly struggled to awaken him" (ibid., 1242). Poe's pun on "re-compose" here reinforces the identity between the tale of "Valdemar" and its title character: if Poe understood tale telling as something quite like mesmerism, he here reverses the equation, characterizing the mesmerist as one concerned with efforts at composition. It is curious, however, that while the narrator says he is unable to "re-compose" his patient because of a "total abeyance of the will," he does not specify whose will is in abeyance. In mesmeric submission, it would usually be the patient's will that would be rendered inoperative, but here the narrator's indecision and "unnerved" state point rather to *his* will as having folded. This punning passage thus serves not only to cement the identification between Valdemar and "Valdemar," and Poe and the narrator, but it also implicates the latter figures in the passivity and helplessness of a mesmeric submission *in articulo mortis,* this composition that seems to insist on its own decomposition.

The reader is implicated as well, for the reader is certainly in a similar kind of "unnerved" submission. The abruptness of the ending, for us as for the "whole company" around the bed, leaves us feeling as though Valdemar's dissolution is the horrifying embodiment not only of the mesmeric communication, but of that which sustains our own rapt absorption in Poe's text: suddenly, at the near edge of the tale, there lies "putridity," a slimy edge. "We two have, together, created this thing." This "thing" is a language-thing, the resubstantialization of an "impossible" communication across the social limit. Poe makes no effort to cover up the impossibility of Valdemar's communication: not only are his statements—*"I say to you that I am dead!*—impossible, but Poe even renders this impossibility, as he does all else in the tale, corporeal: how is articulation possible when it emerges from "the tongue and not the lips?" This "vibratory motion" (ibid., 1240) of the black tongue is, to play on Poe's title, the kind of articulation one is likely to get *in articulo mortis.*[17] And I suggest that a powerful element in the revulsion we feel is linked both to this impossibility and to the pleasure we take in it. This pleasure is linked simultaneously to a symbolic discourse, the lure of an "impossible" metalanguage that might speak from beyond death, that might contain and cover the social limit, and to the failure of that discourse. Zizek paraphrases Lacan: "*jouissance* is the basis upon which symbolization works, the basis emptied, disembodied, structured by the symbolization, but this process produces at the same time a residue, a leftover, which is the surplus-enjoyment" (Zizek 1989, 170). This "surplus-enjoyment" of the sensational, the kind of horrified pleasure taken in sudden nosebleeds, liquefying corpses, exploding heads, what have you, is a truly threatening pleasure taken in the idea that *something remains,* that insofar as there abides a corporeal or material or affective leftover, the Symbolic cannot entirely coordinate the body of the social.

NOTES

1. But not only his. Poe famously borrows from, and parodistically recycles, the style of *Blackwood's* short sensation pieces. In general, and with important exceptions (Gothic fiction, Collins's sensation novels) it seems that devotees of the exploration of heightened affect, of shock and horror, are also drawn toward shorter forms. Such at least is the argument of David G. Hartwell in the editorial introduction to his anthology of short fiction, *The Dark Descent* (Hartwell 1987).

2. The relevant passage in Kant, quoted by Lloyd, is as follows: "By the name *sensus communis* is to be understood the idea of a *public* sense, i.e., a critical faculty which in its reflective act takes account (*a priori*) of the mode of representation of every one else, in order, *as it were,* to weigh its judgment with the collective reason of mankind, and thereby avoid the illusion arising from subjective and personal conditions which could readily be taken for objective, an illusion that would exert a prejudicial influence upon its judgment. . . . This . . . is effected by so far as possible letting go of the element of matter, i.e., sensation, in our general state of representative activity, and confining attention to the formal peculiarities of our representation or general state of representative activity." Kant, *Critique of Judgment,* para. 40, cited in Lloyd 1989, 36 (Lloyd quotes from the James Creed Meredith translation).

3. The role of writing and printing in colonial America's construction of a liberal public sphere marked by just the formalizing and abstracting tendencies I here ascribe to the liberal example is well examined in Warner 1990.

4. Baym 1978. Baym sets these novels specifically against a Richardsonian heritage: "The disappearance of the novel of seduction is a crucial event in woman's fiction, and perhaps in women's psyches as well" (26). "Seduction" here means successful seduction, or perhaps, as in *Clarissa,* just plain rape. What Baym wishes to emphasize is that, while such seduction novels inevitably entail the destruction of the female hero, "Woman's Fiction" novels tell the story of her incredible, and finally successful, resistance to both temptation and overt aggression. Although *Clarissa* is obviously the model for the seduction plot, the resistance plot can, I think, also be legitimately traced back to Richardson, and *Pamela.*

5. In a longer version of this essay, I examine in some detail the ways in which sentimental novels project certain figures—the censorious matron, the naive female reader, the foolishly romantic girl—that, precisely because they are treated ironically by the text, are ambivalently invested by the reader, an ambivalence that coincides with the reader's identification with the ironic symbolic discourse, that is, the voice that knows the rules of the genre. What I have been calling the form's duplicity is what makes the sentimental novel such a preeminently liberal form, for as Lloyd remarks at the end of his essay "Kant's Examples," "such an ironic disposition is the fundamental prerequisite

for the inculcation of ideology since it assumes, as an internal mechanism of the most formal and 'transferrable' kind, the subordination of the individual to the universal" (Lloyd 1989, 48). Moreover, as I develop in *Poe and the Imagination of Mass Culture*, this ironic disposition is the sine qua non of mass-cultural forms. That is, there is no mass culture without liberalism.

6. In both its recalcitrance and its intensity, mourning's affect is coded feminine, in particular by Protestant discourse. See Breitwieser 1990, where he organizes a highly textured interpretation of Rowlandson's narrative around Hegel's fundamentally Protestant anxieties in *The Phenomenology of Spirit*, when faced by the recalcitrant figure of Antigone.

7. Fisher 1985, 106–7: "little Eva who watches and learns the stories of the slaves is, because she is a child, unable to change what she sees around her. She is for that reason like the reader and the prisoner. Because she cannot act, she must suffer. She must, literally, die of the stories that she hears. The mysterious illness [not so mysterious, after all!] that carries her away is a symbol of knowledge itself, unendurable knowledge in the absence of the power to act."

8. The quotations are from George Turnbull, writing in 1740, and are cited in Fiering 1976, 197–98. Jay Fliegelman contends that the supposition of an innate "moral sense" in the Scottish moral philosophy of such figures as Adam Ferguson and Francis Hutcheson constituted an attempt to mitigate what they took to be the dangerous rationalism of Lockean psychology and its "identification of virtue with self-interest" (Fliegelman 1982, 23). The source of this "moral sense" was accordingly located outside both the individual and the calculation of reason: it was an "innate principle of sociability" (ibid., 24), an "instinct," in the words of Hutcheson, "antecedent to all reason from interest, which influences us to the love of others" (Fiering 1976, 207).

9. Brown discusses this shift in the first six chapters of Brown 1940. Other accounts can be found in Brissenden 1974; Todd 1986; and Ermamesta 1951. A thorough account of the development of sentimentalism in American periodicals can be found in Doyle 1941.

10. See Baym 1984, 27. In his compendious account of mass literary practices in the antebellum period, David Reynolds uses the metaphor of "liquidity" to describe the relations of influence among those mass literary genres. See Reynolds 1988.

11. Eva Cherniavsky's treatment of Legree's haunting by various maternal imagoes has helped me see here the indissoluble link between the affective and the feminine as they are deployed both by sentimental and by sensational literature; I thank her here for her readings and her writings. See her essay in this volume.

12. This passage is repeated almost verbatim in Poe's cosmological "poem" *Eureka* (1848), which could be said to map the affective aesthetics of "Mesmeric Revelation" onto the attractions and repulsions of the universe's "masses."

13. Townshend 1982, 313. Charles Caldwell, an American champion of mesmerism, also speaks of the "instinctive or natural language" that is purely physiological. See Caldwell 1982, 46–47.

14. See the appendices in Townshend 1982 for a typical series of case studies. For a historical account of mesmerism that stresses these mimetic phenomena, see Fuller 1982, esp. chaps. 2–4.

15. Another perspective on the nature of this social fusion in the mesmeric state can be found in the third part of Hegel's *Encyclopaedia* (1830) (Hegel 1970), where he discusses

at some length the phenomena of mesmerism, which he calls "animal magnetism." For Hegel, the individual "in such a morbid state stands in direct contact with the concrete contents of his own self." These "contents" consist in the first instance of the individual's social determination, the "essential and the particular empirical ties which connect him with other men and the world at large." In the normal waking state, adult human beings understand these ties as a "complex of interconnections of a practically intelligible kind," intelligible, that is, according to categories of externality, cause and effect, means and end. Individuals in "direct" (hence unmediated) contact with these "concrete contents," on the other hand, discover themselves "in the very heart of interconnection" rather than on one end of a mediated relation. To be thus in the "heart of the interconnection" is to be in "identity with the surroundings," is in fact to inhabit the social limit, that space from which individuality is filled and determined by its prior sociality. As Hegel says, although to the adult waking consciousness the social world seems external, in fact "this world which is outside him has its threads in him to such a degree that it is these threads which make him what he really is: he too would become extinct if these externalities were to disappear, unless by the aid of religion, subjective reason, and character, he is in a remarkable degree self-supporting and independent of them." In this last clause can be discerned once again the appeal to a kind of disciplinary mastery over the social ties that make an individual "what he really is." The identification with the social, "identity with the surroundings," is once again invoked only to be suppressed, a suppression that, in Hegel as in the sentimental tradition, is effected through a disciplinary agency that can indifferently take form as "religion" or "subjective reason." Given my previous examination of sentimental termination, then, it is no surprise that Hegel finds evidence of this "identity with the surroundings" not only in mesmeric suspension, but perhaps most powerfully in "the effect produced by the death of beloved relatives, friends, etc. on those left behind."

Because it is a realm in which both psychological boundaries (between egos) and philosophical ones (between categories) are overcome or erased, Hegel figures this mesmeric "identity with the surroundings" as a *liquid* in which the individual is "immersed." What is more, because this liquid is not a simple medium of dissolution but is rather the environment of identification and convergence, it is characterized as a "mass"—to be specific, an "inarticulate mass." Hegel's qualification here of the "mass" as "inarticulate" suggests that the limit opened up by mesmeric identification is one that either stops short of or exceeds discursive control, that it is, perhaps, the point at which discursive recuperation has not yet triumphed over an identifying imitation. Hegel 1970 (all quotations are taken from 101–3).

16. Given Poe's tale's richness for any investigation of the limits to discourse, it should perhaps not be surprising how often references to the tale show up in French critical thought of the past forty years. (Still, I was surprised.) See Lacan 1988a, 231–32; Derrida 1973; Barthes 1985.

17. To make Valdemar's voice come not from his lips but from the blackened tongue that normally lies hidden and ventriloquizing behind them is to figure, with an extraordinary condensation, the way in which the normally feminized dying body is in fact made to utter the masculine discourse of the Symbolic, a discourse phallic and deathly, and strictly speaking, impossible: a black tongue talking on its own.

Revivification and Utopian Time

Poe versus Stowe

EVA CHERNIAVSKY

Out of Eden: The Utopian Mother

It is only the utopian in some archetypes that enables their fruitful citation when looking forward, not backward. That has already occurred in the apparent interlocking of the phantasmagorias and in the dissolution of that appearance. All those rationalisms concerning mothers, *as those who are still giving birth*, show a light shining in from utopia, even during romanticism with the yearning graves and underworld lantern. The particular brooding in archetypes, and especially that, shows their incompleteness. (Bloch 1988, 121)

In this stunningly obscure and resistant passage from Ernst Bloch, which itself seems shrouded in the murky half-light of the crypt, of the underworld it so mysteriously invokes, I recognize a familiar discourse, one in which contradictory cultural codes are aligned; I recognize something that I want to define, in what follows, as the logic of sentimentalism. Bloch's remark about mothers, appended apparently by way of example to a discussion of the utopian components of certain archetypes, puts several terms into play: on the one hand, something he calls "rationalisms" of motherhood, associated here with "utopian light"; on the other hand, the "phantasmagorias," or archetypal images, of the Gothic romance. Bloch fails to elucidate this odd configuration of terms; still, in the very linking of "rationalisms" to Gothicism, incidental as the locution "even during" may make their historical relation appear, a useful (re)construction of his elliptical allusion to motherhood suggests itself. A specifically modern rationalization of motherhood intersects with the emergence of the Gothic in late-eighteenth- and early-nineteenth-century Western culture, one that serves the Enlightenment project of rationalizing the social body. In this construction of motherhood—which made its appearance in the literature of the United States precisely in the period of the nation's founding—the mother becomes the transparent mediator of democratic social and political ideologies, the privileged agent of her children's socialization, the producer of the rational citizen.[1] This identification of the mother with social norms, to which her potential difference, her particularity, is sacrificed, arguably engenders the antithetical and complementary excesses of the Gothic, the imagery of subterranean maternal presence, of the "yearning grave." The kinship, or congruence, of the rational and the phantasmatic, of the social and the buried mother, reveals itself decisively in sentimentalism's figuration of the good Christian mother, as one whose moral influence extends beyond the grave, affecting her children's actions long after she herself is dead.

But where is the "utopian" in the mother's (re)production of the rational social body? I insist on the question because it does more than address the validity of a particular, cryptic example: Bloch's more or less casual reference to the utopian resonance of the mother's (re)productive role conceals the centrality of this maternal function to his conception of a utopian drive, as he elaborates it throughout *The Utopian Function of Art and Literature*. The utopian drive, Bloch contends, inheres in particular signifiers that contain in embryo the possibility or prospect of difference. In the form of the not-yet-known, of its "not-worked-through, non-mythical surplus," the utopian signifier incorporates that which is alien to it, which remains in excess of its historically delimited meaning, of the false, the merely partial, consciousness it displays (Bloch 1988, 120). Thus, inasmuch as the archetype exemplifies this utopian function, its importance rests in its immanent alterity. In Bloch's construction of the utopian function, the metaphorical nature of gestation is unmistakable: the utopian signifier brings to term within itself the potential form of the other. The "rationalisms concerning mothers, *as those who are still giving birth*," bearing new forms of being within, in fact furnish the conceptual model of the utopian drive; as Bloch conceives it, the "utopian function" is a function of the maternal body.

Bloch's model for the cultural production of utopia, in other words, is itself the product of the "rationalisms concerning mothers," which he acknowledges here as an instance only of another, presumably transhistorical, cultural logic. Or rather, his model is the product of these "rationalisms" at their point of juncture with the Gothic archetype of "the yearning grave," a juncture that I have proposed to locate in the logic of sentimentalism.[2] To designate Bloch's model of the utopian drive as sentimental is not to diminish its political resonance: on the contrary, I argue that sentimentalism *is* a utopian discourse, precisely insofar as its figuration of the good Christian mother is pregnant with a radically other possibility. Unlike Bloch, however, I locate the good Christian mother's alterity not in her rationalization of the Gothic phantasm, but in her rendering of a motherhood that inhabits and exceeds both the rational and the Gothic planes of the mother's sentimental portrait. More concretely, the sentimental discourse of the early- to mid-nineteenth-century United States can be seen to have led a varied life: as a "rationalism concerning mothers," operating in the service of democratic ideologies; as a (Gothic) mythology of motherhood, which ostensibly undermines this rationalization of the maternal, but ultimately bears its stamp; and finally, as the utopian, or "non-mythical," surplus of democratic motherhood, which speaks to the incompleteness of this very image of the mother and indeed exposes as merely partial the consciousness that informs the democratic social and political order itself.

Thus, with respect to the figure of the mother in the culture of nineteenth-century democracy, to locate her "non-mythical surplus" is to see not only beyond her social rationalization, but beyond her highly mythologized excess. Indeed, beyond her theorized excess: in its representation of the social subject that nineteenth-century liberal culture engenders, psychoanalysis insists both on the mother's central role in the constitution of her child's subjectivity, and on her phantasmatic position outside the social-symbolic order. The utopian component of sentimental motherhood is immanent within, but not reducible to, the imagery of the "yearning grave"; neither is it reducible to the psychoanalytic encoding of that "yearning grave" as womb, or origin, as the Edenic space of the pre-Oedipal mother-infant dyad. Constituted as anterior to language (anterior, that is, to the infant's acquisition of language/subjectivity), the pre-Oedipal mother-infant connection (or, more succinctly, the maternal) is finally the negation of any form of consciousness we might want to claim it represents; to know the maternal is to be outside the dyadic enclosure—to know it as a lack.[3] While Bloch's utopian prospect, then, is there in what one says, unheard or underheard, but always (potentially) enlightening, the maternal, so conceived, is what is not there insofar as one is in a position to say anything at all.

Not surprisingly, sentimental fiction represents the pre-Oedipal mother as either dead or dying; she is the iconic absence in and of the sentimental narrative, the cameo, the memory, the deeply affecting, compulsively reproduced image of one who is, literally and symbolically, not of this world.

A densely symbolized lack, this occupant of the "yearning grave" is the inverse and double of the self-effacing wife and mother, her social analogue and the all-too-present embodiment of democracy's moral norms. As a moral example to her offspring, the sentimental mother is perhaps "still giving birth," not to new forms of being but to the normative social subject. To state the case schematically, though not, finally, to overstate it, sentimental fiction figures a mother who is imagined as present insofar as she remains transparent—the mere conduit of morality—or absent insofar as she retains her material specificity. This sentimental economy comes nicely into focus in Margaret Fuller's construction of motherhood as moral influence.

Man is of Woman born, and her face bends over him in infancy with an expression he can never quite forget. Eminent men have delighted to pay tribute to this image. . . . The rudest tar brushes off a tear with his coat-sleeve at the hallowed name. . . . Some gleams of the same expression which shone down upon his infancy, angelically pure and benign, visit Man again with hopes of pure love, of a holy marriage. Or, if not before, in the eyes of the mother of his child they again are seen, and dim fancies pass before his mind, that Woman may not have been born for him alone, but have come from heaven, a commissioned soul, a messenger of truth and love; that she can only make for him a home in which he may lawfully repose, in so far as she is "True to the kindred points of Heaven and home."
   In gleams, in dim fancies, this thought visits the mind of common men. It is soon obscured by the mists of sensuality, the dust of routine, and he thinks it was only some meteor or ignis fatuus that shone. But as a Rosicrucian lamp, it burns unwearied, though condemned to the solitude of tombs. (Fuller 1971, 49–51)

Fuller arranges this portrait of ideal motherhood along the trajectory of the masculine social subject. In her first, pre-Oedipal avatar, the mother here embodies the possibility of presymbolic or nonsymbolic "expression"; her face, and metonymically her body, is itself a communication, so replete with meaning for the supine infant that its "message" never fully ceases. Yet this verbal image of the mother's body is predicated on the child's loss; maternal "expression," conceived as embodied meaning, as the impossible healing of the breach between the signifier and the signified, obtains only in the inaccessible beyond of language. To re-member the mother's body, to symbolize this mute and ineffable maternal "expression," is to commemorate the absence of what cannot be spoken. In fact, the symbolization of the maternal in this passage effects precisely an emptying out of anything that might mark the mother's "expression" as her own: maternal "expression" becomes the medium of the normative social imagination. Thus the mother's face is now "commissioned," made the bearer of another's message, the purveyor of the father's truth, casting the sanction of divine authority on the domestic realm. From this perspective, the memory of his dead mother recalls her son to the "truth and love" of paternal law, the benignity of moral limits.

Still, in another sense, the mother Fuller imagines here is not simply the reflection of the other she brings into the world, even though her own identity appears determined by her infant's evolving relation to the symbolic. More than a recollected "expression" or an internalized moral norm, the mother Fuller summons in this passage is a *visitation*, a spectral presence, a "gleam" emanating from *outside* her child's consciousness and passing through it. Thus this luminous mother is at once internal to the structures of the filial self, and irreducibly other, both a mere memory, which the nostalgic son projects onto another woman's face, and more than that, an apparition, a reanimated being, teasing and goading her son as she manipulates the play of light in another woman's eyes. Ambiguously positioned both within and without the adult son's psychic economy, this spectral mother disturbs the boundaries of his illusory interiority, and thus begins to expose the autonomous masculine subject as a contingent entity within an intersubjective field.

In this sentimental portrait, Fuller practices an authentically utopian politics of (re)animation: a "non-mythical surplus" arises from the figure of the sentimental mother, something that inhabits but exceeds the normative feminine positions that sentimental discourse encompasses. A figure emerges in this portrait too present to be identified with the pre-Oedipal mother (discursively constituted as absent), and too invasive with respect to masculine subjective boundaries to be identified with the Oedipalized mother (whose prohibited body becomes the embodiment of prohibitions, of moral limits). Rather, this emergent figure occupies the fissure between these two mythologized positions, between the Gothic mother and the domestic angel, and thereby "anticipates," to use Bloch's term, the potential difference of a maternal subject. It is not the mother's position in excess of the social and symbolic order—in the Eden of a lost expressiveness—that opens up a utopian perspective in Fuller's portrait of motherhood, but rather the mother's spectral existence in excess of her socially determined selves. This reanimated mother, arisen from the grave, denaturalizes the social determinations both of her pre-Oedipal and Oedipal selves and of the social subject she engenders.

If the historical contingency of the social subject, and by extension of the liberal order she or he inhabits, is made audible in the sentimental text, it is audible as well in the weeping of its reader, at least as she or he is figured within the text (in the guise of "the rudest tar," for instance). The reader's dissolution in tears of sympathy acknowledges the partiality and prefigures the undoing of his or her identity; it constitutes a wordless recognition of the underheard alternative, of a purely prospective yet already affecting difference. The identities in question when we invoke "the reader" are delimited by race and especially by class, although sentimental authors liked to imagine that susceptibility to the portrait of ideal motherhood transcended social divisions. In the figure of "the rudest tar," the wizened old sailor moved to tears at his mother's name, Fuller subtly argues for (by celebrating) the universally affecting qualities of sentimental motherhood. But the actual "rudest tar" was most likely no sentimentalist; sentimentalism remains a race- and class-bound discourse, grounded in domestic ideology and middle-class family structures. As Christine Stansell has shown, for instance, working-class women—whom the middle-class consumers of sentimental fiction periodically undertook to save—easily intuited that the discourse of sentimentalism presented as Christian charity what remained in fact a mission of "social domination" (Stansell 1987, 66). Still, if the tear of sympathy was not the balm that healed all social divisions, the glue that bound together all races and classes, as sentimentalists sometimes sought to claim, if sentimentalism could indeed be made to serve egregiously racist and classist polemics (often in the very rhetoric with which it espoused such causes as abolition), sentimentalism need not therefore be read as a univocal affirmation of middle-class ideologies.[4]

The sentimental authors' claim for the socially leveling effect of sentimental writing reappears in the lament of the modern mass-culture critic, for whom the popularity of the sentimental novel marks a leveling of discursive forms, a "feminization" of United States culture.[5] Oddly enough, what turns out to have been "feminized," as this argument goes, is precisely not the "high" cultural domain that is traditionally gendered male; on the contrary, sentimental fiction's mass circulation appears restricted, conveniently, to the "masses" and the masculine preserve of "high" culture is thus maintained intact. If sentimentalism is a feminized discourse, however, it permeates and, I contend, reconfigures this "high" cultural ground and inflects the literary productions of those white middle- and upper-class men who are seen to write within other, nonsentimental literary genres. Thus Poe can inhabit the same conceptual frame in this analysis as Stowe does—even if, as I aim to show, the politics of "revivification" elide the utopian perspective onto which reanimation opens.

Poe's Hideous Drama

The tale of Ligeia's resurrection, her reincarnation in the body of another, represents, in the narrator's own words, "a hideous drama of revivification," hideous in the insistence of Ligeia's demand for life, a demand articulated in the material idiom of the flush and the tremor, and in the resistance of Rowena's frame to these incursions of being.

At length it became evident that a slight, a very feeble, and barely noticeable tinge of color had flushed up within the cheeks, and along the sunken small veins of the eyelids. Through a species of unutterable horror and awe, for which the language of mortality has no sufficiently energetic expression, I felt my heart cease to beat, my limbs grow rigid where I sat. . . . In a short period it was certain, however, that a relapse had taken place; the color disappeared from both eyelid and cheek, leaving a wanness even more than that of marble; the lips became doubly shrivelled and pinched up in the ghastly expression of death; a repulsive clamminess and coldness rapidly overspread the surface of the body. . . . But why shall I minutely detail the unspeakable horrors of that night? Why shall I pause to relate how, time after time, until near the period of the gray dawn, this hideous drama of revivification was repeated; how each terrific relapse was only into a sterner and apparently more irredeemable death; how each agony wore the aspect of a struggle with some invisible foe; and how each struggle was succeeded by I know not what of wild changes in the personal appearance of the corpse? (Poe 1984b, 274–75)

A twin horror shapes the narrator's sensations in this final section of "Ligeia": the horror of the corpse itself, of the hardened pallor and cold texture of its flesh, a horror rehearsed and intensified with every reenactment of death, and the horror of its revivification, of a self-induced resurgence of being—a demand for life ultimately complicit with the narrator's desire, yet dangerously and appallingly alien in origin. Even before Rowena's shroud comes undone to reveal Ligeia's distinctive features, apparent in this drama of revivification is the telltale "vehemence of desire for life" that the narrator earlier attributed to the dying Ligeia, which thus discloses Ligeia's part in this drama prior to the body's actual unveiling. If from the first, then, the narrator, like the reader, must intuit Ligeia's return, recognize in the transformations of Rowena's corpse Ligeia's indelible will to live, his intuition only accentuates the spectacle's horrific nature. In fact, I suggest, it is exactly because the narrator discerns Ligeia's agency in the antics of Rowena's corpse that his own will is suspended, that the symptoms of life in the corpse produce in the teller of this tale the very symptoms of death.

This relation of mutual exclusion, in which the masculine narrator cannot sustain his identity vis-à-vis a feminine presence, is the hallmark of sentimentalism in its masculine (or "high" cultural) inflection—as read and reproduced by a class of male writers who emphatically dissociate their own literary practice from that of contemporary women novelists. "Ligeia" is the narrative of sentimental motherhood told from the perspective of the ambivalent son, whose desire for an impossible return to the maternal—a *safely* impossible return, since the son's inscription in the symbolic order is plainly irreversible, the (phantasmatic) integrity of the maternal not recoverable—matches only his terror of that other possibility, that the maternal would *come back to him*. Rather than a return to a condition of imagined wholeness, the lost mother's resurrection would signify the disintegration of the autonomous self, the termination of masculine subjective mastery—not the satisfaction, but the transformation of desire in the face of what masculine desire consistently negates: difference, particularity, presence. More concretely, the mother's (re)animation would bring into existence the very thing that the phantasm of the maternal functions to erase—namely, the "lost" mother herself.

Kaja Silverman offers a particularly tidy and compelling explanation of how the mother disappears from the maternal in classic psychoanalytic discourse: "The child's discursive exteriority—its emergence from the maternal enclosure—can be established only by placing the mother herself inside that enclosure, by relegating her to the interior of [Julia Kristeva's term for this enclosure] the *chora*, or—what is the same thing—by stripping her of all linguistic capabilities" (Silverman 1988, 105). Because in the mythology of the subject as constituted in democratic culture—and articulated in the ideal of the bourgeois family, in the discourse of the "domestic" novel, and in the psychoanalytic narrative of the subject's formation—the child's differentiation from the mother inaugurates his or her relation to the symbolic, the mother's own relation to language is falsified. Rather than appear an individuated being, herself inserted in the symbolic order, whose body assumes specific affective dimensions for her infant, the mother is identified with the space of the maternal itself, with the infant's position of disempowerment, with his or her place outside language. In this frame, the son's desire to return to the origin, to the "maternal enclosure," may be read less as a desire for phantasmatic connection, for the perfect identification of self and (m)other, than as an extension of the desire for autonomy, a desire for reassurance that his own infantile incompetence is now and forever hers, a desire to preside anew over the (m)other's silencing—as a desire for a transcendence of the symbolic that is less the negation of his discursive history than of his mother's.

Conversely, the lost mother's (re)animation would signify her (re)inscription in history, her (re)instatement as a subject in and of discourse— neither in excess of nor (therefore) reducible to the social, but rather marking a site where the social fails to coincide with its own boundaries, where the necessary and original contingency of the masculine social subject becomes visible. In its implicit contradiction of pre-Oedipality, its (retroactive) negation of masculine subjective primacy, its (re)construction of the maternal as a relation between mother and infant (better still, as a relational field) or as a social space, the mother's (re)animation displaces the very limit of the social, and thus opens onto that utopian perspective where her not yet articulated difference becomes (potentially) articulable.

The utopian perspective of Poe's "Ligeia" is as fragile and elusive as the status of Rowena's body is undecidable: as a masculine medium, sentimentalism at once opens and forecloses on the possibility of the mother's return, a possibility mediated for us here by the overinvested narrator/son. Insofar as the son narrates the tale, the mother's return is enacted, and contained, within the frame of filial desire; thus this reviving mother remains internal to the masculine subject, not a ghost on the point of speaking, but a hallucination on the verge of fading out. Or rather, the mother's return is *almost* contained in this narrative frame, since "Ligeia" hinges precisely on the ambiguity of containment. By dutifully conceding his addiction to opium, affirming his tendency to delusion, to the "waking visions of Ligeia" in which he indulges while sitting watch over Rowena's corpse, by demonstrating, in short, a healthy skepticism about his own perceptions, the narrator effectively derails the very reading he appears to advance: the conscientious acknowledgment of his impaired condition no less plausibly attests to the narrator's rationality, to his unimpeded capacity for self-evaluation, for distinguishing between his "visions" and reality. Interrogating his own authority, then, the narrator legitimates the other possibility—that the sounds and motions from the bed, which have every appearance of interrupting his "revery," do in fact emanate from beyond, from Ligeia herself.

Significantly, commentators on the tale, few in number and startlingly peremptory in tone, bracket this carefully cultivated irresolution, and conflate Ligeia with the narrator in the most reductive and monological ways. John Irwin, for instance, asserts that Ligeia is "a Psyche-figure for the narrator," a reading he derives, as far as textual evidence goes, solely from her description in the tale as a person of "gigantic volition" (Irwin 1980, 227).

Donald Pease, on the other hand, identifies Ligeia with a primal loss, with an ineffable "something" the narrator no longer possesses: "In such tales as 'Ligeia,' 'Morella,' and 'Berenice' . . . [Poe] created settings where fallen nobility could recover relation with someone or something lost" (Pease 1987, 189). The narrators of these tales "displace their present world by acting according to the demands of an archaic and infinitely more powerful past" (ibid., 190). For Irwin, then, Ligeia's "gigantic volition" is categorically subordinate to the masculine authorial voice, while for Pease Ligeia's power, abstracted as the attraction of the narrator's prelapsarian past, in no sense compromises or limits the narrator's discursive mastery.

Thus, ironically, while neither Pease nor Irwin reads the figure of Ligeia as a mother, they assign her a mother's destiny in the social-symbolic order of nineteenth-century democracy; she is either the reflection of the masculine subject, or conflated with the place of the subject's origin.[6] But it is precisely this destiny, and this order, that "Ligeia" ambiguously contests and (re)affirms. On the one hand, then, the narrator's reminiscences of Ligeia and of his relation to her insist on her extrasymbolic status, and so on her necessary inscription as absence within the symbolic order. In this frame, the narrator's enervated diction, his obsessively refined style of portraiture—the plainly feigned naiveté with which he aspires to a mimetic perfection that the very self-consciousness of this discursive posture undermines—functions to evacuate Ligeia from the site of her re-presentation.

In beauty of face no maiden ever equalled her. It was the radiance of an opium-dream—an airy and spirit-lifting vision more wildly divine than the phantasies which hovered about the slumbering souls of the daughters of Delos. Yet her features were not of that regular mould which we have been falsely taught to worship in the classical labors of the heathen. "There is no exquisite beauty," says Bacon, Lord Verulam, speaking truly of all the forms and *genera* of beauty, "without some *strangeness* in the proportion." . . . It might have been too that in these eyes of my beloved lay the secret to which Lord Verulam alludes. They were, I must believe, far larger than the ordinary eyes of our own race. . . . The "strangeness," however, which I found in the eyes was of a nature distinct from the formation, or the color, or the brilliancy of the features, and must, after all, be referred to the *expression*. Ah, word of no meaning! behind whose vast latitude of mere sound we intrench our ignorance of so much of the spiritual. (Poe 1984b, 263–64)

In the first moment of this portrait, Ligeia's physical beauty negates her materiality, as though perfection of form could only exist in the insubstantial medium of the vision, in the fluid dimensions of imaginary space. And while beauty in this initial moment still refers to form—Bacon's "strangeness" rests in proportions—the narrator ultimately deploys Bacon's aesthetic to locate Ligeia's beauty in what altogether exceeds her material "formation," in her "expression." Having transmuted Ligeia's beauty into a beauty of "expression," moreover, the narrator ambiguously registers the loss, abruptly emptying her "expression" of its meaning, so that this signifier of excess, of an excess that still assumed at the outset a certain material specificity, becomes a cipher—the signifier of that which remains *in excess of* signification. Thus Poe, like Fuller, invests in the "expression" of a mother's face, with the fine if poignant distinction that what was in Fuller's construction the sign of a vanished plenitude becomes in Poe's a "vast latitude" of absence—of something always already unspoken.

Still, the plenitude of embodied meaning Fuller associates with the mother attaches to Poe's Ligeia as well. As one who exceeds the symbolic order, exceeds all discursive determination of meaning, Ligeia becomes the repository of all meanings—the body of the signifiable itself:

I have spoken of the learning of Ligeia: it was immense—such as I have never known in woman. In the classical tongues was she deeply proficient. . . . Indeed upon any theme of the most admired because simply the most abstruse of the boasted erudition of the Academy, have I *ever* found Ligeia at fault? . . . I said her knowledge was such as I have never known in woman—but where breathes the man who has traversed, and successfully, *all* the wide areas of moral, physical, and mathematical science? I saw not then what I now clearly perceive, that the acquisitions of Ligeia were gigantic, were astounding; yet I was sufficiently aware of her infinite supremacy to resign myself, with a child-like confidence, to her guidance through the chaotic world of metaphysical investigation at which I was most busily occupied during the earlier years of our marriage. . . . Without Ligeia I was but as a child groping benighted. (Poe 1984b, 266)

Ligeia is thus coextensive here with the space through which this "childlike" narrator moves "benighted"; she traverse[s]" a universe that he merely inhabits. In the frame of her "gigantic acquisitions," moreover, the figure of Ligeia herself begins to elude us, as all possible articulations of her "gigantic volition" seem *ab ovo* exhausted. Ligeia vanishes in the face of her own "infinite supremacy," of an unboundedness that is the negation of her subjectivity, a plenitude that leaves no room for her partiality, for her voice. Instead, it is the figure of the narrator whom we distinguish, projecting himself down the "all untrodden path" of a strangely vacant "vista":

With how vast a triumph—with how vivid a delight—with how much of all that is ethereal in hope—did I *feel*, as she bent over me in studies but little sought—but less known—that delicious vista by slow degrees expanding before me, down whose long, gorgeous, and all untrodden path, I might at length pass onward to the goal of a wisdom too divinely precious not to be forbidden. (Ibid.)

In this idealized presymbolic realm of the maternal, where learning is encoded in sensory rather than discursive registers—where knowledge is felt—the figure of the mother is already fading from view, losing the status of guide, of interlocutor, of mother, to become instead the matrix of a masculine protosubject, of a not-yet-subject already invested here, however, with the social and discursive primacy of the normative (white, middle-class) adult male.

Inasmuch as the pre-Oedipal, at least as the narrator figures it in this passage, is already informed by the logic of a social symbolic system that privileges masculine autonomy at the expense of feminine presence, the dissolution of the maternal at Ligeia's death appears not so much to inaugurate as to bring to term the development of the masculine subject. Still, the crisis assumes conventionally Oedipal dimensions: thus death acquires a phallic shape in the verses of Poe's "Conqueror Worm"—which the narrator attributes to Ligeia in Poe's revision of the tale—while the dying Ligeia's frantic invocation of paternal authority on hearing her poem recited only confirms the (until now nonexistent) father's role in this event. However, to the primal horror of the worm's incursion ("But see, amid the mimic rout / A crawling shape intrude! / A blood-red thing that writhes from out / The scenic solitude!"), Ligeia responds with a rage ambiguously plaintive and admonitory in quality, at once providing and contesting the recognition of paternal ascendancy that this patriarchal God appears to exact: " 'O God!' half shrieked Ligeia, leaping to her feet and extending her arms aloft with a spasmodic movement, as I made an end to these lines—'O God! O Divine Father!—shall these things be undeviatingly so?—shall this conqueror be not once conquered?' " (ibid., 269). Ligeia's question is none the more answerable for being ostensibly rhetorical in nature; inasmuch as it solicits an unequivocal response, it asks for the resolution that this narrative drama of revivification defers. Yet the tale's undecidability disturbs the social-symbolic order even as it eclipses its own utopian "light." Although to replace the socially unplaced figure of Ligeia—the narrator notes early in the tale that he never learned her "paternal name"—he purchases a bride whose title resonates with all the fine distinctions of social class, the "Lady Rowena Trevanion, of Tremaine," it is to Rowena's paternally inscribed body that Ligeia so insistently, and interminably, lays claim.

Stowe's Authentic Ghost

In the chapters of *Uncle Tom's Cabin* set on Simon Legree's plantation, Poe's drama of revivification is rescripted to accommodate the possibility that "Ligeia" at once envisions and negates—the possibility, that is, of the lost mother's (re)animation as a powerful, articulate, "authentic" presence. Inasmuch as Stowe authenticates the spectral mother whose status Poe carefully refuses to determine, however, she implicitly repudiates the affirmative construction of the social subject. Thus the proof of the mother's authenticity in this instance turns on the *nonidentity* of her avatars, rather than on the congruence of her selves over time: when Legree's "pale mother" rises up from the grave to reproach her hard-hearted son, her reappearance, and its effects on the otherwise intractable Legree, inspire his black slave Cassy to impersonate the pallid ghost, and thereby reenact her (re)animation, this time as an unimpeachably self-conscious and material entity. Moreover, it is Cassy's travesty of the resurrected white mother to which Stowe gives the title "An Authentic Ghost Story," so that in this episode of the novel, at least, the reanimated mother's authenticity comes to rest squarely on her *difference* from her prior incarnations.[7] Legree's (re)animated mother is a visibly hybrid subject, constituted in and by the newly articulated relation of what she was to what she is (not).

If Legree's susceptibility to Cassy's stratagem turns on his horror of his dead mother's reappearance, Stowe appears to impute to the sadistic slave driver something more than the generic susceptibility of the masculine subject to a terror of maternal (re)animation. The etiology of Legree's revulsion is thus more obscure than in the case of Poe's narrator, whose horror at the mother's return hinges simply on his own status as a now properly socialized male. Legree's history is complicated, however, by an absolute lack of nostalgia for the maternal enclosure, by an eager acquiescence in paternal law that results, paradoxically, in his repudiation of all that his mother represents, not excluding the moral norms that sustain a patriarchal democratic order.

Hard and reprobate as the godless man seemed now, there had been a time when he had been rocked on the bosom of a mother,—cradled with prayers and pious hymns,—his now seared brow bedewed with the waters of holy baptism. . . . Far in New England that mother had trained her only son, with long, unwearied love and patient prayers. Born of a hard-tempered sire, on whom that gentle woman had wasted a world of unvalued love, Legree had followed in the steps of his father . . . and at an early age, broke from her, to seek his fortunes at sea. (Stowe 1982, 528)

Still, what may appear by the standard of the realist novel to be Stowe's flimsy characterization of a wantonly cruel son is in fact consistent with the logic of a culture that exacts the male child's separation from the mother, if not precisely in such baldly violent terms. Indeed, the son's trajectory away from the mother and into the symbolic is already inscribed in Stowe's representation of the maternal. As in Fuller's portrait, maternal love here finds its voice in the presymbolic idiom of the mother's body, of her rocking and cradling; yet the maternal body is itself almost immediately refigured as (mere) language, as the medium of the infant's initiation into the soothing rewards of piety. In this frame, Legree's idiosyncrasy rests not with his rejection of his mother, but rather with his unaccountable failure to senti-mentalize her loss, to participate in his culture's idealization of a figure that it thereby ruthlessly effaces. Legree's brutality, in other words, consists in making visible the violence of an erasure that sentimental discourse serves, at least in part, to naturalize.[8]

As Stowe intuits, then, Legree's repudiation of sentimental idealization in no sense subtracts him from sentimentalism's cultural logic; in fact, it only serves to situate him more decisively within the social-symbolic structure that sentimental narrative articulates even as it moves to contest. In the figure of Legree, Stowe, *with* Poe, aligns the terror of a sentimental haunting with the very terms of the masculine subject's inscription in the social order. It is in this sense that I understand what would otherwise appear to be the simply ludicrous receptivity of the unrepentant and callous Legree to what is coded here, at least, as his mother's *moral* reproaches, symbolized in a lock of golden hair that she encloses in her parting letter:

> Legree burned the hair, and burned the letter; and when he saw them hissing and crackling in the flame, inly shuddered as he thought of everlasting fires. He tried to drink, and revel, and swear away the memory; but often, in the deep night, whose solemn stillness arraigns the bad soul in forced communion with herself, he had seen that pale mother rising by his bedside, and felt the soft twining of that hair around his fingers, till the cold sweat would roll down his face, and he would spring from his bed in horror. Ye who have wondered to hear, in the same evangel, that God is love, and that God is consuming fire, see ye not how, to the soul re-solved in evil, perfect love is the most fearful torture, the seal and sentence of the direst despair? (Stowe 1982, 529)

The terror of this apparition derives not from the saintly mother's media-tion of a morality Legree rejects, but from her contestation of an erasure in which Legree is all too willingly complicit: Legree cannot "swear away" his mother's memory, because this "memory" here assumes a will of her own, compromises the closed communion of Legree with himself, and erupts into the precinct of his subjective interiority, which his mother's presence now effectively reconfigures as an intersubjective space. As in the "solemn stillness" of the night Legree's mother comes (back) to life, he loses himself in the most material sense; shocked past control of his body's functions, he breaks out in cold sweat and leaps up in horror.

This is the scene into which Cassy inserts herself. Witness to his frenzy at the sight of Eva's blond locks, which Legree's overseers have snatched from Tom and dutifully delivered to their master, Cassy infers the cause of Legree's terror and turns it to her own advantage. Draped in a white sheet, she impersonates Legree's pale mother and, having reduced him to an impotent and inarticulate fury, walks off the plantation unmolested. Significantly, however, Cassy's affinity for the part hinges for Stowe on the "influence" she already commands over Legree, an influence in turn attributed to Cassy's specifically verbal instability.

> The influence of Cassy over him was of a strange and singular kind. He was her owner, her tyrant and tormentor. . . . When he first bought her, she was, as she said, a woman delicately bred; and then he crushed her, without scruple, beneath the foot of his brutality. But, as time, and debasing influences, and despair, hardened womanhood within her, she had become in a measure his mistress, and he alternately tyrannized over and dreaded her. This influence had become more harassing and decided, since partial insanity had given *a strange, weird, unsettled cast to all her words and language.* (Ibid., 567, emphasis added)

Although in and of itself this account of Legree's and Cassy's dialectical relation is certainly compelling, Stowe here curiously falsifies the history of Cassy's "partial insanity" as it emerges from other moments in the narrative. As Cassy herself explains to Uncle Tom, Legree is only the last in a chain of abusive masters who have "crushed her, without scruple," for their own aims. Thus Cassy's first episode of abandoned rage is directed at the master who sells off her children despite her careful negotiations to prevent this act, and thus finally imparts to Cassy what she had been at once unwilling and unable to see: her erasure from the social-symbolic order, the absolute failure of her voice to signify. Cassy's "unsettled" language, then, marks her liminal relation to an order in which, though she may say what she will, she *means* nothing at all. Yet, as though unwilling to realize the connection between Cassy's maternal grief, the horror of her recognition that in a slave economy her claim to her children is unintelligible, and her "unsettled" language, Stowe suddenly telescopes a history that elsewhere she finds useful to develop.

Indeed, to trace the genesis of Cassy's "unsettled" language in this manner is to reverse the implication of the edited account Stowe offers us here: in this larger frame, Cassy's lapse from a normative feminine/maternal discourse—a discourse in which Cassy, as a slave mother, was never inscribed—is less remarkable than her capacity to preserve any connection at all to white motherhood's discursive logic, to address Legree in the decisively maternal idiom of "influence." "Influence" here ceases to refer to maternal mediation of generalized social norms, to "moral influence," in short; rather, Cassy's "influence" over Legree mediates nothing but her own partial and particular history—the history of her erasure from the social and symbolic site of motherhood, the history encoded in the "weird cast" of her language. Yet it is exactly by rehearsing the narrative of her silencing that Cassy staves off silence, and it is by staging her disappearance that Cassy makes herself visible.

It was a cloudy, misty moonlight, and there [Legree] saw it!—something white, gliding in! He heard the still rustle of its ghostly garments. It stood still by his bed;—a cold hand touched his; a voice said, three times, in a low fearful whisper "Come! come! come!" And, while he lay sweating with terror, he knew not when or how, the thing was gone. He sprang out of bed, and pulled at the door. It was shut and locked, and the man fell down in a swoon. After this, Legree became a harder drinker than ever before. . . . There were reports around the country, soon after, that he was sick and dying. Excess had brought on that frightful disease that *seems to throw the lurid shadows of a coming retribution back into the present life.* (Ibid., 596, emphasis added)

But *who* speaks in this black mother's travesty of a (re)animated white mother who is herself merely immanent in a discourse that inters her? I suggest that from this locus of disjuncture a maternal subject rises: vanished beneath the sheet, the face of "Cassy" marks the place where the sentimental image of an expressive maternal countenance evaporates, leaving only a voice, and its resonant articulation of the mother's social and symbolic power. Sentimentalism expires here in the shoddy trappings and crude devices of a haunting that in the very banality of its artifice abdicates a mythologized reality and authenticates the material remainder: a deadly command that Legree cannot mute, temper, or resist.

If Ligeia warps the limits of the filial self, "Cassy" (re)possesses the vicious son, in the name of the histories of erasure she articulates here. And while there is no place for her to go, exactly, she is also impossible to efface. Indeed, for all Stowe's apparent desire to redomesticate Cassy, to position her in the reconstituted familial sphere to which the freed black women in this novel accede, the figure Cassy cuts in that white sheet is beyond recall. For as much as Stowe seeks to reinscribe Cassy's face with the tender expression of white motherhood, and engineers the altogether implausible return of Cassy's children to her, Cassy stands out, apart, in the scenes of familial reunion that follow, a strange, unsettled figure, marking time on a utopian clock.

NOTES

This essay stands in a dialogical relation to "Terminate or Liquidate" (see chap. 4). Jonathan Elmer shared with me an early draft of his essay at around the same time I was beginning an initial version of my own. While I situate Stowe quite differently in relation to Poe, and indeed situate the social limits on which we both agree that sentimentalism plays quite differently in relation to gender, I want to acknowledge a formal and conceptual indebtedness that no doubt (at this point) the reader of these essays will be better able to delineate than either of us can.

1. For a full account of the concept of "Republican Motherhood," see Kerber 1981.

2. Hence the peculiarly elusive phrasing of this passage, in which Bloch points us to the very thing he seems reluctant to concede—namely, the historical frame of his own transhistorical analytical project. The historical contingency of these "rationalisms," implied in their congruence with Gothicism, thus remains nevertheless unspoken.

3. Thus I would suggest that the valorizations of the maternal as an extradiscursive space in (so-called) French feminism, and particularly in the work of Julia Kristeva, finally only serve to reinstate the logic of bourgeois subjectivity. While Kristeva's models help articulate the (masculine) bourgeois subject's relation to the maternal, they offer little or no ground for the contestation of a masculine subjectivity constituted at the price of maternal silence. Insofar as the maternal represents for Kristeva a "heterogeneity that cannot be subsumed in the signifier," Kristeva—following Freud and especially Lacan—adopts as transhistorically valid a historically specific essentialization of motherhood. Yet as nineteenth-century sentimentalists themselves intuited, the idea of the maternal as the "in-excess" of the social-symbolic order is itself a social and cultural code that may, as such, be unsettled, contradicted, and eroded. My citation is from "Stabat Mater" in Kristeva 1987, 259.

4. While I agree, then, with Hazel Carby's assertion that "the conventions of True Womanhood" serve to uphold a "racist, ideological system," I suggest that the discourse of sentimentalism is not finally reducible to the discourse of True Womanhood, though it does, certainly, participate in this fundamentally racist and classist discourse. However, the extent to which nineteenth-century African-American writers could appropriate and radically reconfigure sentimental narrative models argues for sentimentalism's dialogical structures. See Carby 1987, 50.

5. See Douglas 1978.

6. Indeed, virtually no critics have perceived Ligeia's maternal characteristics. I find one exception, however, in Daniel Hoffman's study of Poe, entitled annoyingly *Poe Poe Poe Poe Poe Poe Poe* (Hoffman 1987). Hoffman acknowledges Ligeia's function as "Mother-Figure" in the tale, but situates the narrator's relation to her within a strictly Oedipal frame. Thus the "problem" turns out to be Poe's impotence (the author being, moreover, entirely conflated with the narrator here).

7. My insistence on Stowe's authentication of a travesty as a strategy for deessentializing female identity is indebted in part to Butler 1990, esp. 43–57.

8. Legree thus speaks to Margaret Homans's sense of the violence of this erasure: "The symbolic order is founded, not merely on the regrettable loss of the mother, but on her active and overt murder." See Homans 1986, 11.

A Clew to a Clue

Locked Rooms and Labyrinths in Poe and Borges

JOHN T. IRWIN

It seems clear that Borges produced his three detective stories—"The Garden of the Forking Paths," "Death and the Compass," and "Ibn Hakkan al-Bokhari, Dead in His Labyrinth" (Borges 1978)—as an antithetical doubling, an interpretive reading-rewriting of the origin of the analytic detective genre, Poe's three Dupin stories—"The Murders in the Rue Morgue," "The Mystery of Marie Rogêt," and "The Purloined Letter." Part of the impetus for this project seems to have been a wish to memorialize the hundredth anniversary of the genre by writing an analytic detective story of his own that would recover what he took to be the genre's original impulses. "The Garden of the Forking Paths" was published in 1941, one hundred years after the appearance of "The Murders in the Rue Morgue." Borges recalls that the English translation of the story was sent to a contest sponsored by *Ellery Queen's Mystery Magazine* and that it won a second prize (see Borges 1948). The magazine had itself been founded in 1941, one of several publications meant to mark the genre's centennial.

I would like to focus on the link between a central image in Borges's detective stories, the image of the labyrinth, and the fact that Poe's first detective story, "The Murders in the Rue Morgue," presents itself as a locked-room puzzle. In his note to the English translation of his second detective story, "Death and the Compass," Borges directs our attention to what he calls "a thread of red" that "runs through the story's pages," a recurrence of the color in crucial passages that is in fact to be found in all three of these stories. However, I am less interested in what this recurrence means in the stories than in Borges calling it to the reader's attention by imaging it as "a thread" running through the tale. What Borges does is give us a clue to the very concept of clues, subtly reminding us of the importance of a thread in the story of the encounter of Theseus and the Minotaur in the labyrinth, and doing so within the context of three detective stories in which the final encounter between the protagonists occurs in a literal or a figurative labyrinth.

The "thread of red" that the author so obligingly isolates from the fabric of his story, as if to suggest that it is a clue whose unraveling will lead to the tale's solution, recalls the origin of a word that, perhaps more than any other, is associated with the analytic detective story. Under the spelling "clew," *Webster's New World Dictionary* gives "1. a ball of thread or yarn; in Greek legend, a thread was used by Theseus as a guide out of the labyrinth; hence, 2. something that leads out of a maze, perplexity, etc., or helps to solve a problem: in this sense generally spelled clue." A clue is literally, then, a ball of thread, and its common metaphoric meaning (as a hint to solve a mystery) is a function of the myth of Theseus and the Minotaur. Given that the thread running through the labyrinth of Borges's detective stories is specifically a red one, it is worth noting that in the ancient world one of the more common color schemes used in visually representing the labyrinth pattern, particularly as a decorative border design (the meander), was a red line on a yellow or pale background, which suggests that for Borges the red line outlining the shape of a labyrinth (for example, the red ink line forming the triangle on the map in "Death and the Compass") and the red thread leading us out of the story's labyrinth may be continuous.

In giving us this clue to the origin of the word *clue,* this hieroglyph of the object from which the common meaning of the word derives, Borges is engaged at once in doubling the Dupin stories and in interpreting them, in the sense that any rewriting of another's work amounts to an oblique reading of that work by the second writer. And what Borges's reading of the Dupin stories focuses on in this instance is Poe's repeated use of the word "clue" in these three tales with what seems to be a clear sense both of its original meaning (a ball of thread) and of the association of its figurative meaning with the myth of Theseus and the Minotaur. The word *clue* or *clew* occurs seven times in the Dupin stories, and at least two of the occurrences are of special significance. In "The Purloined Letter," for example, the word is used only once, but in a position of great formal importance (the story's final paragraph). Oddly enough, however, it does not occur in a context where one would have expected it—that is, Poe uses *clue* to refer, not to the hints that lead Dupin to solve the mystery of where and how Minister D— has hidden the purloined letter, but rather to the trace Dupin himself leaves in the substituted letter to reveal his identity to his double. Explaining his decision not to leave the interior of the substituted letter blank, Dupin says:

That would have been insulting. D——, at Vienna once, did me an evil turn, which I told him, quite good-humoredly, that I should remember. So, as I knew he would feel some curiosity in regard to the identity of the person who had outwitted him, I thought it a pity not to give him a clue. He is well acquainted with my MS., and I just copied into the middle of the blank sheet the words—

—Un dessein si funeste,
S'il n'est digne d'Atrée, est digne de Thyeste.

They are to be found in Crébillon's "Atrée." (Poe 1969–78, 993)

This reference to Dupin's manuscript, that is, to his immediately recognizable handwriting, as a "clue" to his identity suggests an imagistic association of that meandering line of ink on paper (which reveals the opponent concealed in the letter) with the meandering line of thread that leads to and from the opponent concealed in the labyrinth, an association clearly present in the detective story that Borges balances against "The Purloined Letter." In "Death and the Compass" the clue Scharlach gives Lönnrot to their meeting place in the maze—a line of red ink on a map—is also a veiled signature, its redness suggesting the doubly red name (Red Scarlet) of the man who is Lönnrot's double.

That Poe associates a line of ink inscribed on a sheet of paper with a line of thread running through a labyrinth seems even more likely when we consider the elaborate hieroglyphic action that he constructs in "The Murders in the Rue Morgue" around the word *clue*. What with the tale's startling device of a simian culprit, we often forget that Poe's first detective story initially presents itself as a locked-room mystery: Dupin's first problem is the murderer's "means of egress" from Mme and Mlle L'Espanaye's apartment. When the police arrive, they find that the "large back chamber in the fourth story," from which the women's screams had issued, is "locked, with the key inside," and upon forcing the door, they find that the front and rear windows are "down and firmly fastened from within." Examining the chamber's two rooms, Dupin satisfies himself that the murderer could not have exited through either of the doors to the hall, since each was locked with the key inside, nor through the chimneys, which are too narrow at the top to admit "the body of a large cat," nor through the windows in the front room, from which "no one could have escaped without notice from the crowd in the street." All of which leads him to concentrate his investigation on the two windows in the back room. Each has a "gimlet-hole" drilled in its frame with "a very stout nail . . . fitted therein, nearly to the head" (ibid., 527–52). The police had tried to raise the sashes but, failing, had concluded that the murderer had exited in some other way. Dupin, however, carries out a more minute examination. With some difficulty, he removes the nail from one of the frames and then tries to raise the sash, only to find that it still cannot be budged. He theorizes that the sash must be fastened by a hidden spring that snaps into place when the sash is lowered. He quickly discovers the spring, but this still leaves him with the problem of the nail inserted in the frame. Even if the sash had latched automatically when lowered, how had the murderer reinserted the nail in the gimlet hole on the inside of the closed window?

With this in mind, Dupin turns his attention to the other window, seemingly identical to the first, with a nail inserted in the frame and a hidden spring that fastens automatically. Dupin reasons that since all other possible means of escape have been logically eliminated, this window must have been the murderer's way out; and though it seems identical to the other one, it must, he concludes, be different in some respect, and the difference must involve the nail in the frame. As he explains to the narrator:

You will say that I was puzzled; but, if you think so, you must have misunderstood the nature of the inductions. To use a sporting phrase, I had not been once "at fault." The scent had never for an instant been lost. There was no flaw in any link of the chain. I had traced the secret to its ultimate result,—and that result was *the nail.* It had, I say, in every respect, the appearance of its fellow in the other window; but this fact was an absolute nullity (conclusive as it might seem to be) when compared with the consideration that here, at this point, terminated the clew. "There *must* be something wrong," I said, "about the nail." I touched it; and the head, with about a quarter of an inch of the shank, came off in my fingers. The rest of the shank was in the gimlet-hole, where it had been broken off. (Ibid., 553)

The murderer had indeed, then, exited through this window, with the hidden spring automatically fastening the lowered sash, and the police mistaking "the retention of this spring" (ibid., 554) for that of the apparently undamaged nail. Dupin's description of the unbroken, step-by-step process that led him to the nail is significant for several reasons. First, "the clew" that terminates at the nail clearly suggests, in the context of the imagery of following a marked path (e.g., tracking a scent), that Poe uses the word *clew* here to evoke both its literal, original meaning and also that mythic account of following a thread out of a labyrinth from which the word derives its standard figurative meaning, and that he is doing so precisely because of (and perhaps to call attention to) the structural similarity between a locked-room mystery and a labyrinth. In both, the problem is one of understanding how an apparently exitless enclosure may be exited, in one instance by following a figurative clue that leads to the discovery of the criminal's "means of egress" (ibid., 555), in the other by following a literal clew that leads out of the maze. (One might note here in passing that Poe's image of a clew terminating at a nail in the exit's frame implicitly raises the question of how Theseus kept the thread in place at the labyrinth's entrance as he unwound the clew along his path. Though the question is not addressed in any of the major classical versions of the myth, the Scholiast on Appollodorus explains that Theseus fastened "one end of the thread to the lintel of the door on entering into the labyrinth" (Appollodorus 1976, 2:135 n. 3), and one might easily imagine the thread's being tied to a nail driven into the lintel.)

What seems clear is that Borges's antithetical reading/rewriting of the Dupin stories registers not only the resemblance between the mystery of a locked room and the puzzle of a labyrinth, but also the resemblance between these two structures and the purloined letter. The basic similarity of the three turns on each figure's problematic representation of the relationship between inner and outer. In a locked-room mystery, for example, the notion that a solid body requires a physical opening to pass from inside a room to outside it seems to have been violated. Inside the room there is physical evidence, usually a dead body, of the earlier presence of another body in the room, that of the killer. But when the room, with all its entrances locked from within, is broken into by the police, that other body is absent—a situation that seems to question assumptions as basic as the physical continuity of inner and outer and the noninterpenetrability of solid bodies. A locked-room mystery confronts us with an enclosure that appears, from both inside and outside, to be unopened, indeed unopenable, without there being left some physical trace of its having been opened, such as a broken lock from the police's forced entry or an unfastened window from the murderer's escape. The solution generally involves showing that the room's appearance of being unopened is only an appearance, an outward illusion that does not represent an inner reality.

In contrast to the locked room, a labyrinth is always open from the outside but appears to be unopenable from within. It permits access to a physical body but denies it exit by subtly disrupting the link between relative and absolute bearing, by confusing the self's control of itself through the disorientation of the body. A labyrinth is in a sense a self-locking enclosure that uses the directionality of the human body as the bolt in the lock.

The relationship of inner and outer is even more problematic in the case of the purloined letter, for there it is a matter not only of the letter's being turned inside out as part of its concealment in the open but also of whether the letter is hidden inside or outside a given physical space, the Minister's house. During the Prefect's account of his minute but unsuccessful search of the Minister's dwelling, the question arises of whether the Minister might in fact carry the letter about with him or whether he might have "concealed it elsewhere than upon his own premises." The Prefect maintains that the letter cannot possibly be in the Minister's possession, since he has twice had the Minister "waylaid, as if by footpads, and his person rigorously searched." As to the letter's being hidden somewhere other than the Minister's house, Dupin reasons that since "the instant availability of the document—its susceptibility of being produced at a moment's notice" is "a point of nearly equal importance with its possession," the letter must be hidden in the Minister's residence.

The mystery depends on this rigorous circumscription of the letter's possible hiding places. If the Minister had the whole world in which to conceal the letter, what would be mysterious about the Prefect's inability to find it? Only because it is logically certain that the letter is hidden in a specific, finite enclosure whose space has been painstakingly searched does its continued nonappearance become mysterious. That is, as opposed to a locked-room mystery in which the criminal's patent absence from an internally sealed space constitutes the problem, the mystery of the purloined letter turns on an object's unperceived presence within what we might call an externally sealed space, a space that is closed off not physically but logically, since all the possible external hiding places for the object must be analytically eliminated if there is to be something odd about the object's nonappearance. A locked-room mystery asks how a solid body got out of (or into) an internally sealed space without violating the space's appearance of closure; a hidden-object mystery asks how a solid object remains present within a finite physical space without, as it were, making an appearance. In one case we are certain that what we seek is not inside a given space, in the other that what we seek cannot possibly be outside it.

Part of the peculiar force of hidden-object and locked-room detective stories is that they seem to present us with a physical embodiment, a concrete spatialization, of that very mechanism of logical inclusion/exclusion on which rational analysis is based; indeed, they present us with this as an apparent confounding of rational analysis. In the case of the purloined letter the problematic relationship of inner and outer takes on an added twist. For while the object must be present *inside* the Minister's house without its making an appearance, the relationship of appearance to reality as outer to inner is itself further put in play because the object is hidden *out in the open* within this enclosed space. That is, the letter is concealed in plain sight on the surface, *on the outside of this inside* (the house), a concealment accomplished by, and symbolized in, the turning of the letter itself inside out. Thus everted, the letter's outside—the part of the letter whose appearance is known to the Prefect and Dupin from the Queen's description, the part that usually serves to conceal, to envelop, the letter's contents—now becomes the content to be concealed from the eyes of the police; while the inside—the reality that gives this letter its special significance, the part of it that is not known to the Prefect and Dupin—becomes a new outside that gives the letter a different appearance.

Analyzing the structure of hidden-object and locked-room mysteries in terms of an inner/outer problematic not only allows us to see that the first and last Dupin stories are variations on the same mystery of consciousness; it also reveals a further link between these stories and the labyrinth, a link involving the intersection between the inner/outer and the right/left oppositions. Poe compares the turning of the letter inside out to the turning of a glove, and the reversal of a glove's inner and outer surfaces is also a reversal of its handedness, a right-handed glove turned inside out becoming a left-handed one and vice versa. But the reversal of inner and outer depends on inner and outer, like the poles of any mutually constitutive opposition, being not separate entities but rather opposing aspects of the same entity. And this sense of inner and outer as opposing appearances presented by a single continuous surface recalls one of the traditional methods for finding both the center of and, more importantly, the exit from a labyrinth, a method that works by aligning the continuity of the inner and outer surfaces with the handedness of the individual exploring the labyrinth. In his classic study *Mazes and Labyrinths,* W. H. Matthews describes the method's application to the navigation of a hedge maze:

When it is impracticable to place marks, or even to use, like Theseus, a clue of thread, it is still possible in the majority of cases to make certain of finding the goal by the simple expedient of placing one hand on the hedge on entering the maze, and consistently following the hedge around, keeping contact all the time with the same hand. Blind turnings present no difficulty, as they will only be traversed in one direction and then in the other. The traveller being guided by his contact with the hedge alone is relieved of all necessity for making a choice of paths when arriving at the nodes.

The only case in which this method breaks down is that in which the goal is situated anywhere within a loop. Where this occurs the explorer adopting the method described will discover the fact by finding himself eventually back at the starting point without having visited the goal. (Matthews 1970, 191)

This method postulates that if the interior and exterior surfaces of a labyrinth are continuous, so that the inner surface inevitably leads back to the outer, then the inner surface can guide one back to the exit, if one can find a way of maintaining the body's orientation in relation to this surface continuity. And that constant orientation of the body is established by the uninterrupted use of the same hand to trace the surface continuity. Suppose, for example, that on entering a labyrinth we decide to use the wall on our right as the guiding thread into and out of the maze, and that as we begin walking, we guide our progress by keeping our right hand in contact with the wall. We will, as Matthews notes, eventually trace the interior surface of the entire labyrinth and return to the entry point. But the wall that was on our right as we entered, and with which we maintained continuous contact, will as we return be on our left, and the wall that on exiting we touch with the right hand will be the one that had been on our left as we entered. That is, on returning to the entry point we will be facing the other way, outward from the labyrinth rather than into it.

This rather involved description is necessary to make clear the connection between the structure of the labyrinth and the structure Poe proposes for the purloined letter by comparing the everting of the letter to the everting of a glove. In everting a glove, its inner and outer surfaces exchange places. This movement reverses not only the glove's handedness, but also the direction in which its fingers point. Imagine a right-hand glove lying palm downward on a flat surface with its fingers pointing away from us; if we turn it inside out while maintaining its palm-downward orientation, we will have a left-hand glove whose fingers point toward us. In following the interior surface of a labyrinth to its exit, we are exploiting the same topological phenomenon that makes possible the turning of a glove—that inner and outer are two opposing aspects of a single continuous surface. The difference is that in turning a glove this continuity is traced by *the movement of the surface itself,* while in navigating a labyrinth the continuity is traced by *the movement of a hand along the surface.* Nevertheless, the various reversals effected by these movements correspond: as the glove's inner surface becomes its outer, the direction in which its fingers are pointing and its handedness are reversed; and as the labyrinth's inner surface leads us back to the entrance, the direction in which we are facing is reversed, as well as what we might call the handedness of the wall (the wall that was on our right on entering is now on our left).

I now return to the thread of my argument and to the passage in "The Murders in the Rue Morgue" where Dupin explains how a process of logical elimination led him to the broken nail in the window frame at which "terminated the clew" (Poe 1969–78, 553). As I suggested earlier, the passage is significant for reasons that go beyond its association of locked room and labyrinth through the image of a threadlike clew leading to an entrance or exit. It marks as well, for example, a crucial moment in the development of the battle of wits between writer and reader in the analytic detective genre. At this point in Poe's first detective story, Dupin is about to reveal the solution to the tale's initial mystery—the locked room—as a prelude to revealing the tale's principal mystery, the identity of the killer. Dupin's method of revelation in both instances is not a sudden announcement of his conclusions but rather a gradual presentation of his train of thought, a retelling of the crime or re-presentation of the scene that indicates and organizes salient points in a way that might, but does not, enable the listener—Dupin's unnamed companion—to anticipate the detective's solution. Moreover, it is quite clear that Dupin conceives of this method of revelation as a game played with his friend the narrator, for besides showing him the clues that influenced his own deductions, Dupin gives the narrator added hints—often in the imagery with which he characterizes a situation—that point to the ultimate solution. For example, in describing the reasoning that led him to the nail, he says, "To use a sporting phrase, I had not been once 'at fault.' The scent had never for an instant been lost. . . . I had traced the secret to its ultimate result,—and that result was *the nail. . . .* here, at this point, terminated the clew" (ibid.). Though Dupin is describing how he solved the locked-room problem, the imagery—"a sporting phrase," the "scent" that "had never . . . been lost"—hints at the solution to the larger mystery of the killer's identity, in that it calls to mind the sport of hunting and suggests that the object of Dupin's pursuit is in fact an animal. And since human hunters do not have the olfactory ability to track game by its scent, there is perhaps a hint here as well of an animal quality to Dupin (the traditional image of the sleuth as bloodhound), of which I will have more to say later. Dupin's suggestion that the culprit is nonhuman is reinforced by the image of the threadlike clew terminating at the nail, for while the clew followed one way in the Theseus myth leads back to the entrance, the clew running the other way marks the track Theseus followed in hunting down the half-human, half-animal Minotaur.

The game Dupin plays with the narrator is at once a part and a figure of the game the author plays with the reader, as Poe suggests by making the terminus of the clew (the problem's solution) a *nail,* thereby testing the reader's linguistic skill and attention. Dupin is French, and though the narrator's nationality is not specified, he does reside in Paris, so we can take it that he is fluent in the language. Consequently, we may assume that Dupin's conversations in English with the narrator represent the tale's "translations," as it were, of ones originally conducted in Dupin's native tongue. Dupin's account of his solution to the locked-room problem minutely describes the two windows at the rear of the victims' chamber, mentioning again and again the nail inserted in the frame of each window. And the French word for "nail," the word Dupin would have used so often, is *clou.* This is simply Poe's way of giving the reader a linguistic clue (hint) that the clew (thread) will ultimately lead to a *clou* (nail)—though even the most alert reader will probably understand this pun only retrospectively, so that Poe remains one up. But there is more at work here than just a pun, for the structure of this linguistic clue—two words with similar sounds but different meanings (a hidden, a metaphysical difference)—mirrors the structure of the solution to which the threadlike clew leads, two windows apparently "identical in character" but with a hidden difference, a concealed break in the *clou* imbedded in one of them. (In this connection it is worth noting that in the bilingual pair clew/*clou,* with their phonetic similarity and their orthographic and lexical differences, the English half is split and doubled again—clew/clue—by an orthographic difference and a phonetic and lexical sameness.) The hidden difference between the windows is hinted at in Dupin's first description of them: "There are two windows in the chamber. One of them is unobstructed by furniture, and is wholly visible. The lower portion of the other is hidden from view by the head of the unwieldy bedstead which is thrust up close against it" (ibid.). The window whose "lower portion . . . is hidden from view by the head" of the bed is the same window in which the broken, lower portion of the nail is hidden from view by the nail's undamaged head. The language of the subsequent passage in which Dupin recounts his discovery of the break in the nail clearly echoes his earlier description of the windows:

I touched it; and the head, with about a quarter of an inch of the shank, came off in my fingers. The rest of the shank was in the gimlet-hole, where it had been broken off. The fracture was an old one (for its edges were encrusted with rust), and had apparently been accomplished by a blow of a hammer, which had partially *imbedded,* in the top of the bottom sash, *the head portion* of the nail. I now carefully replaced the head portion in the indentation whence I had taken it, and the resemblance to a perfect nail was complete—the fissure was invisible. Pressing the spring, I gently raised the sash for a few inches; the head went up with it, remaining firm in its *bed*. I closed the window, and the semblance of the whole nail was again perfect.

The riddle, so far, was now unriddled. (Ibid.; emphasis added)

Clearly, Poe is playing a game of verbal clues with the reader in having the head of the bed conceal the portion of the same window in which the head of the nail, "firm in its bed," conceals the broken shank. Moreover, in the very act of unriddling one riddle, he leads us to another, for he offers a clue not just to the solution of the locked-room problem (the broken *clou*) but also to a larger pattern of imagery that runs through the entire story and hints at both the identity of the killer and the meaning of the tale—I refer to the tale's recurring allusions to decapitation, the separating of a higher portion from a lower portion. The most striking instance is literal, the corpse of Mme L'Espanaye. In the words of the newspaper account of the body's discovery:

After a thorough investigation of every portion of the house, without farther discovery, the party made its way into a small paved yard in the rear of the building, where lay the corpse of the old lady, with her throat so entirely cut that, upon an attempt to raise her, the head fell off. The body, as well as the head, was fearfully mutilated—the former so much so as scarcely to retain any semblance of humanity.

To this horrible mystery there is not as yet, we believe, the slightest clew. (Ibid., 538)

Poe indicates the significance of this head/body separation when he notes that the corpse was so badly mutilated "as scarcely to retain any semblance of humanity": that is, in the differential relationship that he sets up between head and body, Poe codes the body as nonhuman (lacking "any semblance of humanity") and thus codes the head as human in opposition—the standard equation of head, mind, rationality, humanity on the one hand and of body, instinct, irrationality, animality on the other. The concluding image of "the clew" links the puzzle of Mme L'Espanaye's corpse being found *outside* the locked room to the nail that is the solution to the locked-room mystery. And this linking of the corpse, whose head has been severed from its body, to the nail, whose head is broken from its shank, reinforces my interpretation of the clew-leading-to-the-nail (i.e., to the entrance) as an echo of the myth of Theseus and the labyrinth. While one end of Theseus's clew marks the labyrinth's entrance and exit, the other marks the location of the corpse of the labyrinth's inhabitant, a creature itself characterized by a head/body separation. (The Minotaur, with its animal head and human torso, symbolizes the destructive reversal of the proper (i.e., master/slave) relationship between mind and body, between the human and animal elements in human beings, the kind of reversal that occurs, for example, when instinctual ferocity masters reason in the taking of a human life. The Minotaur is killed because it is a mankiller, the slaughterer of the Athenian youths sent to Crete every nine years as tribute.) And this same master/slave reversal is symbolized by the humanlike killer-animal of "The Murders in the Rue Morgue," an animal whose cries are mistaken for human speech, whose name "orang-outang" literally means "man of the forest," and whose murderous rampage is triggered by its attempt to mimic a self-reflective action, its master's shaving his face in a mirror.

Dupin does not engage in a battle of wits with the unthinking killer of "The Murders in the Rue Morgue." Rather, in the absence of a rational culprit in the first analytic detective story, the mental duel between detective and criminal that will become the genre's mainstay is replaced by, or displaced into, Dupin's outwitting of both the ape's master and the Prefect of police. Dupin does not himself capture the ape; indeed, he never even sees it, so that it is only by outwitting the animal's master through a false advertisement that lures him to Dupin's lodgings that Dupin is able to verify his theory of the killer's identity. We should also note that when Dupin later reveals the solution to the police, the Prefect reacts to the amateur detective's analytic success as if it were a defeat for himself. Unable to "conceal his chagrin at the turn which affairs had taken, " he remarks on "the propriety of every person minding his own business" (ibid., 568). Poe's description of the battle of wits between Dupin and the Prefect seems to associate the Prefect with Theseus's opponent in the labyrinth, even to the point of using a head/body separation to characterize the Prefect's methods. Dupin says of the Prefect:

I am satisfied with having defeated him in his own castle. Nevertheless, that he failed in the solution of this mystery, is by no means that matter for wonder which he supposes it; for, in truth, our friend the Prefect is somewhat too cunning to be profound. In his wisdom is no *stamen*. It is all head and no body, like the pictures of the Goddess Laverna,—or, at best, all head and shoulders, like a codfish. But he is a good creature after all. (Ibid.)

As Theseus overcame the Minotaur in its own dwelling, so Dupin defeats the Prefect "in his own castle." And as Theseus's opponent was a creature with an animal head and a human body, so Dupin's opponent the Prefect, "a good creature after all," is compared to a mythical being traditionally represented as a head without a body (Laverna, the Roman goddess of thefts) and to an animal that is "all head and shoulders," the codfish. The point of this comparison, which figures the Prefect's reasoning as "cunning" rather that "profound" (Latin *profundus,* deep, low), higher rather than lower ("all head and no body"), seems to be the same point Dupin makes in "The Purloined Letter"—that the Prefect cannot imagine the workings of a mind substantially different from his own, a rule always true when the level of the other's intellect is above his own "and very usually when it is below." These two extremes are illustrated by the Prefect's failure to comprehend the operations both of a mind (the Minister's) that is almost superhuman in comparison to his own and of a "mind" that is literally subhuman, that of the ape.

That Dupin *does* recognize in the savagery of the L'Espanaye murders the signature of an animal mind is in some degree a function of Dupin's own doubleness—not that doubleness of the creative and resolvent elements in the self personified as poet and mathematician that Dupin discusses in "The Purloined Letter," but rather a doubleness that makes the detective and the criminal antithetical mirror images, reciprocals of one another precisely because the impulses that have mastered the criminal are those that have been mastered in the detective. Dupin recognizes the marks of "*brutal ferocity*" in the deed because it is an animal ferocity, an irrationality that he recognizes within himself as within everyone, an irrationality that grounds rationality as the physical body grounds the human mind. Summing up the distinctive marks of the criminal—"an agility astounding, a strength super-human, a ferocity brutal, a butchery without motive, a *grotesquerie* in hor-ror absolutely alien from humanity, and a voice foreign in tone to the ears of men of many nations, and devoid of all distinct or intelligible syllabifica-tion"—Dupin asks the narrator what this combination of features suggests, and the narrator replies, "A madman . . . has done this deed—some raving maniac, escaped from a neighboring *Maison de Santé.*" The response is significant because earlier, in describing his and Dupin's shared style of living as a reflection of "the rather fantastic gloom" of their "common temper," the narrator says, "Had the routine of our life . . . been known to the world, we should have been regarded as madmen—although, perhaps, as madmen of a harmless nature" (ibid., 558). That the ape's rampage and Dupin's fantastic temperament both suggest madness to the narrator underlines the instinctual, not to say irrational, element shared by the culprit and the detective. Indeed, one might interpret the intellectual power that both Poe and Dupin consider to be the culmination of rational analysis—the power of intuition—as being in large part the rational mind's reliance on, its translation into consciousness of, the animal instincts of the body in which it is lodged, the kind of physical intuition whose lack prevents the Prefect, with his all-head-and-no-body reasoning, from recognizing and interpreting the signs of "*brutal* ferocity" in the crime.

What all this ultimately suggests, then, is that in deciding to write a group of stories aimed at analyzing the analytical power, at discovering why, as he says at the start of the first Dupin story, the analytical power should itself be so little susceptible to analysis, Poe attempted to embody in the very structure of the genre the high level of self-consciousness inherent in such a project. As Poe practices it, the detective story is a literary form closely aware of its own formal elements, its antecedents, its associations—indeed, so much so that it subtly thematizes these as part of the textual mystery that the reader must unravel in the tale. And that is why Poe draws our attention in the very first Dupin story to the word *clue* and its origin in the myth of Theseus and the Minotaur, for what he gives us is a clue not just to the source of a notion that is synonymous with the genre itself but also the source of the plot with which he chose to originate this genre. In following the thread of allusion wound around the word *clue,* he allows us to see that Dupin's adventure, with its locked-room puzzle and humanlike killer-ape, rewrites Theseus's encounter with the labyrinth and its half-human, man-killing Minotaur—that is to say, precisely the scenario that Borges makes explicit in his own rewriting of Poe.

Detective Fiction, Psychoanalysis, and the Analytic Sublime

SHAWN ROSENHEIM

"We have gone so far as to combine the ideas of an agility astounding, a strength su-
perhuman, a ferocity brutal, a butchery without motive, a grotesquerie *in horror ab-*
solutely alien from humanity, and a voice foreign in tone to the ears of men of many
nations, and devoid of all distinct or intelligible syllabification. . . . What impression
have I made upon your fancy?" I felt a creeping of the flesh as Dupin asked me the
question. "A madman," I said, "has done this deed—some raving maniac escaped
from a neighboring Maison de Santé.*"*
> —Edgar Allan Poe, "The Murders in the Rue Morgue"

Though "The Murders in the Rue Morgue" may be said to have initiated the
genre of detective fiction, many twentieth-century fans have been put off by
what seems like Poe's capricious violation of an implicit narrative convention. The ape, it is alleged, represents an instance of bad faith, since no
reader could reasonably be expected to include animals in a list of potential
murderers. More generally, we may take Poe's ape story as an index of a
deeper bad faith on the part of the whole genre, in its frequent imbalance
between the detective story's protracted narrative setup and its often un-
satisfying denouement. There is often an embarrassing sense on the part of
readers of detective fiction that its typically Gothic revelations are incommensurate with the moral weight suggested by the genre's narrative form.
In this sense, too, Poe's orangutan is an emblem of readers, who—their
attention solicited by an unworthy narrative dilemma—find that the real
crime has been practiced on their own sensibility. In the words of Geoffrey
Hartman:

The trouble with the detective novel is not that it is moral but that it is moralistic;
not that it is popular but that it is stylized; not that it lacks realism but that it picks

up the latest realism and exploits it. A voracious formalism dooms it to seem unreal, however "real" the world it describes. . . . The form trusts too much in reason;
its very success opens to us the glimpse of a mechanized world, whether controlled
by God or Dr. No or the Angel of the Odd. (Hartman 1975, 225)

Though well taken, Hartman's caution is hardly original: already in the first
detective story, Poe recognized the problem. As Poe indicated in a letter to
Phillip Cooke, he was aware that the promise of detective fiction to unriddle
the world was ultimately tautological: "Where is the ingenuity of unravelling a web which you yourself have woven for the express purpose of unravelling? These tales of ratiocination owe most of their popularity to being
something in a new key. I do not mean to say that they are not ingenious—
but people think they are more ingenious than they are—on account of the
method and *air* of method" (Poe 1966, 2:328).

Poe's comment interests me because, while he demystifies the detective
story, insisting that the narrator's solution to the crime is, in fact, no "solution" at all, but a *coup de théâtre* staged by the author from behind the
scenes, he also recognizes the willingness of readers to be deceived by the
story's "method and *air* of method." Such an air of method might also be
described as the genre's penchant for analysis, a term that recurs throughout
the Dupin stories.[1] "Rue Morgue" begins with a discussion of "analysis," and
in a letter describing "Marie Rogêt," Poe emphasizes the same term: "under
the pretense of showing how Dupin . . . unravelled the mystery of Marie's
assassination, I, in fact, enter into a very rigorous analysis of the real tragedy
in New York" (Poe 1969–78, 3:718). Though it may at first seem curious that
the literary genre most vocally devoted to the powers of the ratiocinative
mind should vex those powers on the mindless acts of Poe's orangutan, on
consideration, Poe's use of the ape in "Rue Morgue" emerges as something
more than a simple narrative miscalculation or mere sideshow. In brief, the
ape permits Poe to elaborate a cryptographic argument about language and
human identity, in which the extreme contrast between the ape's physicality
and Dupin's inhuman reason tells us something about the constitutive
oppositions of the genre. And since detective fiction in general, and Poe's
more particularly, has enjoyed a long and privileged relation to psychoanalytic reading, Poe's experiments with the monkey may tell us something
about how we, as readers, are ourselves made to ape his ape.

"Analysis" in several senses has been a key to the theoretical ubiquity
of "The Purloined Letter." But while that story is unquestionably a great
achievement, Poe purchases the analytic force of his narrative only by purging the text of any attempt at realist representation (Limon 1990, 103).

Hence, Barbara Johnson's too-familiar claim that Minister D——'s letter is "not hidden in a geometrical space, where the police are looking for it . . . but is instead located 'in' a *symbolic* structure" is correct only because of Poe's refusal to engage the difficult project of representing the texture of social experience (Johnson 1980). In sharp contrast to the outdoor settings of "Marie Rogêt," or even to the street scenes in "Rue Morgue," "The Purloined Letter" retreats from the boulevards, parks, and waterways of the teeming city, with their social and sexual ambiguities, into the enclosed and private spaces of Minister D——'s chambers. Hence, the remarkable success of "The Purloined Letter" as a locus for literary and psychoanalytic theory— indeed, as one of *the* venues by which French theory has translated itself into America—begins to seem the consequence of playing cards with a stacked deck. The tale's theoretical richness derives from the fact that Lacan, Derrida, Johnson, and the others who have written in their wake have chosen a text that is already supremely two-dimensional, already overtly concerned with allegorizing the operations of the signifier.

In fact, the semiotic purity of "The Purloined Letter" is an exception in Poe's detective fiction, which focuses more generally on the tension between representations of three-dimensional bodies and language, which is either two-dimensional in its printed form or, as speech, proves uncannily disembodied and invisible. The dominant form of the genre is far closer to "Rue Morgue" or, in its true-crime mode, to "The Mystery of Marie Rogêt," in which Poe is less concerned with the "itinerary of the signifier" narrowly conceived than he is with the problems posed by the difficult intersection between the human capacity for language and the brute fact of incarnation. Poe's obsession with corpses, especially prominent in the late fiction, reveals his continuing anxiety over the body's refusal to suffer complete encipherment into language. Significantly enough, Poe's deaths are almost invariably associated with injuries to the organs of speech. The horror of Valdemar's mesmeric dissolution in "The Facts in the Case of M. Valdemar" stems from the grotesque contrast between his putrefying body and his "wonderfully, thrillingly distinct—syllabification" (Poe 1984b, 839–40), as "ejaculations of 'dead! dead!'" burst "from the tongue and not the lips of the sufferer" (ibid., 842). In "Rue Morgue" the strangled Camille L'Espanaye's tongue is "bitten partially through" (ibid., 410). Marie Rogêt bears "bruises and impressions of fingers" about her throat, and "a piece of lace was found tied so tightly around the neck as to be hidden from sight; it was completely buried in the flesh, and was fastened by a knot which lay just under the left ear" (ibid., 513). And in "Thou Art the Man," often considered Poe's fourth

detective story, the narrator ("Mr. P.") exposes and destroys the murderer
Charley Goodfellow by confronting him with the speaking corpse of his
victim, who bursts out of a wine cask with impressive consequences:

There sprang up into a sitting position, directly facing the host, the bruised,
bloody and nearly putrid corpse of the murdered Mr. Shuttleworthy himself. It
gazed for a few moments . . . with its decaying and lack-lustre eyes . . . uttered
slowly, but clearly and impressively the words, "Thou art the man!" and then, falling over the side of the chest as if thoroughly satisfied, stretched out its limbs
quiveringly. (Ibid., 740)[2]

Such obsessive instances of mutilated language suggest that for Poe the
disjunction between linguistic and physical identity was always traumatic.
As in so much detective fiction, the violence attendant on social relations in
"Rue Morgue" results from the represented encounter between two-dimensional signs and three-dimensional bodies, and might properly be described
as cryptonymic. I borrow the term from Nicholas Abraham and Maria
Torok, who in their reinterpretation of Freud's case study hypothesize that
the Wolf Man's physical symptoms stem from a punning, multilingual "verbarium" of key (or code) words, which indirectly name the principal trau-
mas of his life. The words are "encrypted" in the self to avoid analysis *by* the
self, for whom they pose insoluble psychic double binds. In consequence, it
becomes an essential but impossible task to say whether the words name a
real event or whether in themselves they produce the symptoms they are
meant to explain.[3] Derrida describes the Wolf Man in language equally well
suited to the involutions of psychic space manifested in, say, Roderick
Usher: he had "edified a crypt within him: an artifact, an artificial unconscious in the Self, an interior enclave, partitions, hidden passages, zigzags,
occult and difficult traffic" (Abraham and Torok 1986, xliv); the only passage through this Gothic architecture of the mind is through the magic
words of the verbarium, coded translingually across English, Russian, and
German, to keep the crypt, that "monument of a catastrophe," imperme-
able (ibid., xlv). As the comparison to Usher suggests, cryptonymy involves
an unambiguously Gothic understanding of language. Not only Derrida's
diction but the case study's corresponding themes of paralysis, violation,
and unspeakability are common property of the Gothic novel and of nineteenth-century hysteria.

As I have noted elsewhere (Rosenheim 1989), to an extraordinary degree
cryptography provides secret organizing principles for Poe's trilogy of detective stories. The cryptograph reflects on the level of the sign what Dupin em-

bodies on the level of character, and what the form of detective fiction im-plies on the level of narrative: the fantasy of an absolutely legible world. As it is encountered in Poe's essays on secret writing, cryptography is the utopian inverse of cryptonymy, since in it reader and writer are fully present to one another within their two-dimensional cipher. Conceptually, analysis is closely associated with cryptography. Both depend on the "separating or breaking up of any whole into its parts so as to find out their nature, propor-tion, function, relationship, etc.,"[4] and both emphasize the abstract, sym-bolic force of mind over matter, which provides a form of mental leverage over the world. But already in the moment of creating the genre of detective fiction, Poe suggests that the only "analysis" it can offer may itself be a fic-tion. While cryptography seems to propose a detour around the Gothic aspects of cryptonymy—a way of avoiding its disturbing physicality—cryp-tography takes on disturbing cryptonymic features whenever Poe attempts to represent actual bodies. The problem is that cryptography provides an *alternative body* in conflict with one's corporeal investment; since even in cryptography language is never truly free of the material shell of the signi-fier, this linguistic self finds itself in tension with one's embodied identity.

Despite the story's promise of legibility, "Rue Morgue" intimates that the triumph of the detective's analytics cannot be clearly distinguished from the effects of the analytics on the reader's body. To the degree that the reader invests his belief in this formal drive toward legibility, he becomes Poe's dupe, for should the reader attempt to imitate Dupin, he quickly finds that his analysis devolves into mere repetition.[5] And yet, to that same degree, these stories threaten to become meaningful: if the uncanny anticipation of the story's own interpretation is at all significant, it is so because the text discloses in the reader's body the nature of the interpretive desires that initiate one's reading. Like the purloined letter, the lesson of "Rue Morgue" is hidden in plain sight, announced in the story's first lines: "The mental features discoursed of as the analytical are, in themselves, but little suscepti-ble of analysis. We appreciate them only in their effects" (Poe 1984b, 397). While our readings certainly produce "effects," the desire to discover the right relation of analysis to literature is ultimately doomed by the impos-sibility of establishing a metalanguage uncontaminated by the materiality of signification. In this respect, the narrator's attempt in "Rue Morgue" to keep his analytic discourse free from the corporeal opacity of his subject resembles Freud's procedure in his case studies. If detective fiction is noto-riously susceptible to psychoanalytic interpretation, this is only because psychoanalysis, too, has often seemed to presume the separation of its analytical procedures from the materiality of its objects—a separation be-tween language and the body that "Rue Morgue" both constructs and, finally, destroys.

II

Following Richard Wilbur, critics have long recognized speech in "Rue Morgue" as a symbolic expression of identification, noting that Dupin's use of a high and a low register links him with the high and low voices of the sailor and the ape (Wilbur 1967). But Poe is finally less interested in pitch than in syllabification, which runs on a continuum from the orangutan's grunts to Dupin's "rich tenor," with its "deliberateness and entire distinct-ness" of enunciation (Poe 1984b, 410–12). Hence Poe's own deliberation in staging the ape's crime within earshot of such a polyglot group of auditors, each of whom hears in the orangutan's voice someone speaking an unfamil-iar language. Henri Duval: "The shrill voice, this witness thinks, was that of an Italian.... Was not acquainted with the Italian language." William Bird: the voice "appeared to be that of a German.... Does not understand Ger-man." Alfonzo Garcia: "The shrill voice was that of an Englishman—is sure of this. Does not understand the English language, but judges by intona-tion" (Poe 1984b, 409–10). Similarly, Isidore Muset, "—— Odenheimer," and Alberto Montani, respectively attribute the voice to Spanish, French, and Russian speakers. Poe even has Dupin supplement his references to the "five great divisions of Europe" with mention of "Asiatics" and "Africans," in what amounts to a Cook's Tour of the varieties of human speech:

> Now, how strangely unusual must that voice have really been, about which such testimony as this *could* have been elicited!—in whose *tones*, even, denizens of the five great divisions of Europe could recognize nothing familiar! You will say that it might have been the voice of an Asiatic—of an African.... Without denying the inference, I will now merely call your attention to [the fact that] ... no words—no sounds resembling words—were by any witness mentioned as distinguishable. (Ibid., 416)

What is at stake in this inventory? As with the case studies of deaf-mutes and feral children that appeared toward the end of the eighteenth century, the orangutan offered Enlightenment thinkers a liminal figure of the hu-man at a time when language was crucially involved in the definition of humanity. By the 1840s, however, the ape had been reduced to a comic or grotesque image. But given Poe's insistence on the syllabic nature of speech, it is also important to recognize the orangutan's affiliation with a tradition of philosophical inquiry.[6] The most comprehensive discussion of the orangutan's relation to language is given in *The Origin and Progress of Language*, by James Burnet, Lord Monboddo, who devotes sixty pages to this question in order to understand "the origin of an art so admirable and so useful as language," a subject "necessarily connected with an inquiry into the original nature of man, and that primitive state in which he was, before language was invented" (Burnet 1974, 1:267). Monboddo hypothesizes that the orangutan is actually a species of humankind, being "a barbarous nation, which has not yet learned the use of speech" (ibid., 270). The taxonomic name of the orangutan, *Homo sylvestris*, is merely a translation of the Malay "Ourang-Outang," which, according to the naturalist Buffon, "signifies, in their language, *a wild man*" (ibid., 272). According to Monboddo, orangutans use tools, grow melancholy when separated from their tribes, and are capable of conjugal attachment and even shame. Monboddo cites an explorer who saw a female orangutan that "shewed signs of modesty . . . wept and groaned, and performed other human actions: So that nothing human seemed to be wanting in her, except speech" (ibid., 272–73).

By enlisting orangutans in the same species as humans, Monboddo intends to demonstrate that what separates the two is less biology than culture, epitomized by the possession of language. For Buffon, this lack of speech discredits the orangutan's evolutionary pretensions. Monboddo ridicules Buffon, however, for making "the faculty of speech" part of the essence of humanity, and for suggesting that "the state of pure nature, in which man had not the use of speech, is a state altogether ideal and imaginary" (ibid., 293). Buffon thus anticipates the current association of language and human origins. For Poe as for Buffon, the "state of pure nature" *is* "altogether ideal" and precisely "imaginary," since, ontogenetically if not phylogenetically, human consciousness is a function of the subject's mirroring in language.

This tradition provides a context for understanding the dramatic process by which the narrator discovers the identity of the killer. From the start, Poe has planted clues: the crime is "brutal," "inhuman," "at odds with the ordinary notions of human conduct." Now Dupin remarks on the crime's strange combination of features:

"We have gone so far as to combine the ideas of an agility astounding, a strength superhuman, a ferocity brutal, a butchery without motive, a *grotesquerie* in horror absolutely alien from humanity, and a voice foreign in tone to the ears of

men of many nations, and devoid of all distinct or intelligible syllabification. . . .
What impression have I made upon your fancy?"

I felt a creeping of the flesh as Dupin asked me the question. "A madman," I
said, "has done this deed—some raving maniac escaped from a neighboring
Maison de Santé." (Poe 1984b, 423)

The narrator's suggestion is close, but "the voices of madmen, even in their
wildest paroxysms . . . have always the coherence of syllabification" (ibid.,
558). Identification of the criminal depends, again, on Dupin's understanding of language; in fact, the testimony of the crime's auditors constitutes an
aural cryptogram. The origin of this moment goes back to "A Few Words on
Secret Writing," in which Poe remarked that of the hundred ciphers he
received, "there was only one which we did not immediately succeed in
solving. This one we *demonstrated* to be an imposition—that is to say, we
fully proved it a jargon of random characters, having no meaning whatsoever." Poe's ability to interpret signs requires him to recognize when a set
of signs violates the "universal" rules of linguistic formation. The claim to
cryptographic mastery depends on the logically prior ability to recognize
when a set of characters is not even language. By having the solution to the
crime in "Rue Morgue" turn on the aural cryptogram, Poe simultaneously
dramatizes both the power of human analysis and his fear of what life
without language might be like.

After its recapture the orangutan is lodged in the *Jardin des Plantes.* Until
his death in 1832, the *Jardin* was Georges Cuvier's center of research; as the
repeated juxtaposition of Cuvier and Dupin indicates, Poe finds in the
zoologist's mode of analysis an analogue to his own technique of detection.[7]
Cuvier was famous for his ability to reconstruct an animal's anatomy from
fragmentary paleontological remains, through systematic structural comparison. As a contemporary of Poe's wrote: "Cuvier astonished the world by
the announcement that the law of relation which existed between the various parts of animals applied not only to entire systems, but even to parts of
a system; so that, given an extremity, the whole skeleton might be known . . .
and even the habits of the animal could be indicated" (Review 1851).[8] Like
Cuvier's bones, and in implicit analogy with them, syllables are for Poe
linguistic universals, basic morphological units that form the necessary
substrate to thought. Individual words possess meaning for the linguist
only through their participation in a global system: "the word is no longer
attached to a representation except insofar as it is previously a part of the
grammatical organization by means of which the language defines and
guarantees its own coherence" (Foucault 1973, 280–81).

Cuvier seems to provide a methodological justification for Poe's cryptographic reading of the world. But if this is so, what should we make of Cuvier's key role in revealing the true nature of the murderer? Having teased the reader's narrative appetite with oblique clues concerning the killer's nature, Dupin introduces the text of Cuvier with a theatrical flourish, sure that his revelation will produce its intended effect: "It was a minute anatomical and generally descriptive account of the large fulvous Orang-Outang of the East Indian Islands. The gigantic stature, the prodigious strength and activity, the wild ferocity, and the imitative propensities of these mammalia are sufficiently well known to all. I understood the full horrors of the murder at once" (Poe 1984b, 424). This is a curious passage, not least because in Poe's version, the description of the orangutan virtually reverses Cuvier's actual claims. Not content to note that the orangutan is "a mild and gentle animal, easily rendered tame and affectionate," Cuvier disparages "the exaggerated descriptions of some authors respecting this resemblance" to humans (Cuvier 1832, 54–55); he at once deflates both the ape's anthropic pretensions and its wildness. That Poe knew this text seems almost certain: M'Murtrie, who translated Cuvier's book, seven years later published with Poe and Thomas Wyatt *The Conchologist's First Book*, with "Animals according to Cuvier." Yet evidently Poe's intellectual allegiance to Cuvier was subservient to his need to magnify the melodramatic and Gothic aspects of the murders. In the final analysis, it is not the crime but the solution that produces the reader's uncanny shiver, not the violence but the minute and clinical attention that Dupin requires of the narrator. To understand why the killer's simian origins produce "the full horrors" of which the narrator speaks, we need first to examine the effects of the revelation that Poe's narrative produces.

III

Throughout the Dupin stories, Poe offers models for the nature of analysis, including games of odd and even, theories of mental identification, and the elaborate comparison of the respective merits of chess and whist. Yet as we discover in "Rue Morgue," analysis itself must remain disappointingly invisible to the reader, except through its intensely pleasing effects:

We know of them, among other things, that they are always to their possessor, when inordinately possessed, a source of the liveliest enjoyment. As the strong man exults in his physical ability, delighting in such exercises as call his muscles into action, so glories the analyst in that moral activity which *disentangles*. He derives pleasure from even the most trivial occupations bringing his talent into play. He is fond of enigmas, of conundrums, of hieroglyphics. (Poe 1984b, 397)

In its basic narrative structure, "Rue Morgue" is itself an enigma whose effects, according to its own logic, should clarify the nature of analysis. But the opening discussion reverses the ordinary process of interpretation: the crime and its solution "will appear to the reader somewhat in the light of a commentary upon the [analytic] propositions just advanced" (ibid., 400), rather than the other way around. Nor is it clear exactly why we should experience "the liveliest enjoyment" from the ensuing tale of violence. Might we understand the tale as an allegory of the superiority of brain to brawn, in which Dupin handily defeats both the sailor's evasions and the ape's brute difference? Certainly; but the pleasure of such a reading is not itself analytical, and hence brings us no closer to understanding the properties that the narrative so ostentatiously foregrounds. Since the narrator has compared analytic pleasure to that enjoyed by the strong man, we ought perhaps to consider the two "strong men" of the tale as guides. The first of these is the orangutan (*Homo sylvestris*), possessed of "superhuman" strength; the second is its owner, "a tall, stout, and muscular-looking person" who comes equipped, as in a fairy tale, with "a huge oaken cudgel" (ibid., 426). But these figures seem to exercise their powers only in violence: the elder L'Espanaye's head is "nearly severed" "with one determined sweep" of the ape's "muscular arm" (ibid., 430), and though the sailor seems amicable by comparison, even he spends his energy whipping the ape into submission, and his muscles tense at the thought of killing Dupin ("The sailor's face flushed. . . . He started to his feet and grasped his cudgel" [ibid., 427]). In practice, while the pleasures of the analyst seem only figurally related to those of his muscular counterpart ("As the strong man exults . . . so glories the analyst"), the narrative that follows demonstrates that the relation between the two is causal: the analyst's skills are called for because of the strong man's exertion, as Dupin pits his thought against the unwitting power of the ape and the sailor's potential for violence.

According to Peter Brooks, any given story has a central metaphor that, however dissolved into the thread of the narrative, articulates the story's primary relationships. And since all narrative can be mapped rhetorically as a relation between the poles of metaphor and metonymy, we can describe the narrative's duration as a metonymic "acting out of the implications of metaphor," which at once reveals the meaning of the impacted initial metaphor and transforms it through its narrative embodiment (Brooks 1985, 13).

Citing the example of Conan Doyle's "Musgrave Ritual," Brooks shows that the obscure and apparently meaningless ritual practiced by the Musgraves is actually a metaphor that condenses and shapes the action of the story. Regardless of whether Brooks is right to contend that the relation between initial metaphor and narrative metonymy holds for all stories, it is undeniably true of detective fiction in general, and of its founding text as well. The first rhetorical figure encountered in "Rue Morgue"—the analogy between the pleasures of analysis and those of strength—provides the story's structuring metaphor; in fact, the tale has everything to do with the proper way of understanding the relationship between the physical and the mental, and the pleasures associated with each.

Take as an emblem of this disjunction the difficulty that the Mmes. L'Espanaye find in keeping head and body together: Camille L'Espanaye is strangled; her mother's throat is "so entirely cut that upon an attempt to raise her, the head fell off" (Poe 1984b, 411, 406). "Rue Morgue" repeatedly stages the violent separation of heads and bodies, literal and figurative, and while Dupin and the orangutan are the most visibly polarized emblems of this split, the form of the tale repeats this pattern, joining its analytic head to the fictive body through the most insecure of narrative ligatures: "The narrative to follow will appear to the reader somewhat in the light of a commentary upon the propositions just advanced" (ibid., 400). However one wishes to allegorize this relation of heads to bodies—as an opposition between spirit and matter, analysis and effects, or ego and id—it is the distinguishing structural feature of the text at every level. But though "Rue Morgue" formally repeats the opposition between body and head in the relationship of narrative and commentary, we can identify Brooks's initial metaphor only in retrospect, since Poe's text conceals its metaphors as metonymies until the narrative's climactic revelation, by which time we as readers have been thoroughly implicated in a scene at which we imagined ourselves only spectators.

Generically, this implication has already been built into the text through its combination of the Gothic with what I call the analytic sublime. Besides its extravagant setting in a "time-eaten and grotesque mansion, long deserted through superstitions into which we did not inquire, and tottering to its fall" (ibid., 400–401), "Rue Morgue" reveals its generic debt in the sensational violence of the killings, the segmentation of space into barely permeable vesicles, and the uncanniness of the crime's resolution. Although Eve Sedgwick argues compellingly that as a genre the Gothic is preeminently concerned with male homosocial desire, Poe's detective stories find their activating tension less in the closeting of sexual difference than in the closeting of consciousness within the body. Despite its overt disavowal of the Gothic ("let it not be supposed," the narrator reminds us, "that I am detailing any mystery, or penning any romance" [ibid., 402]), Poe employs an aura of analytical reason only to intensify the reader's experience of violence and disorder.

In the Gothic's implicit spatial model, Sedgwick suggests, an "individual fictional 'self'" is often "massively blocked off from something to which it ought normally to have access": air, personal history, a loved one. Regardless of the specific lack, it is the unspeakability of this occlusion that is generically distinctive: "The important privation is the privation exactly of language, as though language were a sort of safety valve between the inside and the outside which being closed off, all knowledge, even when held in common, becomes solitary, furtive, and explosive" (Sedgwick 1986, 17).[9] Thus although the detective story, with its long retrospective reconstructions, seems par excellence the genre in which language is adequate to its task of description, in the end, the apparent rationality of the detective is a device used to create Sedgwick's Gothic division. Far from offering a safety valve between inner and outer, language itself separates the analyst from the object, thereby creating the pressure differential between self and world that language is pressed to describe. The impalpable tissue separating inside and outside is consciousness itself, which can never be identical either with itself or with the body. The more intensely Poe thematizes disembodied reason (the analytic sublime), the more powerfully Gothic will be the moment in which our identification with the body of the ape is revealed.

This use of reason against itself appears with particular clarity in the episode in which Dupin discovers the exit by which the killer escaped from the quarters of the Mmes L'Espanaye. In this first instance of the locked-room mystery, the doors to the L'Espanaye home are locked; there are no secret passages or "preternatural events"; and the condition of the bodies rules out suicide. The two windows are shut, each fastened by "a very stout nail" pushed into a gimlet hole drilled through frame and casement. Yet on visiting the house, Dupin displays absolute confidence in his logical powers: "The impossibility of egress, by means already stated, being thus absolute, we are reduced to the windows. It is only left for us to prove that these apparent 'impossibilities' are, in reality, not such." Reasoning that "the murderers *did* escape from one of these windows," Dupin decides that the sashes *must*, then, have the power of fastening themselves. There was no escape from this conclusion. I had traced the secret to its ultimate result—and that result was *the nail*. It had, I say, in every respect, the appearance of its fellow in the other window, but this fact was an absolute nullity (conclusive as it might seem to be) when compared with the consideration that here, at this point, terminated the clew. "There *must* be something wrong," I said, "about the nail." I touched it; and the head, with about a quarter of the shank, came off in my fingers. The rest of the shank was in the gimlet-hole, where it had been broken off. (Poe 1984b, 419)

This is what Freud called the "omnipotence-of-consciousness" with a vengeance: the evidence of the senses is "an absolute nullity" against the locked room of Dupin's logic ("There was no escape from this conclusion"). As predicted, and in apparent confirmation of his hypothesis, the nail-head pops off at Dupin's touch, as if his analysis was a type of narrative thaumaturgy, able to bring about changes in the world through mere enunciation ("'There *must* be something wrong,' I said, 'about the nail'"). Such confusion of causes and effects is a version of the tale's split between analysis and action, an indication that Poe's analytical sublime contains the seeds of its own undoing. The abstract introduction to a tale of horror (also familiar from "The Imp of the Perverse") intensifies the shock of the narrative by increasing the contrast between the narrative's ratiocinative calm and the brutality to follow. And since excessive contrast is itself a Gothic convention, "Rue Morgue" stages the relation between the story's introduction and its main body as another instance of the Gothic. Indeed, the nail itself anticipates my conclusion: its status as a token of the power of reason is immediately undermined by Dupin's recognition that the nail itself is fractured. Like everything else in "Rue Morgue," the nail—an apparent integer —splits into head and body.

IV

This constant recurrence of heads and bodies is structurally parallel to the separation in detective fiction of the metonymic and metaphoric poles of language. Working with clues associated with the narrative's originating crime, the detective's analytical method is primarily a form of metonymy, which is, in turn, associated with the frame narrative of the detective's analysis, and with its origins in cryptography. Conversely, the core narrative of most detective stories obsessively concerns itself with bodies, most commonly with their violation and murder. Metonymy, Lacan suggests, is evidence of the displacement of desire for the mother onto the signifying chain itself. As the law of the signifier, the law of the father separates the infant from the mother at the moment when Oedipal injunctions manifest themselves in, and as, the child's newly acquired language. The child attempts to recapture its original plenitude through the use of language, but this displaced search turns into an identification of suspended desire with the process of signification itself:

And the enigmas that desire seems to pose for a "natural philosophy"—its frenzy mocking the abyss of the infinite, the secret collusion with which it envelops the pleasure of knowing and of dominating with a jouissance, these amount to no other derangement of instinct than that of being caught in the rails—eternally stretching forth towards the *desire for something else*—of metonymy. (Lacan 1977, 166–67)

In place of the child's imaginary, there are only the "rails" of metonymic linkage, which, far from leading back to the mother, constitute the bars separating one from her being. But this "desire for something else" is not without compensatory pleasures, chief among which is the "jouissance" of employing language to structure the observable world, investing it with the sense of an almost tangible approach to the object of desire. The rails teeter constantly along the edge of remembrance, "at the very suspension-point of the signifying chain" (ibid.).

In its concern with evidence, the detective's search is a variation on the metonymic suspension displayed by the narrator of the Gothic romances, who tends "to muse, for long unwearied hours, with [his] attention riveted to some frivolous device on the margin or in the typography of a book" (Poe 1984b, 227). This obsessive attention is a defense mechanism designed to turn the mind away from something that must seem to be repressed, but which, in fact, hovers teasingly close to consciousness:

There is no point, among the many incomprehensible anomalies of the science of mind, more thrillingly exciting than the fact . . . that in our endeavors to recall to memory something long forgotten, we often find ourselves *upon the very verge* of remembrance, without being able, in the end, to remember. And thus how frequently, in my intense scrutiny of Ligeia's eyes, have I felt approaching the full knowledge of their expression—felt it approaching—yet not quite be mine—and so at length entirely depart! (Ibid., 264–65)

Compare this to the narrator's reaction to Dupin's description of the strength, ferocity, and "harsh and unequal voice" possessed by the orangutan: "At these words a vague and half-formed conception of the meaning

of Dupin flitted over my mind. I seemed to be upon the verge of comprehension, without power to comprehend—as men, at times, find themselves upon the brink of remembrance without being able, in the end, to
remember" (ibid., 421). In both cases, the quality of this near-memory, and
the habits of both excessively attentive narrators, correspond to Lacan's
metonymic subject "perversely" fixated "at the very suspension-point of the
signifying chain, where the memory-screen is immobilized and the fascinating image of the fetish is petrified" (Lacan 1977, 167).

Lacan's rhetorical analysis permits us to see how completely the metonymic frame narrative of the tale disembodies both analyst and reader, even as
the Gothic narrative core of the detective story foregrounds metaphors of
the body.[10] This metaphoric pull toward embodiment is crystallized in the
basic scenario of "Rue Morgue," which, as Marie Bonaparte noted long ago,
is a particularly nasty Oedipal triangle. For Bonaparte, the orangutan represents the infant, whose obsession with the question of the mother's sexual
difference is only settled through the symbolic castration involved in Mme
L'Espanaye's decapitation. Bonaparte's reading depends on a style of anatomical literalization now out of fashion, discredited in an era in which
psychoanalytic critics rightfully prefer textual and rhetorical criticism to
readings that, as Brooks notes, mistakenly choose as their objects of analysis
"the author, the reader, or the fictive persons of the text" (Brooks 1987, 2).
The problem is that "Rue Morgue" continually *solicits* what can only be
described as bad Freudian readings. Bonaparte's biographical interpretation of Poe's fiction is, in the main, enjoyably unconvincing, but her monomaniacal inventory of sexual symbols (of, for instance, the L'Espanayes'
chamber as a gigantic projection of the interior female anatomy) is difficult
to dismiss. From the rending of the double doors of the L'Espanaye home
("a double or folding gate . . . bolted neither at bottom nor top" forced
"open, at length, with a bayonet"), to the ape's futile ransacking of Mme
L'Espanaye's private drawers ("the drawers of a *bureau* . . . were open, and
had been, apparently, rifled, although many articles still remained in them"
[Poe 1984b, 421]), to the identification of the broken and the whole nail, the
story overcodes its anatomical symbols. Discovered in its crimes, the orangutan's "wild glances" fall on "the head of the bed, over which the face of its
master, rigid with horror, was just discernible." The ape stuffs Camille
"head-down" in the chimney; the L'Espanayes live in a room "at the head of
the passage"; the nail in the window behind the bed is fixed "nearly to the
head"; Dupin looks over "the head-board minutely"; the other nail too is
"driven in nearly up to the head." The ape flees from its master's bed to the

L'Espanayes', where it swings itself through the window "directly upon the headboard of the bed." "Head" is used twenty times, "bed," "bedstead," or "bedroom" seventeen times; as well as rhyming aurally, "head" and "bed" continually chime through their contiguity in the text, inviting the reader to link them through metaphor. Even the fractured window-nail can represent the mother's phallus: "Il y a le mystère du clou mutilé d'une des fenêtres, sans doute symbole, sur le mode 'mobilier,' de la castration de la mère." Dupin's inductions about the broken nail constitute a *fort-da* game in which he resolves the question of the maternal phallus by both denying its presence ("'There *must* be something wrong,' I said, 'about the nail.' I touched it; and the head . . . came off in my fingers") and affirming it ("I now carefully replaced this head portion and . . . the fissure was invisible"). Such an explanation helps clarify why the analysis of the nail musters such weird intensity: "There *must* . . . be something wrong with the nail" (Bonaparte 1949, 439).

My claim is not that such anatomical allegorizing substantiates psychoanalytic criticism, but that Freudian readers have long been attracted to detective fiction just because the genre's structure and themes so often echo central psychoanalytic scenarios. What looks like Poe's eerie anticipation of psychoanalytic motifs may say as much about generic as about psychic structure. Certainly, the literary interest of Freud's case studies depends in no small part on an essentially cryptographic sense of power over the body. Despite Freud's frequent attempts to distance himself from writers of fiction, his early conception of psychoanalysis as "the task of making conscious the most hidden recesses of the mind" (Freud 1963a, 96), of rendering the body transparent to language, is driven by the same themes of cryptographic interiority at play in Poe's detective fiction. And Dupin's boast that "most men, in respect to himself, wore windows in their bosoms" (Poe 1984b, 401) is actually a more modest version of Freud's famous declaration in his study of Dora: "He that has eyes to see and ears to hear may convince himself that no mortal can keep a secret. If his lips are silent, he chatters with his finger-tips; betrayal oozes out of him at every pore" (Freud 1963a, 96).

Although critics have remarked on the embarrassing frequency with which detective stories draw on stock psychoanalytic imagery, no one has yet called attention to how thoroughly "Rue Morgue" seems to gloss the analytic process itself. Freud describes the "essence of the psychoanalytic situation" as follows:

The analyst enters into an alliance with the ego of the patient to subdue certain uncontrolled parts of his id, i.e., to include them in a synthesis of the ego. . . . [If] the
ego learns to adopt a defensive attitude towards its own id and to treat the instinctual demands of the latter like external dangers, this is at any rate partly because it understands that the satisfaction of instinct would lead to conflicts with
the external world. (Under the influence of its upbringing, the child's ego ac-
customs itself to shift the scene of the battle from outside to inside and to master
the *inner* danger before it becomes *external.*) (Freud 1963b, 253)

Freud's clinical observations would serve almost equally well to describe the
sailor's visit to Dupin, with Dupin standing in for the analyst, the sailor for
the analysand, and the orangutan as a figure for the remembered "primal
scene." In *Dora,* Freud notes that "the patients' inability to give an ordered
history of their life insofar as it coincides with the story of their illness is not
merely characteristic of the neurosis," but is, in fact, a defining feature of
mental illness; and Freud's essential test for recovery simply *is* the patient's
newfound ability to narrate his or her life, to "remove all possible symptoms and to replace them by conscious thoughts" (Freud 1963a, 31, 32). In
this case, the sailor must recount under duress the story of the crime, which
is formally parallel to the dreams that provide the analytic material for
Freud's case studies. His wish to hide his knowledge makes sense in terms of
the plot, but it is less easy to explain away Dupin's insistence, at once
solicitous and stern, that the sailor narrate what he knows. Dupin, one
might say, enters into an alliance with the sailor in order that he might
"subdue certain uncontrolled parts of his id," unmistakably represented by
the ape. As a corollary, Dupin repeatedly insists that the sailor acknowledge
the beast as his own: "Of course you are prepared to identify the property?"
(Poe 1984b, 427), even as he declares that the sailor is both innocent and
complicit: "You have nothing to conceal. You have no reason for concealment. On the other hand, you are bound by every principle of honor to
confess all" (ibid., 428). Pressed to take a reward for ostensibly recovering
the ape, Dupin continues the same theme: "You shall give me all the information in your power about these murders in the Rue Morgue" (ibid., 427).

Forced at gunpoint to answer, the sailor responds first by losing the
ability to articulate ("The sailor's face flushed up, as if he were struggling
with suffocation. . . . He spoke not a word" [Poe 1984b, 427]), and then by
threatening compensatory violence ("He started to his feet and grasped his
cudgel" [ibid.]), as the story of the ape homeopathically reproduces itself in
the sailor's telling. The stress of confession threatens to produce a repetition

of the original crime, but Dupin's mixture of firmness and kindness ("I perfectly well know that you are innocent of the atrocities in the Rue Morgue. It will not do, however, to deny that you are in some measure implicated in them" [ibid., 427]) permits him to redirect his symptomatic repetition into narrative—precisely the result of a successful analytic intervention predicted by Freud. The sailor explains how, having brought the ape from Borneo to Paris in order to sell it for profit, he returned one night to find that the orangutan had escaped into his bedroom,

> into which it had broken from a closet adjoining, where it had been, as was thought, securely confined. Razor in hand, and fully lathered, it was sitting before a looking-glass, attempting the operation of shaving, in which it had no doubt previously watched its master through the key-hole of the closet. Terrified at the sight of so dangerous a weapon in the possession of an animal so ferocious, and so well able to use it, the man, for some moments, was at a loss what to do. He had been accustomed, however, to quiet the creature, even in its fiercest moods, by the use of a whip, and to this he now resorted. Upon sight of it, the Ourang-Outang sprang at once through the door of the chamber, down the stairs, and thence, through a window, unfortunately open, into the street. (Ibid., 428–29)

Having only heard up to this point about the animal's "intractable ferocity," this image of the orangutan is rather touching; even when the ape imitates "the motions of a barber" with the Mmes L'Espanaye, its purposes, we are told, are "probably pacific" (ibid., 430). Poe offers us a Darwinian revision of Freud, a primate scene in which the ape—still "in the closet," forced to peep through a keyhole—sees its master shaving, and tries to imitate him. Shaving codes the body as a part of culture, not nature; and as in David Humphreys's contemporary poem "The Monkey" (printed in Duyckinck and Duyckinck 1875, 1:392), the ape takes up the razor out of a wish to be human.[11] But without language, the developmental scenario implied by the ape's mimicry stalls: whatever its "imitative propensities," as a mute, the ape cannot readily make its intentions known. The ape's frustrated turn from gesture to violence reveals the abject inadequacy of mimesis in comparison with speech. Unable to manipulate abstract symbols, the ape takes out its rage on the flesh; and while the story's focus on injured mouths and throats may be an instance of displacement upward, it is also a direct attack on the organs of speech. The orangutan represents both Bonaparte's murderous infant, poised at the moment of discovering sexual difference, and a liminally human, highly evocative image of the body's resistance to signification. These elements are synthesized in a Lacanian revision of the primal scene as the entry into signification. Poe's use of the orangutan serves as his own myth of human origins, which condenses within itself both individual and evolutionary history, both linguistic and sexual desire.

Thanks to Dupin's narrative therapy, the sailor is afforded the opportunity to break the cycle of repetition through the type of analytic transference that, in Brooks's words, "succeeds in making the past and its scenarios of desire relive through signs with such vivid reality that the reconstructions it proposes achieve the *effect* of the real" (Brooks 1987, 13). Although it is meaningless to speak of curing a fictional character, this protoanalytic scene is one way in which Poe stages the reader's textual cathexis, though such a proleptic parody may suggest that, like "Rue Morgue" itself, the psychoanalyst's function is to manufacture a narrative rather than to reveal one. The sailor's mistake has been to assume that once he had succeeded in lodging the ape at his own residence, the danger that it posed was over. The sailor has yet to learn to "treat the instinctual demands of the [id] like external dangers." Hence, the captive ape escapes from the sailor, forcing him to face the violent consequences of its acting-out. The process of admitting his possession of the ape is a precondition for its taming, which requires that the sailor objectify and confront as an external danger ("no mean enemy") the fact of the bodily unconscious. The recapture of the erstwhile brute (a story Poe does not even bother to recount) represents the sailor's psychic reintegration. As Freud writes: "The struggle between physician and patient, between intellect and the forces of instinct, between recognition and the striving for discharge, is fought out almost entirely on the ground of transference-manifestations. This is the ground on which the victory must be won, the final expression of which is lasting recovery from the neurosis. . . . in the last resort no one can be slain *in absentia* or *in effigie*" (Freud 1963b, 114–15). By implication, literature might be said to stage *in effigie* just such ego-training sessions, teaching the reader "to shift the scene of the battle from outside to inside": from behaviors to an internalized encounter with the text.

Once the sailor confesses, and thereby owns up to his implication in the killings, the story is finished; the narrator has "scarcely anything to add," and hastily concludes by noting that the ape "was subsequently caught by the owner himself, who obtained for it a very large sum at the *Jardin des Plantes*. Le Bon was instantly released, upon our narration of the circumstances (with some comments from Dupin) at the *bureau* of the Prefect of Police" (Poe 1984b, 431). Since the real story of "Rue Morgue" concerns the production of uncanny effects in the reader, Poe has no qualms about violating the principles of narrative construction. Instead, the extreme brevity of the denouement, and the untidiness of the story's conclusion, remind us that Poe's characters are merely puppets, technical apparatuses deployed in the attempt to intensify our affective transference onto his tales. Although the allegorical reading sketched here could be elaborated further, the parallels between Freud's method in the case studies and Poe's narrative are clear. The elaborate sexual symbolism, the fetishization of analysis, the literalization of the "talking cure," and, above all, the story's peculiar staging of metaphor and metonymy are coordinated devices through which Poe enhances the reader's identification.

Thus far, the reader has had little incentive to identify with anyone except Dupin. But though Dupin's cryptographic power is specifically predicated on his linguistic prowess, the resolution of this case is not a matter of language alone. Instead, Dupin now finds himself confronting the tangible world, carefully measuring the "impression" made by the orangutan's fingers on Camille L'Espanaye's neck against the span and pattern of a human hand, only to find that the prints on the strangled woman are not even approximately the same (" 'This,' I said, 'is the mark of no human hand' " [ibid., 423]). Dupin continues his physical investigation: " 'Besides, the hair of a madman is not such as I now hold in my hand. I disentangled this little tuft from the rigidly clutched fingers of Madam L'Espanaye. Tell me what you can make of it.' 'Dupin!' I said, completely unnerved, 'this hair is most unusual—this is no *human* hair' " (ibid.). Recall that in the opening paragraph of the story, the analyst is said to glory "in that moral activity which *disentangles*": just the word Dupin uses to describe the process of physically extracting his tuft of hair from the "rigidly clutched" hand of the corpse. For all the text's insistence on the separation between the pleasures of the strong man and those of the analyst, the solution of the Rue Morgue murders requires that Dupin make forceful, even violent, contact with the traces of the ape.

After producing his assembled physical evidence, Dupin asks the narrator: "What impression have I made upon your fancy?" repeating as a metaphor the word used to refer to the uncanny and inhuman marks left on the dead woman's neck. Prior to the moment in which Dupin histrionically reveals the orangutan as the culprit, the reader's body has been anesthetized by Dupin's disembodied analytics (an anesthetization also evident in Dupin, who in moments of excitement becomes "frigid and abstract," his eyes "vacant in expression" [ibid., 401, 415]). In the "creeping of the flesh" that follows (ibid., 423), the narrator's body identifies with the ape through Dupin's recreation of the crime, revealing that he, too, through his direct somatic response, is implicated in the narrative to which he listens. "A symptom," writes Lacan, is "a metaphor in which flesh or function is taken as a signifying element" (Lacan 1977, 166); and in the moment when the reader's skin shivers in sympathy with the narrator, we witness the overthrow of the metonymic order. In the shift to the metaphoric, in the symptomatic reproduction within the reader's body of a sensational response, the reader reveals his collaboration with the ape. Through the creation of this response, Poe circumvents Freud's complaint that in analysis "the patient hears what we say but it rouses no response in his mind" (Freud 1963b, 251). To rouse the mind, a text must also arouse the body: only through the symptomatic commitment of the reader's flesh can the text realize its transferential effects.

Appropriately, it is the knowledge of his own embodiment that permits Dupin to solve the mystery of the L'Espanayes' deaths. This is the implication of Dupin's final comments on the Prefect, in which he takes pains to emphasize the futility of the latter's "bodiless" wisdom: "In his wisdom is no *stamen*. It is all head and no body, like the pictures of the Goddess Laverna—or, at best, all head and shoulders, like a codfish. But he is a good creature after all. I like him especially for one master stroke of cant, by which he has attained his reputation for ingenuity. I mean the way he has '*de nier ce qui est, et d'expliquer ce qui n'est pas*'" (Poe 1984b, 431). Though figured as a "creature," it is just the Prefect's failure to negotiate between head and body that prevents him from imagining the animal nature of the killer. As a kind of walking bust, all head and shoulders, the Prefect, not Dupin, is an emblem for excessive rationality, unable to accommodate the ape's physical presence. By contrast, Dupin twice notes his admiration for the animal. "I almost envy you the possession of him," he admits to the sailor (Poe 1984b, 431); and we may suppose that Dupin longs for the animal's intense physicality, even as he revels in the physical effects, the "creeping of the flesh," he produces in his listeners. (Once more, Dupin appears as a stand-in for Poe, who also relies for his very bread and butter on the ability to conjure identification.) "Where is the ingenuity of unravelling a web which you yourself have woven for the express purpose of unravelling?" Poe asked of Cooke; we may now be able to answer that it lies in having in the meantime caught something in that web. In the present case, Dupin's greatest exertions are not to catch the monkey, but its owner, lured in by the text placed in the newspaper. Just so with the story's readers: drawn in by another piece of paper, by another thread or web, we find ourselves trapped within its self-dissolving structure, as any assumptions about the nature of analysis are undone by our own somatic performance.

As "The Murders in the Rue Morgue" concludes, the divergent senses of the word "stamen" crystallize its irreconcilable oppositions:

"stamen, n.; pl. stamens rare stamina, [L., a warp in an upright loom, a thread; lit., that which stands up, from *stare*, to stand.] 1. a warp thread, especially in the ancient upright loom at which the weaver stood upright instead of sitting. [Obs.] 2. in botany, the male reproductive organ in flowers, formed principally of cellular tissue.[12]

Insofar as "stamen" refers to the male generative organ of a flower, it marks the (male) reader addressed by the text; call this the Freudian reading, in which to have a male body seems inseparable from complicity in the orangutan's gendered violence. But the first meaning, now obsolete, indicates the warp thread in a loom; and through familiar paths (loom, weaving, text), we arrive at the stamen as the narrative thread running throughout Poe's text. The story's overdetermined treatment of heads and bodies, words and things, analysis and its effects, implies the close association of the origins of narrative with the discovery of sexual difference, though it is impossible to tell which came first. Instead of reinforcing an evolutionary hierarchy that would separate us from our simian relations, the cryptographic narrative structure of "Rue Morgue" acts to remind us of our corporeal investment: through the story's enacted rhetoric, the reader lives out the distance between the tale's opening metaphor and its closing one— between the simile comparing analysis and the strong man's pleasure, which safely separates its terms even as it joins them, and the metaphor of the stamen, which reveals the degree to which the reader, too, finds himself hopelessly entangled.

NOTES

1. It is a cliché of detective-fiction criticism that its most avid readers are professionals distinguished for their own analytic abilities—doctors, lawyers, and the like. W. H. Auden, one remembers, was a compulsive reader of detective fiction, as is failed Supreme Court nominee Judge Robert Bork, who consumes at least one a day.

2. The deception is accomplished by thrusting "a stiff piece of whalebone" down the throat of the corpse and doubling it over in the wine cask, so that it springs up when

released. As for Mr. Shuttleworthy's impressive accusation, the narrator "confidently depended upon [his] ventriloquial abilities" (Poe 1984b, 742).

3. "It is not a situation *comprising* words that becomes repressed; the words are not dragged into repression by a situation. Rather, *the words themselves, expressing desire, are deemed to be generators of a situation that must be avoided and voided retroactively*" (Abraham and Torok 1986, 20). For hints of a cryptonymic reading of Poe's writing, see Riddel 1979.

4. *Webster's New Twentieth-Century Dictionary*, s.v. "analysis."

5. I use the male pronoun as a way of recognizing how extremely "The Murders in the Rue Morgue" genders its readers. While it would be profitable to investigate how the female reader locates herself in Poe's text, I am concerned here to elucidate the dominant assumptions of the genre, which begins with this story.

6. For a collection of eighteenth-century treatments of feral children, see Malson 1972, which includes Jean Itard's famous treatment of the Wild Boy of Aveyron. Shattuck 1980 offers a detailed but dull interpretation of Itard's work. The idea of a criminal orangutan was not original to Poe: Peithman records that Poe "very likely saw an article, 'New Mode of Thieving,' in the *Annual Register for 1834* . . . which tells of an 'extraordinary burglary' in which a woman entering her bedroom is attacked by a 'Monkey (or a Ribbed-face Baboon) which threw her down, and placing his feet upon her breast, held her pinned firmly to the ground.'" The animal, it turns out, belonged to "itinerant showmen" from whom it had "been let loose for the sake of plundering" (Poe 1981a, 196–97).

7. Cuvier actually boasted about the superiority of his method to that of the detective: "This single track therefore tells the observer about the kind of teeth; the kind of jaws, the haunches, the shoulder, and the pelvis of the animal which has passed: it is more certain evidence than all of Zadig's clues" (Coleman 1964, 102). Voltaire's novel is typically cited as the source for the detective's method, in the inferential reasoning by which three brothers perfectly describe a horse they have not seen, relying only on the circumstantial traces that remained.

8. Foucault suggests the intellectual ties between Dupin and Cuvier by using a quotation from Schlegel: "the structure or comparative grammar of languages furnishes as certain a key of their genealogy as the study of comparative anatomy has done to the loftiest branch of natural science" (Foucault 1973, 280).

9. Sedgwick's emphasis on male homosocial desire initially seems like a promising way of reading Poe's detective stories, which manifest many of the gendered conventions—including the doubling of criminal and detective, the detective's social and physical alienation, and the violence directed against female bodies—that have long characterized crime fiction. Yet Poe's homosocial pairs keep turning into repetitions of a single self (Dupin and the narrator, Dupin and Minister D——, D—— and his imagined brother), without the triangulation of difference needed to set sexual desire in play. On the Gothic and male homosociality, see Sedgwick 1985, 83–117.

10. Reacting against this type of tropic determination, Geoffrey Hartman warns critics not to move too quickly from rhetorical analysis to narrative significance: "The detective story structure—strong beginnings and endings and a deceptively rich, counterfeit,

'excludable' middle—resembles almost too much that of symbol or trope. Yet the recent temptation of linguistic theorists to collapse narrative structure into this or that kind of metaphoricity becomes counterproductive if it remains blind to the writer's very struggle to outwit the epileptic Word" (Hartman 1975, 214). Hartman's caution is well taken, but the meaning of the detective story's rhetorical form lies primarily in its somatic effects on the reader, and not in its unsustainable claims to revelation.

11. Attempting to imitate its master, Humphreys's animal accidentally cuts its own throat (Poe 1981a, 197). Poe habitually associates hair, the sexualized body, and violence. The first thing discovered at the crime scene are "thick tresses—very thick tresses—of grey human hair . . . torn out by the roots," "perhaps half a million of hairs at a time" (Poe 1984b, 422); and Marie Rogêt's jilted paramour identifies her body by stroking her arms to see if they have her characteristically luxuriant hair.

12. *Webster's New Twentieth-Century Dictionary*, s.v. "stamen."

PART THREE

IMAGINING GENDER

Amorous Bondage

Poe, Ladies, and Slaves

JOAN DAYAN

The order of nature *has, in the end, vindicated itself, and the dependence between master and slave has scarcely for a moment ceased.*
— Thomas R. Dew, *Review of the Debate in the Virginia Legislature* (1832)

It Doth Haunt Me Still

In October 1989 I presented the annual Poe Lecture at the Enoch Pratt Free Library in Baltimore. As part of the memorial to Poe's death, we walked to the grave, put flowers on the ground, wondering if Poe was really there—for some say the body has been removed—and then proceeded to the library, where I was to deliver the sixty-ninth lecture on Poe. I had titled the talk "Poe's Love Poems." In writing it, in thinking about those difficult last poems of Poe—unique in the history of American poetry—I turned to what I called "his greatest love poem," the much-contested review of Paulding's *Slavery in the United States*, published in the *Southern Literary Messenger* in April 1836, the same year as Lydia Maria Child's *Anti-Slavery Catechism.*[1] Traditionally these talks are published as monographs by the Poe Society of Baltimore. A month after my talk, I received a letter saying that the society wanted to publish the proceedings, but advised that I limit the paper to the "fine analysis of the love poems" and cut out the dubious part on slavery.

I realized then that the process of how we come to read or understand our fondest fictions results from a sometimes vicious cutting or decorous forgetting. I have not been allowed to forget my attempt to talk about the "peculiar institution" behind Poe's most popular fantasies. I received letters from male members of the Poe Society arguing that Poe did not write the proslavery review. Three years ago, after I spoke on Poe at the Boston

Athenaeum, an unidentified man appeared before me, saying: "I enjoyed your talk, but Poe had nothing to do with such social issues as slavery." He then referred to an ongoing communication he had had with another Poe critic following my talk in Baltimore, adding that I had "overstepped the bounds of good taste and discretion, by contaminating the purest love poems in the English language."[2]

What matters in these continuing altercations is the way in which the very questioning of authorship prods us to ask questions about Poe, property, status, superstition, and gentrification that put Poe quite squarely in dialogue with the romance of the South and the realities of race. Just as the ideology of southern honor depended on fantasies of black degradation, racist discourse needed the rhetoric of natural servility to confirm absolute privilege. As I will argue, the cultivation of romance and the facts of slavery are inextricably linked.

I do not want to sound like Poe in his protracted discussion of his infamous performance at the Boston Lyceum in the *Broadway Journal* for two years, but I do want to draw attention to the coercive monumentalization of certain writers—specifically, how necessary Poe and his "ladies" remain as an icon to the most cherished and necessary ideals of some men. Here is Floyd Stovall in "The Women of Poe's Poems and Tales": "They are all noble and good, and naturally very beautiful. . . . Most remarkable of all is their passionate and enduring love for the hero" (Stovall 1925, 197). It is perhaps not surprising that some Poe critics—the founding fathers of the Poe Society, for example—sound rather like the proslavery ideologues who promoted the ideals of the lady, elegant, white, and delicate.

Poe's ladies, those dream-dimmed, ethereal living dead of his poems, have been taken straight as exemplars of what Poe called "supernal Beauty" —an entitlement that he would degrade again and again. Think about the idea that was "Lady Madeline Usher" returning from the grave as a brute and bloodied thing, the frenziedly iterated "*it*" of her brother Roderick. Many of the dissolutions and decays so marked in Poe's tales about women subvert the status of women as a saving ideal, thus undermining his own "Philosophy of Composition": the "death of a beautiful woman is, unquestionably, the most poetical topic in the world" (Poe 1984a, 19). No longer pure or passive, she returns as an earthy—and very unpoetical—subject.

Let us take my experience as prelude to a rereading of Poe that depends absolutely on what has so often been cut out of his work: the institution of slavery, Poe's troubled sense of himself as a southern aristocrat, and finally, the precise and methodical transactions in which he revealed the threshold separating humanity from animality in an unsettling way. His most unnatural fictions are bound to the natural histories that are so much a part of their origination. Read in this way, Poe's sometimes inexplicable fantasies—for example, a general's artificial body parts named, claimed, and screwed on by a black valet in "The Man that Was Used Up"—become intelligible. Poe's Gothicism is crucial to our understanding of the entangled metaphysics of romance and servitude. What might have remained local historiography becomes a harrowing myth of the Americas.

When we read about masters and slaves in the justifications of slavery that proliferated following the Nat Turner rebellion in Virginia on 21 and 22 August 1831, called by most southerners the "insurrection" or "servile insurrection," women are often absent from the discussion. Yet the southern lady, pure, white, and on her pedestal, remained the ground out of which developed the proslavery philosophy. It was she, that amorphous yet powerfully contrived vessel of femininity, who represented the refined and artificial wants of civilized society ever threatened by the projected desires of brute creation. The patriarchal defense of the intimate relation between master and slave found itself coordinate with the insistence on the subordination of women. Here is George Fitzhugh, writing in 1850 what would become part of his acclaimed *Sociology for the South*:

A state of dependence is the only condition in which reciprocal affection can exist among human beings. . . . A man loves his children because they are weak, helpless and dependent. He loves his wife for similar reasons. When his children grow up and assert their independence, he is apt to transfer his affection to his grandchildren. He ceases to love his wife when she becomes masculine or rebellious; but slaves are always dependent, never the rivals of their master. (McKitrick 1963, 45)

I now turn briefly to the disputed review of James Kirke Paulding's *Slavery in the United States* and William Drayton's *South Vindicated from the Treason and Fanaticism of the Northern Abolitionists* (Poe 1979, 8:265–75). Here, Poe explicitly makes philosophy out of color: turning the Negro inside out, he makes metaphysics out of a biological trait. The mark of blackness compels him to elucidate the propriety of possession, a belief that underlies his most popular rituals of terror. Poe begins his review with the French Revolution, arguing that "property" is what everyone wants most, and that such desire is dubiously called the "spirit of liberty." He calls this revolution, which made its first triumph "the emancipation of slaves," "this eccentric comet," nearly the same words used by Thomas Jefferson in *Notes on the State of Virginia* to describe the Negro's imagination.[3]

But the crucial section of the Paulding review remains Poe's analysis of the "patriarchal character." His strangely sober take on "moral influences flowing from the master and slave" depends on what he calls "the peculiar character (I may say the peculiar nature) of the negro" (Poe 1979, 270). Poe suggests that the enslaved want to be mastered, for they *love*—and this is the crucial word for Poe—to serve, to be subservient. Dependence is necessary to reciprocal affection, yet note that Poe does not comment on Paulding's excursus on women as "guardian angels," whose "appropriate sphere is their home, and their appropriate duties at the cradle of the fireside." Indeed, Poe says nothing about what preoccupies the conclusion of Paulding's book: his disquisition on women abolitionists who have "prostituted" (his word) themselves by "assuming the character of a man" (Paulding 1836, 309). What Poe does do, however, before getting back to Paulding, is describe the *essential* Negro. He notes an inscrutable power "which works essential changes in the different races of animals." Like Jefferson he faces the conundrum of color, pausing to consider "the causes which might and should have blackened the negro's skin and crisped his hair into wool" (Poe 1979, 270–71).

Poe then turns to the well-worn familial argument, which he describes as the "loyal devotion on the part of the slave" and "the master's reciprocal feeling of parental attachment to his humble dependent." These "sentiments in the breast of the negro and his master," Poe explains, are stronger than they would be under like circumstances between individuals of the white race. "That they [these sentiments] belong to the class of feelings 'by which the heart is made better,' we know. How come they?. . . . They grow by the habitual use of the word 'my,' used in the language of affectionate appropriation, long before any idea of value mixes with it. It is a term of endearment. That is an easy transition by which he who is taught to call the little negro 'his,' in this sense and *because he loves him*, shall love him *because he is his*" (ibid., 271–72). The language of "affectionate appropriation," says, it seems at first, simply that you love most what you own. But Poe goes further: you own what you love. Poe, unlike George Fitzhugh, Thomas Dew, or Beverly Tucker, is not simply speaking of desirable and ready submission; he is busy making convertible love and possession.

Mud and Spirit

I might have titled this essay "Mud and Spirit," for Poe's textual cruxes have always to do with conversions between matter and spirit, between the utmost carnality and absolute ideality. The debate in *Eureka* about the suspension in cosmic rhythms between matter and not-matter is grounded in enlightened disquisitions on the physiognomies of "man and brute" and, more precisely, in the character of a human and the nature of the Negro. In most "natural histories," for example Buffon's *Histoire naturelle*, or those other strangely unnatural natural histories of the Caribbean, as in the works of southern theologians and proslavery advocates, the Negro approximated the most destitute and most needy of all animals. For Edward Long in his extraordinary *History of Jamaica* (1774), Negroes, excluded from the rest of humankind, were signal because of a particular kind of exaltation. According to Long, from these degradations, from "mere inert matter," we can ascend "into the animal and vegetable kingdoms," until finally we proceed "from analogy" to "matter endued with thought and reason!" (Long 1774, 2:356, 372).

What is most striking and most infamous in Long's meditation is that the word *Negro* calls up a disturbingly minute analysis of body parts and gradations of being, until finally he draws an analogy between the Negro and the orangutan. "The oran-outang's brain," he claims, "is a senseless *icon* of the human; . . . it is meer matter, unanimated with a thinking principle" (ibid., 30). Thomas Dew, Poe's friend and a professor of political economy at William and Mary College, warned that even with "the free black . . . the animal part of the man gains the victory over the moral, and he, consequently, prefers sinking down into the listless, inglorious repose of the brute creation" (McKitrick 1963, 20–33).[4]

When Long wrote about what he called the progression "from a lump of dirt to a perfect human being," he meant the move from matter to human. But what is the relation between those "creatures" constituted as brute exemplars of matter and the rarefied vessels of spirit, those species of "true womanhood" who haunt the learned discourse on race as the absolute perfection so antithetical to—and yet as subordinated as—that lump of dirt? What do we gain by forcing proximity on those categories and claims the naturalists so rigorously separated?

Perhaps all of Poe's work is finally about radical dehumanization: one can dematerialize—idealize—by turning humans into animals or by turning them into angels. As Poe proves throughout *Eureka* and in his angelic colloquies, matter and not-matter are convertible. Further, both processes, etherealization and brutalization (turning into angel or brute), involve displacement of the human element. We are dealing with a process of sublimation, either up or down. Animality, after all, emerges for most nineteenth-century phrenologists, theologians, and anthropologists in those beings who are at once man and beast: lunatics, women, primates, black men, and children. What remains unmentioned, and unencoded, is the *manhood* at the center of these operations. It is this powerfully absent construction that Poe intentionally probes. He, the white epistemologist of the sublime, the Enlightenment "universal man," haunts Poe's writings. It is his divisions, as well as his projections, that Poe confounds.

Thus the unbelievable overturning of the *law of identity and contradiction* that I have argued to be central to Poe's work can now be considered as more than a fable of mind. Poe's reconstructions depend on experiences that trade on unspeakable slippages between men and women, humans and animals, life and death. Poe deliberately undermines the taxonomic vocations of male supremacy, and thus attributes to it a troubling, ambiguous vitality.

My Tantalized Spirit

The tales about women, "Morella," "Ligeia," "Berenice," "The Fall of the House of Usher," and "Eleonora," are about men who narrate the unspeakable remembrance: not the gun-toting, masterful cavaliers or gentlemen of southern fictions of the gentry, but the delicate acolytes of erudite ladies or the terrified victims of the lady revenants. In these tales, possession, multiple hauntings, and identity dissolutions suspend gender difference as a component of identity. The memorial act demands a willing surrender to an anomalous atmosphere where one thing remains certain: the dead do not die. They will not stay buried. In Poe's tales, these awfully corporeal ghosts are always women. As we read the compelling narratives of the men who wait and watch for the inevitable return, we sense how much the terror depends on the men's will to remember, their sorcererlike ability to name and to conjure the beloved, who is, of course, the exemplar for later "white zombies."

Poe's ideal of "indefinitiveness," his turn to the "ethereal," "ideal," "breath of faery," or "mystic," is most weirdly disrupted in his poetry. The three poems that trouble me most are the second "To Helen," "For Annie," and "To——." Terms such as "saintliness," "sweet," "ideal," or "feminine perfection" (often used by critics when referring to the women of Poe's poems) obscure how deliberately Poe fragments and dissolves conventional images of "womanliness." In these poems Poe reveals the progress of perfection: its absolute dependence on the imperfect. In "To Helen," we move from a lady's "upturn'd" face in a landscape of dying, smiling roses, with faces also "upturn'd," to the progressive elimination of the world of nature: "The pearly lustre of the moon went out: / The mossy banks and the meandering paths, / The happy flowers and the repining trees, / Were seen no more." Every part of the lady is obliterated, except for her eyes: "*Only thine eyes remained. /* They *would not* go—they never yet have gone." "They follow me—they lead me through the years. / They are my ministers—yet I their slave" (Poe 1984b, 95–96).

There is something less than ideal or sanctifying about these eyes. They recall the eyes of the Lady Ligeia or Berenice's teeth forever imprinted on the narrator's mind. In the process of abstraction, once every piece of nature named is blotted out, no woman remains, but only what Poe calls "less than thou." Woman, "the fair sex," and the "romance" she bears can only be experienced as fragment. Freed from marriage, domesticity, and any possible relation to property, the beloved is reduced to a haunting remnant. But what happens to the poet? Yielding himself passive to the love-light, as the death-obsessed imaginer of "For Annie," Poe renders himself up as "slave" to those omniscient eyes: "Their office is to illumine and enkindle— / My duty, *to be saved* by their bright light" (Poe 1984b, 96–97). The bereaved lover thus figures himself through a servitude articulated as salvation.

As a way to read the surrender of these love poems, I want briefly to recall the rhetoric of redemption in Poe's Paulding-Drayton review. In the scenes of suffering that conclude the review, Poe appreciates the all-consuming etiology of possession. As the master weakens, the servant remains fixed in a relentless, nearly superhuman deathwatch. How different are such spectacles of feeling from Poe's representation of the compulsive lover in these poems, or in the bedside vigils of "Ligeia" and "Morella"? For Poe, adoration is always a deadly business. When he wrote his review, Poe merely reiterated the sentimental decor necessary for maintaining the illusion of mastery. But by the time he composed these late poems, he had apprehended the ruse of sentiment and not only exposed but satirized the inalienable connection between the illusions of reverent attachment and the matter of human bondage.

In "To——," written to Marie Louise Shew in 1848, Poe fantasizes about being swallowed up by the object of his affections. A strange turn takes place midway through the poem. He takes the name that he will not name, "two foreign soft dissyllables"—Lady "Marie Louise" (unnamed in the published version)—as prod to his undoing:

. . . And I! my spells are broken.
The pen falls powerless from my shivering hand.
With thy dear name as text, though bidden by thee,
I cannot write—I cannot speak or think,
Alas, I cannot feel; for 'tis not feeling,
This standing motionless upon the golden
Threshold of the wide-open gate of dreams,
Gazing, entranced, adown the gorgeous vista,
And thrilling as I see upon the right,
Upon the left, and all the way along
Amid empurpled vapors, far away
To where the prospect terminates—*thee only.*

(Ibid., 88)

Here we have another strange vanishing ritual, which like that of "To Helen" seems to mock the progress of corporeality from matter to human. The more closely Poe analyzes and purifies his notions, the more he tries to establish a solid foundation, the more he loses himself in fantasy. Poe's unlinked Great Chain completely mixes man, nature, women, reason, and dreams. Not only does feeling summon dissolution, but Poe takes heartfelt affection and turns it into lust. What southerners dignified by the name love, Poe rather unceremoniously presents as fierce, inhuman desire. In "To—" he animates not feeling or thought, but instead wildly physicalized passion that has far from salutary effects on the soul.

The poet trades his subjectivity, his very power to speak or write, for the most *sensible* part of his beloved, looking into her *heart of hearts.* Poe has coerced feeling into image; and as in "To Helen," we are left with a strangely fetishized kernel of womanhood, those scintillant "star eyes." Here, "thee" is implicitly the "heart" that can be reached only through penetration "adown the gorgeous vista" into a tunnel-like space that thrills as it constrains, "upon the right / Upon the left, and all the way along / Amid empurpled vapors, far away / To where the prospect terminates—."

Why does Poe so often present himself in these later poems as a "slave" to the images he has created? What does he mean by this posture of enfeeblement, his claim of impotence? I suggest that Poe articulates a specific relation of domination, where the speaker who has defined himself as possessor is in turn defined by his possession. I quote two passages of variously willed passivity: a stanza from "To Annie" and a passage from a letter to Sara Helen Whitman.

Sadly, I know
   I am shorn of my strength,
And no muscle I move
   As I lie at full length—
But no matter!—I feel
   I am better at length.
              (Ibid., 98)

Oh God! how I now curse the impotence of the pen—the inexorable *distance* between us! I am pining to speak to *you*, Helen,—to you in person—to be near you
while I speak—gently to press your hand in mine—to look into your soul through
your eyes—and thus to be *sure* that my voice passes into your heart. (Poe 1966,
2:396)

To gain a voice, the writer must become the beloved. Getting into her mind
will ensure that his voice gets into her heart. To *want* to be in the place of
another is to be possessed. Or put another way: If you cannot have her, then
you can become her. Poe understands *the law of the heart*, the power in the
word *my*. And in nearly all of Poe's dealings with ladies, whether in letters
(recycled to various "real" beloveds), poems, or tales, he has possessed all
the others so fully that they become the same, not only interchangeable with
each other, but with Edgar Poe.

Yet if we put "To Helen" or "For Annie" in the southern context, we can
go further. Beverly Tucker, proslavery apologist and professor of law at
William and Mary, who befriended Poe and was his greatest supporter
when Poe edited the *Southern Literary Messenger* in 1835–36, wrote much
about "obedience to the law of Love." In his "Moral and Political Effect of
the Relation between the Caucasian Master and the African Slave," the
terms of contrast are again limited to the paradigm of the benevolent master and the grateful servant. But in *George Balcombe*, a romance of Missouri
and Virginia, published in 1836, he included women, and especially "genuine feminine devotion," in his philosophy of feeling. He asked his male
readers to seek those women who reject the "'ologies" of female radicals,"
and prefer "to learn the housewifely duties and plain old fashioned sense of
a Virginia lady." Referring to unmarriageable "learned ladies," George Balcombe warns that there are "secrets in heaven and earth not dreamed of in
their philosophy." Instead, the uncorrupted—and "uncultivated"—woman
will beware "*intellectual distinction*, or *distinction* of any kind," for such "a
feeling unsexes her." This *real* woman "reads her Bible, works her sampler,

darns her stockings, and boils her bacon and greens together" (Tucker 1836, 1:88, 277, 275, 278).

Before turning to Poe's review of Tucker's *George Balcombe*, I want to emphasize that Tucker's portrayal of the lady depends for its effect on another favorite subject of the gentleman George Balcombe: the zealous and appreciative Negro. Balcombe's longest disquisitions concern wives and slaves. What is the "noblest of God's works"? Balcombe has the answer: "—a *right woman—a genuine unsophisticated woman*" (ibid., 273). The "established order of the universe," Balcombe's magisterial hierarchy, depends absolutely on distinguishing superior and inferior beings: "I see gradations in everything. I see subordination everywhere." Within this created order, rising in a climax of subordination, white men are on top. Men of "delicacy" marry only women who know their place. Only these women can enjoy the bonds of matrimony, and only grateful Negroes can be graced with "that strong tie . . . spun out of the interchange of service and protection." Those born slaves actually "feel themselves inferior," and that sentiment alone is "the *rationale* of the filial and parental bond" (ibid. 2:164–65). Finally, Balcombe clinches his argument about Negroes, tradition, and "inextinguishable affection" by joining women with blacks in happy servitude:

Is gratitude abject? Is self-abandoning, zealous devotion abject? If the duties of heaven require these sentiments, and its happiness consist in their exercise, which of us is it that is but a little lower than the angels—the negro or the white man? . . . Let women and negroes alone, and instead of quacking with them, physic your own diseases. Leave them in their humility, their grateful affection, their self-renouncing loyalty, their subordination of the heart, and let it be your study to become worthy to be the object of these sentiments. (Ibid., 166)

Poe reviewed *George Balcombe* in the *Southern Literary Messenger* in 1837. Most of the review is plot summary. Although Poe says nothing about Tucker's theory of servitude, he does pay attention to the women characters. The ever-blushing Mary Scott, who was "beautiful and intelligent—gay, sprightly and impassioned," Poe praises as "imbued with the spirit of romance." Remarking on Elizabeth, whom he describes as "the shrinking and matronly wife of Balcombe," he concludes: "She is an exquisite specimen of her class, but her class is somewhat hacknied." Poe's favorite character is Ann, the proper Virginia lady, who in Balcombe's words is "wise, generous, and delicate." Poe concludes his judgment of Tucker's ladies by asserting: "Upon the whole, no American novelist has succeeded, we think, in female character, even nearly so well as the writer of George Balcombe" (Poe 1984a, 956, 975–76).

Tucker's proper ladies are passive and accommodating, utterly dependent on the men who regulate their destiny. In *George Balcombe*, Tucker's portrayal of the ideal wife reflects the character of her husband: "while her husband's light was above the horizon, [she] hid herself beneath it, or if she appeared at all, modestly paled her lustre in his presence" (Tucker 1836, 1:275). But when Poe yields himself up to the "bright light" of Helen, he shifts the entire patriarchal argument to the domain that seems relevant to him, namely, the reversibility of supremacy. In Poe's mechanics of love, heartfelt men become vague and impotent, while beloved women become shadowy or reduced to pieces of prized and sexualized symbolic matter. In a time when many argued for sharper categorizations and more hierarchy, when ladies, slaves, and men endured ever more difficult trials of definition, Poe managed to confound and denaturalize the "natural order" of things. In prostrating himself before the fetishized women of his poems or creating powerful intellects, mystics, and witches like Ligeia and Morella, Poe worked changes on the subservient women praised by his fellow southerners.

Poe is preoccupied with repeated and varied postures of enfeeblement, a deliberate weakness that leaves only feeling, an obsession with the heart that links the white male writer, the white woman of his dreams, and the ungendered, unmentioned black. Without mentioning blacks, Poe applies the accepted argument on the "nature" of Negroes and the "spirit" of women—both feeling, not thinking, beings—to the white men usually excluded from such categorization.[5]

When Poe dwells repeatedly on the extremes of savagery and cultivation, brute possession and tender affection, he refers to a long history of racialist writings, including those of George Buffon and Edward Long. Buffon describes "Negroes" as "naturally compassionate and tender" (1831, 1:163). Edward Long discusses at length the "courteous, tender disposition" of the orangutan, debasing black women in the process. Long tells his readers that orangutans "sometimes endeavour to surprize and carry off negroe women into their woody retreats." He then turns to these Negroes, to whom he grants not a trace of affectionate feeling, describing them as "libidinous and shameless as monkeys, or baboons." No longer questioning whether a black female would accept an ape for a husband, Long assures his readers that "hot" Negro women seek out these animals to "embrace" (Long 1774, 2:360, 364, 361, 383).

White women were imagined by advocates of slavery as emptied of all qualities that could attach them to physical reality, while black women became vessels for the carnality that was expelled from icons of pure womanhood. Poe takes the blushing belle and makes her both passionate and suspiciously white, with a deathly, unnatural pallor that makes whiteness as negative and opaque as what Jefferson had described in *Notes on the State of Virginia* as an "immoveable veil of black" (Jefferson 1975, 189). Further, Poe's voice as poet reconstitutes itself, the male lover in nineteenth-century America, as a wholly negative consciousness, obeisant to the *law of the heart.*[6] The law, as Poe defines it, however, has more to do with lust than with propriety, and he substitutes monomaniacal frenzy for the delicately modulated feelings of the "civilized" southerner.

There is a two-pronged program here. First, Poe plays with the possibility of one thing passing into another—the *convertibility* so much a part of his project. The superior male mind, erected over the bodies of women continuously purified or defiled and blacks alternately sentimentalized or cursed, turns into the very objects once posited as external to it. Second, Poe repeats, exaggerates, and transforms the immutable, romanticized attributes white women are granted by men. He dramatizes the fact of appropriation, and thereby undefines the definitions that mattered to civilized society. It is not surprising, then, that one reviewer of Poe's work writing in 1856 reflected: "In perusing his most powerful tales, the reader feels himself surrounded by hitherto unapprehended dangers; he grows suspicious of his best friends; all good angels appear turning to demons" (*North American Review* 432).

Dying to Serve

To read much of nineteenth-century literature is to encounter conceits of servitude. From Caleb Williams's anguished and ambiguous declaration to Falkland, "Sir, I could die to serve you!" to Jane Eyre's "I'd give my life to serve you," to a Bartleby who quite literally dies to serve while refusing to, scenes of mastery and servitude greeted readers who thought they would escape to fictions or romances. Even the supernatural in many Gothic tales had its real basis in the language of slavery and colonization, put forth as the most natural thing in the world. One has only to read the 1685 *Code noir* of Louis XIV, that collection of edicts concerning "the Discipline and Commerce of Negro Slaves in the French Islands of America," to understand how what first seems phantasmagoric is locked into a nature mangled and relived as a spectacle of servitude. Its surreally precise conditions for human reduction (how best turn a man into a thing), like Long's anatomical permutations on monkey, man, horse, and Negro, demonstrate how unnatural the claims to right and property actually were.

The *Code noir* or *Black Code* is a document of limits.[7] Unlike the racist disquisition on blacks as lacking the finer feelings of a tender heart, the code is not concerned with the tangled semantics of charitable servitude or lurking debauchery. One reads instead sixty articles that take one into a chilling series of qualifications: prohibitions that permit, limitations that invite excess, and a king's grandiloquence that ensures divestment. There is no time for discussions of innate inferiority, natural difference, or nightmares of contamination. The blacks and slaves in French America are introduced not as persons, but as a special kind of property: a "thing," according to Roman law, juridically deprived of all rights. Once acquired by a planter, legally divested of their selfhood and removed from their land, slaves became the planter's possession. Alternately defined as chattels and as real property, they were sometimes movable assets (part of the planter's personal estate) and sometimes unmovable, disposed of as if real estate, or in especially macabre cases, as if garbage.

If the *Black Code* turned a human into a thing, a piece of movable property, it could be argued that the law of the heart accomplishes the same end; the law of the heart remains inseparable from the fact of property. Southern proslavery apologists appreciated the special privileges that accompanied possession, as did some abolitionists, who could never quite liberate their objects of pathos from domination. The acclaimed dispossession of Stowe's *Uncle Tom's Cabin* works only so long as the "Negro" is kept forever separate in essence from the Anglo-Saxon, locked in the precincts of affectionate service, impressionable spirituality, and childlike simplicity. Stowe's fantasy, brimful of just pity, remains entirely affirming and satisfying to the "superior" white ego. How different, after all, is Stowe's representation of Tom stretched out supine on the veranda in order to be close to the dying Eva—what Miss Ophelia calls "sleeping anywhere and everywhere, like a dog"—from Poe's portrayal in the Paulding-Drayton review of the bond between master and servant?

Poe's dramatizations of possession—a reciprocal devouring of self and other—remind us of the force of language, especially literary language, to allow the covert continuation of domination. Fictions of sentiment and idealizations of love, which are the special realm of right-minded women and domesticated blacks, are linked in unsettling ways to the social realities of property and possession. Poe knew how the sanctifying of women depends on a more sinister brutalization, or spectralization. His narrators in "Ligeia," "Berenice," and "Morella," for example, demonstrate how the language of love can animate and sustain utter servility.

Sentiment, as Poe confirmed in "The Black Cat," is not only coercive but also despotic. The rare and special love between slave and master, and between man and wife, based on the law of property, becomes the medium by which perfect submission becomes equivalent to a pure but perverse love. A slave, a piece of property, a black pet, once loved in the proper domestic setting, effects an excess of devotion, an inextricable bond that proslavery apologists, and even Captain Delano in Melville's *Benito Cereno*, argued, can never be felt by two equals. Poe wrote "The Black Cat" to demonstrate how destructive is the illusion of mastery: just as the pet of perfect docility turns into "a brute beast," "a man, fashioned in the image of the High God," is dependent on and utterly enslaved by the very thing he has so lovingly brutalized (Poe 1984b, 603).

No Place of Grace

We need to reread Poe's romantic fictions as bound to the realities of race, keeping "every thing . . . within the limits of the accountable—of the real," as he urged in "The Philosophy of Composition." There is a logic to his excessive attention to blood, things dirtied, and bodies mutilated. Lurking in every effusion of ennobling love is the terror of literal dehumanization: not only the Burkean sublime or the Calvinist's rhetoric of sensation, but that most terrific conversion, the reduction of human into thing for the ends of capital.

Think about the degradation and rot, the "premature burial" in the confines of the Grampus in *The Narrative of Arthur Gordon Pym*, in terms of the slave ship: the "close atmosphere of the hold" where Pym hides; drinking water "putrid and swarming with vermin"; Augustus's body "loathsome beyond expression," reduced finally to a "mass of putrefaction." When Pym describes the ship of the dead, he uses rhetorical strategies characteristic of an apocalypse, but the ultimate disclosure here is the stench of a slaver (a return to the "skeleton ship" of Coleridge's *Ancient Mariner*): "Of a sudden, and all at once, there came wafted over the ocean from the strange vessel (which was now close upon us) a smell, a stench, such as the whole world has no name for—no conception of—hellish—utterly suffocating—insufferable, inconceivable" (ibid., 1085). In reconsidering Poe's relentlessly circumscribed settings, the pits of unspeakable crimes, we recall the holds of slave ships, those "dens of putrefaction" as C. L. R. James described them in *The Black Jacobins*, his history of the revolution in Saint-Domingue (James 1980, 137).

I take as parable for the late-in-coming recognition of the African American, Poe's "Morning on the Wissahiccon," his strange meditation on the hidden though "real Edens" of the United States. Those ignored areas, less traveled than those on the northern and eastern seaboard, are located in "the gorgeous interior . . . of some of our western and southern districts" (Poe 1984b, 939). But Poe finally chooses a "pedestrian tour" along the Wissahiccon, "a brook . . . which empties itself into the Schuylkill, about six miles westward of Philadelphia" (ibid., 942).

After describing the typical walk, he recounts his own visit to the stream, where, rapt in dreams of the "good old days," he saw "or dreamed that I saw" an elk from the days when "the red man trod alone." His fantasies of those idyllic days before the land had been marred "by the stern hand of the utilitarian" were curiously interrupted. He suddenly heard a furtive "hist! hist!" "In an instant afterwards, a negro emerged from the thicket, putting aside the bushes with care, and treading stealthily." The "noble animal" did not escape, but attracted by the offering of salt from the Negro, bowed, stamped, and "then lay quietly down and was secured with a halter." So ends the "romance of the elk" (ibid., 944). The Native Americans have vanished, but their elk is now kept as a pet, domesticated by a wealthy family, whose black servant delivers the animal into bondage. The romance of the Americas, as Poe knows, depends on a sequence of subordinations, variously called love, care, and devotion. An entire history of violence, genocide, and slavery, it could be argued, is hidden in Poe's apparently tame and visionary landscape sketch.

The facts of race intrude almost imperceptibly yet persistently into Poe's romance. "God's plan for securing the hearts of his creatures" (Poe 1984b, 964), to quote George Balcombe, Poe insists is analogous to the polemicist's plot to justify human bondage. But he reserves his greatest scorn for those who condemn slavery while continuing to restrict blacks to the status of objects: recipients of the charity of white men who continue to be masters. As a critical reader of the transcendentalist ideologies of his time, Poe's compulsive satire on the pundits, on their mystifying language and cant, was fueled by the abolitionist leanings of those he called the "Frogpondians": Emerson, Thoreau, Lowell, and especially Longfellow.

Emerson's 1884 address in Concord on the tenth anniversary of the emancipation of the Negroes in the British West Indies preceded Poe's Lyceum debacle by about a year. For Emerson, the mettle of white men has been proved by their largess on "behalf of the African": "Other revolutions have been the insurrection of the oppressed; this was the repentance of the tyrant. It was the masters revolting from their mastery." Not only is Emerson idealizing, and decontextualizing, a far more disturbing history, but what he calls "elevation and pathos" keeps whites quite secure in their superiority while blacks, though no longer called slaves, remain inferior. Invited to the Boston Lyceum, Poe deliberately insulted his audience by reading "Al Aaraaf" (which he introduced by saying he wrote it at nineteen years old), renamed "The Messenger Star of Tycho Brahe" for that "drunken" specta- cle.[8] Poe's blustering and offensive performance no doubt had its sources not only in envy, insecurity, and aesthetic debate, but in his disapproval of Emerson's high-minded celebration of West Indian emancipation as a "piece of moral history" (Emerson 1904, 146).

Poe's attack in *Eureka*, carrying further his condemnation of those he called the oracles of "higher morality," those "thinkers-that-they-think," who wander "in the shadowy region of imaginary truth," remained grounded in his disdain for those he condemned in his reviews as "the small coterie of abolitionists, transcendentalists and fanatics in general." After all, what he attacked as "the frantic spirit of generalization" was one of the major accusations of proslavery advocates in the South, who called the northern abolitionists fools of abstraction, who knew nothing of the particulars of southern slavery. In order to understand Poe's unceasing condemnation of the Bostonians, we need to reread literary history as regional debate.

Poe's obsessive attacks on Longfellow—and especially his critique of the poem "The Slave in the Dismal Swamp" in his 1845 review of Longfellow's *Poems of Slavery* (1842)—come not only from envy or aesthetic discretion, as some have suggested, but also from the acute knowledge of the facts behind Longfellow's romantic sentimentalism. The Dismal Swamp, sometimes called "the Great Dismal," was for a long time the refuge for runaway slaves in the South. Poe no doubt read Samuel Warner's "Authentic and Impartial Narrative," an account published in 1831 of Nat Turner's "Horrid Massacre." Warner's description of the "very large bog, extending from N. to S. near 30 miles, and from E. to W. at a medium about 10 miles," where cypress and cedar cast an "everlasting shade," could well have been a source for the ghastly landscape of "Silence—A Fable" (composed in 1832 and published in 1835). Even birds do not fly over this gloomy swamp, "for fear of the noi- some exhalations that rise from this vast body of filth and nastiness. These noxious vapors infect the air round about." Warner then exclaims, "It is within the deep recesses of this gloomy Swamp, 'dismal' indeed, beyond the power of human conception, that the runaway Slaves of the south have been known to secret themselves for weeks, months, and years, subsisting on frogs, terrapins, and even snakes!" (Warner 1971, 296–98).

Poe must have known about the scouring of the swamp in pursuit of slaves, of the hounds that unsuccessfully followed the scent of Nat Turner. Yet, as so often in his writings, Poe misrecognizes or disavows the facts he knows, condemning Longfellow for writing "a shameless medley of the grossest misrepresentation. When did Professor LONGFELLOW ever *know* a slave to be hunted with bloodhounds in the *dismal swamp*? Because he has heard that runaway slaves are so treated in CUBA, he has certainly no right to change the locality" (Poe 1984a, 763). But some of what Poe says matters, for Longfellow's poem purifies the place. He cleans up the mire. The vessel for squalor, the bearer of putrefaction in "The Slave in the Dismal Swamp" is his "poor old slave, infirm and lame," who hides in an unreal landscape:

> Where will-o'-the-wisps and gloworms shine,
>   In bulrush and in brake;
> Where waving mosses shroud the pine,
>   . . . .
> All things above were bright and fair,
>   All things were glad and free;
> Lithe squirrels darted here and there,
> And wild birds filled the echoing air
>   With songs of Liberty!
>   (Longfellow 1886, 285)

Longfellow's picture of the "hunted Negro," like other portraits of the pathetic hero so popular in the North, allows the reader pity, but also distance from the poeticized object of emotion.[9]

Poe did not accept Longfellow's translation of the Dismal Swamp into an Edenic scene contaminated by one spot of deformity, the slave. Indeed, Poe's dark, stagnant waters, and the "morass" and "wilderness" in "Silence —A Fable" at "the boundary of the dark, horrible, lofty forest," reiterate the locale of the hunted. It is "The Island of the Fay," however, that communicates something of the terror felt by those southerners who read accounts of black "monstrosity" and feared insurgent slaves hiding in the shadows of the Dismal Swamp. Poe's voyager observes "in a single view both the eastern and western extremities of the islet." The two ends mark two extremes of landscape, and two myths of the South: one a "radiant harem of garden beauties," a piece of heaven, filled with flowers, butterflies, and sun; the other "whelmed in the blackest shade." The voyager dreams about the dark side. In the gloom of the cypress he forces a merger between his idyll of innocence and an unrelenting dirge. Seen after "the light," the shadow upon shadow on this end of the island move Poe to fancy a place of enchantment. But what kind of enchantment? "This is the haunt of the few gentle Fays who remain from the wreck of the race." As in *Pym*, the narrative depends on a crisis of black and white, but here what was white becomes utterly imbricated with and absorbed by blackness. And yet the shadows that overtake the imagined "Fay," identified by Poe as "Death," are part of her very substance, what had made her "magic": "her shadow fell from her, and was swallowed up in the dark water, making its blackness more black" (Poe 1984b, 937–38).

In what should be reread as Poe's fantasy of the South, the shadows of those who once lived "sweet lives" gradually dissolve "into the ebony water" and become "absorbed into its blackness," until finally, "the Fay, now the mere ghost of her former self, went disconsolately with her boat into the region of the ebony flood—and that she issued thence at all I cannot say,— for darkness fell over all things, and I beheld her magical figure no more" (ibid., 938). The spirit's magic, her enchanted beauty, is hybrid, an amalgam of black and white. Poe rewrites the cult of purity central to southern romance. All that remains of the master race are these spirits. But in this fable of color, the white fays, in getting back their bodies, merge into blackness. No longer pure, they disappear, blending with what had been construed as their antithesis in the "natural" order of things.

When we note varying denigrations of blacks, especially in Poe's early works, it becomes even more unsettling that issues of race, like those of gender, have not figured much in criticism of Poe's writings.[10] But then, much that is necessary to the sanctification of something called "literariness"—those texts that are praised as art, not as politics—is risked if we put Poe in his place, if we avoid the romantic image of a genius in "Dream-Land," "Out of SPACE / out of TIME" (Poe 1984b, 79). For instance, in "The Journal of Julius Rodman," the "faithful negro" Toby is described "as ugly an old gentleman as ever spoke—having all the peculiar features of his race; the swollen lips, large white protruding eyes, flat nose, long ears, double head, pot-belly, and bow legs" (Poe 1984b, 1242). And there is the orangutan in "The Murders in the Rue Morgue," whose strange gibberish at first suggests "primitive" vocables: "it might have been the voice of an Asiatic— of an African" (ibid., 416).[11] In Poe's review of Robert Bird's *Sheppard Lee*, a story of metempsychosis, lost bodies, and wandering spirits, an obvious source for Poe's "Gold Bug"—Poe discusses the "negro servant, Jim Jumble . . . a crabbed, self-willed old rascal, who will have every thing his own way." In Bird's story, as Poe represents it in his review, Jim Jumble "conceives that money has been buried by Captain Kid, in a certain ugly swamp, called the Owl-Roost. . . . The stories of the negro affect his master to such a degree that he dreams three nights in succession of finding a treasure at the foot of a beech-tree in the swamp" (Poe 1984a, 390–91). Sheppard Lee's failing to find the treasure, falling dead, and then turning into a ghost and looking for yet another body to inhabit (briefly possessing the corpse of a "miserable negro slave" called "Nigger Tom"), will be revised in Poe's tale of Legrand, who does the conceiving, and the manumitted black servant Jupiter, who knows (*nose*) nothing—he is unable to tell his left eye from his right—concluding with a final, successful treasure hunt.

Yet even though Poe used racist stereotypes in such stories as "The Man that Was Used Up," "The Gold Bug," and "The Murders in the Rue Morgue," I suggest that he exercised these images in order to tell another story. Consider "The Man that Was Used Up: A Tale of the Late Bugaboo and Kickapoo Campaign" (1839). Not only does Poe describe the dismemberment and redemption of Brigadier General John A. B. C. Smith, but he writes the "other" into the white hero's tale, putting those called "savages" or "things" into the myth of Anglo-Saxon America. Reduced to "an odd looking bundle of something" by the Bugaboo and Kickapoo Indians in a "tremendous swamp-fight away down South" (doubtless an allusion to the Dismal Swamp), the general is put together every morning by Pompey, his black valet. With each successive body part replaced, the general regains the voice of the consummate southern gentleman while remaining utterly dependent on the "old negro" he debases. He calls Pompey "dog," then "nigger," then "scamp," and finally, once all his parts are reassembled, "black rascal" (Poe 1984b, 315–16).

When Poe was "dying" for "Annie," he was writing his most horrible tale of retribution, "Hop-Frog; or, The Eight Chained Ourang-Outangs" (1849). What Mabbott regards as merely "a terrible exposition of the darkness of a human soul" (Poe 1969–78, 3:1344) is Poe's envisioned revenge for the national sin of slavery. As we have seen, orangutans were deemed the most appropriate analogues for blacks. Here Poe literalizes what natural historians perceived as bestial similitude and prophesies the apocalypse of "servile" war, so feared by southerners. In the fiery climax of "Hop-Frog," eight cruel masters get turned into orangutans by an enslaved dwarf "from some barbarous region . . . no person ever heard of" (Poe 1984b, 900). Just as the unidentifiable "gibberish" of the orangutan murderer in "Rue Morgue" "might have been the voice of an Asiatic—of an African," this unheard-of place refers implicitly to Africa. Tarred and flaxed, the masters are burned to "a fetid, blackened, hideous, and indistinguishable mass" (ibid., 908). The blind spot of most critics to slavery and its justifications as grounds for the turn in "Hop-Frog" is exemplified when Mabbott reflects: "The manner of chaining apes described is not mentioned by any authorities consulted" (Poe 1969–78, 3:1344).

The dependence of much Gothic fiction on Calvinist theology and apocalyptic text can be particularized as the relation between a "suffering"— alternately degraded and idealized—"servant" and an omniscient master. In Poe's relation of domination, enslavement compels convertibility, where, as Hegel argued in his *Phenomenology of Mind*, the distinction between master and slave is transformed: "just as lordship showed its essential nature to be the reverse of what it wants to be, so, too, bondage will, when completed, pass into the opposite of what it immediately is" (Hegel 1970, 237). Aware of the perils of mastery, Poe repeats the conversion narrative that is so much a part of material possession. As with Poe's tales about avenging women— those beloveds who haunt and possess the lover—"Hop-Frog" inverts and reconstitutes what Orlando Patterson has called "the idiom of power" (Patterson 1982, 17–34).

When Ladies Did Not Walk But Floated

In the fantasy of dissolution that concludes "The Island of the Fay," the fairy reveals her essence in dying. Her gist is black, and hence her death is a darkening. In this final spectralization, Poe responds to racial taxonomies that depend for their effect on precariously rarefied white women. This spirit exudes the shadows that had always filled her. Poe's "ladies," once returned to their home in the South, urge us to think about the way rituals of purity depend on reminders of dirt. In 1852, three years after Poe's death, George Frederick Holmes reviewed *Uncle Tom's Cabin* in the *Southern Literary Messenger*. Holmes moves from the descent of the novel "from its graceful and airy home" to "a more vulgar mission," thus tainting its "robe of ideal purity" to "that sex," who must be protected by "the lords of creation," unless she, like her fiction, "deliberately steps beyond the hallowed precincts—the enchanted circle—which encompasses her with the halo of divinity."

What Poe called the "circumscribed Eden of dreams" he knew encompassed more than just maiden purity. Women can be granted "spirit" by men only because these men delimit ceremonies of subordination that include women, blacks, dogs, and children. Just as slaves earn benefits when they labor and obey, women deserve gallantry as long as they are inert or inactive vessels. But if these privileged women interact with their masters, or get too close to the men who act on them, men could be threatened with the foul contamination they fear. In love stories that become ghost stories, Poe's narrators first look upon, idealize, and *feel with the mind*, hollowing out the beloved image, and then turn on the object of their affections, only to suffer retribution for their conversion, or "alternation," as the narrator of "Berenice" puts it (Poe 1984b, 229).

In "Our Cousin, Mr. Poe," Allen Tate writes that Poe's "exalted idealiza-tion of Woman" was "more intense than the standard cult of Female Purity in the Old South." Tate suspects that Poe "was not quite, perhaps, a South-ern gentleman." He turns his dead ladies into vampires, and most impor-tant, these erudite women could never be part of the social and economic life of antebellum Virginia. After all, Virginia perpetuated itself "through the issue of the female body, while the intellect, which was public and political, remained under the supervision of the gentlemen" (Tate 1967, 41).

What then is the nature of Poe's intensity in writing about women? In his private dealings with women, Poe was excessively polite, if not chivalric, in courtly, southern style. In his personal life, he appreciated the value of recycling terms of endearment, the more romantic the better. It did not matter what he did to his ladies—whether he courted more than one at the same time, lied to them, or betrayed them—so long as he remained genteel. Yet Poe's objects of affection should not blind us to Poe's serious attention to women writers, or to his awareness of society's mechanisms of control. Writing about Elizabeth Barrett Browning, he laments that a false code of gallantry prohibits the serious critique women deserve as much as men do. Poe as critic does not want to subject women to "the downright degradation of mere puffery," and when he turns to Barrett's *Drama of Exile*, he does not spare her his critique. He praises her "very extraordinary resources," but condemns her for representing Eve not as "a woman," but instead as "a mystical something or nothing, enwrapped in a fog of rhapsody about Transfiguration." Unlike his cloying and sentimental reviews of Frances Sargent Osgood and Lydia Huntley Sigourney, Poe's review of Barrett is tough, no doubt because her "obscurity" reminds him of "the cant of the transcendentalists" (Poe 1984a, 116, 118, 119).

Like those southern gentlemen who kept "black wenches" and "white ladies" neatly separated into categories, Poe does not explicitly connect the idea of race to that of gender, yet he suggests such a coupling in his fiction and poetry. Although he reviews both Margaret Fuller and Lydia Maria Child, he never mentions their essays against slavery, or their comparison of slaves violated to women subordinated in marriage. Only once in a review does Poe link the institution of marriage to that of slavery. Reviewing Longfellow's *Poems on Slavery*, he describes "the Quadroon Girl" as "the old abolitionist story—worn threadbare—of a slaveholder selling his own child." He adds, "a thing which may be as common in the South, as in the East, is the infinitely worse crime of making matrimonial merchandise—or even less legitimate merchandise—of one's daughter" (ibid., 285).

What Poe seldom did in his criticism, he accomplished in his fiction. In "Ligeia," Poe's blond Lady Rowena of Tremaine is married off for money: "Where were the souls of the haughty family of the bride, when, through thirst of gold, they permitted to pass the threshold of an apartment *so* bedecked, a maiden and a daughter so beloved?" A "lady" such as Ligeia becomes the site for a crisis of racial identity. In life, Ligeia "came and departed as a *shadow*," and before her bodily "return," the narrator envisions "a *shadow* . . . such as might be fancied for the shadow of a shade." That Ligeia would not tell her lover about her family, or ever reveal her "paternal name," makes this lady sound as if she might well be Poe's rendition of the favorite fiction of white readers: the "tragic mulatta" or "octoroon mistress."[12]

In "Ligeia," Poe signals the same physiognomic traits as did taxonomists of color in the Caribbean and the South: hair, eyes, and skin. Ligeia has "the raven-black, the glossy, the luxuriant and *naturally-curling tresses*" that would be used by Stowe when describing Harry in *Uncle Tom's Cabin* and by Child in her portrayal of Rosabella in *A Romance of the Republic* and Rosalie in "The Quadroons," with her "glossy ringlets of . . . raven hair." In *A Romance of the Republic* miscegenation is safely reinscribed as nature's delightful caprice and the charming ability to speak many languages, to be mixed up or polyglot. The female products of white-and-black couplings are represented as compounds of flowers blended, shaded, or striped in "mottled and clouded" hues and color naturalized as an "autumnal leaf" or the color of a pear made golden by the sun. Here, the origin myth for the mulatta is a "tropical"—never African—"ancestry."[13]

Ligeia's eyes, like those of Creole beauties described by numerous observers, are large and expressive. But Poe goes further: "far larger than the ordinary eyes of *our own race*. They were even fuller than the fullest of the *gazelle eyes* of the tribe of the valley of Nourjahad" (emphasis added). Mabbott notes that Poe alludes "to *The History of Nourjahad* by Sidney Biddulph (Mrs. Frances Sheridan)" and then quotes from this text, which describes Nourjahad's "seraglio" as "adorned with a number of the most beautiful female slaves, . . . whom he purchased at vast expense" (Poe 1969–78, 2:332). Ligeia's sirenlike voice, the reiterated "strangeness" in her beauty, and her passion all suggest a racial heritage that would indeed be suspect, but Poe's rhapsodic and tortured circlings around the "whatness" of eyes that are linked to those of a dark tribe suggest how masterful had become the euphemisms for marks of blackness in a land preoccupied with construing purity out of impurity. If we recall Poe's elaborate, phantasmagoric decor of the bridal chamber wrought for the new bride Rowena, with its "few otto-mans and golden candelabra, of Eastern figure" (Poe 1984b, 271), we are reminded that the scene for Ligeia's resurrection is indeed a harem devoted to the memory and perpetuation of a submission far more grounded in a particular and "peculiar" institution than has previously been noted.

Could a white lady have such reiterated "wild eyes," "wild desire," "wild longing"?[14] Ligeia's "skin rivalling the purest ivory" links her further to women of color. How can you detect color in a white "suspect"? As colors faded and hair and eyes became closer to those of "pure" whites, new distinctions had to be invented. The attempt to name, label, and classify the degrees of color between the extremes of black and white resulted in fantas-tic taxonomies of a uniquely racialized enlightenment. The epistemology of whiteness, absolutely dependent for its effect on the detection of blackness, resulted in fantasies about secret histories and hidden taints that would then be backed up by explicit codes of law. And since it was not always possible to detect black blood in light skin, natural historians assured their readers that the tone of whiteness was different: unnatural, less animated, dull, or faded, white but pale or closer to yellow, with a tint from grayish yellow to yellow-ish white like ivory. This Gothic obsession with identity and origins, for example, the indeterminacy of Isabella with "dark, olive cheek" in Melville's *Pierre* ("I seem not of woman born" [Melville 1929, 213]), gets its metaphors and ambiguities from the mottled discourse of racial identity.

The return of Ligeia's spirit through the body of Rowena is heralded by the fall of "three of drops of a brilliant and ruby colored fluid" into Rowe-na's wine goblet. The "shadow" or "shade" is corporealized as drops of blood. Blood is the sign by which the spectral presence of race becomes incarnate as an ineradicable stain. What became known in the South and the Caribbean as "the law of reversion" certified the futility in trying to remove blackness, even the least molecules of black blood, by successive alliances with whites. The concept of blackness had to be reinforced, made absolute and unchangeable against the prima facie evidence of fading color, and the strategy was to call this idea *blood*. Once turned into a metaphysical attribute, blood provided a system for the classification of a mythical essence: blood equals race. Poe's Gothicism literalizes the terror in the metaphor of the blood taint. Recall the particularities of "The Masque of the Red Death": "Blood was its Avatar and its seal—the redness and the horror of blood." No longer concealed, blood breaks through the skin, the disguise or mask of whiteness, leaving "scarlet stains upon the body and especially upon the face of the victim."

Even a southern writer like Tucker in *George Balcombe* suggests, though indirectly, the horrific slippages that Poe deliberately intensifies. According to Tucker's gentlemen, a proper woman is endowed with primitive qualities that civilized society hones into generous sentiments. Docile, she learns to cherish her husband's superiority and subordinate herself to the "master feeling of her heart." A turn to God, "the great King above all gods," clinches these bonds of affection. God loves and asks nothing in return from "us helpless worms" except "our hearts" (Tucker 1836, 2:51–52, 1:71–72). Poe takes this fiction and exposes it as coordinate with the most terrifying possession. In Poe's tales about women, marriage turns what was cherished into what is scorned. In this process of reciprocal repulsions, the "Conqueror Worm" gets into the heart, "seraphs sob at vermin fangs," and as beastliness reveals itself to be the true, if concealed, ground of immaculate femininity, the Great House collapses (Poe 1984b, 269).

Poe demonstrates that just as justifications of slavery depended on making the black nonhuman and unnatural, women were also subject to the minds of men. Women would always remain on the side of the body, no matter how white, rarefied, and ethereal, or how black, earthy, and substantial. They can be hags or beauties, furies or angels. They are nothing but phantasms caught in the craw of civilization, and Poe's Gothicism literalizes the way in which racialist terminology—and the excesses of a system that depended on discourses of gender purity for its perpetuation—generated its own gods and monsters.

Getting Back to Richmond

Though Poe left Richmond in 1827, he returned home in 1835 and became editorial assistant, principal book reviewer, and finally editor of the *South-*

ern Literary Messenger. In 1830 the total population of Virginia was 1,211,405, of whom 694,300 were white, 47,348 were "free persons of color," and 469,757 were black slaves. Further, the 1820 census figures for Richmond demonstrate the high percentage of African Americans in the city of Poe's youth: about two-thirds of the households owned slaves (Wade 1964, 20). So it could be argued that Poe's Virginia was a very African place.

Nat Turner's 1831 rebellion—in Southampton, some seventy miles south of Richmond—gave rise to accounts of butchery and blood, and often to stories of the "unoffending women and children" victims. These accounts were summoned whenever the question of emancipation was raised. And since emancipation in the British West Indies had been made final in 1834, a year before Poe's return, one can imagine that many proslavery advocates found themselves faced with a double bind: rebellion or emancipation. It could be argued that people in the Virginia Tidewater knew more about the revolution in Saint-Domingue than many in the northern states, since pro-slavery newspapers and pamphlets compared "General Nat's" failed insurrection to the successful working of blood by Dessalines in Haiti in 1804, "when in one fatal night more than 1,000 of the unfortunate white inhabitants of the island of St. Domingo (men, women and children) were butchered by the Negroes!" (Warner 1971, 293–94).

Some Virginians even feared that some of the refugees of Saint-Domingue who settled in Southampton had brought their Negroes with them. "Over ten thousand émigrés from that island fled to the southern States, bringing with them new elements of fear of slave uprisings" (Eaton 1964, 90). The *Virginia Gazette and General Advertiser,* for example, published frequent accounts of women tortured by black insurgents, their eyes gouged out with corkscrews and their bellies ripped open to reveal unborn children to their dying mothers (Jordan 1968, 375–80). Although southern newspapers tended to underplay white atrocities during the last years of the war for independence, they did report General Rochambeau's use of bloodhounds from Havana, Cuba, to disembowel black prisoners in his spectacular arena set up on the grounds of the old Jesuit monastery at Cap Français. Most of the French colonists—nearly 25,000—seeking refuge in the United States ended up in Virginia, mostly in Norfolk, since, as the exiled white Martiniquan historian and lawyer Médéric Louis Elie Moreau de Saint-Méry wrote, "the inhabitants of this place have shown a constant affection for the French" (de Saint-Méry 1913, 55–56).

Poe returned to Richmond as the fear of black terror and retribution spread. Note that in the review of *Slavery in the United States,* though Poe

refers to "recent events in the West Indies" and talks of "the parallel movement here," he nowhere refers to the Nat Turner insurrection. Perhaps Poe
knew that his readers would too readily recall the Turner rebellion and
white vengeance in southeastern Virginia, the inhuman carnage that finally
cost many innocent blacks—some estimate two hundred—their lives. As
Poe worked on the *Southern Literary Messenger*, increasing circulation from
five hundred to about thirty-five hundred, what became known as the Great
Southern Reaction of the 1830s and 1840s created a closed, nearly martial
society intent on preserving its slave-based civilization.

The slave trade in the city of Richmond was active and had reached its
height in Virginia during the 1830s. Some have argued that Virginia slave-
traders enjoyed an affluence rivaled only by the tobacco merchants of the
previous century. "Prior to 1846, the Bell Tavern, on the north side of Main
just below Fifteenth, was the scene of a great many of these deplorable
spectacles" (Dabney 1976, 111). Poe must have frequently walked past the
Richmond slave market, which was only two blocks from the offices of the
Southern Literary Messenger. He doubtless witnessed slave auctions, and
experienced the terror of those led through the streets, chained in slave
coffles, readied for their journey to the Deep South. Thomas Jefferson
Randolph, nephew of Thomas Jefferson, announced in the Virginia Legislature in 1832: "The exportation has averaged 8,500 for the last twenty years.
. . . It is a practice and an increasing practice, in parts of Virginia to rear
slaves for market. How can an honorable mind, a patriot and a lover of his
country, bear to see this ancient dominion converted into one grand me-
nagerie, where men are to be reared for market, like oxen for the shambles?"
(*Workers' Writers' Program* 1940, 162).

We have evidence of Poe's relationships with the leading proslavery advocates in Virginia, but what about those variously represented in the Virginia
slavery debate of 1831–32 as "pets," "playmates of the white children," "the
merriest people in the world," "valuable property," or "monsters"? How can
we begin to think about those who left no written records but were a
constant presence, whose existence, though distorted or erased, informed
Poe's unique brand of Gothic narrative in ways that have been ignored?

Poe's guardians, the Allans, had at least three household servants (all
slaves, but at least one of these was owned by someone else and bonded to
Mr. Allan). On 1 January 1811, Mr. Allan hired a woman named Judith from
Master Cheatham for twenty-five pounds, "to be retained and clothed as
usual under a bond of 50 [fifty pounds sterling]."[15] According to some
accounts, Judith was Edgar's "Mammy"; other accounts note the names

"Juliet" and "Eudocia" mentioned in receipts and bills of sale as being in John Allan's household. Whatever her name, she sometimes took Edgar to the "Old Church on the Hill" grounds, where he spent many late afternoons. His foster mother Fanny Allan was often too ill to attend to Poe. Though we hear about Poe's dead mother Eliza and all those subsequent, surrogate pale mothers (especially Jane Stannard and Fanny Allan in Richmond), we are never reminded of the black woman in the house. When Poe was awaiting entry into West Point in 1829, living with Maria Clemm in Baltimore, he sold a slave. In April 1940, the *Baltimore Sun* published the record of the bill of sale of "a negro man named Edwin," calling it an "Item for Biographers." The article begins: "While examining some entries in an underground record room at the Courthouse a few days ago a Baltimore man who wishes his name withheld quite by chance came across an old document relating to Edgar Allan Poe, which seems thus far to have entirely escaped the poet's biographers."[16]

Many Virginia accounts of the Nat Turner rebellion blamed its occurrence on superstition and religious fanaticism. But these written accounts of the "extraordinary" beliefs of Negroes, shared by many whites, probably mattered less to Poe than his daily encounters with slaves in his own house or on the plantations he visited. Poe's Gothicism and his unique tools of terror finally have less to do with "Germany" or the "soul," as he proclaimed in the preface to his "Tales of the Grotesque and Arabesque," than with African American stories of the angry dead, sightings of teeth, the bones and matter of charms, and the power of conjuring. Such stories, merging with early Christian folk beliefs transplanted to the South, as well as the frenzy of revivals with whites and slaves caught up in the Holy Spirit, might also have encouraged the strangely sentient landscapes of Poe, his obsession with the reciprocities between living and dead, human and animal, and the possessions and demonic visitations of his best-known tales.[17]

Dialogue with the Dead

In writing *Fables of Mind: An Inquiry into Poe's Fiction* (Dayan 1987), I struggled with the philosophical and religious cruxes in Poe's tales. Philosophy meant Locke. Religion meant Calvin and Edwards. The path to enlightenment was clear. I could explain the dark hauntings, the spectral return of a Ligeia who took possession of the physical Rowena, by looking at Calvin's insistence on visibility in the flesh, Locke's paradoxes of identity, and even Newtonian mechanics. Yet what if we turn to the equally critical ground in

Poe's past, that of African American belief? In "Unspeakable Things Unspoken," Toni Morrison notes the presence, the shadow, the ghost from
which most critics have fled (1989, 12). In a world where identities wavered
between colors, where signs of whitening and darkening were quickly apprehended by all inhabitants, enlightenment depended on shadows. The
gods, monsters, and ghosts spawned by racist discourse redefined the supernatural. What the white masters called sorcery was rather an alternative
philosophy, a set of spiritual experiences shared by blacks and whites. The
most horrific spirits of the Americas were produced by the logic of the
master filtered through the thought and memory of slaves.

After "Ligeia" was published in 1839, Poe sent it to Philip Cooke and
asked whether or not the ending was intelligible. What most dismayed
Cooke about the ending was the way "the Lady Ligeia takes possession of
the deserted *quarters . . .* of the Lady Rowena." He explains, "There I was
shocked by a violation of the ghostly proprieties . . . and wondered how the
Lady Ligeia—a wandering essence—could, in quickening *the body* of the
Lady Rowena . . . become suddenly the visible, bodily, Ligeia" (Mabbott
1942, 50).[18] Consider the ending. Ligeia with her "huge masses of long and
dishevelled hair" and "wild eyes" enters and takes the place of the "fair-
haired, the blue-eyed Rowena." Seeing the quickening, risen flesh, the narrator thinks, "Can it be Rowena?" only to recognize Ligeia. Familiar with
stories of the returning dead, Poe worked them into the tale he called his
"best." The spirit so fills the living body that no trace remains of the once-
alive vessel; taken by the spirit, the body reacts. Its gestures and lineaments
conform to ghostly demands. We are no longer dealing with a narrator in a
trance, a mad person who hallucinates, a drugged murderer, but the scene
of possession. Not by a white master—the affectionate appropriator of Poe's
disputed review—but by a spirit, conjured and rising up, like Ligeia, from
quiescence to revenge.

I grew up in the South and recall the terrors that constitute knowledge,
the awful concreteness of the spirit, and theories that needed no John Locke
to reveal wandering souls or shape-shifting identities. Who are the ghosts to
drag you down? Blood on the carpet, a look at the moon that could kill you,
circumscribed by fear of women who left their skin at the door, haints more
present than the living. The question is how to bring what has been constituted as mere foolishness or worse into the study of a literary text without
turning practice into cliché, without turning African American belief into a
trope in yet another scholarly exercise. I conclude with two slave stories
recorded by Moreau de Saint-Méry, before he left Saint-Domingue for the

United States. These stories of genesis suggest that cosmologies of color were not the property of whites alone.

According to them [the blacks], God made man and he made him white; the devil who spied on him made another being just the same; but when he finished the devil found him black, by a punishment of God who did not want his work to be confounded with that of the Evil Spirit. The latter was so irritated by this distinction, that he slapped the copy and made him fall on his face, which flattened his nose and swelled his lips. Other less modest negroes say that the first man came out black from the hands of the Creator and that the White is only a negro whose color has deteriorated. (De Saint-Méry 1913, 58)

Poe's racialized Gothicism—the terrors of whiteness in Poe's *Pym*, the shadows and shades in fairyland, the blurring of privilege and perversion in tales about ladies who turn into revenants and lovers who turn into slaves—requires that we rethink the meaning of color and the making of monsters, as well as question the myths of the masters who still haunt the halls of the academy.

NOTES

A somewhat different version of this essay was published in *American Literature* 66, no. 2 (June 1994).

1. Poe, "Review of J. K. Paulding's *Slavery in the United States* and *The South Vindicated from the Treason and Fanaticism of the Northern Abolitionists*" (Poe 1979, 8:265–75). Although the review is often referred to as the "Paulding review," Bernard Rosenthal argues that it is more accurate to refer to it as the "Paulding-Drayton review," since the other book under review, *The South Vindicated from the Treason and Fanaticism of the Northern Abolitionists*, once thought to be anonymous, is known to be by William Drayton, to whom Poe dedicated his *Tales of the Grotesque and Arabesque*. See Rosenthal, 29–38. Here, I refer only to Paulding, since I believe that Poe responds primarily to his text. For my full analysis of Poe's review, see Dayan 1991.

2. Until 1941, with William Doyle Hull's claim that Beverly Tucker wrote this review, scholars did not question Poe's authorship. The review was included in Harrison's Virginia edition of Poe's work, and both Hervey Allen in *Israfel* in 1927 and Arthur Hobson Quinn in his critical biography in 1941 discuss Poe's review on slavery. The institutional erasure of Poe, slavery, and the South continues in the Library of America edition of Poe's *Essays and Reviews* (Poe 1984a), which omits the review. I cannot now discuss the argumentation for and against Poe's authorship, but direct the reader to the still unsurpassed analysis by Bernard Rosenthal cited in note 1. Rosenthal's essay remains the most convincing unraveling to date of the enigmatic review. Besides emphasizing Poe's friendship with such proslavery apologists as Dew and Tucker and his attachment, even if vexed, to the idea of Virginia aristocracy, Rosenthal demonstrates that the letter of 2 May 1836, used by Hull and others to prove Tucker's authorship of the review, must

refer to a different essay. Rosenthal demonstrates that there remains a "basic chronologi-cal inconsistency in relation to the letter and the appearance of portions of the April *Messenger* in the *New Yorker*" (31–32). For a review of Nelson's *Word in Black and White: Reading "Race" in American Literature* and my "Romance and Race" (Dayan 1991) see Ridgely 1992. Ridgely concentrates on the attribution of authorship, while boldly refus-ing to ignore that the questions these interpretations ask go beyond the issue of the "Paulding-Drayton review." This focus on a single review continues the "masking" of the more substantial socio-ontological contexts that both Dana Nelson and I have at-tempted to provide for the study of Poe's "fictions."

3. In *Notes on the State of Virginia*, Jefferson talks about the "wild and extravagant" imagination of the Negro, which, "in the course of its vagaries, leaves a tract of thought as incoherent and eccentric, as is the course of a meteor in the sky" (Jefferson 1975, 189).

4. After the Nat Turner rebellion, Virginia's legislators debated openly during January and February 1832, with antislavery spokespeople arguing for colonization of the blacks in Liberia and stressing the destructive effects of slave labor. In the end, most delegates accepted the proslavery argument that colonization was too costly to implement. It is generally agreed that Dew's expert analysis of the debates, with his conclusions and recommendations, defeated once and for all western Virginia's gradual emancipationists and ushered in a decade of repressive slave controls (the "black laws"), and expanded patrol and militia systems.

5. Some proslavery advocates, however, deprived the black even of feeling. William Beckford (not the author of *Vathek*) argued against emancipation in the West, writing that "a slave has no feeling beyond the present hour, no anticipation of what may come, no dejection at what may ensue: these privileges of feeling are reserved for the enlight-ened" (Beckford 1788, 84).

6. Besides Hegel's elaboration on "The Law of the *Heart*, and the Frenzy of Self-Conceit" (Hegel 1970, 391–400), his concept of the "beautiful soul" in his *Phenomenol-ogy of Mind* is also useful here. For Hegel the "identity" of the "beautiful soul" comes about "merely in a negative way, as a state of being devoid of spiritual character. The " 'beautiful soul' . . . has no concrete reality" (ibid., 676).

7. Note that in three hundred years the *Code noir* has not been translated into English, but most significantly, this codification of methodical divestiture remains so difficult to find that it has vanished from historiography. I first read the *Code noir* in a collection that included the additional royal edicts, 1699–1742: *Recueils de reglements, edits, declara-tions et arrêts . . . concernant le commerce, l'administration de la justice, la police des colonies françaises de l'Amérique . . . avec Le Code Noir et l'addition au dit Code.*

8. Poe then retold the story in two consecutive articles of the *Broadway Journal*. For an account of this episode, see Quinn 1941, 487–89.

9. No one has demonstrated more powerfully than Winthrop Jordan in *White over Black* how excessive sentimentality diminished the possibility of action or ethics in the antislavery program. "A romantic sentimentalism was a symptom of, and perhaps a subtle yet readily intelligible social signal for, a retreat from rational engagement with the ethical problems posed by Negro slavery" (Jordan 1968, 370–71).

10. Nelson's *Word in Black and White* (1992) came to my attention after I completed this essay. Her rigorous redefinition of "race" in both fictional and nonfictional works of

Anglo-American writers is crucial to understanding the metaphysics of whiteness, the rewriting of race as aesthetics, and the connections in America among race, romance, and nation. See especially 90–109.

11. As I have argued in "Romance and Race" (Dayan 1991), Poe's Dupin knows how to detect unadulterated barbarism, and the descriptions of the affectionate yet easily enraged orangutan who loves to mimic his master and violate women refer readers to the familiar fantasies of consanguinity between black men and apes. As Edward Long puts it in his *History of Jamaica*: "an oran-outang . . . is a human being . . . but of an inferior species . . . he has in form a much nearer resemblance to the Negroe race, than the latter bear to white men" (Long 1774, 1:103).

12. Note that the offspring of a "misalliance" between a white man and a black slave followed the condition of the mother. Under the laws trying to curb interbreeding, a light-colored woman was prohibited from using the name of her father. Especially problematic is the use of the term *mulatto*. Virginia Domínguez writes in *White by Definition: Social Classification in Creole Louisiana*, "Limited lexical options meant that the term *mulatto* was used to denote anyone who did not appear all white *or* all black" (1988, 49). In Europe and the United States, and in most of the Caribbean by the late 1700s, the general term *mulatto* was used to metonymize varying nuances of skin color and extents of blood mixture. Note, however, that colonial taxonomies were far from lexically limited; they bear witness to a frenzied nomenclature of color. According to Moreau de Saint-Méry's theoretical taxonomy of color in *Description de la partie française de l'Isle Saint-Domingue*, mulatto was one of eleven categories of 110 combinations ranked from absolute white (128 parts white blood) to absolute black (128 parts black blood), pushing the invisibility of color differentiation to fantastic extremes. Such a system not only displaced the human element from the hybrid offspring of colonial couplings, but became a desperate attempt to redefine whiteness. This analysis of rituals of color and black codes is elaborated in my *Haiti, History, and the Gods* (Berkeley: University of California Press, 1994).

13. Surely one of the most problematic uses of women by well-intentioned abolitionists was made when they converted the racist portrayal of a demonic and lascivious ape-woman into a sentimental female hero, processed as the refined, potentially salvageable, but ever fallen "tragic mulatta."

14. I am indebted here to my student Jennifer Ellis's analysis of Ligeia in her paper, "Rereading Poe's Textual Body in 'Ligeia,' and Ligeia's Body as Text: Doubling and the Racial Unconscious" (University of Arizona, December 1992).

15. I am grateful to Jean M. Mudge for this information.

16. I thank Jeffrey Savoy of the Poe Society of Baltimore for sending me this article.

17. The biography that deals most with the contact between the young Poe and slaves is Hervey Allen's *Israfel* (1927). Note that the revised, one-volume edition of *Israfel* issued in 1934 excludes these discussions of Poe and his African American surround.

18. Philip Cooke to Poe, 16 September 1839, in Poe 1966, 1:231.

Poe and Gentry Virginia

DAVID LEVERENZ

Allen Tate's remarkable 1949 essay, "Our Cousin, Mr. Poe," defines Poe as southern not only for his high sense of a writer's calling but because Poe understood better than anyone else that the modern world was going straight to hell, or to the bourgeois, commodifying North. For Tate, a culture not controlled by leisured gentlemen means Dante's *Inferno*, which Poe rewrites: a disintegration from reason and community into machine-like, alienated egotisms of the will, vampiric women, and cravings for sensations. Tate mournfully concludes, however, that Poe lacked the stylistic and moral control to be a true southern gentleman. His "early classical education and a Christian upbringing" (49) simply did not stick.

Recent southern critics have been considerably more sensitive to the patriarchal and racist idealizations in such elegizing of gentry traditions. They tend to locate Poe's southernness paradoxically and peripherally, in his marginality to gentry status. Louis Rubin links Poe's characteristic vitality of the "beleaguered intellect" to his less than legitimate status as an orphan in the home of John Allan, who himself felt alien to the Tidewater gentry and unappreciated by his wealthy uncle, William Galt. In the five years in which Allan was trying to make his mark in England, for instance, Poe was boarded out from the age of seven. His guardian also made it clear that the boy was not to be treated as a member of the family.[1] Others have made cases for Poe's southernness through his conservative, antidemocratic values. As Stuart Levine has summed them up, Poe was "a reactionary, a snob, and a racist" (Levine 1990, xxx).

Yet Tate's sense of Poe as a kind of demonic, premodernist visionary, at best a marginal or negative southerner, still holds. G. R. Thompson puts the problem succinctly: "Poe is the antebellum South's one original writer, and he is the one writer whose Southernness is suspect" (Thompson 1988, 264). Except for three glancing allusions, Richard Gray leaves Poe out of *Writing the South*, a mute testimony to Poe's flight from regional entrapment.[2] Resolutely antiprovincial in nearly every literary way, Poe spent most of his professional life moving from northern city to northern city, vainly seeking capital and cultural authority to edit an elite, five-dollar magazine for civilized gentlemen, in the spirit of Tate's ideal.[3]

The deconstructive and ideological turns of the past twenty years invite us to read Poe's southernness more thoroughly. This essay argues that Poe was more than a marginal visionary, and that the southern ideal of the gentleman plays a crucial role in his writings as well as in his life. Poe's mix of claustrophobic Gothicism, arcane reasoning, and cosmopolitan satire both exaggerates and undermines the gentry fictions of a doubly dependent postcolonial region. On the productive periphery of the emerging capitalist North, the South also produced tobacco and cotton for the world's capitalist center, in London. There John Allan came close to bankruptcy, much as William Byrd II had failed to make his London mark almost two hundred years earlier. Allan returned to inhabit the compensatory fiction that Byrd had helped establish: a paradoxical self-image of the gentleman in the provinces, proud yet touchy, cool yet combative, masterful yet keenly defensive about any slights to his honor.

In *Imagined Communities*, an influential study of the interplay between colonialism and nationalism, Benedict Anderson suggests that "tropical Gothic" is enabled by metropolitan capital, and further, that racism is a way to "play aristocrat off center court." He goes so far as to say that colonialism invented racism, as a fallback strategy to establish and maintain dominance within provincial dependence (1983, 137, 139).[4] Throughout the South, racism and slavery allowed white English emigrants to foster an Anglophilic social fiction of imitative pseudoaristocracy for squires and would-be squires, and to preserve that fiction in amber against historical change.

William Byrd II helped make Virginia the apex of the pseudoaristocracy's hegemonic arch. After his return from London in 1726, he turned life at his home at Westover into his ideal of what a planter's life in the provinces should be. Witty, urbane, civic-minded, he wrote his *History of the Dividing Line* in large part for his London friends; it was not published until 1841. Yet as Kenneth Lockridge suggests, Byrd also strove to adopt "a rigid, almost unbending set of poses" defined in part by his struggles at the margins of London's high society. His coded diary became his secret mirror to reassure him that every day, in every way, he did what gentlemen do. Not only his

179,000 acres, from which Richmond and Petersburg were created, but also his public persona as the classic Virginia patriarch secured his position at the top of the provincial gentry hierarchy, despite his enormous debts. When John Allan suddenly inherited his uncle's riches, saving him from ruin, Allan also inherited three large estates: Lower Byrd, Little Byrd, and Big Byrd.[5]

Poe inhabits and undermines gentry fictions of mastery, not least by exposing the gentleman as a fiction. Typically, he displays cultivated narrators unable to master themselves. An "imp" seems bent on their destruction, as if self-directed malevolence rather than socially virtuous benevolence constituted the "sixth sense" of Scottish moral philosophy. Or Poe celebrates masterful intellects, such as Dupin or himself, who keep resentments at bay with their powers to transcend subjectivity through mental mirroring. Poe's narratives exaggerate gentry contradictions, especially the double imperatives of cool reasoning and impulsive bravado. His tales do not simply shame gentlemen of honor; he constructs, then deconstructs, their private lives, by transgressing the great social divide between public displays of mastery and an inwardness felt as alien to oneself. Arabesques of public leisure become grotesque enslavements to obsession. Finally, Poe plays with gentry specters of a debased capitalist future to put his own indulgent yet satiric spin on nostalgia for an idealized aristocracy. He is especially keen to make textuality itself the source for true aristocracy, a status to which only his genius can pretend.

In so doing, Poe gives an American twist to the mode that Michael McKeon has labeled "extreme skepticism." To simplify the neo-Marxist argument of McKeon's *Origins of the English Novel*, the rise of the novel reflects and mediates the rise to domination of class and individualism as social categories of self-perception. Capitalist dynamics challenged traditions of status that emphasized deference, kinship, and lineage. To apply McKeon across the Atlantic a hundred years later, Poe expressed "the untenably negative midpoint between these two opposed positions" (1987, 118–19).[6] Poe negates a progressive ideology of individualism by emptying out the meaningfulness of the self as a social construct. He exposes subjectivity as a collage of derivative literary conventions and a chaos of senseless, self-destructive desires. Simultaneously, Poe negates the regressively prescriptive idealizations of the public man of honor animating Allen Tate's critique yet another century later.

To advance these arguments, I have divided my essay into four parts. The first discusses Poe's life in relation to gentry fictions and contradictions, with a look at reductive northern readings of Poe and the South. The second part considers Poe's playful textuality as his version of true aristocracy. Here I touch on "Ligeia," "The Fall of the House of Usher," and Pierre Bourdieu. In the third part, I apply my reading of gentry dynamics to a more full-scale reading of "The Man of the Crowd," with some attention to the Dupin stories and "The Cask of Amontillado." At the end, using "Hop-Frog," I consider Poe as a gentry trickster.

II

In the late fall and early winter of 1828–29, the Virginia legislature held a constitutional convention to consider the overrepresentation of Tidewater and Piedmont gentry in state politics. Resentful yeoman delegates from the West argued for representation based on the white male population, while plantation gentry delegates from the East argued that representation should also be based on property, including slaves. As the Tidewater delegates declared with special intensity, the gentry on larger plantations feared that more equal representation would slowly shift power westward. Then the great tradition of gentry leadership, symbolized by the presence of the aged James Monroe as nominal presider and James Madison as chair of the key committee, would come to an end.

John Randolph, who probably served as one of the models for Roderick Usher, delivered the climactic gentry speech. Randolph, a delicate, even effeminate man who liked to ride in an old-fashioned English coach drawn by four English Thoroughbreds, affirmed his class consciousness as clearly as the yeoman delegates voiced their class resentments. "I am an aristocrat," he liked to say. "I love liberty. I hate equality." His speech warned that stripping the gentry of privileged property status would sound the "tocsin of civil war" (Freehling 1982, 63–64). Randolph meant class war, in Virginia.

Despite Randolph's ominous invocations of Armageddon, the gentry's case for mixed-base representation lost, twice, forty-nine to forty-seven. Finally the gentry salvaged a compromise apportionment based on a favorable 1820 census, after a more progressive motion to use subsequent census reports had been defeated by a tie vote, forty-eight to forty-eight. The final vote was still a cliff-hanger: fifty to forty-six (ibid., 65–69, 70–78).

In Alison Freehling's account of these debates, *Drift toward Dissolution*, the rhetoric of the convention delegates exposes three or perhaps four Virginias: the empowered eastern gentry from Tidewater and Piedmont; the resentful artisans, farmers, and mechanics of the West; and the more heterogeneous mix in the valley, spilling over into the Piedmont region, including Richmond, the capital, right on the fall line between Piedmont and Tidewater. In Richmond, Poe's hometown and still not much more than a town, these political tensions were exacerbated by other tensions between two kinds of gentry: the old plantation elite, and newer Scottish merchants such as John Allan who were challenging the elite for economic dominance.

After Nat Turner's south Tidewater revolt in August 1831, another special legislative session was held. It ought to surprise northerners, as it did this Yankee, to learn that a great many delegates favored "expedient abolition," including Thomas Jefferson's grandson and (behind the scenes) governor John Floyd. Not one delegate declared slavery to be a positive good, though many eastern delegates proclaimed slavery indispensable to the gentry way of life. If the Virginia House had been apportioned on the 1830 census, Alison Freehling concludes, the overwhelming proabolition sentiment from the West would have brought the final tally within one vote of success. As it was, the vote was seventy-three to fifty-eight, East defeating West. Everyone agreed that abolition and the recolonization of free blacks and slaves to Liberia should be fully explored. When Jefferson's grandson was subsequently reelected, though only by ninety-five votes, this champion of abolition acknowledged that his support had come primarily from the "poorer" whites sympathetic to his unflinching position against slavery (Freehling 1982, 123–65, 201, 260–62).

In both legislative sessions, the eastern Virginia gentry seemed on the verge of losing a class war, yet preserved their power handily. The dreams of colonization soon failed; the western part of the state eventually seceded in 1861 to become West Virginia. In *Southern Capitalists*, Laurence Shore argues that again and again the gentry found ways to absorb assaults and justify its right to rule. Part of the gentry's success came from its ability to promulgate an Anglophilic fiction of leisured honor, a fiction masking often conflicting merchant, plantation, and yeoman interests.[7] It preserved the power of perhaps a twentieth of the adult white men by encouraging other white men to feel mastery over women and African Americans. Slavery gave the gentry ample time to jockey for status, while racism gave status to every white who was not a slaveholder.[8] In a still broader sense, slavery helped preserve habits of stratification and deference against the growing pressures of class consciousness and entrepreneurial individualism.

By 1830 the code was clear. Any man who owned ten or more slaves and a hundred or more acres of land—the slaves were considerably more important to the title of "master"—could aspire to gentry status. Any man with more than twenty slaves had secured his position as a gentleman. To rise higher up the ladder built on that floor of natural and human property, a man had to display his status publicly, particularly through rituals of virility: "Fighting, horse racing, gambling, swearing, drinking, and wenching," as Bertram Wyatt-Brown describes young men's mutual testing (Wyatt-Brown 1982, 164).[9] At the same time, a man had to embody a persona of cool, dispassionate, civic-minded reasonableness.

It was not simply a matter of conscious role-playing and masquerading, Wyatt-Brown argues, that made southerners so famously touchy about their virility. Southern men lived their code of honor as a constant test of manhood (Wyatt-Brown 1982, 35). In the North, normative middle- and upper-class families forsook the rod to internalize self-control through conscience and guilt. Virginia gentry families encouraged contentious acting out, with shame, not guilt, as the mediating agent for social control. It did not draw much comment when a professor at the University of Virginia was hit with a slingshot by a student who then tried to bite off the teacher's thumb. During one of the riots in the school's first year, 1825—Poe enrolled the next year—a student tossed a bottle filled with urine through a professor's window.[10] Nose pulling among adult males was an instantaneous invitation to a duel. In Poe's short story "The Business Man," a shyster narrator signals his plunge toward dishonor by mentioning that he tried and failed to get someone to pull his nose. The exceptionally large-nosed narrator of "Lionizing" loses his duel for prestige to a baron with no nose at all—which meant it could not be pulled.[11]

Incipient class conflicts and diffuse social tensions could be subsumed in this ideology of patriarchal, hierarchical honor, with its contradictory dynamics of deference and strutting, dignified gentility and combative competitiveness. Steven M. Stowe details the intricate dance of decorum and insults that led to the death of Hawthorne's friend, Representative Jonathan Cilley, in an 1838 duel (1987, 38–49). It was a resolutely public decorum, as Stowe emphasizes, and a derivative one as well, since it explicitly upgraded the English squire to lordly status with a variety of classical models for civic conduct. George Washington invented himself as that remote, dollar-bill facade by emulating his text for true virtue, Joseph Addison's *Cato*. Addison's play, which he probably read rather than saw, depicts a heroic Roman who mastered all personal passions to achieve lasting honor through dedication to public duty. Such assiduous self-fashioning to prepare a man for civic leadership depends on burying unpresentable feelings "living in the tomb" (Poe 1984b, 98) of self-mastery, much as the social hierarchy stifled potential challenges from slaves, women, or men with creative imaginations.[12]

In his life, Poe frequently adopted the poses of the southern gentleman and his alienated intellectual double, the Byronic poet, often to near parodic excess. At the University of Virginia, the most expensive school in the nation, his extravagant aping of gentry manners ran up at least two thousand dollars in debts in just one year. As Kenneth Silverman's biography displays, Poe also vacillated among the contradictory expectations of gentry roles. He could be charming and courtly with the ladies, including female poets; a bantam cock in contending with his male literary peers; a dandy wearing abstruse learning on his fastidious sleeve; a heavy if intermittent drinker. Only in his seemingly asexual relations with women, including his sisterly wife (appropriately named "Virginia"), did Poe fail to comply with the basic model set by William Byrd so long ago, and present near at hand in John Allan's illegitimate twins. Otherwise Poe loved to brag about his physical prowess, emulating Byron's swimming feats and sometimes inflating his remarkable running broad jump of twenty feet six inches at the university (Silverman 1991, 30, 123, 197, 332).[13]

Not infrequently, Poe conspicuously lost self-control. He prompted at least two fistfights, and launched a full-scale libel suit after the second one, when two men impugned his virility in print. One said Poe was an impotent coward, a forger, and a plagiarist who could not hold his liquor and reneged on his debts. The other published a parodic "Literati" sketch describing Poe as "about 5 feet 1 or two inches, perhaps 2 inches and a half," instead of his actual five feet eight inches (Silverman 1991, 93, 289–91, 307–15, 327–28). For any southern man attuned to honor and reputation, these were fighting words.

Michael Allen has emphasized Poe's "acquired Southern values and haughty temperament" as one of his key strategies to secure aristocratic status for gentleman poets (1969, 201). Poe's journalism also fed the market's avidity for fighting words.[14] As Poe confidently told the first magazine publisher who employed him, Virginians thought they wanted "simplicity" but really enjoyed what the English magazines supplied: sensational subjects in a heightened style (Silverman 1991, 101). Poe's Eurocentric role as a cosmopolitan man of letters rather than provincial apologist seemed grossly ungentlemanly, especially to the writers he gored. His "tomahawking" reviews lacked southern courtesy, tact, or generosity, William Gilmore Simms tried to tell Poe ten years after receiving one of the tomahawks (Rubin 1989, 131). Yet Virginia gentry contradictions impelled his choice of weapons in his fight to fulfill his enormous desire for a high-status literary reputation. In creating "sensations" through his pugnacious reviews, Poe acted the adolescent Hotspur, while his otherworldly poems presented him as a Byronic southern Hamlet.

From a distance, the contradictions and derivativeness in Poe's behavior seem less striking than the childishness. This too was conventional. One of Emerson's most supercilious journal entries records his response to a young "snippersnapper" from the South who "demolished me" in public (Emerson 1982, 170). The southerner, he vengefully mused on 8 October 1837, is "a spoiled child . . . a mere parader. . . . They are mere bladders of conceit. . . . Their question respecting any man is like a Seminole's, How can he fight? In this country, we ask, What can he do? His pugnacity is all they prize, in man, dog, or turkey." Emerson's comparisons reduce the southerner to a child, an Indian, a turkey, or just hot air, filling "bladders of conceit."[15]

Venting his own conceits on southern heads restores Emerson's dignity. More subtly, his sense of North-South power relations emerges through clashing ideals of manliness, as Emerson's most telling phrase, "In this country," intimates. The phrase sets two postcolonial regions on a collision course. Yet New England, or "we," represents the only true country. We have men who do and talk, not children who fight and parade. New England has "civil educated . . . human" adults, Emerson says elsewhere in the entry; southerners act like Indian braves and barnyard brats. In later journal meditations, Emerson sometimes worries that the southern politician's "personality" and "fire" will dominate northerners in Washington (Emerson 1982, 411). At bottom, however, he has the calm of an absentee landlord. As he wrote in May–June, 1846, if the southerner "is cool & insolent" while northerners "are so tame," "it is because we own you, and are very tender of our mortgages, which cover all your property" (ibid., 358).

Emerson's landlord presumption helps explain Poe's vitriolic attacks on the Boston literati, especially Longfellow. Repeatedly asserting his public "personality" with "fire," Poe accuses Longfellow of gross plagiarism as well as bad writing. In the context of Emerson's entry, the controversy dramatizes two regional codes for the gentleman. On the Virginia side, an ambitious, insecure provincial aggressively lords it over his big-city betters. On the Massachusetts side, both Emerson and Longfellow attempt to respond with a studied calm, at least in public. One of the most astonishing moments in Silverman's biography comes after Poe's death, when Longfellow actually visits Poe's beloved mother-in-law, "Muddy" Clemm, tells her that Poe had been the greatest man living, and invites her to visit him in Cambridge, which she does.[16] Longfellow's generosity went far beyond Emerson's public serenity and private snottiness.

Emerson's South-baiting anticipates a recurrent note in criticism of Poe's work: a thinly disguised critical disdain for the writer's poses and posturings. Harold Bloom all but accuses Poe of being unmanly: he "fathered precisely nothing" (1985, 5), and his criticism was right only about silly women writers, for whom he was "a true match" (ibid., 12). These innuendoes buttress Bloom's claim that, like others in the South, Poe preferred "the Abyss" to the strong Emersonian self (ibid., 11). Such snide strictures about unmanly behavior and weak writing miss Poe's exaggerations of gentry postures. Bloom's New England mode of high seriousness about the self also misses Poe's profoundly skeptical play with social fictions of self-making. What Bloom calls the Abyss needs to be historicized rather than dismissed.

A complementary New England tradition searches for the presence of secret guilt in Poe's writings. In the late 1950s, for instance, Harry Levin first suggested that Poe displaced concerns about slavery onto blackness, and that "The Fall of the House of Usher" can be read as an allegory of feudal plantation culture in its death throes (1958, 160). The latter still seems right. One could expand Levin's insight, using Rhys Isaac's *Transformation of Virginia*, since the web-work of fungi defining both Roderick's house and Roderick's hair parallels the gentry's fashionable display of twining vines on their plantations, modeled on English country houses (1982, 35–39). Even so, the sociological allegory remains just what Daniel Hoffman says it is: a "ripple of meaning" (1972, 315–16), more tangential than primary to the hyperliterary vortex that disorients the narrator's senses.

Psychoanalytic investigations of incest have yielded at last to more sophisticated explorations of Poe's mourning for lost mothering. But postabolitionist expectations of hidden gentry guilt about slavery continue to shape northern attitudes to the South as well as to Poe. I was first disabused of the presumption of such guilt when reading a diary entry written by a young Englishman who visited a Virginia plantation in the 1780s. Robert Hunter's day began with Montesquieu, then tea, then fun with friends. At the end of the day, "we supped en famille, played some tricks at cards, gave the Negroes an electrical shock, and went to bed at eleven" (May 1976, 136).

Faced with moments like that, modern democratic certainties about slavery and guilt falter. Various of Poe's writings reflect a pervasive gentry opinion that humans with black skins were less than human, though other tales, such as "The Man that Was Used Up" or "The Gold Bug," can be read more ironically at the gentry's expense. Critics who have read a great many southern diaries report with some wonder that slaves and free black people are rarely mentioned, even in passing.[17] If Poe's scrabbling, marginal life intermittently imitates gentry codes of behavior, his fictions put his culture's greater fictions at risk.

In *Life on the Mississippi*, Mark Twain inflates a cultural insight as well as the power of writers when he blames Sir Walter Scott for having caused the Civil War (Twain 1980, chaps. 40, 46). Scott's model of medieval chivalry provided only one of many sources for the gentlemanly roles encouraged by the Anglophilic fiction of patriarchal honor. George Washington might read Cato, and James Madison might read Roman histories, but when the Virginia squires turned antisocial enough to read at all, they were most likely to pick up *Tom Jones*.[18] Most members of the gentry lived the fictions they rarely read. After learning to read his culture, Poe shifted the ground and raised the stakes for the game of being a provincial gentleman.

III

Pierre Bourdieu's *Distinction* can help situate Poe's writings in their post-aristocratic context, beyond dismissive Yankee dichotomies of childish versus adult, play versus high seriousness, Abyss versus self. Bourdieu's presumption that court society persisted in the Parisian *haute bourgeoisie* of the 1960s has considerably more applicability to antebellum Virginia than to the contemporary United States. In a postaristocratic society, he argues, "cultural capital" secures and conveys the highest social status. Aesthetic aptitude "rigorously distinguishes the different classes" (1984, 40) by dividing the naive from the sophisticated. Aesthetic detachment brings distinction: "a distant, self-assured relation to the world" (ibid., 56).

Bourdieu's emphasis on the uses of cultural capital to gain social distinction seems to have almost nothing to say about the flagrantly anti-intellectual behavior of many members of the antebellum southern gentry. As William Gilmore Simms memorably concluded, being a southern intellectual was as rewarding as "drawing water in a sieve" (Faust 1977, 148). Despite the examples of Washington, Madison, Jefferson, and others, cultural capital flowed more from cock fighting than from the writing of poems. To apply Bourdieu's principles is to expose the pseudoaristocratic norms generating the South's postaristocratic stratification. Beginning with his youthful pose as a Byronic poet, Poe sought relatively conventional ways of aggrandizing his marginal status through cultural capital, or at least literary image making, much as Simms and other intellectuals invoked Byronic genius to exaggerate their feelings of exile and dislocation. Only Poe, however, took a decisive step beyond provincial conventions of cultural capital, by making textuality itself the source of true aristocracy.

One of Bourdieu's most provocative passages illuminates the sheer sport accompanying Poe's textual poses. "The *petit bourgeois* do not know how to play the game of culture as a game. They take culture too seriously to go in for bluff or imposture or even for the distance and casualness which show true familiarity." Because such people anxiously identify cultural capital with the accumulation of knowledge, Bourdieu continues, "they cannot suspect the irresponsible self-assurance, the insolent off-handedness and even the hidden dishonesty presupposed by the merest page of an inspired essay on philosophy, art or literature. Self-made men, they cannot have the familiar relation to culture which authorizes the liberties and audacities of those who are linked to it by birth" (1984, 330–31).[19]

If we transpose these observations from fact to wish-fulfillment, we have the right context in which to explain a wide range of Poe's literary styles, from his plagiarisms to his critical panache to his fascination with style itself. His claims for beauty and aesthetic purity against the New England heresies of the didactic and the moral exalt abstracted intellectual control to an invulnerably elite status, beyond any taint of subjectivity or bourgeois values. Poe's intellectual audacities and insolent irresponsibilities authorize the rebirth of his family romance, much as the narrator of "Ligeia" invokes "Romance" to preside over his first marriage, which gave him both upward mobility and the adoration of a learned, passionate parent-spouse. No longer one who was born in Boston of disreputable parents in the theater, Poe uses his offhanded familiarity with European cultural capital to leap beyond the Virginia squirearchy. Using textuality as capital, he transforms mourning and marginality into the kind of cultural play that signifies aristocratic status.

One can see this, for instance, in Poe's intellectual strutting, the leisured glitter of high-culture allusions unmaking their meanings. From Mallarmé and Baudelaire to Derrida and Lacan, Poe has been cherished in France for just what normatively American readers—even expatriates such as James and Eliot—try to reduce to adolescent posturing: his hoaxie-Poe trickeries, his melodramas of intellectual excess, the mind games. Poe fuses the bogus with the serious. His moments of maximum horror are also moments of maximum literary artifice. "MADMAN! I TELL YOU THAT SHE NOW STANDS WITHOUT THE DOOR!" (Poe 1984b, 335). Capital letters—a typographical frisson as well as a cry. "Madman"—a more startling surprise, since mad Roderick now accuses the commonsensical narrator of having lost his senses. But "without the door"?

The meanings surge in, to be sure. The "tottering of his lofty reason upon her throne" prefigured in Roderick's rhapsodic poem about "monarch Thought" (ibid., 326) culminates in a further confusion of "his" and "her," as Madeline falls "heavily inward upon the person of her brother" (ibid., 335). In this Gothic plantation house, being a (male) "person" depends not only on property and patriarchal lineage, but also on internal doors that divide honor and reason from passions and the body. In Roderick's poem, a "throng" of forces (ibid., 327) imagined as lower class and chaotic overwhelms the house of the rational mind from within. Now the assault returns as the still more intimate threat of a dead-undead sister who falls inward on the dichotomies that have constructed some persons and dispossessed others. Madeline's body, too, has lost its "door," suggesting both coffin and hymen, and further implying incest. Yet "without" sounds ridiculously hyperliterary, as if Roderick had become spellbound by the "Mad Trist." The climactic moment's linguistic posturing undercuts its Hawthornean proliferation of meanings.[20] The horror builds on a pun; the pun trumpets textuality.

What Poe exposes in such moments, and they are legion, is a sudden Lacanian estrangement from words themselves. The reader's mind—like the narrator's—has been reduced to an infant's cribbed gazing, as if the endless incomprehensibility of big people's overly big words buzzes about a vacuum of staring. Poe does not make readers feel adult, the way Hawthorne and Emerson can do. Instead of offering complex self-reflexiveness, Poe builds to disorienting theatrics of helplessness or mastery, in which language itself becomes alien and theatrical. In Louis A. Renza's fine phrase, Poe's stories are "self-distracting artifacts" (Renza 1985, 82).

If the pleasure in aesthetic detachment consists of "refined games for refined players," as Bourdieu puts it (1984, 499), Poe's erudition ostensibly intensifies the sense of "membership and exclusion" on which distinction depends.[21] Yet his texts grossly flirt with the vulgar. His gentlemen come to look like apes and criminals. Although the elevated style of Poe's narratives keeps lay readers at a respectful distance, just as Bourdieu says it should do in *Language and Symbolic Power* (1991, 152–53), the narratives undercut their own philosophical dignity by employing excessive artifice as well as grotesquely shameful characters. Not by accident has Poe's work become most honored in France, the greatest postaristocratic residuum in the Western world. Poe's theatrics of horror also circulate as mass-market cultural capital. Contemporary opposition between "high" and "vulgar" uses of Poe can be historicized as a dynamic embedded in his own uses of aristocracy, toward the end of the long historical moment that challenged the social constructions legitimating aristocracy as the ultimate symbol of high status.

For Poe and the gentry, aristocracy signifies an idealized realm dislocated from specific social contexts. Like Romance, it functions as what Michael McKeon calls an antithetical simple abstraction, used to elevate high culture above history. If the romance of the gentleman displaces a yearning for high metropolitan status, its theatricality signals self-consciousness about social conventions that were beginning to seem more alien than natural (McKeon 1987, 45–46, 168–89). Unlike the gentry's chivalric posturings, Poe's aristocratic textuality intimates not simply a muted inauthenticity but its own self-destruction.

In the opening paragraph of "Ligeia," for instance, Poe flamboyantly transfers aristocratic status from property, lineage, and kinship to a world elsewhere in the pure textuality of Romance. The narrator declares his transcendent mastery of cultural capital by not being able to remember any details that linked his adored first wife to the world, not even her paternal name. He recalls the full name, place, and kin of his despised second wife, "Lady Rowena Trevanion, of Tremaine," without effort. In subverting the traditional underpinnings of aristocracy, Poe exalts his narrator's conception of true aristocracy as abstractly textual. Like Roderick Usher, the world's first abstract expressionist painter, Poe's narrator implies that the highest status can come only from an art of aesthetic detachment, with no sordid connections to family, money, bodies, or social status.

Yet "Ligeia" becomes a story about inheritance, property, and various kinds of "will": Ligeia's will to resist and conquer death; Ligeia's will bequeathing vast riches to a narrator seemingly above such concerns; the will of faceless, spiritless Rowena's family, who "permitted" their daughter to marry him "through thirst of gold" (Poe 1984b, 270). Most undecidably, the hidden will of the antipatriarchal narrator may have led him to the ultimate patriarchal act of killing one or both wives. Cynthia Jordan suggests that the narrator may have willed Ligeia's death and carried it out, the act being hidden from his consciousness as well as his narrative (1989, 135–39).[22] One need not go that far to see that the narrator deconstructs as well as dishonors his own subjectivity. He presents himself first as an antipatrilineal exaltation of childish dependence on textuality, personified as Mother Wisdom, then as two incompatible versions of possessed destructiveness: a drugged, hallucinating murderer, or a medium for a demonic woman's will. In either case, the narrator has been reduced to a craving for two black eyes.

"The essential Poe fable," writes Michael Davitt Bell, "is a tale of compulsive self-murder" (1980, 99). Placing Poe's dramas of self-murder in their gentry context highlights Poe's transgression of the gendered border between public and private life. In the vortex of Poe's yearning skepticism about aristocratic status, female self-empowerment becomes an alien signifier for contradictory psychological and social meanings: uncontrollable passions, and uncontrollable patriarchal decay. Poe's tales of self-murder expose gentlemen in private, often doing and being done to by women, whose bodies if not voices struggle to be felt at the tales' destructive centers. "Berenice, "The Fall of the House of Usher," and "Ligeia" can be read not only as allegories of the male psyche's attempts to confront the inward female, but as deconstructions of how antebellum gentry culture produced the categories of "gentleman" and "lady" along with its production of the more starkly binary opposition, "black" and "white."

IV

My argument implies the paradox that we can tease out Poe's historicity more fruitfully through the seemingly ahistorical linguistic pleasures celebrated in Poe's long-running French connection than through an analysis of his conscious southern values, his unconscious childhood or social guilts, or his indirect dramatizations of master-slave issues. As a self-made aristocrat, Poe uses textuality to improve his status while subverting the meanings of status stratification. Poe's best tales invite an undecidable doubleness of interpretation, pointing simultaneously to idealized gentry traditions of aristocratic contemplation and demonized mass-market conditions for literary production.

Four stories from the early and mid-1840s illustrate Poe's making and unmaking of gentry meanings. "The Man of the Crowd" (1840), "The Murders in the Rue Morgue" (1841), "The Purloined Letter" (1845), and "The Cask of Amontillado" (1846) each dramatize a gentleman down on his luck, who sees a modern urban world threatening the hierarchies on which he depends for social status. Each man tries to resurrect his sense of mastery, or self-respect, with what amounts to a solo duel. A displaced clash between northern and southern values frames the success or failure of each duel. Or rather, the stories present the northern future as versions of Allen Tate's myth of the Fall into a rootless chaos of mobile urban masses avid for sensations. Perhaps not surprisingly, most modern critics read these stories—especially "The Man of the Crowd"—forward into 42nd Street, not backward into gentry Virginia.

The first half of "The Man of the Crowd," as almost every critic has noted, presents what seems "a stable hierarchy" of descending social types, all "based on an aristocratic set of assumptions," in Jonathan Auerbach's words (1989, 28).[23] The narrator begins as a conventional man of the Enlightenment, classifying "the tumultuous sea of human heads" outside his coffeehouse window with "abstract and generalizing" observations (Poe 1984b, 389). Soon he "descended to details," in order to produce a hierarchy of types. His first two groups set the standard for "the decent," or what he later calls "gentility." Strangely, his details disorient the stability of the hierarchy he thinks he asserts.

The first large group "had a satisfied business-like demeanor," the narrator summarizes. Yet "their brows were knit, and their eyes rolled quickly," whenever they felt pushed. Nevertheless, showing "no symptom of impatience," they "adjusted their clothes and hurried on." To say "symptom" rather than "sign" implies that any sign of feeling, especially annoyance, betokens disease and disorder. Even at the top of the social hierarchy, bodies betray what adjusted clothes conceal, while a "business-like demeanor" belies gentility (Poe 1984b, 389).

The second large group of "the decent" intensifies the tension between bodies and self-control. These people seemed "restless," with "flushed faces," "muttering" and redoubling "their gesticulations" when the crowd impeded them. They bowed "profusely" when jostled, "and appeared overwhelmed with confusion." Having said all that, the narrator finds "nothing very distinctive about these two large classes." Their clothes enable him to blend "two classes" into one class: "Their habiliments belonged to that order which is pointedly termed the decent" (ibid.).

Already contradictions abound. Two hierarchized groups, or classes, are really one class; men who have businesslike self-control also have bodies out of control; the narrator defines them as the standard, yet those who represent the standard have "nothing very distinctive" about them; decent clothes stabilize perception, yet behavior seems on the edge of both hotheadedness and excessive deference. Moreover, the word *habiliments* implies a dressing up for public display, as if looking decent requires a facade.

Next he undermines the division he has tried to reestablish. "They were undoubtedly noblemen, merchants, attorneys, tradesmen, stock-jobbers— the Eupatrids and the commonplaces of society—men of leisure and men actively engaged in affairs of their own—conducting business upon their own responsibility. They did not greatly excite my attention." A finely tuned, five-rank hierarchy briefly supplants the two groups. Clearly "noble-men" are at the top, while "stock-jobbers" and "tradesmen" are at the bottom. But where do "merchants" and "attorneys" go? Where did John Allan fit, in London? With "Eupatrids," or with "commonplaces"?

Eventually, the dichotomy between "leisure" and "business" all but disappears. At least, the narrator forces a paradox: only leisured noblemen and Eupatrids truly exhibit "a satisfied business-like demeanor." The actual men of business, from merchants on down, look increasingly unsatisfied and anxious. On the other hand, even stock-jobbers threaten the edge of true gentility. No wonder all this bores him; to analyze it would be to expose gentility as both normative and nonexistent.

The narrator has already described himself in doubled terms, as a leisured gentleman at his coffeehouse, recovering from illness, on the edge between ennui and happiness, pain and pleasure, looking at "two dense and continuous tides of population." Now he has come close to emptying out his simplifying dichotomies. Worse, he also implies that only clothes can be "read" without contradiction. His act of reading, and only his act of reading, makes gentility seem stable and commanding. At the top, not one person he sees inhabits that category without ambiguity, either between clothes and body movements or between business and leisure. The narrator's reading of types shows him not only imposing an uninhabited yet hegemonic social abstraction, the ideal gentleman, but reinventing the fiction with greater and greater assurance as his types deviate from his imagined norm.

Such ambiguities characterize a pseudoaristocrat, in terms close to those used in Richard Gray's history of the gentleman-planter ideal in early Virginia. As "a compound of gracious feudal patriarch and bluff English squire," the planters were "always primarily businessmen" and "entrepreneurs," yet "anxious to assume the trappings of an aristocracy." In the early nineteenth century, those who sought to inhabit that contradictory, imported ideal were "a conscious and declining minority," as the two constitutional conventions in Richmond signify (Gray 1986, 9, 12–13, 23). The narrator's assessment of London's two standard-bearing groups expresses tensions in Virginia, not only in status ranking and class conflict but among hotheadedness, deference, and respectability.

Two more Virginia gentry tensions intensify as the narrator describes London's lower orders. First, he scorns the ungenteel, yet relishes their attempts at upward mobility. Second, he shows inordinate contempt for men who work with their hands, while he defines women who work as prostitutes in the making. Significantly, the words "gentility," "gentlemen," and "gentry" do not appear except as stabilizing fictions of scheming aspiration for the hopelessly deviant. On "the scale of what is termed gentility" (Poe 1984b, 391), various groups display "idiosyncratic" efforts to "be mistaken for gentlemen." Junior clerks who "wore the cast-off graces of the gentry," and senior clerks with the "affectation of respectability" (ibid., 390), struggle without success to measure up. Further down the scale, the narrator comfortably calls pickpockets "these gentry," and gamblers "gentlemen who live by their wits" (ibid.). Their fraudulence licenses his mocking labels while subtly exposing the cultural fiction.

Then come "Jew pedlars," street beggars, invalids, and at last, women, all of whom work: "modest young girls returning from long and late labor," who shrink "more tearfully than indignantly" from presumably leering and lustful men. The girls' lack of anger signals their coerced, sexualized future in the world's oldest profession, already paraded by "women of the town . . . [their] interior[s] filled with filth," and the "paint-begrimmed beldame," no better than an "utterly lost leper in rags" (ibid., 391). Women who use their bodies for money—what worse violation of patriarchal protectiveness could there be?

Only one type is in fact lower on the narrator's scale: white men who work with their hands. Here Virginia gentry values become most manifest, diverging strikingly from urban class consciousness. Subhumans—that is, slaves or animals—should do physical labor. But the narrator sees a disorienting profusion of workers, none of whom seems to have the slightest regard for gentility: "pie-men, porters, coal-heavers, sweeps; organ-grinders, monkey-exhibitors and ballad-mongers, those who vended with those who sang; ragged artizans and exhausted laborers of every description, and all full of a noisy and inordinate vivacity which jarred discordantly upon the ear, and gave an aching sensation to the eye." What would excite Walt Whitman, romantic "artizans" who sell and sing, makes the narrator feel depersonalized—"the ear," "the eye"—as well as "jarred" and aching, pushed against by the crowd for the first time, through his glass window. "As the night deepened," and the crowd's "harsher" features displaced the "gentler" and "more orderly portion of the people," he felt almost enslaved by "wild" light upon blackness: "All was dark yet splendid—as that ebony" of Tertullian's; it all "enchained me . . . to the glass" (Poe 1984b, 392).

"To work industriously and steadily, especially under directions from another man," wrote Frederick Law Olmsted in 1861 in *The Cotton Kingdom*, "is, in the Southern tongue, to 'work like a nigger' " (1984, 19). William Byrd II anticipated the danger of this attitude in a 1736 letter: slaves "blow up the pride and ruin the industry of our white people, who, seeing a rank of poor creatures below them, detest work for fear it should make them look like slaves" (Simpson 1989). Not surprisingly, then, Poe's narrator brings closure to his list of social types by sliding from manual labor down to blackness. As Olmsted later pointed out, members of the Virginia gentry typically denied their immigrant origins as indentured servants, "tinker and tailor, poacher and pickpocket." Lacking true "manners" and "lineage," most wealthy planters struck him as more "ridiculously" pretentious than Fifth Avenue's "newly rich . . . absurdly ostentatious in entertainment, and extravagant in the purchase of notoriety" (1984, 562–63). While Olmsted's assessment exudes an Emersonian scorn at the edges, Poe's narrator confirms the young traveler's sense of the inauthenticity of the gentry.[24]

A progressive reading of "The Man of the Crowd" could build an incipient class conflict here. Only the workers reject upward mobility toward the culture's hegemonic fiction of "the decent" as a mode of self-definition, and only the workers teem with vital, singing, romanticized life. Threatened into individuality and class consciousness by such a spectacle, so the argument could run, Poe's narrator experiences "a craving desire" to keep in view the strange old man who embodies the now "wild" extremes of the crowd, as if class conflict could be avoided by reading the man's compounded energy. But the story quickly abandons workers to their "temples of Intemperance" (Poe 1984b, 396). The old man's unreadable idiosyncrasy prefigures urban anomie, not class war. Wearing dirty yet beautifully textured linen, hiding a diamond and a dagger, anomalous to every category yet rushing from aloneness, the old man reduces progressive readings of individuality and class to a spectacle of unresolvable contradictions. He, too, is a self without subjectivity.

To the narrator, the old man represents something much more unsettling than one of the urban homeless produced and abandoned by capitalist dynamics. As the narrator's double, the old man represents the contradictions already half-voiced at the generative center of the gentry hierarchy. In provincial Virginia, the display of face and clothes required not only a collective fiction of gentry honor and shaming rituals, but also an envious, imitative group of white men below the elite, a petty bourgeoisie of clerks, schemers, and frauds, as the narrator contemptuously describes their urban equivalent. Otherwise, the gentry's pseudoaristocratic pretensions would lose cultural legitimacy.

Finally, the narrator's traditional status orientation blocks his ability to read "crime" in the modern way, as individual guilt. Rather, the narrator defines crime as a refusal to be alone. The old man's wild behavior continually animates yet empties out progressive and regressive readings of his motives, because his mobility seems neither downward nor upward, but rather a simple and continuous desire *to belong* to a group, any group. At the interface between two comprehensive, antagonistic modes of social knowing, the old man comes to represent the narrator's own fear of solitary individuality.

Trying to regain interpretive mastery, the narrator conflates the old gentry role of duelist with the new lower-class role of gumshoe detective, unwittingly mirroring the contradictory mix of diamond and dagger in the old man's clothes. His self-stabilizing abstraction of gentility disappears in his increasingly frenzied bodily behavior, just as the opening details about him anticipate. The narrator ends in the doubled place of the title figure, on the other side of the glass. Moreover, he all but dares genteel readers to "read" either man of the crowd better than he can, by proclaiming at the beginning and the end that his story "does not permit itself to be read." As the readers puzzle themselves about that, he tauntingly solicits their own craving to fend off their self-deconstruction.

What Auerbach nicely calls Poe's characteristically disembodied first-person self that lacks a self (1989, 21) also fits M. Dupin, whose interpretive mastery depends on his ability to empty out his subjectivity and make his mind exactly congruent with that of his opponent. Sociologically, Dupin seems ripe for intense status anxiety. "The Murders in the Rue Morgue" introduces him as a "young gentleman" who "had been reduced to such poverty that the energy of his character succumbed beneath it, and he ceased to bestir himself in the world" (Poe 1984b, 400). Where conventional gentlemen would feel humiliated and vengeful, Dupin merely uses his small "patrimony" to live as a leisured, bookish gentleman, drawing the narrator into a world of his own. Soon, however, he becomes "enamored of the Night," with her "sable divinity." The pliable narrator yields to Dupin's "wild whims," much as the loyal friend of Roderick Usher feels insensibly caught up. The two men "counterfeit" the night by day in their "grotesque mansion," and then walk the streets in "true Darkness" to seek an "infinity of mental excitement" (ibid., 401). If the night is a black, beautiful woman, then out of wild womanly blackness, like an uncanny womb, comes Dupin's analytic vitality.

As Jordan points out, Dupin's receptivity to androgynous images gives him mental resources beyond those of conventionally socialized people (1989, 145–49). When he was at the highest pitch of observation, Dupin seemed "a double Dupin—the creative and the resolvent." He became "frigid and abstract; his eyes were vacant in expression"; his voice, usually "a rich tenor" though with an oddly "low chuckling laugh," sometimes "rose into a treble," and he looked at ordinary men as if they "wore windows in their bosoms." His doubled or emptied subjectivity gives Dupin the ability to reconstruct the behavior of orangutans, or outfox men of genius.

The argument for Dupin as an androgynous figure can be joined with John Irwin's analysis of Dupin as a "fallen aristocrat" (Irwin 1992, 205).[25] In my reading, he taps alternative, subversive sources of intellectual power in blackness and femaleness only when those qualities have been abstracted and textualized. A contemporary critical tendency to dichotomize these moments in Poe as a struggle between masculine and feminine modes needs to be situated more particularly in relation to the antebellum gentry's construction of gender and racial dichotomies. Dupin appropriates blackness and womanly night not to attack masculinity but to remasculinize his mental powers as a gentleman of leisure, in a world that disempowered that gentry role. Transforming marginality into intellectual mastery, Dupin becomes the letter and spirit of pure reasoning, with just a touch of revenge.

At the climax of the second tale, the armchair gentleman defeats his unwitting double and adversary, Minister "D——," by substituting a "letter," to the book-length delight of Lacanian and Derridean critics. Dupin's success depends on his ability to be a poet and mathematician, a mirror for the minister's mind, and a duelist without the minister's knowledge. As in "The Man of the Crowd," a gentleman seeks to read, which is to say master, a character at the center of social dynamics, either urban life or court politics. Unlike the earlier story's narrator, Dupin triumphs, with no less than a gunshot. The musket's explosion not only lures the minister to the window, enabling Dupin to substitute his letter, but also signals the symbolic culmination of the "solo duel." In patiently waiting to avenge himself for an insult long forgotten by his dupe, Dupin fulfills gentry expectations about honor and shame. At the same time, as if to reverse Irwin's ingenious explication of "low-to-high" associations in the tale, Dupin debases ritualistic dueling to the level of mobocracy on the streets. Moreover, the musket proves "to have been without ball" (Poe 1984b, 697).

"The Cask of Amontillado" similarly turns on a duelist, one with a more ambiguously successful revenge. Though the story is displaced to Renaissance Italy, Montresor's grievances reflect gentry tensions between old and new money, subsumed in a rhetoric of honor. Like Dupin, Montresor has borne the "thousand injuries of Fortunato" with suppressed resentment. Then a nameless "insult" spurs Montresor to plan revenge (ibid., 848). Luring his unwitting antagonist by asking whether a wine is genuine or fraudulent, Montresor describes Fortunato as a successful social fraud, like the new men who have merely "adopted" enthusiasm about wine in order "to practice imposture upon the British and Austrian millionaires" (ibid.). Yet Fortunato cannot quite be reduced to such a category, at least in wines. "In painting and gemmary, Fortunato, like his countrymen, was a quack," presumably practicing his arts on rich foreigners. But "in the matter of old wines he was sincere." Wearing carnival "motley," with "a tight-fitting parti-striped dress" and "conical cap and bells" (ibid.). Fortunato fits all modern convivial occasions, as a man of "fortune" should, yet with motley ties to the old aristocratic order.

Montresor lives on the edge of his social category, but not by choice. Like Dupin, he is a fallen aristocrat, barely able to hold on to his palazzo; unlike Dupin, his dignity lies only in his past. His sense of the cultural insult to his position slowly emerges in his dialogue with Fortunato, as Montresor entices him deeper and deeper into the palazzo's wine cellar. "You are rich, respected, admired, beloved; you are happy, as once I was. You are a man to be missed. For me it is no matter" (ibid., 850). Fortunato drinks "to the buried that repose around us"; Montresor drinks, with several kinds of irony, "to your long life," while noting that the Montresors "were a great and numerous family" (ibid.).

Then comes a dramatic moment that encapsulates the clash between old and new money in nineteenth-century Virginia gentry terms. Fortunato drank, and "threw the bottle upward with a gesticulation I did not understand." He repeated the "grotesque" movement, clearly surprised. "You do not comprehend?" It is a secret sign of "the brotherhood." Still Montresor did not comprehend. "You are not of the masons." "Yes, yes," Montresor responds, and with one of Poe's most infamous puns, he produces a trowel.

The simple irony is that Montresor will as an artisan mason use the trowel to wall up Fortunato, burying him alive. The complex social irony exposes Montresor as bewildered by the new rituals solidifying male bonds and alleviating tensions in the power elite. Montresor's revenge against Fortunato avenges the outsider status of old money, displaced by men who wear urban motley and deal in international finance.

Psychologically, one could build a strong Oedipal reading from John

Allan having been a Mason (Silverman 1991, 13). Sociologically, the growth of the Masons in American urban centers began to take off in the 1830s and 1840s, reaching its golden age after the Civil War. Literarily, as Silverman argues, the story takes Poe's revenge for the "thousand" insults the writer had endured at the hands of reviewers (ibid., 316–18). Ideologically, Montresor's trowel could represent an idealized union of gentry and artisan values now threatened by a new world of mobile fakes and fortune hunters.

That fourfold allegorical reading, however, depends on readerly sympathy for Montresor. At the end, the revenge preserves the allegories while emptying out subjective coherence on both sides of the wall. As Montresor began to place the last stone, he heard "a low laugh that erected the hairs upon my head. It was succeeded by a sad voice, which I had difficulty in recognizing as that of the noble Fortunato" (Poe 1984b, 853). Previous screams and clanking chains, eerily evoking slavery, had made Montresor hesitate, then redouble his strength. Soon disparate sounds became not-Fortunato, subsiding to an absence of voice, "only a jingling of the bells." The narrator's "heart grew sick; it was the dampness of the catacombs that made it so" (Poe 1984b, 854).

Then he reinforced not only the wall but the social allegory: "Against the new masonry I re-erected the old rampart of bones" (ibid.). If Montresor's "re-erected rampart" subdues not only the "new masonry" elite but also his "erected hairs," it does so by walling up his own heart and burying himself in the past, with the "old bones" of his ancestors. Stripped of subjectivity, Montresor's family bones parallel Fortunato's disintegration into sounds, then silence. Montresor's last line—"*In pace requiescat!*"—wishes R.I.P. to himself as well, in a dead language.

V

Poe fails at longer narratives, whether philosophical or fictional, especially in his arbitrary plotting of *The Voyage of Arthur Gordon Pym*—a story that only critics relish, for what they can do with it. His emptying out of "character" into detached intellectual mastery or passionate self-destruction cannot generate momentum in a longer genre. What can be riveting or shocking in the short story seems nihilistic and capricious in the novel. Faced with incipient bourgeois expectations for linear narratives about the social and moral education of complex selves, Poe presents a new aristocracy, one of intellects without subjectivity, or an old aristocracy that uses reason to be sensationally unreasonable. Yet Poe also toys with gentry expectations of status hierarchy by teasing out the unstable fictionality of gentry self-constructions. Not even textuality can sustain his cultural elitism for long.

Poe's contradictory mix of textual aristocracy and falling aristocrats puts regressive and progressive stabilizations of subjectivity into linguistic difficulty. To return to McKeon's analysis of "extreme skepticism," the postcolonial elite with which Poe consciously affiliated himself tried to fend off the social dynamics at stake a century earlier in England by preserving its status hierarchy through the institutions of rural household patriarchy and slavery. In Michael Allen's summary, Poe grew up "in a South that was extending an aristocratic code from the original Virginia gentry to the whole region to consolidate it against Northern pretensions" (1969, 133). British sources and models were crucial to the consolidation. On the edge between northern journalist and southern gentleman, Poe exaggerated the honor and dishonor of the cultivated mind at leisure, a distinctive role enabled by slavery and urged by southern intellectual reformers as the height of social aspiration. Although he shared their delusive dreams of elitist intellectual community, Poe's more profound hopes for aristocracy lay with the gentleman-genius, ultimately a club with one person as member.

Poe's ideal gentleman, as Allen astutely observes, should be a reader, not a writer, since writers have to work with their hands. But Poe's definition of such a gentleman insists on a circular fictionality. For him, "gentlemen of elegant leisure" are those "who can live idly and without manual labour, and will bear the port, charge, and countenance of a gentleman" (ibid., 192). Poe's language itself bears a redundant "port" and "charge," intimating contradictory imperatives: a genius needs an audience of gentlemen, yet writers forsake that status; elegant leisure requires a strenuous charade. These tensions also characterize his skepticism, which continuously veers toward solipsistic grandiosity, then settles back to a kind of transcendent despair that his mind has nothing authentically in common with any order of empirical or fictional validation. McKeon's argument for extreme skepticism as a double reversal, parodically undermining both romance idealism and naive empiricism, complements Joan Dayan's analysis of Poe's linguistic despair, and Stanley Cavell's suggestion that Poe's skepticism betrays his need for love and his fear of being loved.[26]

Historicizing Poe's skepticism need not diminish its force. In a prize-winning essay, Bertram Wyatt-Brown argues that the southern "Sambo" figure plays a role common to all honor-shame cultures: the shameless trickster. Sambo's mimicry of his unpredictable master acts as a signifying mirror for the "patriarchal, male-dominated, honor-obsessed" pecking order (Wyatt-Brown 1988, 1246).[27] To extend Wyatt-Brown's argument, such mirroring becomes a central mode in Poe's narratives, with a difference: he mimics mastery in decline. Honoring and undermining gentry constructions of social identity, Poe's textuality also subverts its own aggrandized aristocratic status. In effect, he plays a trickster role at the alienated margin of gentry culture.

In Poe's hypertextualized world, his fictions invite a skeptical indeterminacy collapsing the southern past and the northern future. More accessibly to us, he satirizes emerging mass-market culture, already filled with readers like the crass king in "Hop-Frog" (1849), who shouts to his trickster-jester, "We want characters—*characters,* man—something novel—out of the way." "Capital!" roars King Audience, when Hop-Frog suggests a game that will turn them into chained orangutans; "I will make a man of you" (Poe 1984b, 904). In sending up these capitalist constructions of manliness and individuality, Poe simultaneously plays with gentry constructions of master-slave relations. By the end of the story, after Hop-Frog grinds his "fang-like teeth" above the masters he has tarred and torched, the trickster becomes a monstrous yet uninterpretable absence. His low-to-high exit through the roof leaves behind eight blackened bodies, whose undecidable identities fuse southern pretenders with northern philistines.

The vengeful allegorizing here, as in "The Cask of Amontillado," bespeaks Poe's writerly rage. It may well be, as Silverman surmises, that Poe's desperate last years drove his final stories into obsessive revenge plots, as if high literary status could be gained only through overkill (1991, 405–7, 316–18). Yet Hop-Frog's trickster escape can stand as a metaphor for Poe's extreme skepticism. While upending idealized southern aristocracy, Poe's fictions depict a world without gentlemen as a descent into Allen Tate's rootless, urban hell. More precisely, trapped between a phantom gentry culture and the mechanistic demands of urban capitalism, gentlemen-narrators discover that their own poses are as nightmarish as the vulgarian scrambling that has contaminated their world.[28]

"The glory of the Ancient Dominion is in a fainting—is in a dying condition," Poe wrote in 1835 (Hovey 1987, 347). By the mid-1840s, his fiction not only deconstructed idealized British models of the gentleman but dramatized the clash of the gentry hierarchy with capitalist dynamics. On the margin of gentry culture, Poe played with his culture's greater historical marginality. Once he had read the gentry as a hegemonic yet beleaguered fiction, he mourned for the postcolonial dreams of aristocracy that he resurrected for himself with textuality. Sensing that his master had two masters, Old and New England, the white Sambo-trickster aped and emptied out his pseudomaster's meanings.

NOTES

1. On Allan and Galt, see Silverman 1991, 12, 27–28; on Allan as foster father and businessman, 9–28. On Poe's marginality, see Rubin 1989, 148–53; on Poe's Byronic poses, 177–78.

2. Gray atones for the omission with " 'I Am a Virginian,' " arguing that Poe adopts various southern personae as well as expressing "profoundly conservative" southern values (1987, 190).

3. On Poe's dreams of an elite magazine, see Silverman 1991, 101–2, 175–76, 408–11); see also Allen 1969.

4. In *American Slavery, American Freedom*, Morgan argues that racism "absorbed in Virginia the fear and contempt that men in England, whether Whig or Tory, monarchist or republican, felt for the inarticulate lower classes," making a rhetoric of liberty and equality possible "by lumping Indians, mulattoes, and Negroes in a single pariah class." This process "paved the way for a similar lumping of small and large planters in a single master class" (1975, 386).

5. On Allan, see Silverman 1991, 20–22, 27–28; on Byrd, see Lockridge 1987, 46, 51; on Byrd as the embodiment of the ideal gentleman, see Gray 1986, chap. 1.

6. On extreme skepticism, see McKeon 1987, 114–19; on the destabilization of social categories, 162–69. McKeon's most prominent English example of extreme skepticism is the third Earl of Shaftesbury. While others have found Shaftesbury more morally coherent than McKeon's analysis of his "indirect discourse of self-conscious and parodic impersonation" implies (118–19), McKeon's historicizing of indeterminacy applies not only to many elements in Swift but also to Poe. At the end, McKeon polemically asserts that extreme skepticism also characterizes contemporary poststructuralism, perhaps with similarly historicizable dynamics (420–21).

7. Other useful studies on gentry leadership and contradictions in Virginia include Breen 1980, esp. chap. 8, on gentry uses of social rituals such as horse racing and gambling, and chap. 9, emphasizing the gentry's "hustler" or entrepreneurial side. Isaac 1982 usefully highlights the gentry's attentiveness to rank and England, but overstates the case for "transformation" by arguing that evangelism and individualism established a competing value system as early as the 1750s. Siegel 1987 similarly argues for the uneasy coexistence of self-made, bourgeois men with gentry paternalism, an Isaac-like dichotomy that most historians see as part of gentry social construction.

8. Kulikoff 1986 defines gentry and yeomen through the relative numbers of their slaves as well as their property holdings (9–13, 262–63, 421–23). As he notes, "perhaps a twentieth of the region's white men" were gentlemen, though half were yeomen, many owning a slave or two (262).

9. See Stowe 1987 on the planter class's celebration of hierarchy, the close correspondence between self-esteem and social order, the public "showiness" in day-to-day life, and the divided gender worlds (5–49, 251–54).

10. On raucous student behavior, see Faust 1977, 9–10; see also Silverman 1991, 31.

11. On nose pulling, see Greenberg 1990, 71; the nose was a "sacred object," the most visible symbol of honor that a man could publicly display. To pull it was to accuse him of lying (68).

12. On Washington and Cato, see Meier 1989, 195–97.

13. Silverman also says Poe's sexual relations with Virginia were "uncertain," perhaps nonexistent (1991, 124), and that his flirtations with other women intimate not sexual desire but his need to be taken care of (282, 289–91, 371, 415). On Poe's student debts, see 32–34.

14. Allen stresses Poe's "desire for British recognition" at least through 1842 (1969, 155), especially in his emulation of John Wilson's critical style. After 1845, Allen suggests, Poe found "a sense of public identity" linked more to his American mass audience than to Wilson (157).

15. On 5 October 1837, Emerson notes how easily "little people . . . demolish me" while "a snippersnapper eats me whole" (1982, 170). His 8 October entry is probably his rejoinder to that experience. In *Mind and the American Civil War*, Simpson reads Emerson's 8 October entry as a reflection of New England scorn for the anti-intellectual South, without noting the previous slight (1989, 48–69). Simpson's analysis of New England nationalism complements my emphasis on contrasting ideals of manliness.

16. On Longfellow's solicitude, see Silverman 1991, 438, 444; on Poe's attacks, 145–46, 234–37. Poe did praise Longfellow in a late public reading (385). Hovey argues, in a fine analysis, that Poe's attempt to free the South from northern thought was at the root of his attempt to free poetry from truth (1987, 349). Hovey also notes that Longfellow may well have retaliated in his novel, *Kavanagh* (1849), by parodying Poe in the character of a poet who poses as "a pyramid of mind on the dark desert of despair" (342).

17. Stowe (1987, 253) notes "the almost complete absence of black people in white accounts of ritual and daily routine." Faust (1977, 116) discusses five southern intellectuals, including Simms and James Hammond, who eventually turned to proslavery arguments to win recognition and respect after failing in other efforts to raise the status of intellectual work.

18. Some years ago a Williamsburg tour guide mentioned that the book most frequently found on Virginia shelves during the late eighteenth century was Fielding's *Tom Jones*. That makes a striking regional contrast to the equivalent secular primacy of *Pilgrim's Progress* and *Paradise Lost* on New England shelves.

19. Culture as "game" recurs throughout *Distinction*; on "the games of culture" as part of the "aesthetic disposition," which "can only be constituted within an experience of the world freed from urgency," see Bourdieu 1984, 54. The value of culture, Bourdieu argues, is generated through the struggle between highbrow and middlebrow, each dependent on the other (ibid., 250–54).

20. Linck Johnson suggests that "without" may seem more archaic now, since Noah Webster's 1828 dictionary gives "on the outside of" as one of its standard meanings, along with "unless," among others (personal communication). At the least, however, the word seems to call attention to Roderick's literary posing. See Cox 1968 for a thoughtful account of Poe's emphasis on excessive impersonations and literary posings.

21. This passage emphasizes the implied yet denied aristocracy in the social game of

taste: "the principle of the pleasure derived from those refined games for refined players lies, in the last analysis, in the denied experience of a social relationship of membership and exclusion. . . . The philosophical sense of distinction is another form of the visceral disgust at vulgarity which defines pure taste as an internalized social relationship" (Bourdieu 1984, 499–500).

22. Jordan notes that the narrator cannot remember Ligeia's paternal name, yet accepts her patrimony. She argues that the story is a fight for narrative authority, which the narrator wins only by silencing Ligeia's story with murderous patriarchal language. Leland Person, in *Aesthetic Headaches*, reads "Ligeia" similarly as the struggle of a man "to define and control a woman" through language (1988, 30), but comes to an opposite conclusion: the woman wins the "battle of wills," rendering the narrator's words impotent as "Ligeia resists objectification, death, and denial" (ibid., 32).

23. Auerbach historicizes Poe primarily as a writer hostile to modernity and Jacksonian democracy (1989, 55–56, 125–26), as does Pease in *Visionary Compacts* (1987, 168–75); see also 199–202 on Poe's taking self-reliance to an extreme of sensational immediacy without personhood. See also Elbert (1991), who argues that Poe's personae alternate between Whig and Democrat modes. Rubin (1989, 138–39), citing Tate, also reads "The Man of the Crowd" in relation to the deracinating modern city, as do many others.

24. Olmsted writes: "It is this habit of considering themselves of a privileged class, and of disdaining something which they think beneath them, that is deemed to be the chief blessing of slavery. It is termed 'high tone,' 'high spirit,' and is supposed to give great military advantages" (1984, 19). For Byrd's letter to the Earl of Egmont, see Simpson 1989, 20.

25. Irwin also calls Poe a "fallen Virginia gentleman" (1992, 205), overstating Poe's childhood status. In "Horrid Laws," Whalen teases out Dupin's progress in the three stories from an aristocrat to a professional who works for money (1992, 400).

26. On the double reversal of romance idealism and naive empiricism in extreme skepticism, see McKeon 1987, 63–64. In *Fables of Mind*, Dayan calls Poe "a philosophical Calvinist" against the American grain, and links his skepticism to that of David Hume (1987, 6–7). She emphasizes Poe's conversion of identity from a philosophic to a linguistic difficulty (201), and writes of Poe's "despair with truth or fiction" (210). For Cavell, see his essay in this collection.

27. To my knowledge, Elizabeth Fox-Genovese is alone among recent southern historians in arguing that "patriarchy" as a term should be restricted to the Roman model, in which a husband could kill his wife, children, and slaves (1988, 63–64). She suggests "paternalism" instead; for an opposite argument that the role of gentleman "derived much of its content" as well as prestige "from the encompassing metaphor of patriarchy," see Isaac 1982, 354–55).

28. For this formulation I am indebted to T. Walter Herbert. For helpful readings of earlier drafts, I am indebted to Frederick Crews, Anne Goodwyn Jones, Linck Johnson, John Seelye, Bertram Wyatt-Brown, and the editors of this volume.

"(Horrible to Relate!)"

Recovering the Body of Marie Rogêt

LAURA SALTZ

Edgar Allan Poe's "Mystery of Marie Rogêt," published serially in *Snowden's Ladies' Companion* in 1842–43, recounts the controversial, unsolved murder of a young New York woman, Mary Cecelia Rogers, whose body was dragged from the Hudson River in July 1841. The unnamed narrator announces that his story is an ideal fictional space—a universe parallel to the real world—in which the previously inexplicable case of Mary Rogers will be recreated and explained as the story of a young Parisian grisette, Marie Rogêt. The narrator claims that "all argument founded upon the fiction is applicable to the truth: and the investigation of the truth was the object" (Poe 1969–78, 3:728). The second of Poe's three detective stories, "The Mystery of Marie Rogêt" (like "The Murders in the Rue Morgue" and "The Purloined Letter") chronicles the extraordinary powers of deduction exercised by the Chevalier C. Auguste Dupin. But despite the narrator's promises and Dupin's preternatural intelligence, the case remains unsolved. Though Dupin produces Marie's body as evidence of a crime, he leaves the nature of the crime, the possibility that she has been violated, and the identity of the culprit disturbingly obscure. His final pronouncement on the case is singularly unilluminating: "Corroboration will rise upon corroboration, and the murderer will be traced" (ibid., 771).

If Dupin fails to resolve the mystery of Marie's disappearance, it is because she vanishes not only from the fictional landscape of Paris but from the text itself. In asking "whodunnit," "The Mystery of Marie Rogêt" poses a riddle of identity that is fundamentally not about Marie but about the author of the crime against her. The story's eponymous victim becomes a kind of reflecting surface on which certain masculine identities are superimposed: the criminal, the narrator, Dupin, even Poe himself. This essay attempts to step through the looking glass, not simply into the Wonderland of history where the "ideal series of events" referred to in the story's epigraph might be revealed, but also in order to ask how Marie's physical disappearance from the Paris streets occasions her textual effacement.

Marie's is a story of love and betrayal, but the implicit romance of her fate is negated by the rationalizing work of detection and displaced onto the relationship between Dupin and the narrator. Since the murders in the Rue Morgue, they have lived a quiet life in their chambers in the Faubourg Saint Germain, "weaving the dull world around us into dreams" (ibid., 724). Despite his retirement, Dupin has become a public figure, and his name has "grown into a household word" (ibid., 725). Prefect G— thus comes to Dupin for assistance with this case. The murderer has eluded the Prefect, with the result that the "eyes of the public [are] upon him" and his reputation is at stake (ibid., 728). He offers Dupin a liberal reward, "which has no bearing upon the proper subject of [the] narrative," and leaves. With the narrator to assist him, Dupin contemplates the case, never leaving his sitting room. The private couple performs the thought-work of detection at home, where they produce not one but many plots of Marie's public life and death. Using newspaper reports of Marie's disappearance as the sole source of information, Dupin conducts an inquest into a world, and a crime, that is entirely textual. He confirms the identity of the corpse; it is the body of a young woman, Marie Rogêt, who had earned a degree of notoriety working behind the counter in a perfume shop. Reading the papers, Dupin traces her path on the morning of her disappearance through Paris to the banks of the Seine, and across it to an inn. He discredits the suspicious testimony of the innkeeper, Madame Deluc, but, reading between the lines, concludes that the dark man she saw with Marie must have been the culprit. This man, concludes Dupin, is one of Marie's three suitors, the same "naval officer" who had been responsible for a previous disappearance three years earlier.

But the clues lead Dupin in different directions; to synopsize "Marie Rogêt" as I have is to confer on it a linear narrative that in fact it lacks. Dupin suggests that Marie met with a "fatal accident" under the roof of Madame Deluc, and alternatively that she was murdered by her lover, the naval officer (ibid., 768). He never resolves these contradictory possibilities, nor does he determine the identity of the naval officer. The murderer is not traced but simply disappears, seemingly into thin air. Rather than provide clarification, Poe, who authorized this vanishing act, interrupts his tale with a statement not about the culprit but about himself. After Dupin's last words, the story reads:

[For reasons which we shall not specify, but which to many readers will appear obvious, we have taken the liberty of here omitting, from the MSS. placed in our hands, such portion as details the *following up* of the apparently slight clew obtained by Dupin. We feel it advisable only to state, in brief, that the result desired was brought to pass; and that the Prefect fulfilled punctually, although with reluctance, the terms of his compact with the Chevalier. Mr. Poe's article concludes with the following words.—*Eds.*] (Ibid., 772)[1]

Under cover of square brackets, in the guise of his editors, "Mr. Poe" intrudes on the fictional frame of his tale and addresses his readers in the textual equivalent of a stage whisper. His frank omission of details covers a covert substitution: rather than disclose a definitive explanation of Mary's murder, "Mr. Poe" exposes an intricate web of authorship. In the center of that web is a private monetary transaction, figured by Dupin's "compact" with the Prefect, and the private transmission of a text destined for public life, "the MSS. placed in our hands." Poe's self-representation, placed at the denouement of the tale, indicates that the mystery of Marie Rogêt is bound not only to the facts of Mary's case—facts that lead away from narrative closure—but bound also to Poe's authorial identity (or double identity as "Mr. Poe" and "Eds."), and to the logistics and economics of publication. The text thus superimposes the shadow of property relations, textual transmission, and authorial exhibitionism over its explanation of a "crime of passion"—the rape and murder of Marie.

How is it that the murder of a young woman occasions oblique speculation on the production of texts? Other readings of "The Mystery of Marie Rogêt" tend to focus on its narrative flaws (it is justly criticized as labyrinthine and incomprehensible) or its logical and historical errors (Poe does not, after all, solve either Mary's or Marie's murder).[2] Although the contradictions of the story are not fully resolvable, they can be made legible. Mary Rogers was generally believed to have perished not at the hands of her lover but under the knife of an abortionist.[3] Though this possibility is driven deeply underground in the text, the perilous cultural space of authorship carved out by Poe must be understood together with the hidden meanings of Marie's carved-up body. The buried abortion serves as a literary site for Poe's inquest into the related problematics of privacy and publicity, self and self-authorship—issues that are raised historically and existentially by controversies surrounding abortion in the 1840s. Poe conceals Marie's "concealment," consigning her terminated pregnancy to a narrative absence, a hidden realm inhabited by secret forms of sexual knowledge.[4] Such knowledge is the unspoken subject of Dupin's ratiocinative investigations. In this view, the evasions and concealments of "Marie Rogêt" are not its flaws, but its structure and obsession.

The effacement of Marie's abortion signals Poe's need to contain and obscure questions about the public visibility of women and their participation in a market economy. The contours of this economy are crucially shaped by the mechanisms of publicity; this cultural dynamic, and the shadow it casts on his own visibility as an author, is a source of profound anxiety for Poe (Whalen 1992). He subordinates Marie and her body's productions to his own literary production, attempting to secure his place in the market that so provokes him.[5] In this essay I situate the scandal of Mary Rogers's disappearance within the context of a publishing market—that of the New York daily newspapers—already engaged in the profitable sensationalization of controversies surrounding abortion. Then I look more closely at the text of "Marie Rogêt," and the contradictory status of female visibility represented there through the peripatetic figure of Marie. Finally, I demonstrate the ways in which Poe's tale, like the newspapers, accrues interest in the form of textual authority by circulating the mutilated body of Marie. Oscillating between the suppression of Marie's abortion and the contemplation of his own authorship, Poe's story never quite comes to life. Marie remains a blank slate, inscribed by Poe with the contradictory plots of an antebellum woman in public.

II

"The Mystery of Marie Rogêt" poses complicated questions; the case of the real Mary Rogers leaves most of them unanswered. When her body was dragged from the Hudson River onto the Hoboken shore in July 1841, Mary's death excited a great deal of interest in the community and in the press. Mary Rogers had lived a public life. She had worked in a cigar store near several newspaper offices, and was well known to newspaper reporters. She was beautiful, and had disappeared once before; although such cases were not uncommon, the attention hers attracted was. The newspapers fueled the excitement through detailed daily coverage, intimating that the police were not acting quickly or responsibly enough. "Who caused any stir to be made to discover the murderers of Mary C. Rogers? The Press!"[6] Spurred to action by newspaper editorials, a committee of private citizens formed to offer a reward for information leading to the capture of Mary's assailant. Mary's betrothed was questioned and released. An unidentified sailor and several other suspects were also questioned, to no end. The possibility of suicide was raised and dismissed. Rumors and theories abounded to explain the disfigurement of Mary's corpse: that the body found was not hers; that she was brutalized by a gang of ruffians; that her body was deliberately mutilated to cover some other crime. This last became the most widely accepted explanation for Mary's death, particularly after the dramatic and widely publicized deathbed "confession" of a certain Mrs. Loss (who corresponds to Poe's innkeeper, Madame Deluc) in November 1842. It was thought almost certain at that time that Mary had died attempting to abort an unwanted pregnancy at Mrs. Loss's inn.

Poe was in Philadelphia during the unfolding of much of the case, but was able to follow it closely through the extensive coverage it received in the Philadelphia papers. Poe wrote his story and submitted it, probably out of financial necessity, to several periodicals for publication in June 1842. The first two installments were published in Snowden's *Ladies' Companion* in November and December 1842; the third, which was to have appeared in January 1843, was delayed until February. John Walsh has argued convincingly that during that month, Poe altered his text so it would not seem completely absurd in the face of Mrs. Loss's testimony, just delivered. Nevertheless, the original text published in 1843 included none of the veiled references to the possibility of "an accident," or to the "concealments" Marie might have effected, references Poe would add before republishing the story in 1845 in *Tales*. The implication of Walsh's findings is that the uncertainty and irresolution of the story can be attributed to Poe's failure to solve the mystery of Mary Rogers correctly—quite simply, Poe got it wrong and later attempted to cover his tracks.

What remains unexplained, however, is the story's blind spot about the abortion. If Poe simply regarded it as one of many wrongheaded theories about the case, why did he not include his rationale for doing so in the tale? Dupin carefully refutes the suggestion of suicide, the possibility that the body found was not correctly identified as Marie, and the popular gang theory, but thoroughly mystifies the question of abortion. In 1848, Poe even admitted abortion as the probable cause of Mary's death in a letter to George Eveleth, "explaining" the questionable omissions in his text: "Nothing was omitted in 'Marie Rogêt' but what I omitted myself—all *that* is mystification. . . . The 'naval officer,' who committed murder (rather, the accidental death arising from an attempt at abortion) *confessed* it; and the whole matter is now well understood; but, for the sake of relatives, his is a topic on which I must not speak further."[7] The whole matter was not then and is not now well understood. Predictably, this letter adds one more layer of mystification to Mary/Marie's story. There is no such confession, except where Poe invents it in the first footnote of "Marie Rogêt."[8] The abortion, which is elliptical in the text, is parenthetical in the letter: Poe is still reluctant to accord it full status in the mystery. He attributes his forbearance from doing so to a desire to shield the naval officer's family. But shield it from what? The officer's deeds? Scandal? Marie herself? Who is the victim of this crime, and who the perpetrator? Poe's protective posturing is no doubt bravado, but it nevertheless accounts for at least some of the confusions of his story. Male honor is at stake, and if the story shields the naval officer and his family, it does so by condemning Marie's relatives to silence through a series of narrative displacements, signaled by the suppressed abortion. The abortion is understood as the private concern of the naval officer—"his topic"—which ought not be brought forward to besmirch his reputation. Rather than probe the intimate details of his violation of Marie, the story reconceives them as a cipher of inviolable privacy. Yet it is Marie who embodies the principle of this concealment. Like the purloined letter, her corpse is visible, but the undisclosed content of the crime against her is held in sufferance by Poe. She becomes an unwitting accomplice to extortion, the real threat being that of the naval officer's exposure.

Poe's investment in protecting the naval officer begins to make sense when seen in the context of anxieties about abortion current in 1840s America. At the same historical moment in which Poe hushed Marie's abortion, supposedly to fend off scandal, the penny press (on which his story depends) began to publicize the practice of abortion, initiating a loud and public debate about it. Until the 1840s, abortion had been largely tolerated, and was legal before "quickening" under common law.[9] Around 1840, however, the number of abortions performed rose sharply. Women increasingly sought them not, as in previous decades, because their pregnancies were illegitimate, but because they wanted to delay having families or limit family size (Smith-Rosenberg 1985; Mohr 1978). Because it allowed married women a certain latitude of power in the home, abortion threatened the "natural" domestic order, and was perceived as a threat to the patriarchal organization of the family: wives might commit adultery without fear of detection; maidens might counterfeit their virtue.

As well as endangering the middle-class institution of marriage from within, abortion signaled the encroachment of women into the economic domain. By the 1840s, abortion had become highly commercialized, and some of its most prosperous practitioners were women. Not simply a lucrative economic enterprise, abortion was a business that infiltrated the domestic realm and played a growing part in answering "domestic" questions regarding childbearing. If Carroll Smith-Rosenberg is correct, female abortionists came to represent in the popular imagination the perniciousness of market forces and their incursion into the private home; the female professional was an oxymoron who figured the violation of boundaries between market and home. However unthinkable, the collective fantasy in which wealthy rakes colluded to procure abortions with the families of the innocent young women they seduced was still more palatable—indeed, it was eminently thinkable through the fictionalizing conventions of sentimental seduction—than the idea that women were performing these abortions. Though most pharmacists and physicians who helped procure abortions were in fact men, it was the female abortionist who was labeled a "monster in human shape" (Dixon 1841, 3). She represented a host of perversions: "commercialization, the unnatural woman, an unnatural world" (Smith-Rosenberg 1985, 226).

Between 1841, the year of Mary Rogers's death, and 1845, the time of the second publication of "Marie Rogêt," the legal as well as moral implications of abortion were changing drastically. By the end of 1845, the state of New York had passed unprecedented legislation that made the woman as well as her abortionist criminally liable. The rapid rise of the antiabortion movement, which lobbied for legislative change, is most often told as a chapter in the history of the professionalization of medicine.[10] This story is incomplete, however, for legislative change would not have come about so swiftly or so early in the century without the involvement of the press. In the late 1830s, the newly emerging penny press sought economic stability and professional legitimacy by experimenting with subjects and styles of reporting that would appeal to a wide readership and simultaneously gain its trust. As part of this bid for cultural authority, the papers activated abortion *as* public, *as* controversial, *as* scandalous: as an issue with which to make good their claims to represent, if not to lead, public opinion. The newspapers became an arena for creating controversy, and the female body proved to be an ideal vehicle through which to market it (Papke 1987; Schiller 1981). Sensationalizing the more or less taboo subjects of sex and violence and selling them as "news," the penny press caught and held the eye, as well as the purse, of the public. The sudden and drastic increase in the public disapprobation of abortion was intimately linked to this media intervention.

In 1841, during the months leading up to Mary's disappearance, New York newspapers trained their readers' attention on the sensational arrest and trial of Madame Restell, New York City's most infamous abortionist.[11] The publication of this and other scandals (involving murder, adultery, and prostitution) helped redefine the previously private exploits of individuals as available for public consumption, and subject to public debate. Construing abortion as something to be exposed, the press helped shift the terms of the debate about it. The newspapers elaborated and expanded the categories of crime and criminal, simultaneously indicating a "public" that they sought to differentiate and protect from the criminal class (Papke 1987). To publicize the trial of Madame Restell was to assist in her demonization: as a practitioner of abortion, she was classed a "vampyre" and a murderess guilty of "demoniac practices" (New York *Tribune*, 30 April 1841).[12]

But even as newspaper reporting condemned abortion, newspaper advertising promoted it. If abortion rates had risen sharply by the 1840s, it was largely because newspaper advertising enabled abortionists to reach larger and larger markets. The contradiction between claims to moral leadership and adherence to the democratic principle of uncensored advertising exploded in a battle for moral authority fought among the dailies. Between James Gordon Bennett's *New York Herald* and Horace Greeley's *New York Tribune*, this battle was especially fierce.[13] The *Herald*, which prided itself on its laissez-faire attitude toward the content of the ads it ran, was one of the major venues for the advertisements on which the success of Madame Restell's business depended.[14] The *Tribune*, along with other publications such as George W. Dixon's *Polyanthos*, agitated public opinion against the *Herald* and the *Sun* (which also carried ads for abortions) and against Madame Restell, calling for her speedy arrest. The *Tribune* leveled serious accusations against the *Herald* and the *Sun*, calling them Restell's "newspaper accomplices," and asking whether "they who for base lucre have wilfully abetted beforehand the crimes of this wretch" ought to escape unpunished (*New York Tribune*, 28 July 1841).

Finding itself in an awkward position, the *Herald* covered Madame Restell's trial, but in less detail than did the *Tribune*, and with much less fervor, tending to mock Restell rather than condemn her outright.[15] In place of Restell, the *Herald* seized another issue with which to promote itself as the guardian of justice and the protector of the public interest: the Mary Rogers affair. Just days before the Restell trial came to a close (29 July), Mary Rogers disappeared (25 July; her body was discovered on 28 July), and the *Herald* could quickly boast the most thorough and consistent coverage of the case in the city. Deaths such as Mary's were not uncommon, but the *Herald* chose to thrust this one into the limelight.[16] Just as the *Tribune* had agitated for Restell's arrest, so the *Herald* took up Mary Rogers's cause. The paper editorialized that

> the entire proceedings—commencing with the finding of the body, the inquest, &c., in their manner, have been most disgraceful. What are our criminal authorities about? . . . The true administration of public justice is shamefully neglected. . . . We hope that the citizens will take this matter up, and call a meeting in the Park or elsewhere, and subscribe a reward for the detection of the murderer of Mary Rogers. . . . Let us subscribe for a reward at once. (*New York Herald,* 3 August 1841)

One week later, the *Herald* reported that a "numerous and highly respectable meeting" was indeed held, at which were adopted several resolutions, including "that the thanks for this meeting be given to the public press of this city, for having repeatedly called public attention to this horrible case; and that all the editors be requested again to aid the Committee in publishing these proceedings" (ibid., 10 August 1841, 2). In the name of the public (its readership), the *Herald* elevated itself above New York City's officials. The allegations of inefficiency and possible corruption with which the *Herald* charged city authorities both echo and deflect the *Tribune*'s charges against the *Herald.* Just as the *Tribune* sought to increase its own circulation through the vilification of Madame Restell, so the *Herald* circulated the story of Mary Rogers in a reciprocal attempt at self-promotion. In each case, the newspapers exhorted their community of readers, in the name of self-policing, to the surveillance and regulation of female bodies. For both Madame Restell and Mary Rogers, notoriety was the condition of public visibility.

This self-positioning of the newspapers as civic leaders and opponents of municipal authorities was evident in a second round of press agitation against Restell in 1845, when the *National Police Gazette* began publication. Initiating its national circulation with a crusade for goodness and right, the *Gazette* brought the name of Restell before the public eye once again. The *Gazette* applied pressure on the police to shut down Restell's business. Resurrecting another high-profile case to raise the stakes of her capture, the paper even blamed Restell for Mary's death. The following excerpt gives a sense of the hysterical pitch of the *Gazette* campaign:

> It is well known that [Restell] keeps a large number of appartments [*sic*] in her golgotha for the accommodation of females in accouchment [*sic*]. . . . How many then who enter her halls of death may be supposed to expire under her execrable butchery. Females are daily, nay, hourly missing from our midst who never return. Where do they go? What becomes of them? Does funeral bell ever peal a note for

their passage? . . . Do friends ever gather round their melancohly [*sic*] grave? No! An obscure hole in the earth; a consignment to the savage skill of the dissecting knife, or a plash in the cold wave, with the scream of the night blast for a requiem, is the only death service ever bestowed upon her victims! Witness this ye shores of the Hudson! Witness the Hoboken beach!

We do not wish to speak in parables. There is a mystery yet to be cleared up which sent a thrill of horror and a sensation of profound excitment [*sic*] through the length and breadth of the land! We speak of the unfortunate Mary Rogers. . . . The wretched girl was last seen in the direction of Madame Restell's house. The dreadfully lacerated body at Weehawken Bluffs bore the marks of no ordinary violation. . . . These are strange but strong facts, and when taken in connection with the other fact that Costello kept an abortion house in Hoboken at that very time, and was acting as the agent of Restell, it challenges our minds for the most terrible suspicions. Such are these abortionists! Such their deeds, and such their dens of crime! (*National Police Gazette*, 21 February 1845)

There is no evidence of Restell's involvement in the Mary Rogers case. But the *Gazette* used the Mary Rogers affair to fuel public hostility against both Madame Restell and the city's officials. In so doing, the *Gazette*, as had the *Herald* and *Tribune* before it, aligned the community's sense of moral responsibility with the textual authority it derived from the power of exposure, and pitted these against the legal authority of the courts and police. The *Gazette* continues:

We now ask again, if a community professing to be civilized will any longer tolerate this wholesale murder under their very eyes? Will a city possessing courts and a police, wink at such an atrocious violation of the laws, and if it will, and the demon murderess Restell be too rich to be within the power of the law, will the community, in the last resort, suffer her to go on unrebuked, by some sudden application of popular vengeance. . . . We call again for action from the authorities in relation to this woman. (Ibid.)

The *Gazette*'s allegations that Restell may have been buying off the authorities, while also unfounded, go to the heart of the issue of her infamy. Certainly the *Herald*'s reticence to speak out against her owes something to the vast amounts of advertising revenue with which she supplied it. But that revenue had broader implications for newspaper publication than the *Herald*'s failure to take a firm stand. If the success of the newspaper advertisements for the services of abortionists such as Madame Restell, Madame Costello, and Mrs. Bird testified to the growing number of women who sought abortions at midcentury, it also testified to the power of the newspapers to reach a growing client class—women. Having professed to make news democratically available to all, the newspapers also provided a public forum for making goods and services commercially available to a diverse public, which included men and women, blacks and whites, journeymen and servants.[17] As a commercial medium, the penny press promoted not only the public exchange of ideas among the citizens of an ideal republic of letters; it also simultaneously promoted and exposed an underground network of consumer-based exchanges among "readers," a category more inclusive than that of "citizens." In such an expanding and diversifying marketplace, the notion of a singular public interest was sorely vexed by the existence of competing interest groups. The public of the 1840s was not only a sphere of publication and debate, but a representational space that overlapped with the marketplace. Ideas were displayed, contested, and circulated along with, not apart from, the bodies, goods, and services that produced them (Habermas 1989; Calhoun 1992; Warner 1990).

The end of abortion's commercial visibility was hastened not by legal sanctions against the practice of abortion or injunctions against its morality, but by prohibitions against its advertisement. In 1873, with the abortion industry still prospering, the nation's foremost antiobscenity crusader, Anthony Comstock, persuaded Congress to pass legislation making the sale or advertisement by mail of any obscene matter a federal offense. This legislation specifically included "any article or thing designed or intended for the prevention of conception or procuring of abortion."[18] In subsuming abortion advertising under the heading of obscene literature, Comstock's avowed concern was not for protecting the life of the mother or the fetus, nor for curbing promiscuous behavior (the results of which could be concealed by abortion), but for what he considered to be the inherent indecency of any public mention of female complaints and cures. What Comstock intuited was the indispensable role of published advertising in opening previously private matters up to public debate. Obscenity or indecency inhered equally in the infiltration of private into public and public into private, and for Comstock, nothing was more private or indecent than the female body. In banning all references to sex, including information about contraception, the new law attempted to legislate the separation of two spheres that were manifestly overlapping by cordoning off so-called private practices, checking them, and keeping them hidden from view. The Comstock law thus reversed the logic of the newspapers, which sought to contain abortion by putting it squarely before the public eye, even as it acknowledged the power of the printed word. The federal policing of the mails severely constricted the abortion industry's avenues of publicity, and in so doing, effectively legislated the demise of the industry itself. Madame Restell's sensational suicide, following her arrest by Comstock in 1878, enacted literally and symbolically his successful removal of the female body from public circulation (Mohr 1978, 199).[19]

Though Poe did not live to see Comstock's antiobscenity laws implemented, his own censoring of the abortion in "Marie Rogêt" analogously removed abortion from the arena of public debate. His public erasure of this controversial issue consigned it to a secret realm potentially untouched by the configurations of market and publicity under which it flourished. Concerned with the marketability of his fiction, Poe shut down the dissemination of the idea of an economically viable woman, and instead explored other plots of female visibility in "Marie Rogêt." In the same way that the excessively private Dupin has inexorably achieved celebrity status and his name paradoxically become a household word, Marie figures the unregulated commerce between public and private selfhood.

III

Unlike the newspapers and Anthony Comstock, Poe is not specifically interested in the policing of virtue. Like them, he understands the ways in which the very indeterminacy of the moral and legal status of abortion provides him with an opportunity to construct authority for his representation of an unspecifiable crime. The anomalous situation of abortion in the 1840s made it as difficult to fit into established categories regarding sentimental womanhood, big business, or medical practice as into classifications of criminality. Writing of the crime in "Rue Morgue" as a violation of categories, Tony Tanner argues:

We find a crime committed by an animal (in effect, a "monster") that the police cannot solve because, as Dupin says, the prefect of the police has a way "*de nier ce qui est, et d'expliquer ce qui n'est pas.*" If, like a good bureaucrat, your thinking is dominated by established categories and classifications, then, by definition nothing can happen or be caused by an agent that falls outside these categories; but the criminal, as metaphorical or literal monster, is precisely that anomaly that the police-bureaucratic mind cannot envisage—it would rather, to translate Poe's words, "deny what is, and explain what is not." Thus, marriage, money, the crime, and the criminal can come to be regarded as monstrous if they do not fit into the theoretical tyranny of established classifications. (Tanner 1979, 196)

If the confusion of categories is criminal, abortion is all the more monstrous because it confounds so many established classifications: home and market, private and public, subject and object, perpetrator and victim, life and death. Turning to "Marie Rogêt," we encounter a narrative that elides the horror of abortion, and so manifestly attempts what Poe disparages: to "deny what is and explain what is not."

As the subtitle of "Marie Rogêt" announces, the story is "A Sequel to 'The Murders in the Rue Morgue.'" "Marie Rogêt" is both different from and the same as "Rue Morgue," which tells the story of the fantastic violation of the private apartments in which Madame L'Espanaye and her daughter live, and, incidentally, of their shocking brutalization. Marie's death, the third following those of Madame and Mademoiselle L'Espanaye, reiterates a paradoxical pattern already in place: the murder of the L'Espanaye women is not properly a murder because the culprit is not a man but an ape; nor is the abortion, judged by the standards of the 1840s, so certainly a crime. In effect, the three murders are the work of a phantom serial killer who, driven to revisit and replay the same scene, never achieves its resolution. To elide the abortion is surreptitiously to introduce new complications into Dupin's ongoing epistemological search for the origins of crime.

The practice of abortion in the 1840s was contingent on marketing and publicity, forces that turn private matters inside out. In "Marie Rogêt," this inversion of public and private is reinscribed on the gendered topography of Poe's fictional Paris, where Marie's is the public sphere of market and streets and Dupin's the private realm of reading and literary production. The unrepresented abortion relocates a species of domestic violence within the nexus of market relations, and in the process figures the emptying out of an identity—Marie's—in her exposure to the vicissitudes of public life. Dupin explores the permeable boundaries among public, private, and market by examining the open borders of the personality of Marie. Through the newspapers, Dupin has access only to Marie's public existence. She is described in extradomestic settings at moments when she is apprehended by the gaze of the public. Nevertheless, Marie's public life is infused with suggestions of her private circumstances. She is a figure who attracts speculation about her sexual history: before Dupin analyzes her case, he delves into Marie's past, which the newspapers have made salient. She has earned her notoriety by working in public at the counter of a perfume shop. As a living advertisement for the store, Marie attracts more and more customers with her great beauty. Her face value, as it were, enters the market, as both a sign and an object of exchange. She lends her tangible beauty to the intangible magnetism of commodities that is so pithily represented as scent. But Marie's visibility behind the store counter makes her vulnerable, liable to be exchanged away. Her disappearance from the perfume shop three years before her murder is a consequence, Dupin believes, of her commerce with the "desperate adventurers" who frequent the shop (Poe 1969–78, 3:725).[20] When Dupin speculates that she eloped with one such adventurer, he blurs her induction into a sexual economy of love and marriage with participation in a market economy of goods and services. Marie's first disappearance, then, is conditional in the text on her public visibility. She is a projection of the mutable desires of consumers that are set in motion by a market in which everything is exchangeable. The objects of these desires, like apparitions, like Marie, appear and disappear before the eye of the public.[21]

Marie could not be more different, it would seem, from the L'Espanaye women in "Rue Morgue," who are the picture of ensconced domesticity. Rarely leaving their home, they are isolated from the traffic of everyday affairs. Not surprisingly, the scene of the murder of this mother and daughter is the large back chamber of their house, which, when discovered by witnesses, is locked from the inside. These murders are characterized by Dupin as "outré," their strangeness accounted for by the unfathomability of so violent an intrusion on such sequestered quarters. In "Rue Morgue" the home is invaded by violence, while in "Marie Rogêt" domestic violence has been turned out of the home and into the streets. Dupin wants to see this explosion as normative. He explains that Marie's case is ordinary, and contrasts it with the murders in the Rue Morgue: "this is a far more intricate case than that of the Rue Morgue; from which it differs in one important aspect. This is an *ordinary*, although atrocious, instance of crime. There is nothing peculiarly *outré* about it. You will observe that, for this reason, the mystery has been considered easy, when, for this reason, it should have been considered difficult, of solution" (Poe 1969–78, 3:736). To displace sexual violation from an inadequately protected home into the public streets and simultaneously transform it from outré to ordinary is to betray a high degree of anxiety about protecting the sanctity of private space.

The "ordinariness" of Marie's murder is specifically related to her pedestrian status. She is an ambulatory character whose walks, her distinctive public behavior, inevitably take her out of the home. Something is outré when it has been pushed out of bounds; someone is outré when she exceeds the limits of conduct or sentiment. Marie, who is killed somewhere on the city streets during the course of her undirected wanderings, has herself transgressed the limits, not only of conduct or sentiment, but also of the imaginary boundary between public and private. That she is pedestrian paradoxically consigns her to the realm of the commonplace while it exiles her beyond the bounds of acceptable behavior. In "Marie Rogêt," the every-day *is* the shocking[22]—the crime against her cannot be outré because in a fundamental way, she already is. Like her unrepresentable abortion, Marie scandalizes because she is so scandalously commonplace.

As a prototype of the mobile subject, the figure of the *flâneur* in the work of Poe has received much critical attention (Benjamin 1973; Brand 1991; Byer 1986). This figure is always significantly male. Janet Wolff argues that the *flâneuse* does not exist in the early literature of modernity because public space, the realm of *flânerie,* was exclusively male, inaccessible to the female observer (Wolff 1985). Yet Marie is a kind of female *flâneur,* a wanderer who habitually leaves the confines of home and neighborhood to traverse the whole of the city. As the female counterpart of the *flâneur* depicted in, for example, Poe's "Man of the Crowd," Marie charts the dangers of female mobility. Her problematic visibility complicates Marie's relation to the in-habitants of the urban streets through which she walks. Where the *flâneur* seeks the spectacles of the metropolis, Marie is herself one such attraction. Though she is an object of observation, collected and displayed behind the store window, Marie's identity becomes scattered and dispersed along the city streets. Wandering through the neighborhoods of Paris, she blends easily into the masses, becoming undifferentiated and unindividuated. Rec-ognition of Marie is contextual, coming easily to customers when she sits behind the shop counter but perhaps not at all when she mingles with the public.[23] She is therefore unsusceptible to public surveillance, simply eclipsed by an unwitnessing urban crowd. Like the *flâneur,* Marie achieves a public anonymity that differentiates her from the "public man" of Poe's Paris, the businessman who, committed to a daily routine, travels "within a confined periphery, abounding in individuals who are led to observation of his person" (Poe 1969–78, 3:749). The public man is stable and recognizable, but Marie is a public woman—unpredictable and out of place. Her chame-leon quality works against her, putting Marie obviously in peril. When she enters public circulation, Marie risks losing herself, both geographically and existentially. She is killed in an unknown public location at an unplot-ted point on the map of Paris.

Marie's apparent aimlessness does not quite obscure her duplicitous, if undirected, desires. Dupin imagines female agency only as betrayal—only, in other words, in the act of breaking out of domestic bounds. He suggests that Marie has been abducted from the city streets, but he also implies her complicity in her own disappearance. Knowing that she cultivates the ad-miration of many men, Dupin ventures that she contrived to elude her fiancé, St. Eustache, on that last morning. As a mobile female subject, Marie abnegates, along with the shelter of the local or domestic, the protection of virtuous womanhood. Combined with her public personae as a seller of wares and a walker of city streets, Marie's mobile sexual desire conjures the specter of prostitution that haunts Dupin's reconstruction of her mysterious death. Like all specters, however, this one fails to materialize fully. Though Marie enjoys the attentions of many men, though she is a shopgirl and a grisette,[24] Dupin labels her decidedly "gay, but not abject" (Poe 1969– 78, 3:768–69). From this, Dupin surmises that Marie's abductor is "above the grade of the common sailor": he is an officer whose companionship with a working-class girl goes without saying (ibid., 769). Construed as an attribute of *her* class, Marie's dangerously mobile sexuality is disarmed. Her desires are predictable rather than criminal; Dupin's study of Marie remains a study of the ordinary.[25]

Although Marie is entirely unlike the "public man" of Paris, she is paradoxically similar to the private men in the tale, Dupin and the narrator. Her walks epitomize her character, identifying her as socially and sexually mutable. Dupin says of these walks that they "may, in general, be supposed discursive" (Poe 1969–78, 3:749). Marie's "discursive" character—what makes her unpredictable—suggests a self that resists purpose or definition. Like Marie's walks, Dupin's method of ratiocination is quintessentially discursive, nonnarrative, passing from premise to conclusion by way of intricate logical peregrinations.[26] Minimizing his discussion of motives, Dupin glosses the relations of cause and effect, and instead employs the "doctrine of chance," or "as it is technically termed, the Calculus of Probabilities" (Poe 1969–78, 3:724). Dupin's "scientific" analysis of each bit of evidence is a local interpretation; as a whole, his argument is a collection of such interpretations, some of which are mutually exclusive. Ratiocination creates an aura of sequential logic, but Dupin's discrete points are non sequiturs; furthermore, "Marie Rogêt" follows no chronological trajectory. The teleological movement of the plot of detection is undermined in the text by the work performed by Dupin. Though he engages the facts of the case serially in order to magnify and focus evidential details,[27] Dupin's argument moves as if from center to periphery: he eliminates particular criminal possibilities without diminishing the concentric circles of total possibility. "Marie Rogêt," which represents worlds within worlds, texts within texts, and selves within selves, thus poses acutely the question of narrative point of view. Dupin's attempts to look at the same event—the crime—from all sides and points of view result in a loss of perspective. As a discursive subject, Dupin doubles and follows Marie. Her traces, the signs of her peregrinations, are the only connecting tissues that hold together Dupin's narrative fragments. Marie's walks, then, dramatize the problem of identity most central to the text: how narrative helps delimit the periphery of personhood.

Marie's discursive identity raises the corresponding specter of unstable masculine identity, and more particularly, of masculine authorial identity. Walking plots the danger of permeable boundaries between urban environments, but as a metaphor for writing, it also suggests the frightening possibilities of indistinct fictional environments. By an act of imagination, or ideality, Dupin can inhabit any body in any place, and his method dictates that he do so in order to solve the case. Dupin himself has no visible body, only a protean intelligence that expands and contracts to fit the minds of his subjects. He variously impersonates Marie and her murderer, giving voice to their innermost thoughts, their secret connivances and schemes of betrayal. Dupin's form of ratiocination necessitates this invasion of privacy, this colonizing of other bodies in exactly those moments of crisis at which they can be said to be out of their minds. But crossing the borders of individual personhood, Dupin demonstrates the sameness of these different identities, and the slippage between woman and man, victim and victimizer, becomes pronounced.

In *Marginalia* Poe disparages this kind of confusion, noting the "sad state of perplexity and promiscuity" attending the unstable representation of gender in Roman depictions of their gods: "Not a quality named that does not impinge upon some one other. . . . Even gender was never precisely settled. Servius on Vergil mentions a Venus with a beard. In Macrobius, too, Calvus talks of her as if she were a man, while Valerius Soranus expressly calls Jupiter 'the Mother of the Gods' " (Poe 1981b, 38). This destabilization of gender categories throws love (Venus) and motherhood (Jupiter) into disarray. Promiscuity designates not wanton sexual behavior but the Romans' incapacity to keep masculine and feminine distinct.[28] Likewise, Marie's promiscuity is an attribute of her discursiveness, a problem of representation rather than sexual behavior as such. "Marie Rogêt" attempts to retard this unseemly blurring of gender roles by fixing them, at least for a moment, into stable images of female victim and male victimizer. Marie's abortion, were it represented, would disrupt this order. To the extent that it signifies a market version of the self that evaporates nostalgic gender categories, the abortion indicts Marie as unwomanly, and therefore remains invisible in this picture. The textual search for new ways to define the self leads away from the sphere of public virtue and the web of domestic ties, and toward a valuation of individual idiosyncrasy, of marks of difference that find their strongest expression in conventionally gendered sex crimes.

Compared with the complexly gendered discursive subject, the gendered body in Poe's text more easily withstands examination. From behind the mask of science, Dupin dissects the body of Marie, unpeeling the layers of her identity, attempting a kind of archaeological inquisition into her constitutional uniqueness. In death, Marie finally transcends the ordinary. Dupin considers her general size and shape, a peculiar hairy mark on her arm, her shoes, the flowers worn in her hat, and her garter—whatever about her that is idiosyncratic—as positive proof in the identification of her corpse. However, the surest signs of Marie's identity are not found on her body, which has been mutilated almost beyond recognition, but in her clothes, which bear the stamp of use. Marie's self-adjusting garters are indisputably Marie's because she has tightened them by setting back the clasp: "what is made to adjust itself, must of necessity require foreign adjustment but rarely. It must have been by accident, in its strictest sense, that these garters of Marie needed the tightening described. They alone would have amply established her identity" (Poe 1969–78, 3:747). Individuality is confirmed along with identity as a mark incidentally inscribed by the body on mass-produced goods. The tale's prurient interest in Marie's garter is mediated not only by Dupin's scientism but by an erotics of things, a fetishism of commodities transformed by personal effects. The desires that chance to be aroused by the market are here transmogrified into accidents of being.[29]

Dupin's concern to identify Marie eventually gives way to the more pressing concern of identifying her assassin. Yet in his search for the murderer, Dupin follows a trail of clues left not by the perpetrator but by Marie. His emphasis on her physical appearance, her quality of being on display, leads Dupin to consider obsessively the visible "traces" of Marie. She leaves a litter of clues, signs of herself, that tell Dupin where she has been. The marks left by Marie are assurances that she once lived and lived *here;* they are contingent reminders that she does so no longer. Like the trail of her petticoats discovered strewn about the thicket, or the lingering scent of the perfume she once sold, these traces of Marie advertise both a private life that remains unintelligible and Dupin's fetishistic desire to explain it. The traces do not begin to settle the question of identity, but reformulate it as a problem of reference: is identity visible or tangible in personal effects? Is Marie's body evidence enough to lend credence to Dupin's speculative explanation of her death?

Dupin follows these traces, charting Marie's path through Paris toward the scene of the crime. He plots the unplotted points of Marie's perambulations on a map of the city, imaginatively satisfying a touristic, voyeuristic impulse toward a kind of literary rubbernecking. The text explicitly identifies all of the New York and the Paris locales that it visits, enlisting Marie's sexual history in the marketing of place. The fascinating "attraction" of the site of Mary/Marie's death not only impels Dupin but impelled many of Poe's nineteenth-century readers to the scene where her body was discovered. The *New York Herald* parodied the bizarre impulse to see in the site a fabricated advertisement for Hoboken that wryly comments on, even as it creates, the public's sense of spectacle: "Hoboken is, in these days, one of the most delightful spots out of town, or under heaven. Its walks—its groves—its sea shores—its fields—its skies—its swings—its murders—its love scrapes— its picnics—its all in all, are unrivalled and unsurpassed" (*New York Herald*, 28 July 1841).

As he draws nearer the scene of the crime, Dupin emphasizes its importance, and so implies his interest in staging Marie's violation—in reproducing and reviewing it—as a private spectacle. A thicket, discovered near the Barrière du Roule by the two small sons of the innkeeper Madame Deluc, is the putative scene of the murder. Dupin's analysis of the thicket, however, is convoluted and contradictory. He convincingly argues that Marie's petticoat, gloves, scarf, and parasol, all of which were found in the thicket, must have been planted there long after her death; he then conveniently forgets this argument and shifts his line of inquiry. Having spent considerable time evaluating the thicket, Dupin states evasively: "We are not engaged in an attempt to discover the scene, but to produce the perpetrators of the murder" (Poe 1969–78, 3:763). Dupin turns the evidence he has adduced against the thicket into evidence against a gang. He asks rhetorically: "What *struggle* could have taken place—what struggle so violent and so enduring as to have left 'traces' in all directions—between a weak and defenceless girl and the *gang* of ruffians imagined? The silent grasp of a few rough arms and all would have been over" (ibid.). The violent and enduring struggle he stages is the struggle between a lone man and a lone woman. The disconcerting female agency of a woman seeking to abort her fetus is overpowered and negated, not massively in a gang rape, but decisively in a confrontation of individuals.[30]

If Dupin suggests that the thicket both must have been and could not have been the scene of the crime, it is because the thicket signifies in two symbolic registers. As a setting in nature, the thicket is inadmissible to Dupin, but as the stage for a domestic drama, he finds it entirely probable.

Dupin describes the thicket in the following fashion: "This thicket was a singular—an exceedingly singular one. It was unusually dense" (ibid., 761). The thicket formed a protective enclosure around an area that Dupin imagines to be a kind of natural parlor: "Within its naturally walled enclosure were three extraordinary stones, *forming a seat with a back and footstool*" (ibid.). Marie's articles of clothing were found there "deposited as if on shelves" (ibid., 762). This "highly artificial arrangement" of clothes decorated the thicket, which was "so full of a natural art" (ibid., 761). Dupin dresses the scene of violation with domestic props, recoding a public space as private and interior. He thus sets the stage for a crime entirely similar to that in "Rue Morgue," where Dupin must discover the mode of ingress into the locked back room of Madame L'Espanaye and her daughter. The back room and the thicket are settings of sexual violation, barely disguised images of the penetrated (maternal) female body.[31]

The equation of masculine sexual desire and the desire for the singular "possession" of a woman in death is made explicit in the 1843 version of "Marie Rogêt": "We are not forced to suppose a premeditated design of murder or of violation. But there was the friendly shelter of the thicket, and the approach of rain—there was opportunity and strong temptation—and then a sudden and violent wrong, to be concealed only by one of darker dye" (ibid., 769). Murder stands in for rape, revising and concealing it. Each is the result of uncontrolled passion, an "accident" of individual desire that is, like Marie's tightened garter, identity's distinguishing mark. Poe removed this passage when he republished "Marie Rogêt" in *Tales*, no doubt because it so thoroughly precludes the possibility of Marie's abortion. Yet even in the 1845 version, Marie's actual death, like her abortion, is unrepresented, taking place in a narrative absence. When Dupin imagines the criminal, alone with the dead, he elides the act of murder and considers only its aftereffects:

> Let us see. An individual has committed the murder. He is alone with the ghost of the departed. He is appalled by what lies motionless before him. The fury of his passion is over, and there is abundant room in his heart for the natural awe of the dead. His is none of that confidence which the presence of numbers inevitably inspires. He is *alone* with the dead. He trembles and is bewildered. (Ibid., 764)

Dupin, leaving behind his pretensions to scientific analysis, impersonates the naval officer after the fact, in his hour of wretchedness. The traces of Marie have led not to the recovery of her corpse, but into the thoughts of her assassin. Dupin gives a surprisingly personal account of the murderer's state of mind—one could say that Dupin identifies with him. In the textual space evacuated of the abortion and filled by a rape and murder, Dupin finds a place for himself. His rendering of the scene inside the thicket is thus both peculiarly introspective (he looks into himself and finds the sentiments of a killer) and voyeuristic (he peers into the dark, secluded thicket and "sees" this scene). Dupin's insistence that a solitary individual must have killed Marie allows him to invest the crime with a human face—with the agency and culpability he will not ascribe to a gang (or to a mother).

The question of identity posed by the peripatetic Marie—the aimless, unintegrated self—is seemingly answered in the unitary and solitary figure of her killer. Dupin recovers masculine individuality in the act of the violent sexual possession of a woman. In the scene Dupin depicts, the killer is "*alone* with the dead." Guilt is experienced as an encounter with oneself, as the anguished reintegration of a divided personality. Apart from a community that might pass judgment on him, the guilty assassin, also the crime's only witness, authorizes his own actions. The real "scene" of the crime is the birthplace of this splintered subject; violence is born in the darkroom of self-exposure. The assassin's act of murder is registered through self-surveillance, through a double consciousness that promotes separate and simultaneous points of view.

Dupin eliminates the gang members as suspects because, not having a collective consciousness, they could never be self-censuring. A gang member seeks the rural precincts of the town "by way of escape from the restraints and conventionalities of society. He desires . . . the utter license of the country . . . he indulges unchecked by any eye except those of his boon companions, in all the mad excess of a counterfeit hilarity" (ibid., 760). Unlike the gang member, the self-disciplining criminal is checked by his own eye, which, as much as the shelf, seat, and footstool, is a sign of domestic order (Brodhead 1988). Though portrayed as individuating the criminal, rape and murder provide him no "escape from the restraints and conventionalities of society." Instead, Marie's violation originates in a thicket, which looks like a parlor, which looks like the den of Dupin.

IV

The scene in the thicket scripts the self-possession of Marie's lover-rapist in the act of "possessing" her body. This body is abducted and held for ransom, the price paid for the stable representation of masculine identity in a market that elicits unpredictable, uncontrollable passions. I want now to look at the economic exchanges in the text that set the circulation of Marie's body in motion. Like her assassin's, the question of Marie's identity is settled by an accident of desire, but this desire is Dupin's rather than her own. Her identity is a stake in the gentlemen's bet Dupin has made with the prefect:

If, dating our inquiries from the body found, and then tracing a murderer, we yet discover this body to be that of some other individual than Marie; or if, starting from the living Marie, we find her, yet find her unassassinated—in either case we lose our labor; since it is the Monsieur G— with whom we have to deal. For our own purposes, therefore, if not for the purposes of justice, it is indispensable that our first step should be the determination of the identity of the corpse with the Marie Rogêt who is missing. (Poe 1969–78, 3:737)

The innumerable bits of evidence that prove that Marie is Marie only confirm a foregone conclusion. Her identity is settled "not for the purposes of justice" but to guarantee Dupin's remuneration. Dupin trades on the certainty of Marie's identity, for it insures him against risk and increases the probability that he will be paid in full for his part in solving the mystery. Unlike exchanges in the impersonal, peripatetic market in which intellectual labor is uncertainly valued, the personal transaction between the Prefect and Dupin creates a private space of economic order sequestered from the random forces of commerce. Marie's body acts as a buffer against these forces, demystifying the process of exchange by assuring the outcome of Dupin's investigation.

Like the solution to the mystery, Marie enters this constricted circuit of exchange as Dupin's invention, and analogously, as Poe's literary property. It is Poe's ability to marshal the facts of Mary Rogers's case into the mediated history of Marie from which he, like Dupin, can expect to profit. This process of mediation is allegorized by the tale's footnotes, which Poe appended to his 1845 revision. The notes represent Mary Rogers and Marie Rogêt as virtually interchangeable. The tale transports Mary from New York to Paris and transfigures her into Marie; the notes then reconsign a textualized, exoticized Marie to the quotidian world of New York newspapers, citing them as the "real" sources for each of the Parisian dailies quoted. The narrator submits that the tale "was composed at a distance from the scene of the atrocity, and with no other means of investigation than the newspapers afforded" (ibid., 723). The footnotes insist on the distance between the scene of composition and the scene of the atrocity, even as the notes collapse the difference between Mary and Marie. What this double dislocation obscures is that Marie has no "real" referent, for the story concerns only an already textualized Mary as she appears in the print world of the newspapers. Marie's identity, once formulated through the trail of her garments as a problem of reference, is finally an issue of textual intercession. The "atrocity" of this crime is committed on paper, where Marie is abducted by the similarly fictional constructs of the newspapers and the tale itself.

Abduction, then, is a media crime, superintended by Poe, in which the outrage against Marie is refracted through too many textual lenses.[32] In a story where murder conceals rape, which in turn stands for a botched abortion, the body of Marie negotiates too many criminal possibilities. As Dupin observes, the difficulty of the case is that one can "picture . . . a mode—many modes—and a motive—many motives" (Poe 1969–78, 3:736). Yet Dupin's discussion of motives is almost nonexistent, while his analysis of modes is so extravagant as to be almost ornamental. Mode and motive are incidental to the crime, which, understood as an accident of passion, remains inexplicable and unrepresentable. Dupin pictures not this criminal incoherence but that which he might render in excessive detail—Marie's corpse:

> The face was suffused with dark blood, some of which issued from the mouth. . . . About the throat were bruises and impressions of fingers. . . . The flesh of the neck was much swollen. There were no cuts apparent, or bruises which appeared the effect of blows. A piece of lace was found tied so tightly around the neck as to be hidden from sight: it was completely buried in the flesh, and was fastened by a knot which lay just under the left ear. This alone would have sufficed to produce death. (Ibid., 730)

The unspeakable crime against Marie is recorded not by Dupin's narrative but in the body language of her mutilated flesh. Here, Marie's neck and throat, not her womb, are the repeated targets of her attacker. Marie's neck is inscribed as origin, then strangled by an emblem of her femininity, a piece of lace "hidden from sight." He who has silenced Marie has forcibly excluded her from language; blood is her mouth's only issue. The literal overkill of the passage does not resolve the discrepancy between rape and abortion, but nevertheless reiterates the exact nature of the atrocity: the struggle between Marie and her assassin is a battle to the death over the authority to produce meaning. The rape of Marie is a literary crime that leaves her linguistically barren; her throat bears the "impressions of fingers" from a hand that well might be Poe's.[33]

Though the epistemology of the autopsy Dupin performs on Marie is a visual one, her corpse, even on close inspection, remains immobile and opaque, a ghastly caricature of the transparency so valued in sentimental womanhood (Haltunen 1982). Marie's condition, like that of the beheaded Madame L'Espanaye, is "(horrible to relate!)" (Poe 1969–78, 2:538). Dupin's parenthetical horror of the female body is emphatic and yet excisable; erupting marginally, it is mingled with his unmistakable relish. His otherwise methodical exposition brackets and contains his attraction-repulsion to the mutilated corpse he envisions, keeping it at a distance. However, Dupin's detachment from his subject—his attempt to rationalize the body—fails to tame its lurid effects: the "language of the evidence" provides no syntax that might make his horror comprehensible (ibid., 3:766). Instead, Marie's excessive visibility acts as a screen that reflects Dupin's horror of relation, a horror that both originates and interrupts the order of his narrative (Jacobus 1990).

Dupin exhumes Marie's corpse and makes its condition public, "not for the purposes of justice" but because, in the sensational economy of the text, the display of her wounds accrues interest for his private investigation. Dupin's horrible relation to the female body, characterized by his rationalizing gaze, provides the most graphic example of the manner in which his evidentiary discourse encodes power relations. Dupin situates himself at the top of a hierarchy of knowledge, unveiling Marie's body and making it available to hypothetical readers as an object of speculation. The story achieves a delicate balance as an artifact of both privately owned and publicly available information: though Dupin and the narrator monopolize the solution to the mystery, they freely divulge the means by which they came to own it. In a gesture of apparent inclusion, for example, the narrator reprints for his readers all of the newspaper excerpts relevant to Dupin: "It will be proper that I submit to the reader some passages . . ." (Poe 1969–78, 3:731). Presumably, the conclusions Dupin draws are recoverable by all equally careful readers.[34] But as a pedagogic model of perfect reading, Dupin is impossible to reproduce. For all his precision, Dupin's analytical abilities are no less mysterious than Madame Rogêt's "singular prophecy" that she would never see Marie again (Poe 1969–78, 3:755). The calculus of probabilities invoked by Dupin throughout the tale as an explanatory device is the tool not of an ordinary reader but of a specialist. While in theory the calculus, unlike intuition or divination, is purely mathematical, its application is highly conjectural: "and thus we have the anomaly of the most rigidly exact in science applied to the shadow and spirituality of the most intangible speculation" (ibid., 724).

Dupin's magical powers of demystification are calculated to yield a profit; his "method" is of central importance to the success of the tale. Poe discussed the popular appeal of his detective stories in a letter to Philip P. Cooke, admitting that Cooke was "right about the hair-splitting of my French friend:—all that is done for effect. These tales of ratiocination owe most of their popularity to being something in a new key. I do not mean that they are not ingenious—but people think them more ingenious than they are—on account of their method and *air* of method" (Poe 1966, 2:328). Poe's canniness about the market value of "method" in fiction indicates his willingness to capitalize on the same cultural valuation of "objective" analysis that the newspapers did, and to invest "method" with new generic possibilities. The newspaper excerpts authorize Dupin's public disclosure of information, while at the same time providing him with a narrative foil. "Marie Rogêt" thus frustrates and satisfies an already existing market of readers by mimicking newspaper representations of the phenomenal world.[35]

Dupin's monopoly of method reflects his mastery of a discourse that commodifies the female body. He resolves the outrage against Marie by understanding the ways in which the crime disturbs patterns of rightful ownership. These economic terms are more susceptible to Dupin's analysis, less horrible to relate, than those that expose the hidden dynamics of power through which Marie is silenced. Dupin transposes the statutory offense of murder into a riddle concerning property ownership: the question of who killed whom is answered only by the question of who owns what. The linchpin of his case connects the perpetrator to a boat that disappears from the dock to which it was anchored. The clue that tips off Dupin is a newspaper advertisement that makes public the theft of the boat, the vessel in which Marie was presumably abducted.[36] This advertisement suggests only —opaquely—that "the rudder is at hand" (Poe 1969–78, 3:770). Dupin reasons that Marie's murderer must be the *owner* of the missing boat, who, anxious to retrieve his property, has stolen it back.

Dupin has no real evidence with which to convict the unnamed naval officer he charges with Marie's murder; Dupin's conclusions are only inferences, but by the end of the tale, he has enough authority to condemn the man without proof.[37] Like Marie, the perpetrator leaves visible traces of himself, but they are categorically different from hers. Marie's clothing and the disfiguring "marks" on her body are signs of a corporality that is ultimately mediated away (ibid., 771). Although Dupin introduces Marie's body as evidence of her violation, he suspends habeas corpus for her assassin, whom he never brings forward to confirm or deny the accusation of murder. Instead, Dupin finds traces of an assassin who exists only in and as text. The murderer is the author of certain "well written and urgent communications to the journals" (ibid., 769), with which he intends to cast suspicion away from himself. But the notes are his only identifying marks; they are the published, public signs that verify his existence.

Incriminated as Marie's assassin, the naval officer is only one of many "guilty authors" who have perpetrated some crime against her (ibid., 761). No less than the naval officer, the narrator and Dupin are themselves strangely implicated in her abduction. The narrator begins the tale by explaining that he feels "called upon to make public" some extraordinary details "which will carry with them the air of extorted confession. Hearing what I have heard lately, it would indeed be strange should I remain silent in regard to what I both heard and saw so long ago" (ibid., 724). The narrator frames Dupin's relation of the tale as a confession, and simultaneously invests himself, the writer, with the corporal authority of an eyewitness. Textual authority, though buoyed by the newspapers, resides in this originary moment of oral transmission, a moment that revises the aborted history of origins represented by the body of Marie.

Dupin's confessions, however, are extorted. Rather than settling the question of his guilt, they raise the problem of the narrator's legitimacy, and of that of the text. Has the text, like Marie, been "despoiled"? There is no way to tell. The circulation of guilt thus becomes central to the story's textual economy. Readers are themselves declared responsible for the text's failings, and denied the right to judge. This is made clear by the narrator's final, exorbitant act of sophistry. Though he initially asked that the history of Marie be read with an eye toward the solution of Mary's murder, he abruptly recants. The error of such a naive reading is "a gross error redolent of mischief—[that] I cannot pretend to expose within the limits assigned me at present; but with the philosophical it needs no exposure" (Poe 1969–78, 3:773). This final exposure of guilt follows quickly upon "Mr. Poe" 's bracketed profession of authorship: "[For reasons which we shall not specify, but which to many readers will appear obvious, we have taken the liberty of here omitting, from the MSS. placed in our hands, such portion as details the *following up* of the apparently slight clew obtained by Dupin. . . . Mr. Poe's article concludes with the following words.—*Eds.*]" (ibid., 772). The proper subject of the narrative is interrupted, and the power vested in the narrator is relinquished, along with the text, to his editors. But "Eds." is only another way to name "Mr. Poe," whose article concludes with his own schizophrenic signature. His final bracketing of self also exposes a splintered personality that is divided among the roles of reader, writer, and editor. In the last analysis, Poe's horror of relation mediates his unspeakable encounter with himself. His autograph inscribes him in "Marie Rogêt" at the very place in which he ought to name the guilty author of a crime against Marie.

In late November and early December 1842, just before publishing the final installment of "Marie Rogêt," Poe himself disappeared. John Walsh hypothesizes that Poe returned to New York from Philadelphia with the desperate hope of uncovering new evidence that might discredit Mrs. Loss's confession (1968, 51–73). But the writer's return to the scene of the crime revealed nothing: the clues died with Mary, and only other texts remained. What Poe could not have known was that his own text would, over time, become more thoroughly integrated into collective memory—more authoritative—than the fragments of newspaper reportage on which it was based. The narrator's idea that "all argument founded upon the fiction is applicable to the truth" is perhaps truer than he knew; the notion that we read history through the lens of fiction is borne out by a whole body of criticism that takes Poe's obituary text, and his Marie, as the point of origin for speculation about Mary and her historical circumstances.[38]

NOTES

Thanks to Lisa Cohen and the many who read previous drafts of this essay, especially Elizabeth Abrams and Rishona Zimring.

1. Except where specifically noted, all citations reproduce Poe's idiosyncratic use of italics for emphasis.

2. Most critical discussions of "Marie Rogêt" evaluate it in terms of its historical accuracy—that is, as a more or less accurate mirror of reality. See, for example, the exchange between William Wimsatt and Samuel Copp Worthen (Wimsatt 1941; Worthen 1948–49; Wimsatt 1949–50).

3. John Walsh traces the history of the disappearance of Mary Rogers, and Poe's attempts to fathom it, in his wonderful book *Poe the Detective* (1968). This essay is much indebted to Walsh's own detective work. It should be clear from what follows that Walsh investigates a historical subject, Mary Rogers, and I am investigating a textual subject, Marie Rogêt.

4. In nineteenth-century usage, "concealment" alluded to birth or pregnancy. See the *Oxford English Dictionary*; see also Mohr (1978, 62, 88), who notes that Alfred G. Hall's *Mother's Own Book* (1843) listed emmenagogic and abortifacient recipes under the heading "secret information."

5. "The Mystery of Marie Rogêt" was the first detective story that attempted to solve a "real" crime, and it advertises itself as such.

6. *New York Atlas*, 8 August 1841; quoted in Walsh 1968 (8). The information in this and the following paragraph is summarized from Walsh, and confirmed by my own reading of the New York dailies.

7. The letter is dated 4 January 1848 (Poe 1966, 2:355–56).

8. Poe self-consciously quotes or paraphrases the contemporaneous newspaper coverage of Mary's case throughout the tale, meticulously footnoting each excerpt. However, he subtly excises, emends, and embellishes the published facts of the case, severing his tale's "ideal series of events" from popular explanations of Mary's death.

9. "Quickening" described the time when the fetus could be felt to move, usually around the fifth month of pregnancy. The time of quickening, however, was difficult to determine except by the mother's testimony. For practical purposes, then, an abortion was illegal only if it resulted in the death of the woman, and in that event the doctor or pharmacist was held liable. It was nearly impossible, however, for pathologists to determine whether an abortion had occurred, and therefore difficult to obtain convictions. See Mohr 1978; Smith-Rosenberg 1985; Olasky 1986.

10. See Mohr 1978 and Smith-Rosenberg 1985; Mohr also discusses the important role of the press.

11. For a complete account of Madame Restell's career, see Browder 1988.

12. The central role played by the press in the trial of Restell was highlighted both in the courtroom and in the dailies. Transcripts of the trial, published by the *New York Tribune* and the *New York Herald*, make clear that the newspapers did not simply report events but altered their course: for the prosecution, one Mrs. Purdy deposed that she had found Madame Restell through an advertisement in the *New York Sun*; and for the defense, because of the extensive and prejudicial exposure of Madame Restell, the selection of impartial jurors was slow and difficult. See *New York Tribune*, 30 April 1841, 20 July 1841; *New York Herald*, 15 July 1841. Restell herself protests the "malevolent falsehoods and intentional misrepresentations" of the press, charging that "its effect is to prejudice and poison the public mind." See *New York Herald*, 3 May 1841.

13. Ads for patent medicines were at the center of these controversies (Schudson 1978). Though the *Tribune* did not advertise abortion, it did advertise patent medicines. The line between abortifacients and patent medicines was thin, especially as advertisements for abortifacients became less and less explicit about the intended use of the product. Referring to "Female Pills," "French Renovating Pills," and so forth, the advertisements nevertheless made their meanings known, as is clear in the following advertisement placed by Madame Costello: "French Lunar Pills . . . [are] so called on account of their efficacy in producing the monthly turn of females. . . . Their effects are truly astonishing. They are never attended with any distressing operation, are always certain, and therefore pregnant women should not take them" (*New York Herald*, 21 August 1841).

14. Marvin Olasky estimates that in the year 1840 alone, Madame Restell bought about $420 worth of advertising, "an appreciable sum, in that Bennett had founded the *Herald* with just $500 in 1835" (1986, 51).

15. The *New York Herald* had earlier called Restell a "learned philosopher in petticoats" (21 August 1839).

16. Walsh notes that the "Hudson River frequently gave up the body of some man or woman who had found a grave in it. . . . Such happenings were usually given one or two paragraphs and no follow-up" (1968, 7–8).

17. For example, at Madame Restell's trial it became clear that a client, Mrs. Purdy, was

referred (without the knowledge of her husband) to Madame Restell and her ad in the *Sun* by her black washerwoman, Rebecca (Browder 1988, 31).

18. The Comstock law is quoted in ibid. (147). See also Mohr 1978 (196–99) on the effects of Comstock's law on the practice and advertising of abortion.

19. Abortion advertising declined precipitously but did not disappear. The language of the remaining ads became so veiled, however, that they were ineffectual as marketing devices.

20. It is not entirely clear why the customers in a perfume shop are "desperate." Poe seems to have collapsed the distance between fact and fiction, forgetting that Marie, unlike Mary, did not work with the sometimes rowdy patrons of a cigar store. Alternatively, Francine du Plessix Gray writes that in Paris in the 1880s, sexual trade was conducted in the back rooms of perfume shops, or "boutiques à surprise"; but this may be anachronistic for New York in the 1840s (1992, 32).

21. I take this formulation from Philip Fisher (1986). The roots of the phenomena of celebrity discussed by Fisher can be found, I believe, much earlier in the century than his article acknowledges, and are more heavily inflected by gender than he admits.

22. Robert Byer (1986) notes the shock of the everyday in his discussion of "The Man of the Crowd."

23. Anne Friedberg argues that, toward the end of the nineteenth century, the department store offered a protected public site that authorized the gaze of the *flâneuse* (Friedberg 1993, 32–38). Marie's gaze is not protected or even represented; in Poe's constellation of consumer culture, Marie emblematizes the desire for commodities, but it is specifically as a desiring subject that she meets her demise. See also Gilman 1993, who sees "Marie Rogêt" as a reading of urban experience.

24. Parisian grisettes were "modest kept women . . . salesgirls or factory workers, so named because many of them were associated with the garment trade, in which gray cloth was widely used" (Gray 1992, 33). On the relations between working-class women and the attentions commonly paid them by upper-class men, see Stansell 1987.

25. Peter Brooks writes that the "prostitute's plot is by definition a deviance" (1985, 156), whereas I have argued that Marie figures the ordinary. Moreover, prostitution signifies a different configuration of female body and marketplace than the one I am interested in here, the one signified by abortion. The problem posed by prostitution is the selling of self, the conversion of sex into a commodity, whereas abortion introduces a related but different epistemological concern about concealment and the reproduction of self. This puts an entirely different spin on the relation of sex to the market; abortion suggests the creation of a market for bastardized forms or texts. Another crucial difference is that while the plot of prostitution relates the impossibility of effacing the marks of vice (see Brooks), the plot of abortion relates the opposite. Thus, the prostitute's body is ultimately immutable and unsusceptible to revision, while an abortion erases the secret past of the woman who has had it.

26. The *Oxford English Dictionary* lists "ratiocinative" as a synonym for "discursive." Paradoxically, the discursive is both aimless and analytical.

27. This is Barthes's phrase (1981, 99). Dupin looks at the facts of the case as if he were looking at a photograph.

28. Poe, according to the *Oxford English Dictionary*, was the first to use the word "promiscuity" in this way.

29. Dupin's "Calculus of Probabilities," or "doctrine of chance," makes accident its field of analysis. The calculus puts statistics at the service of the prediction of otherwise unpredictable behaviors, including both criminal and economic ones. But the economic man posited by Dupin as Marie's murderer (discussed later in the essay) meets his match in Marie, who embodies and elicits "illogical" market behavior. Her decision to terminate her pregnancy, for example, remains outside the provenance of Dupin's social-scientific analysis.

30. There was no decisive evidence, no way to tell, whether Mary/Marie had been violated, and if she had been, how many times. The signs of sexual violation were not appreciably different from signs of abortion. Dupin summarizes: "We will resume this question by mere allusion to the revolting details of the surgeon examined at the inquest. It is only necessary to say that his published *inferences*, in regard to the number of the ruffians, have been properly ridiculed as unjust and totally baseless, by all the reputable anatomists of Paris. Not that the matter *might not* have been as inferred, but that there was no ground for the inference:—was there not much for another?" (Poe 1969–78, 3:763).

31. It is possible to read the scene of Marie's rape and murder in the thicket through the lens of psychoanalysis—as a primal scene that is repressed and replayed throughout the text.

32. Abduction is a logical category elaborated by Peirce that Nancy Harrowitz (1983) identifies as the particular brand of ratiocination employed by Poe—not deduction or induction but, suggestively, abduction. Abduction is the retroactive explanation of an observed fact with a "known law of nature" or "general truth." Abduction is the perceptual jump that allows one to posit the origin of a fact, an origin that can then be tested to prove or disprove a hypothesis. In my view, logical and sexual abduction are two inseparable phenomena in Dupin's double search for criminal and sexual origins.

33. Freud's Dora provides another clear example of the displacement and reinscription of sexual desire from womb to throat: "the conclusion was inevitable that with her spasmodic cough, which, as is usual, was referred for its exciting cause to a tickling in her throat, she pictured to herself a scene of sexual gratification *per os* between the two people whose love-affair occupied her mind so incessantly" (Freud 1963a, 65). In Dora's case, as in Marie's, this displacement fulfills equally the desire of her analyst, who wrestles with her to control the meaning of her stories.

34. On the high premium placed by nineteenth-century sentimental culture on transparent forms of "seeing," and especially on the triumph of transparency over deception, see Wolf 1992.

35. In *Marginalia*, Poe outlines a new science of reading produced by and for the magazine market. He describes a world of proliferating "facts" that must be both disseminated and apprehended with increasing speed. The new journalism processes and packages the facts in order to circulate them more effectively—in other words, in order to exchange them on an ever spiraling circuit of information (1981b, 91).

36. John Walsh concludes that this newspaper excerpt was fabricated by Poe (1968, 43). Poe infrequently tampered with the "facts" of the case, but his invention of this one

points to his need to understand this crime in terms of property ownership and publication.

37. It is entirely unclear, for example, why a naval officer would be stationed in Paris; Dupin's indictment of the officer only really makes sense if his case is set in New York. This oversight indicates the extent to which the "facts" of the case become irrelevant to its solution.

38. Walsh notes several critics, including himself, who have attempted to track down the naval officer in Poe's text and correlate him with Mary Rogers's murderer. Walsh is the only one who made a serious attempt to connect Mary's death with circumstances *not* elaborated in the tale—despite the existence of several nineteenth-century fictional and documentary reconstructions of Mary's death (J. H. Ingraham, George W. Walling, Thomas Byrnes, Andrew Jackson Davis), at least one of which explicitly depicts Mary's abortion (Davis 1869).

PART FOUR

READING CULTURE

Poe, Literary Nationalism, and Authorial Identity

MEREDITH L. MCGILL

But, before we have an American literature, we must have an American criticism.
—James Russell Lowell, "Our Contributors"

Even when their intent is to place Edgar Allan Poe's career and writings within the context of antebellum publishing, biographical and critical studies generally produce an image of Poe standing apart from the institutions and practices through which authors gained access to the reading public. Characteristically, Poe is depicted in staunch and principled opposition to the coteries that dominated the literary marketplace (Moss 1963), or calculatedly or desperately conceding to their demands (Richard 1968). Such critiques try to preserve Poe's integrity by insisting that his work remains detachable from the well-orchestrated "puffing" and cliquish favoritism that largely controlled the market for books in that period. Poe's prominent attacks on this system and his persistent advocacy of an analytic and impartial criticism have enabled literary historians to portray him as a figure of heroic resistance despite the sometimes damning details of his literary and critical practice.

The critical investment in Poe as a figure who could remain detached from the conditions of production finds its origin in the intersection of Poe's career with the very coteries from which critics have tried to distance him. Rather than isolating him from his milieu, Poe's insistence on critical impartiality enabled him to be taken up as an exemplary subject by an influential group of literary nationalists, the Young Americans. Poe's sudden rise to prominence in the early months of 1845 and his spectacular decline in the autumn of that year were crucially mediated by his association with the cause of American literary independence. I will analyze the terms of this alliance as it was forged in an influential biography, tested in the "Little Longfellow War," and fractured by Poe's scandalous performance at the Boston Lyceum. Rather than being a story of heroic resistance, unavoidable complicity, and unfortunate psychological collapse, Poe's implication with the coteries and with the cause of literary nationalism forms a crucial chapter in the history of the production of Poe as a subject who stands outside history.

James Russell Lowell and the "Be-Mirrorment" of Poe

James Russell Lowell's biographical essay "Edgar Allan Poe" not only served to announce Poe's arrival on the increasingly important New York publishing scene; it also marked the incorporation of the figure of Poe into the discourse of literary nationalism, and the public identification of his writings and career as chief casualties of, and possible solutions to the problem of, a national literature. Written at Poe's request for a *Graham's Magazine* series called "Our Contributors," Lowell's essay was immediately reprinted in two installments on the front page of the *New York Evening Mirror,* and widely noticed in New York, Philadelphia, and Baltimore papers. Read in the context of the circumstances of its composition and first printing, Lowell's essay might be regarded merely as a friendly critique and informative summary of Poe's life and work written for the benefit of the readers of *Graham's,* the popular Philadelphia monthly of which Poe had been an editor and to which he continued to contribute regularly. Yet Lowell's essay took on its primary significance for Poe's career and for the cultural legacy of the figure of Poe in the context of its New York reprinting. It is not simply that the republication of the essay and its endorsement by a group of influential editors and reviewers—N. P. Willis, Margaret Fuller, Charles Briggs, and Evert Duyckinck—gave this critique added prestige and contributed to its wider distribution. The embrace of Lowell's version of Poe by these literati, all of whom had close ties to the literary nationalist program of the Young America movement, placed Poe's New York debut firmly within the context of the highly politicized struggle to define the terms of American literary independence.

The publication of Lowell's essay was a pivotal event in Poe's struggle to gain recognition for and to profit by his writing. In addition to praising Poe's abilities as a poet, critic, and writer of tales, Lowell reprinted selections from the poetry and provided a comprehensive list of the uncollected and anonymous tales, marking the first time on the national stage that a description of Poe had been identified with a body of writing.[1] The essay, then, represented a significant consolidation of Poe's identity as an author, and a milestone in the popularization of this identity. It also enabled Poe to acquire a new form of property in his writing. Lowell's good opinion served as a valuable entrée for Poe into New York literary society and the powerful publishing network of the Young America movement. Charles Briggs, for one, was so impressed by Lowell's essay that he took Poe on as a contributor and editor of the *Broadway Journal,* marking the first time in Poe's career that he was able to acquire a proprietary stake in the periodical in which his writing appeared. This was an important achievement in an era when magazine authors were frequently unpaid, and, when paid, traditionally ceded control over publication to editors in exchange for their pay.[2] Poe took advantage of his new position by performing his own act of consolidation, using the pages of the *Broadway Journal* to print revised versions of a considerable number of his poems and tales, creating a series of authorized texts that continue to form the basis of the Poe canon. In addition, Poe's association with the Young America movement—in particular, his patronage by Evert Duyckinck—opened up the columns of the prestigious *Democratic Review* and *American Review* to his poems and essays, ensured a large crowd and favorable reception for his lecture called "The Poets and Poetry of America," and secured a place for two volumes of his work, *Tales* and *The Raven and Other Poems,* in Young America's flagship publishing venture, the Library of American Books.

One must be careful, however, to read this evidence of Poe's increasing self-possession not only in light of the complicating factor of his dependence on Young America's patronage, but also in the context of the rhetoric of literary nationalism in which the figure of Poe became thoroughly enmeshed. As Claude Richard has demonstrated, the consolidation of Poe's authorial identity came at a significant cost to his critical independence: gaining control over his body of writing, by being publicly identified as its author and by controlling its dissemination as editor and litterateur, meant ceding control over the content of his criticism. The period from March 1843, when Poe began courting their favor, through the collapse of the *Broadway Journal* in late 1845 can be read as a narrative of Poe's long-sought achievement of authorial identity, and as the space of an embarrassing surrender. Within this period, Poe repeatedly compromised his critical principles to curry favor with the Duyckinck circle, sacrificing his independent critical voice to promote the literary and political goals of the Young Americans.

Poe was certainly an unlikely recruit to this cause, which combined the bombastic promotion of a national literature with the vigorous advocacy of an international copyright agreement. Although a lifelong supporter of international copyright, Poe had repeatedly come out against the simple-minded endorsement of books with "strictly 'American' themes," ridiculing the critical tendency of "liking, or pretending to like, a stupid book the better because (sure enough) its stupidity was of our own growth, and discussed our own affairs" (Poe 1984a, 1027). Poe's hostility to the national-ist program suffused his critical practice and took the New York publishing scene as a specific target. Not only had he written a scathing critique of "Wakondah," a nationalist epic written by Young America's leading spokes-person, Cornelius Mathews, but he had identified the *Mirror* as a primary locus of the corrupt links between critics and the book trade that made the commercial success of such literature possible. The founding editors of the *Mirror* had hoped the journal's name would represent the democratizing power of print; they saw it as an instrument "for reflecting back to many, the intellectual treasures of the few" (Chielens 1986, 273). Poe, however, took the *Mirror* to represent the corruption of the many by the few, the "manufacture" by a coterie of critics of "a pseudo-public opinion by whole-sale." For Poe, "be-Mirrorment" came to signify the entrapment of an author within the iterative but ultimately self-serving power of the press (Poe 1984a, 1007).

How are we to understand the transformation of this resolute opponent of literary nationalism into one of the "merest and maddest *partizans* in letters" (ibid., 1027) he had so vigorously condemned? Richard's answer is to dismiss Poe's conversion as opportunism. He depicts Poe's sudden sup-port of Young America as a calculated move, an unfortunate but necessary step toward his lifelong dream of establishing his own elite literary maga-zine.[3] However, to regard Poe's relation to the literary nationalist movement purely from the standpoint of Poe's own motives is to overstate his ability to dissociate himself from the terms by which he was embraced by this move-ment, and through which he gained access to a wide reading public. In spite of Poe's motives and his increasingly veiled differences with the nationalist program, it remains the case that nearly all his production in this period was put forward under the aegis of Young America, a point graphically demonstrated by the title pages of the only books written by Poe to have been widely circulated in his lifetime (and the only books for which he was paid a royalty): the 1845 *Tales* and *The Raven and Other Poems*. Both vol-umes, as part of Duyckinck's nationalist publishing project, the "Library of

American Books," bear on their covers an inscription from the *Address of the American Copy-Right Club*: "Sundry citizens of this good land, meaning well, and hoping well, prompted by a certain something in their nature, have trained themselves to do service in various Essays, Poems, Histories, and books of Art, Fancy, and Truth" (Thomas and Jackson 1987, 541).

That Poe's writing was widely disseminated under Young America's imprimatur should suggest that his connection with the literary nationalist program was not something he could easily negate. Critics who focus on Poe's duplicity in undertaking this alliance not only mistake Poe's desire to hold himself apart from this movement for his ability to do so; they also misstate the consequences of this alliance. The crisis for Poe was not that he was forced to embrace literary nationalist ideals in order to advance his career. Rather, his autonomy was jeopardized when the literary nationalists embraced *his* principles, invoking him as an idealized figure of independent judgment within their discourse. Poe did not abandon his critical ideals so much as he lost control over them as they were translated into the literary nationalist idiom. By examining the complex mediations performed by Lowell's essay, one can uncover how Poe's critical independence, the originality of his productions, even the details of his biography, became tied to the problem of American literary independence.

Lowell begins his essay with an analysis of the then current state of literary production in America, casting his account of the life and writings of Poe as a polemic on the question of a national literature. This analysis is a particularly volatile one in that it steers a course rhetorically between nationalist and antinationalist positions: it adopts the urgency of nationalist appeals, and is structured as a declaration of crisis and a call to arms, yet its key metaphors imply a powerful indictment of efforts to construct an independent literature out of American materials. This equivocation is not surprising, since Lowell composed his biography of Poe at a stage of his career when he had fallen out of favor with the Duyckinck circle because of his failure fully to endorse their cause in his short-lived periodical the *Pioneer*.[4] Lowell's biography of Poe became an occasion for him to reconceptualize his relation to the discourse of literary nationalism in the light of Poe's increasing influence. It offers a refraction of Poe's critical ideals through the lens of Lowell's disillusionment with the proposals of the Young Americans.

The extent of this disillusionment is apparent from the opening set of images, a description of cultural dislocation that, while it is indebted to the generic pronouncements of Young America, signals a shift from even the muted nationalism of the *Pioneer*. In a rhetorical move common to advocates of literary nationalism, Lowell identifies the failure of American literature as a geographical and political one, a failure to bring culture, politics, and landscape into proper relation:

The situation of American literature is anomalous. It has no center, or, if it have, it is like that of the sphere of Hermes. It is divided into many systems, each revolving round its several sun, and often presenting to the rest only the faint glimmer of a milk-and-watery way. Our capital city, unlike London or Paris, is not a great central heart, from which life and vigor radiate to the extremities, but resembles more an isolated umbilicus, stuck down as near as may be to the center of the land, and seeming rather to tell a legend of former usefulness than to serve any present need. (Lowell 1943, 5)

Lowell presents the relation of American literature to nationhood as a series of apparently insuperable disjunctions: publishing centers are detached from each other, and from the seat of government, while the government itself is cut off from "present need," situated at a geographical center that has become peripheral. Read against the conventional proclamations of the Young Americans, this emphasis on detachment and internal disarray becomes all the more pronounced. Nationalist manifestos customarily began with a condemnation of American subservience to British literary models, and finished with a call for a literature commensurate with the majesty of American scenery and the ideals of republican institutions. Throughout, the emphasis was on independence and self-sufficiency figured as the ties among art, land, and state. Duyckinck called for "such an image of rural life, of men in cities . . . as the wide area of the land should reflect in the broad shield of the state" (Miller 1956, 111); Lowell himself had declared in the *Pioneer* that he "would no longer see the spirit of our people held up as a mirror to the OLD WORLD;—but rather lying like one of our own inland oceans, reflecting not only the mountain and the rock, the forest and the redman, but also the steamboat and the railcar, the cornfield and the factory" (1843, 2). In Lowell's revised account of the national predicament, however, the lack of connection among geographical, political, and cultural systems is so severe as completely to disable political patronage. Not only does the "isolated umbilicus" of the nation's capital fail to nurture the various centers of literary production, but literature itself is rendered incapable of reflecting back the image either of the land or of the state. We are left, not with an invocation of imminent cultural independence, but with the disturbing image of a literary culture cut free and yet unnourished.

Lowell then shifts from this figure of maternal abandonment to a scene of stillbirth, replacing the accusation of a failure to nourish with the charge of a disastrously misplaced affection: "Meanwhile, a great babble is kept up concerning a national literature, and the country, having delivered itself of the ugly likeness of a paint-bedaubed, filthy savage, smilingly dandles the rag baby upon her maternal knee, as if it were veritable flesh and blood, and would grow timely to bone and sinew" (1943, 5). While Lowell's ultimate target of contempt seems to be the motherland's deranged approval of its offspring, his disgust at American literary production registers most powerfully as a proliferation of representations of crudity and inauthenticity. The "isolated umbilicus" of the state has delivered itself not of an infant, but of a rag baby, and, as if the figure of an inhuman miscarriage were not enough, Lowell adds that this surrogate child is a likeness of a savage, and an ugly one at that; that it is filthy, and yet also obscured with paint, a paint that may seek to cover, but which is also the hallmark of the primitive. The figure of the savage is a loaded one for the former editor of the *Pioneer*, as it was for all the Young Americans who repeatedly called for a literature that would embody the wildness of the American Indian as well as the American landscape (Miller 1956, 96). Lowell uses this grisly image to ridicule and renounce the program of the Young Americans. His emphasis on the lingering horror of maternal approval pointedly shifts the target of his critique from nationalist authors to the editors and critics who celebrate such grotesque productions. From the materials of a conventional nationalist appeal—one that calls for the recognition and celebration of the "anomalous" state of American literary production—Lowell has fashioned an indictment not unlike Poe's attack on Young American critics and editors for "liking, or pretending to like, a stupid book the better because . . . its stupidity was of our own growth, and discussed our own affairs."[5]

Lowell's assessment, however, is more severe than Poe's, whose characterization of literary nationalism as a form of willful self-delusion suggests its eventual dissipation. Within the figural logic of Lowell's essay, the image of the nation's delight in its inanimate child-surrogate intensifies his initial emphasis on maternal abandonment by categorically denying the possibility of growth and maturation. Rather than summoning the conventional figure of a late-adolescent nation, one that has dwelled too long in a state of extended dependence, Lowell acknowledges the fact of independence but insists not merely on the failure, but on the *impossibility* of America nurturing its literary offspring. He has arrived at an impasse from which it seems impossible to proceed.

At this point, Lowell suggests a reversal of terms. In a dramatic change of registers, he asserts that "before we have an American literature, we must have an American criticism" (1943, 5–6). This reversal makes little sense when read against the imagery that precedes it. Even if it is interpreted as a transposition of nationalist priorities (Duyckinck had insisted in an early review that "it is the office of the critic to follow, not to lead. We need authors first, and critics will follow afterwards" [1840, 24]), Lowell's insistence on the impossibility of sustenance makes it difficult to place any confidence in the generative power of criticism. It is only when Lowell invokes Poe as a figure of parthenogenesis that it becomes clear that the possibility of a prior, independent criticism offers him a welcome escape from the insoluble problem of maturation.[6]

Lowell's initial description of Poe is oddly anticlimactic: he introduces Poe as "the most discriminating, philosophical, and fearless critic upon imaginative works who has written in America," largely on the ground that he is "a man who thinks for himself, and says what he thinks, and knows well what he is talking about" (1943, 7). Read in the context of the essay's opening images, however, Lowell's stress on Poe's self-sufficiency seems more important than his superlatives. Indeed, in describing Poe as a man who thinks for himself, Lowell personifies the goals of criticism Poe had set forth in his "Prospectus of *The Stylus*." In this abstract (which he sent to Lowell), Poe expressed the hope that his magazine would "assert in precept, and . . . maintain in practice, the rights, while, in effect, it demonstrates the advantages, of an absolutely independent criticism;—a criticism self-sustained" (Poe 1984a, 1035). While his goals are certainly idealistic ones—this criticism would "[guide] itself only by the purest rules of Art" (ibid.)—Poe's immediate reference is to his promise that the *Stylus* would be sufficiently capitalized to forswear compromising connections with the book trade, what he called in an earlier version of the prospectus reading "through the medium of a publisher's will" (Poe 1984a, 1025). For Poe it was ultimately financial independence that guaranteed unbiased reviews. In the context of Lowell's analysis, however, the image of self-sustenance takes on a biological resonance. Throughout his exposition of Poe's works, Lowell offers the figure of Poe as a response to the problem of a literature cut free from all sources of support. In the rhetorical economy of the essay, the grounding power of Poe's authorial and critical practice is directly linked to his ability to counter the opening images of impossible growth.

Poe is able to perform this function for Lowell because of his call for critical self-sufficiency, and because of the contingencies of his own biography. Poe is the type and figure of maternal abandonment: first orphaned, then disinherited, Poe personifies the national predicament. Lowell suggests as much when he locates Poe's turn to authorship at the point when he was "cut off [from] his expectations as an heir" (1943, 7) by the birth of a son to his adoptive father, the artificiality of his lineage exposed and displaced by a natural filiation. Poe's biography is both the occasion for Lowell's meditations on the state of the national literature and his template for understanding it. However, if the details of Poe's biography shape Lowell's literary-political analysis, the idea that Poe is a subject with a history all but disappears from his account of Poe's literary production. Lowell represents Poe not merely as an autonomous critic, but as a figure of impossible maturity, one who seems never to have passed through a state of dependence or incompletion.

This figuration of Poe is most legible in Lowell's long digression on the juvenile poems of famous poets, each of which fails in some regard to anticipate the virtues of the poet's mature verse. After a litany on the failed precocity of Shakespeare, Milton, Pope, Collins, Chatterton, Southey, Coleridge, and others, Lowell praises Poe's early poems as "the most remarkable boyish poems" he has ever read. In "the rudest verses" Lowell finds he can "trace some conception of the ends of poetry," a phenomenon he "can only express by the contradictory phrase of *innate experience*" (ibid., 10). Lowell sees in Poe's early verse not merely the traces of his mature production, but the ends of poetry itself. Lowell has found proof for his maxim that calls for principle to precede practice: before Poe had a mature poetry, he had incarnate in his juvenilia a "conception of the ends of poetry" that renders moot the question of comparative strength or degrees of development.

The source for Lowell's trope of reversal becomes apparent in his account of Poe's prose. In a passage that echoes Poe's nascent theory of the "unity of effect or impression" (Poe 1984a, 571), Lowell observes that in the composition of his tales, Poe's "mind at once reaches forward to the effect to be produced" (1943, 14). This depiction of Poe as the embodiment of his critical ideals bears the marks of Lowell's characteristic overreaching. Poe's version of his poetics of effect recognizes the contingencies of the compositional process even as it seeks to displace its account of origins with the image of a perfectly reproducible effect. In his early review of *Twice-Told Tales,* Poe had stressed the "deliberate care" (Poe 1984a, 572) required of the artist in selecting an effect, while in his "Philosophy of Composition" he would expand upon the "elaborate and vacillating crudities of thought, . . . the true purposes seized only at the last moment . . . the innumerable glimpses of idea that arrived not at the maturity of full view" (ibid., 14). Lowell, however, has Poe arrive at his intended effect "at once." Lowell attributes to Poe such control over the reaction of the reader that he redraws self-sufficiency as a kind of self-enclosure. Poe is both author and critic, creator and "spectator *ab extra*"; his autonomy is so complete as to suggest the replacement of the image of biological with that of mechanized production:

[Poe] analyzes, he dissects, he watches,

'—with an eye serene,
The very pulse of the machine,'

for such it practically is to him, with wheels and cogs and piston rods all working to produce a certain end. It is this that makes him so good a critic. (Lowell 1943, 14)

Whatever pulse remains of Wordsworth's "perfect Woman, nobly planned" —the "Phantom of delight" behind the quotation (Wordsworth 1984, 293)— is all but extinguished by Lowell's emphasis on Poe's careful supervision of his textual machine. The machine *is* a perfect woman insofar as it promises production without dependence. Thus even the creative practice that underwrites Poe's criticism is assimilated to a regulatory function. Lowell's dominant image of Poe is that of effect without cause and without access: "Mr. Poe has that indescribable something which men have agreed to call *genius*. No man could ever tell us precisely what it is, and yet there is none who is not inevitably aware of its presence and its power" (1943, 12).

Poe seems to have found the terms of Lowell's praise extravagant and amusing; he satirized this line in particular in his comic tale "The Literary Life of Thingum Bob, Esq." (Quinn 1941, 786). However, the New York literati who reviewed Lowell's essay reinforced his claims, stressing Poe's extraordinary maturity and the absolute independence of his criticism, and linking him to a powerful but untraceable effect. N. P. Willis, for example, welcomed Lowell's "biographical and critical sketch of the American Rhadamanthus," asserting that this "*coup d'oeil*, of the position and powers of Mr. Poe . . . is of great interest to the public that *feels* him" (Thomas and Jackson 1987, 491). Poe's authority is established by the sudden disclosure that it is already in effect.

Willis's notice permits us to trace the trajectory of Poe's critical ideals through the mediating accounts of those who promoted his career. In Lowell's hands, Poe's ambitions for his unrealized magazine were recast as an indictment of American culture for failing to have nourished these ambitions. Lowell saw in the collapse of the *Stylus* a missed opportunity for the instant achievement of a critical mastery that would have rivaled that of England, claiming that "had Mr. Poe had the control of a magazine of his own, in which to display his critical abilities, he would have been as autocratic, ere this, in America, as Professor Wilson has been in England" (1943, 7). Willis transforms this complaint into a renewed call for an editorship for Poe, one that he claims would have the power to undergird the New York publishing world. Echoing Lowell on Poe's self-sufficiency, Willis argues that "Poe has genius and taste of his own . . . and the finest discriminative powers; and such a wheel of literature should not be without axle and lynch-pin" (Thomas and Jackson 1987, 491). It remains to be seen why Lowell's portrait of Poe as a critical autocrat should have been so warmly received and vigorously promoted by a group dedicated to fostering democratic principles in art.

Removing the Anonymous: Young America and the Control of Dissemination

Evert Duyckinck's favorable notice of Lowell's essay provides a context for understanding how Poe could have appeared to arrive on the New York scene fully formed, in command of an extensive *oeuvre* without ever having passed through the process of production. His comment provides a historical correlative for Lowell's and Willis's association of Poe with an effect that cannot be traced to its origin. Less than a week after the publication of Lowell's essay, Duyckinck editorialized in the columns of the *Morning News:*

We cordially give welcome to the distinct recognition of Mr. Poe's merits. Whenever his name is mentioned it has been with the comment that he is a remarkable man, a man of genius. Few knew precisely what he had written, his name was not on Library catalogues or any of his books on the shelves. His influence has been felt while the man was unknown. Lowell's article removes the anonymous and exhibits the author of some of the most peculiar and characteristic productions in our literature. (Thomas and Jackson 1987, 492–94)

It is striking that, given the scope of the essay, Duyckinck should choose to call attention to the role it played in matching the figure of Poe with the texts he had written. After all, at this stage of his career Poe had published three books of poetry, *The Narrative of Arthur Gordon Pym,* a series of gift-book contributions, a school text on conchology, two volumes of collected tales, a serial issue of prose romances, and, according to Lowell's calculations, fifty-five individual tales and extravaganzas. Yet, given the extraor-

dinarily volatile publishing climate of the 1830s and 1840s, it is not altogether surprising that Poe, who was well known as a critic, could remain
relatively unknown as an author, his writing dispersed but his reputation
indeterminate.[7] Duyckinck celebrates the removal of an anonymity that,
though it was frequently manipulated by Poe to his advantage, was an
inescapable condition of publishing in that era.

"Precisely what [Poe] had written" could remain a mystery not simply
because of the limited circulation of his works, but because of the decentralized publication of his poems and tales, and because many were
initially printed or reprinted without his name attached. Poe conducted
most of his career during a boom period in magazine publishing, when
economic depression and the lack of international copyright brought on an
extraordinary demand for cheap publications and fostered the regulariza-
tion of the system of reprinting. Although legally possible, domestic copyright of magazine pieces was relatively rare, even after *Graham's* and *Godey's*
began to seek copyright for their contents in 1845. Magazines such as the
Southern Literary Messenger, which printed predominantly "original" articles, were the exception, not the rule. Republication without payment and
often without attribution was standard practice in miscellanies, such as
Littell's Living Age, which were made up entirely of reprints from foreign
and American magazines, and in mammoth weeklies, such as *Brother Jonathan,* which reprinted yards of material—even entire books—on enormous
folio pages. At the other end of the publishing scale, the editors of prestigious journals such as the *American Review* insisted on concealing the
identities of their contributors as the hallmark of gentlemanly publishing
(Barnes 1974; Mott 1957).

The system of reprinting was encouraged by the existence of disparate
publishing centers—Lowell's distant, disjointed orbits—that saw themselves
as catering to a regional readership, and thus took on the responsibility of
excerpting poems, tales, and essays from the periodicals of other regional
presses. Under this decentralized system of production and reproduction,
texts were frequently subject to circulation without editorial or authorial
control. Textual integrity and authorial identity were common casualties of
the reprint process, as the publishing history of some of Poe's most famous
tales will attest. "The Fall of the House of Usher," for example, was reprinted
anonymously in the London monthly *Bentley's Miscellany* six months after
its collection in Poe's *Tales of the Grotesque and Arabesque,* and then reprinted in the *Boston Notion* under a heading that suggested British authorship—"From Bentley's Miscellany for August." "The Purloined Letter" un-

derwent a similar purloining, suffering abridgment—with attribution—at the hands of *Chambers' Edinburgh Journal*, reprinting in its altered state in *Littell's Living Age*, and then a third reprinting in two installments in the *Morning News*, with the headnote "From Chambers' Journal, via Littell's Living Age." Given such complex textual itineraries, it is not surprising that all kinds of confusions about authorial identity should have arisen, misattributions that twentieth-century readers with stable texts might find unimaginable. Poe's career illustrates the difficulty of establishing an authorial identity under such conditions. As Lowell remarked of Poe, "he has squared out blocks enough to build an enduring pyramid, but has left them lying carelessly and unclaimed in many different quarries" (1943, 7).

Indeed, it is difficult to overstate the importance of anonymity and pseudonymy as mediating factors in Poe's career. Even bracketing the pseudonymous strategies deployed by Poe relatively successfully for effect ("Arthur Gordon Pym") or self-protection ("Tamerlane" and "By a Bostonian"), a broad range of his texts and textual practices drifts free from the confines of individual authorship. A representative list of these practices might include: a successful newspaper piece such as "The Balloon Hoax," which, in taking the form of a report, is necessarily unsigned; a review, such as Poe's of Lowell's *Poems*, which remains unsigned either by editorial fiat or by personal choice; the unsigned reviews, such as C. J. Peterson's of the works of Rufus Griswold, or Thomas Dunn English's of Poe's *Tales*, which have been attributed to Poe to his disadvantage; Poe's pseudonymous authorship of *The Conchologist's First Book*, a product of its true author's attempt to circumvent the restrictions of copyright; the unlocatable quotations from nonexistent authors used as epigraphs for numerous tales and for the "Prospectus of *The Stylus*"; the anonymous and pseudonymous contributions to the *Broadway Journal* that were Poe's, but were disguised as the work of "††" or "Littelton Barry" to give the impression of a varied authorship; the anonymity of Poe's work as a "mechanical paragraphist," condensing statements and writing announcements for the *New York Mirror;* and the implicit pseudonymy of his work for the journals entitled *Burton's* and *Graham's*, magazines for which Poe at times had full editorial responsibility, and which were frequently reviewed by other periodicals issue by issue, as if they were individual books.

The broad range of these practices underscores the ease with which Poe seemed to inhabit them, and the difficulty of finally extricating his persona and his writing from the complex forms of empowerment and disablement they represent. Poe is commonly seen only as a victim or a critic of the publishing practices of his era, imagined to have been crushed by these systems, or to stand somehow outside them, looking in. And yet it was from the vantage point of a full participant that he launched his critique of such practices. Poe bitterly attacked the use of anonymity in criticism, as when he complained of the quarterlies, "Who writes?—who causes to be written? Who but an ass will put faith in tirades which *may be* the result of personal hostility, or in panegyrics which . . . may be laid, directly or indirectly to the charge of the author himself?" (Poe 1984a, 1009). Yet he also used it to his advantage, first publishing "The Literary Life of Thingum Bob, Esq." anonymously in the *Southern Literary Messenger,* then calling attention to it anonymously in his capacity as paragraphist for the *Mirror:* "A broadly satirical article, oddly entitled 'The Literary Life of Thingum Bob, Esq.' has been the subject of much comment, lately . . . and the question is put to *us* especially, here in the North,—'who wrote it?' Who *did?*—can any one tell?" (Thomas and Jackson 1987, 487).

"Can anyone tell?"—a question that still troubles bibliographers of Poe—was a question that horrified Young Americans such as Duyckinck when they confronted the welter of texts produced by the culture of republication. A brief account of the anxieties that propelled the Young American platform will help explain Duyckinck's relief at the canonizing function that Lowell's essay on Poe performs, and the role Poe was to play for the movement from his outpost at the *Broadway Journal.* Understanding the shift in rhetoric that occurred as the Young Americans took on the question of international copyright will help clarify why the sudden appearance of Poe as a fully formed author and critical autocrat should seem so appealing.

While the Young America movement was always an elitist undertaking—its founding members were a group of affluent *litterateurs* who had formed themselves into an exclusive private association—their rhetoric distinguished itself at the start by its populism, their project drawing strength and gaining prominence from its connection with the radical wing of the Democratic party and with its chief publishing venture, the *Democratic Review.* This alliance was at first a happy one; the core of the movement—Duyckinck, Mathews, and William A. Jones—joined forces with editor John O'Sullivan to promote a literature that was committed to republican institutions, one that would instill in American youth the proper democratic habits. In terms of literary politics, the Young Americans allied with O'Sullivan against the elitist pretensions of the Whig *Knickerbocker* and the Boston press: it was the "better-educated classes," after all, who, by aping British refinement, were giving such a tone to "our literary institutions and . . . learned professions" as to "[poison] at the spring the young minds of our people" (O'Sullivan 1837, 15). In *Arcturus* and the early *Democratic Review* it was a general maxim that achieving literary independence was a matter of transforming the content of literary works; one established "the true glory and greatness of the democratic principle, by *infusing* it *into* our literature" (ibid.; emphasis added). The terms of O'Sullivan's praise for the Democratic party's content-hero, Nathaniel Hawthorne, are indicative of the broad politics of this position: in a comment that seems less a critical assessment than proof of a political commitment to domestic manufacture, O'Sullivan praises Hawthorne for not having "imported his literary fabrics, nor made them after patterns, to be found in either obscure or noted foreign warehouses" (Miller 1956, 111).

It was, in the end, the conflict between this commitment to domestic manufacture and the adoption of an international copyright law that finally drove a wedge between the Young Americans and the Democratic party. Crudely put, the lack of international copyright was good for American manufacture. In a declaration called "The International Copyright Question," which marked an important rift in their relations, O'Sullivan concluded that democratic principles lay more with supporting the system of cheap publication than they did with promoting a literature that was democratic in content alone. O'Sullivan theorized that the adoption of international copyright (and with it, payments to British authors) would so raise the cost of books as to create "an aristocracy of readers" (O'Sullivan 1843, 118). Instead, O'Sullivan placed his faith in the democratizing power of new technologies of print, praising "this revolution in the book trade" whereby large editions could be produced at a low per-volume cost and sold at a low price, thereby achieving a wider circulation. He speculated that literature with democratic content would naturally emerge from a system of democratic publishing. If the price of domestic publication were made low enough by high-volume printing, the American author, possessing "advantages of national sympathy and patriotic pride on the part of the people" as well as "comprehension of the character and taste of his countrymen" (ibid.) would automatically outsell his British competitor.

O'Sullivan's firm stand against international copyright put Duyckinck and his circle in an awkward position: their own party had abandoned their platform, while the argument in favor of a literature with a discernibly democratic content began to be taken up by the Whigs as a protectionist measure. The *Knickerbocker*, for example, came out in favor of a national literature on decidedly conservative grounds. Its chief concern was not with the representation or maintenance of republican institutions, but with a possible outbreak of licentiousness. The republication of foreign works exposed the public to a dangerous "sensuality" and "immorality," whereas "Home literature"—of the proper refinement—promoted "good taste, and a sense of fitness and propriety" ("Necessity for a National Literature" 1845, 416–17). This new alignment of politics and rhetoric prompted Duyckinck to direct his appeal to a Whig readership in the pages of the newly formed monthly the *American Review*. In an article in the February issue, "The Literary Prospects of 1845" (which appeared, incidentally, directly after "The Raven—by Quarles"), Duyckinck laid out the terms of a regrounding that had already begun to take place, shifting his rhetoric from the promotion of works with American content to an attack on the immorality of the system of republication.

Duyckinck's appeal to the Whigs brought out the elitism that had been implicit in the Young American position all along, a condescension toward the masses the group was trying to elevate that had been only partially concealed by their association with the radical democrats. In this essay, Duyckinck gives expression to anxieties about the rapid expansion of print culture that had provided a steady background hum in Cornelius Mathews's many speeches on the need for international copyright. Duyckinck's projections for the coming year evince a deep-seated contempt for the popular press, a disgust with the scope and extent of mass production, and an overriding concern about imposture:

> We would fain hope that the literary system which has been distinguished by the epithet 'cheap and nasty' is pretty much at an end. . . . Nothing has been too mean or poor-spirited for that system to produce. It was pregnant in nauseous puffs, unworthy of a mountebank. . . . Native authors were neglected, despised, insulted; foreign authors were mutilated, pillaged and insulted besides. Ingratitude was among the least of the current vices. Misrepresentation and falsehood were its companions. The good writers were not only taken possession of, their works altered and thrown upon the public without their just honor and responsibility, but they were made the cover for the circulation of the worst licentiousness. (Duyckinck 1845, 148)

Read against O'Sullivan's resounding confidence in the liberating powers of the press, Duyckinck's hopes can only be termed reactionary. In fact, toward the end of the passage he draws dangerously close to the position of the *Knickerbocker* Whigs, with an important distinction: it is not the circulation of licentiousness that is the crime here, but the mutilation and misrepresentation of the texts of the "good writers" under whose cover this illicit traffic takes place. On the whole it is *not* foreign sensuality or even the foreign itself that troubles Duyckinck. What the reprint trade threatens to produce in American readers is an inability to discriminate. The popular press is all-encompassing and nondiscriminating: nothing is "too mean" for it to publish. Like Lowell, Duyckinck figures American publishing in terms of a monstrous female reproductive power, but his focus is on restraining rather than subverting or replacing this power. Duyckinck sees the regulation of the reprint trade as the remedy for the press's grotesque overcapacity; he longs for a press that "will bear the natural and just fetters of order, benevolence, refinement" (ibid., 150).

Duyckinck's generalized fear of the indiscriminate can be seen in his obsession with inauthenticity and in his fervent hope that an international copyright agreement will remove this state of uncertainty: "the line will in future be more strongly drawn between honesty and fraud in publishing" (ibid., 148). Here Duyckinck's tone is restrained and his prognosis hopeful, but Cornelius Mathews's widely circulated "Appeal" demonstrates how easily the Young American defense of literary property could slide into epistemological panic. In a characteristically dramatic and inconclusive passage, Mathews proclaims:

This—an invasion of property—is only one of the external evils growing out of a false and lawless state of things. Of others, which strike deeper; which create confusion and error of opinion; which tend to unsettle the lines that divide nation from nation; to obliterate the traits and features which give us a characteristic individuality as a nation—there will be another and more becoming opportunity to speak. (Mathews 1842, 122)

Duyckinck's preoccupation with textual uncertainty—the inability in an age of cheap republication to tell a book by its cover—manifests itself in Mathews's prose as a more fundamental anxiety about cognition, individual difference, and the instability of national identity.

It is a persistent irony of this rhetoric that those who agitated most fiercely for international copyright should find national identity in writing so precarious as to be hardly worth protecting. And yet what Duyckinck's and Mathews's rhetoric exposes is the crisis of judgment that attended the rapid expansion of the trade. It was not simply the importation of foreign values that the reprint trade promoted, but the possibility that citizens might no longer be able to tell the difference between domestic and foreign; it was not so much dependence with which the Young Americans were concerned, but indistinction.

Duyckinck's "Literary Prospects" essay announced a shift in strategy and served as a call to action, a call for renewed efforts to make discriminations among texts. This was the year, after all, in which he was to launch both his "Library of American Books" and a companion series of reprints, the "Library of Choice Reading," which somewhat nervously advertised its selections under the slogan "Books Which Are Books" (*Wiley and Putnam's Literary Newsletter* 1845, 306). As both the series title and the slogan suggest, Duyckinck had become less concerned with pretense than with indiscrimination. This was also the year of Poe's spectacular emergence on the New York literary scene, his access to the nationalist publishing machine paved by the lavish praise given in Lowell's biography. The terms of Lowell's praise and the shift in Young American rhetoric should explain why this essay was so persuasive. Given their opposition to the unchecked productivity of the press and their fears of the indiscriminate, one can see why the Young Americans might fail to read the opening of the essay as an attack on their policies. Indeed, the proliferation of images of inauthenticity in Lowell's critique of literary nationalism could have been enough to convince them that he was actually on their side. The shift in their rhetoric from the support of democratic content in literature to an attack on the reprint trade perfectly positioned them to receive and to replicate the kind of coterie-critique that Poe had been honing in his struggles with various editors. In fact, Duyckinck echoes this critique in a passage in "Literary Prospects" in which he alludes to the arrival of Poe on the New York literary scene. After a lengthy discussion of the way in which a misguided "feeling of nationality" had prompted editors to praise works with American content without regard to their merit, Duyckinck suggests that these "false defenders of mediocrity" are actually puffing plagiarisms: "A pungent and rather startling essay might be written on this prolific theme; and such we are given to understand by a hint in a late number of our contemporary, the 'Democratic,' is already prepared, by a writer whose pen 'hath a taste to it,' under the pleasant title of 'American Cribbage!'" (1845, 149).

Duyckinck's response to the "overproduction" (ibid., 148) of the press is technologically reactionary: it is a return to the pen, and to one that "hath a taste to it"—both courage and cultivation. The resort to the pen is a necessity, given the thorough corruption of the practice of puffery and its links to the system of republication. The resort to *Poe's* pen represents an attempt to get outside the system by enlisting the help of someone long known as its critic, someone who appeared to have produced a large corpus of work without its assistance, someone who had promised to provide a "criticism self-sustained."

Poe's relative anonymity as an author was a practical disadvantage, and yet it was indispensable to his construction by the Young Americans as a figure with redemptive power. When they advocated a literature with American content, their rhetoric had often taken on an extravagant, messianic tone, invoking the truly native author as one who, like Christ, was in the world, but not of it. The Young Americans' rhetorical assumption of the role of prophet and precursor gave expression to their sense of the nation's urgent need for salvation, and to their own need to be legitimated as the sole critics capable of recognizing this author-savior. Lowell's construction of Poe as a figure of parthenogenesis, one whose works demonstrated impossible, instant maturity, played directly into this formation. Lowell's reversal of the priorities of the literary nationalist program—his insistence that a literary criticism with integrity would necessarily precede the advent of the Master Genius—reinforced Young America's newfound commitment to discrimination and to the restraint of the system of republication, and placed Poe in a difficult position—in Willis's words, as a possible "axle and lynch-pin" for their entire system.

Narratives of Absolute Possession and Dispossession: Authorial Identity in the "Little Longfellow War"

Lowell invoked the figure of Poe as a solution to a series of seemingly insoluble cultural problems: the problem of national integrity and political authority in a culture characterized by decentralization; the problem of the growth of a literature mapped onto these fragments, and thus detached from centralized support; and the problem of literary production in the context of a criticism that would celebrate inauthenticity rather than pass through a period of unbearable dependence. Lowell's embrace of Poe as a self-originating poet and self-sustaining critic neutralized, by containing, the centrifugal forces that threatened to shatter Lowell's fledgling career as poet and editor. Poe's instant maturity eliminated dependence by obviating the need for growth.

Duyckinck's celebration of Poe's emergence from anonymity and his invocation of Poe's powers of discernment fulfill a similar function within his narrative of national crisis. For Duyckinck, Poe's achievement of authorial identity is not a process but a sudden unveiling, the differentiation and consolidation of texts out of a field of indifference. Within the logic of "Literary Prospects of 1845," Poe's proposal for a chapter on "American Cribbage" stands in for the principle of differentiation itself; the ability to distinguish between original and copy is appealed to as a kind of interim regulatory measure in lieu of the passage of an international copyright law. And yet what is perhaps most striking about Duyckinck's essay is the incommensurate nature of this substitution, the inadequacy of individual judgment (no matter how unimpeachable) as a solution to the problem of uncontrollable production. To begin with, Duyckinck has no clear idea how the regulation of the circulation of texts in the literary marketplace will produce an original genius. In a characteristic gesture of obfuscation he exclaims, "We cannot say of genius, it will be here or there, but the spirit of God breathes it, and lo! a Homer, a Shakspeare [*sic*]" (1845, 150). He can only reassure himself, by insisting on the making of distinctions, that he has taste enough to recognize a work of genius when it comes along. Poe's proposed "Chapter on American Cribbage" is indispensable to him in this regard, in that it projects a generalized posture of absolute judgment, one of extraordinary accuracy and dependability.

It is, however, unclear how the ability to adjudicate between texts could keep in check the overproduction of the press, how Poe's promise to expose the derivative nature of American literary production would succeed in drawing the line more clearly between "honesty and fraud in publishing" (ibid., 148). Duyckinck's hope seemed to be that Poe's exposure of the fraudulent relations between pairs of texts would disarm the system of puffery by drawing attention from the suspect texts themselves to the corrupt practices of those who promoted them. Yet not only does this model gloss over vast differences in scale, proposing to address the problem of mass production by the exercise of subtle differentiations at the point of reception; it also represents a retreat from the problem of scale to the simpler terrain of authentic and derivative, an imposition of absolutes of honesty and fraud, guilt and innocence, on what Duyckinck repeatedly acknowledges to be a vast, undifferentiated middle ground of textual production. Duyckinck was attracted to Poe's proposal because it promised a systematic and irrefutable exposure of textual fraud: "The beauty of these *exposés* must lie in the precision and unanswerability with which they are given—in day and date—in chapter and verse—and, above all in an unveiling of the minute trickeries by which the thieves hope to disguise their stolen wares" (Poe 1984a, 1346). And yet he invokes Poe's powers of discernment as a means of wresting American literature from the hands of the "false defenders of *mediocrity,*" those critics who fall into "paroxysms of admiration" over what is essentially a "minor literature" (1845, 148–49). Duyckinck proposes addressing the delicate problem of recalibrating the inflated claims for American texts with the sledgehammer distinction of original from copy.

Poe's proposal for the "Chapter on American Cribbage" meets Duyckinck's rhetorical needs because of the posture of absolute judgment it projects, and because of the self-authorizing strategies of the fiction of which it is a part. Poe suggests this project in the context of his *Marginalia,* a series of book annotations that purport to be the work of a gentleman of excessive leisure and impossible erudition. Poe's preface to the series suggests that these notes derive their authority from their status as handwritten adjuncts to printed texts. This idle scribbling exceeds even the immediacy of speech in its utter privacy and inutility; paradoxically, it is the aimlessness of the marginal notes that grants them value. In his *Marginalia,* Poe opens up a textual space that seeks to exempt itself from the corrupting forms of self-interest that suffuse the world of print. That these are *printed* marginalia circulating in a popular magazine, however, belies their claim to represent the pure exercise of judgment performed within the confines of the margin, the virtuous space of gentlemanly seclusion. As Stephen Rachman has observed, Poe exploits the equivocal status of his published marginalia, both posing as a literary gentleman and self-consciously exposing this posture as masquerade. Poe's marginalia serve to parody as well as to exemplify gentlemanly discernment.

However, as Lowell's misreading of Poe's theory of effect makes clear, Poe's characteristic deflationary gestures do not prevent his fictions from being taken up in other discourses. Irony is an insufficient defense against appropriation. Although it seems implausible, a false aristocrat was precisely what literary nationalist rhetoric demanded. Poised between a condemnation of the literary elite and an attack on the popular press, the Young Americans required discrimination of a pedigree that could not be traced back to Britain. Only a performance of literary judgment that was cut off from the historical grounds of its authority could be certifiably American.

The promotion of Poe's late-February lecture, "The Poets and Poetry of America," graphically demonstrates that he was cast in this role. Willis's announcement of the lecture transforms Duyckinck's enlistment of Poe's critical pen into the acquisition of an even sharper instrument: "The decapitation of the criminal who did not know his head was off till it fell into his hand as he was bowing . . . conveys an idea of the Damascene slicing of the critical blade of Mr. Poe" (Moss 1963, 167), while Duyckinck's review of that same lecture makes it abundantly clear that this blade was employed in direct support of the principles he had laid out in the "Literary Prospects" essay:

In the exordium [Poe] gave a great and cutting description of the arts which are practised, with the aid of the periodical press, in obtaining unmerited reputation for literary worth. His observations upon this division of his subject extended also to the pernicious influence of coteries, and he did not hesitate to point to the Capital of New England as the chief habitation, in this country, of literary hucksters and phrase mongers. Mr. Poe's manner was that of a versed and resolute man, applying to a hideous sore a keen and serviceable knife. (Thomas and Jackson 1987, 509)

Here Duyckinck celebrates Young America's assimilation of Poe's coterie-critique, newly deflected from New York to Boston. Poe's retargeting of his critique demonstrates more than his expedient embrace of local antagonisms; it marks his incorporation into the regional struggle to control national literary culture, a struggle largely fought over the proper terms of literary assessment. And yet it was as much the performance of judgment as the judgments themselves that Duyckinck and his circle welcomed—it was the fact of the cutting that got most of the attention. Poe had become an icon of the act of literary judgment itself, in Willis's words, the "statuary embodiment of Discrimination" (ibid., 510).

Poe's extended attack on Longfellow both confirms and tests the limits of this appropriation. Longfellow was not only a key member of the Boston literary elite; he had become the standard-bearer for a literary culture that rejected the proposals of the Young Americans. As Perry Miller has noted, Boston and New York conservatives saw in Longfellow's "ever-widening popularity a proof of the 'universality' which is the mark of genuine poetry, . . . [a poetry] which has nothing to do with nationalism" (1956, 99). In one sense, then, Poe's attack on Longfellow's poetry constitutes the strongest proof of his loyalty to the Young Americans: it represents both a strategic strike on behalf of their critical authority and an act of courageous discrimination. Yet even a cursory look at the texts that make up the Longfellow War suggests that this debate is not a straightforward display of personal or regional rivalry. In spite of Poe's title, his antagonist in this debate is not Longfellow himself, but a pseudonymous interlocutor who personifies and defends common property in writing. Poe's rebuttal is not an attack on Longfellow per se, but an elaborate defense of the grounds on which a charge of plagiarism may be made.

What most critics consider the opening salvo of this war was issued in mid-January in a short critique of Longfellow's *Waif*, published anonymously in the *Evening Mirror* a full week before the publication of Lowell's biography, and two weeks before the appearance of "The Raven." While this initial review created a minor sensation, resulting in a series of letters to the editor and editorial responses, six weeks passed before Poe recommenced the battle in the pages of the *Broadway Journal*. The gap between this initial, anonymous critique and Poe's full-fledged five-part excursus marks the space in which the figure of Poe as original author and independent critic is delivered up. The *Waif* review, then, serves as an important pretext for the concerns of the Longfellow War. It provides a commentary on the construction of authorial identity that would haunt the later production.

Poe's chief target in this review is what he sees as Longfellow's strategy of anonymity in publishing *The Waif*, a collection of fifty "fugitive" poems, seventeen of them anonymous, prefaced by a proem that is identified as Longfellow's work. Poe's odd response to this volume is to insist that all the unsigned poems were written by Longfellow himself. The volume thus constitutes both a powerful act of consolidation and an unaccountable ambiguation, a failure on Longfellow's part to speak in the fullness of his poetic voice. In the context of Poe's review, all suspensions of identity are suspect, conspiratorial. For instance, in commenting on the structure of the volume, Poe asks suspiciously "How does it happen . . . that the name of each author in this volume is carefully omitted from its proper place, at the head of his poem, to be as carefully deposited in the index?" (Poe 1984a, 698). Poe seems to be accusing Longfellow of claiming authorship of all of the poems in the volume simply by making it difficult for the reader to determine their "paternity" (ibid.). He implies that *The Waif* is a false orphan, a text that exploits the condition of namelessness to which he and other lesser poets are subjected.[8] Poe's anxiety about the deployment of anonymity as a textual effect stretches to his assessment of formal aspects of the volume: Longfellow's book is assembled "purposely at random," and the meter of his proem provides the perfect counterpoint for this controlled surrender of control—it is a model of "dexterously executed *slip-shod-iness*" (Poe 1984a, 696).

It is in the context of an obsessive circling around questions of anonymity and identity, surrender and control, that Poe raises the issue of whether Thomas Hood's "Death Bed" has been plagiarized by another poem, and the larger question of Longfellow's imitation. It is not the derivative nature of Hood's or Longfellow's poetry that initially irks Poe; it is Longfellow's emergence as an author against a backdrop of undifferentiated and unacknowledged fellow poets. Here Longfellow's crime is not theft, but a crucial act of erasure figured as theft: "there does appear, in this exquisite little volume, a very careful avoidance of all American poets who may be supposed especially to interfere with the claims of Mr. Longfellow. These men Mr. Longfellow can continuously *imitate* (*is* that the word?) and yet never even incidentally commend" (ibid., 702). Poe's coy play on the imprecision of "imitate" as the word for the phenomenon of which he speaks reaches forward to the palpable crime of plagiarism even as it reaches back toward an undifferentiated field, the repression of which constitutes the grounds of the poet's emergence.

Poe in the *Waif* review seems to be working out the problem of his own obscurity in relation to Longfellow's maddeningly empowered use of anonymity as a literary device; he would transform this scenario into an accusation of direct theft in the five installments of the Longfellow War. Poe emerges as a full authorial subject in this series, throwing off the editorial "we" (ibid., 705), while insisting unconditionally on the existence of plagiarism. The example Poe repeatedly resorts to in order to make good on this unwavering claim, however, is the frequent theft by "authors of established reputation" of "recondite, neglected, or forgotten books" (ibid., 718), an example that, rather than substantiating his claim, points to the difficulty of an author's coming into ownership of a text in the first place. Poe's repeated toying with the limits of literary property finally transforms his absolute insistence on the crime of plagiarism into a startling defense.

The Longfellow War was structured as an elaborate response to a letter challenging Poe's judgments in the *Waif* review. This letter, signed "Outis" —Greek for "nobody"—was first published in the *Evening Mirror*, but Poe reprinted it in its entirety as part of his step-by-step refutation of its claims.[9] Speaking as a representative of the generalized public (nobody in particular) as well as no-body, a personification of the depersonalized medium of print, Outis stands up to Poe's insinuations, undermining the critical project of separating original from copy by suggesting that plagiarism simply does not exist. According to Outis, "Images are not created but suggested" to authors by events (Poe 1984a, 710); similarities between poems are coincidental, the product of poets' shared language and shared experience. Recognizing that this attempt to undermine the grounds of the charge of plagiarism also threatens the grounds of authorial identity, Poe attacks Outis's claim that images are common property as a deflection of responsibility for poetic language from the authorial subject, and insists on an author's relation to language as a taking of possession. Poe portrays Outis's appeal for common property in writing as an avoidance of the moment of discrimination, a refusal to perform the adjudication between texts that is required of criticism.

At such moments Poe seems clearly to be performing the work of discrimination set out in the "Chapter on American Cribbage" and endorsed by the Young Americans. He provides an item-by-item comparison of the similarities between contending poems (ibid., 732–35), and establishes a general formula for the weighing of evidence generated by such comparisons (ibid., 736). His concern throughout the debate is to distinguish his own careful unfolding of critical principles from Outis's anonymous and unsubstantiated assertions, insisting on the exercise of judgment in the face of unidentified and undifferentiated aggression.[10] Yet Poe's position in this debate drifts from the idealized posture of "Discrimination" not merely through an occasional resort to personal invective, but as a consequence of his broader argument. Describing the vector of literary theft, Poe insists that "of the class of wilful plagiarists nine out of ten are authors of established reputation" (Poe 1984a, 718) who plunder the work of "poverty-stricken" and "neglected" men of genius (ibid., 720).

This allegation has the power to unsettle the Young American agenda not because it transforms an attack on the popular press into an attack on the elite, but because it reveals, beneath the narrative of a struggle between authors, a counternarrative of the struggle of authors to emerge in the first place, to distinguish themselves out of an indistinguishable mass of texts. Poe's insistence that plagiarism is most often the work of the "gentleman of elegant leisure" calls attention to the unstable grounds of literary property, and implies that literary judgment is consequently unreliable. In a series of melodramatic narratives, Poe suggests that in spite of his careful explication of the nature of this crime, the plagiarist can operate with impunity. According to Poe, the author of established reputation "pilfers from some poverty-stricken, and therefore neglected man of genius, on the reasonable supposition that this neglected man of genius will very soon cut his throat, or die of starvation . . . and that in the meantime he will be too busy in keeping the wolf from the door to look after the purloiners of his property" (ibid., 720). For Poe, the immorality of this form of plagiarism is linked to the invisibility of the theft. The confidence and self-possession of the author of established reputation is a by-product of the virtual nonexistence *as property* of the texts of the neglected author. Poe situates his account of literary crime at the vanishing point of the subjectivity of its victims, suggesting the tenuousness of poor authors' attachment to their texts, and the precariousness of considering plagiarism as an intersubjective relation. Far from creating an "American Cribbage" fantasy, where thefts can be exposed with the precision of chapter and verse, day and date, Poe constructs a narrative in which the absorption of one text into another is done with ease, and the detection of the crime seems all but impossible.

Poe's concern with the vulnerability of the authorial subject to the circulation of texts is most evident at the moments when he invokes the act of plagiarism and the accusation of plagiarism as intersubjective struggles. For instance, at the beginning of the third installment of the debate, Poe cites Outis's text in order to demonstrate the emergence of a personal threat out of the apparent impersonality of his prose. Calling attention to Outis's strange capitalization of "THE DYING RAVEN," Poe suggests that the title of Dana's poem was "so printed for the purpose of safely insinuating a charge which not even an Outis had the impudence openly to utter" (Poe 1984a, 726). Yet as soon as he has conjured personal impudence out of the impersonality of Outis's typography, Poe withdraws the charge, claiming that he cannot be sure that "any such thoughts as these ever entered the brain of Outis," that such a charge must remain "purely suppositious," and that, should he insist on the allegation, he would "furnish ground for a new insinuation of the same character, inasmuch as [he would] be employing Outis' identical words" (ibid.). This is undoubtedly lighthearted wordplay, yet it is also an acknowledgment of the more threatening possibility that their positions might ultimately be indistinguishable. Insofar as Poe's principled stand is constructed as a rebuttal to Outis's letter, and is interlaced throughout with quotes from this anonymous text, it is dependent on the very anonymity it eschews. And what is worse, because the form of Poe's rebuttal involves a repetition of the charges of his opponent, the very antagonism that marks their difference is capable of disappearing in the reiteration of "identical words."

It is not altogether surprising, then, that in the final installment of the Longfellow War, Poe should construct an alternate context for understanding plagiarism, one in which authorial identity is linked not to the forcible taking of possession, but to a form of radical dispossession. In this installment, Poe shifts from his attempt to prove the legitimacy of the grounds of the *charge* of plagiarism to an attempt to construct a narrative in which the *practice* of plagiarism could be considered legitimate. In what appears to be a dramatic reversal, Poe argues that plagiarism can be viewed not as malicious theft, but as the product of a heightened sensitivity to beauty that is the hallmark of the true poet:

What the poet intensely admires, becomes . . . a portion of his own intellect. It has a secondary origination within his own soul—an origination altogether apart, although springing from its primary origination from without. The poet is thus possessed by another's thought, and cannot be said to take of it, possession. But, in either view, he thoroughly feels it as *his own*—and this feeling is counteracted only by the sensible presence of its true, palpable origin in the volume from which he has derived it—an origin which, in the long lapse of years it is almost impossible *not* to forget—for in the meantime the thought itself is forgotten. But the frailest association will regenerate it—it springs up with all the vigor of a new birth—its absolute originality is not even a matter of suspicion—and when the poet has written it and printed it, and on its account is charged with plagiarism, there will be no one in the world more entirely astounded than himself. (Ibid., 759)

What is perhaps most striking about this defense of plagiarism is the utter passivity of the offending poet. He is not only fully possessed by another's thought in the act of reading, he is subject to a kind of hair-trigger reproduction of this thought—"the frailest association will regenerate it." While Poe's emphasis on the helplessness of the plagiarist completely absolves the true poet of responsibility for literary theft, the absolute terms in which he casts his apologia indicate that this is not a retraction of his initial position, but its reassertion in inverted form. In this passage, authorial possession appears as its Gothic opposite—the haunting by another—yet these states are curiously reciprocal. Dispossession is experienced by the author as proprietorship until the moment of going into print: the thought may be another's, but the poet "thoroughly feels it as *his own*." In the absence of the book that secures the textual origin of the poet's thought, its derivation is convincingly restaged as biological origination: it "springs up with all the vigor of a new birth." Poe identifies the poet as wholly deluded (the "absolute originality" of his thought is "not even a matter of suspicion"), and yet the extent of his deception bestows on him a paradoxical uniqueness: at the moment of exposure there is "no one in the world more entirely astounded" than the plagiarist himself. Poe's representation of the poet wholly overtaken by another's thought allows him to maintain his initial insistence on the fact of possession as the ground of authorship, while at the same time acknowledging the constant vulnerability of the author to self-loss. His model of legitimate literary theft works to contain the threat posed by anonymity, recasting the displacement of the authorial subject that Outis advocates and represents within the domain of personal property. In his narrative of authorial possession, Poe identifies the circulation of texts with a surrender of autonomy (the loss of the "sensible presence" of the book and the moment of going into print are the twin sites of the poet's betrayal). And yet he seeks to convert this lack of agency into a mark of identity, suggesting that a helpless subjection to iteration is the condition of true poetry.

This redefinition of plagiarism as the provenance of the true poet, however, utterly jeopardizes Poe's commitment to adjudicating between texts. Rather than unfolding a means by which the critic can separate original from copy—his promised digest of the techniques by which authors perpetuate textual fraud—Poe leaves the critic with no means of distinguishing the debased practice of plagiarism from the inspired one, except perhaps by the frequency of its occurrence. As Poe suggests in his closing argument, the true poet is actually *more* apt to plagiarize: "the liability to accidents of this character is in the direct ratio of the poetic sentiment—of the susceptibility to the poetic impression" (ibid.). Despite the promise of mathematical precision conveyed by Poe's "direct ratio," the true poet's mark of distinction is ultimately inaccessible to the critic and to the poet himself: it is a primary vulnerability to imprinting.

Disowning Ownership: Poe's Evasion of Identity at the Boston Lyceum

In the Longfellow War, Poe defends the author as a proprietary subject by portraying him as subject to a primary appropriation. Poe relies on the convertibility of these states and of the absolute terms he invokes to describe them, yet this relentless and recessive logic ultimately collapses the distinctions it sets out to enforce: plagiarism and true poetry become indistinguishable. In light of these interchangeable models of authorship as absolute possession and dispossession, Poe's controversial performance at the Boston Lyceum seems an extraordinary attempt to undo the tyranny of these options, to step outside the realm of literary property. Poe's acceptance of an invitation to deliver an original poem before the Lyceum represents the authorial correlative to his attempt to perform an act of absolute critical judgment in the Longfellow War. Reportedly unable to compose an original poem for the occasion (Thomas and Jackson 1987, 573)[11] Poe committed an act of self-plagiarism, delivering an unidentified early poem, "Al Aaraaf," as if it had been expressly written for this event. According to Poe, the initial reception of the poem was cordial, if reserved, and the affair only erupted into a scandal after he admitted "over a bottle of champagne" that he had written the poem in his youth (Poe 1986, 299).

What is remarkable about this violation of decorum is both Poe's drive toward self-exposure and the intensity of public reaction to reports that the poem had been written *"before its author was twelve years old"* (Thomas and Jackson 1987, 579). Although Poe's arrogance and longstanding antagonism toward Boston certainly fueled the scandal, public outrage over the impropriety of his performance exceeded the offense, spilling over into criticism of Poe's inclusion of juvenilia in *The Raven and Other Poems*. In the newspaper and magazine commentary that followed the affair, Poe was repeatedly decried for permitting immature and fragmentary verses to circulate in the public sphere (ibid., 593–95; Walker 1986, 226–30, 240–45).

James Russell Lowell's careful elimination of all traces of incompletion and dependence from Poe's biography enables us to read Poe's embrace of the juvenile as a significant threat to the mandate for American originality with which he had become identified. In the words of a critic who wrote in Poe's defense, the Lyceum had called on Poe to "deliver himself in poetry" (Thomas and Jackson 1987, 588): he was expected not only to present his work for their judgment, but to perform an act of autogenesis that would support the claim to literary autonomy—his own and America's—that had been made on his behalf. Instead, Poe recited a poem that he insisted was the work of a nonproprietary subject, a juvenile poet—one in the midst of a process of development. Like "Al Aaraaf" itself, which represents a mythical middle ground between heaven and hell, salvation and damnation, Poe's recitation of a juvenile poem eludes the absolutist imperatives of the rhetoric in which his identity as an author had been forged. Neither fully formed nor belated, the trope of juvenility hovers somewhere between the impossible alternatives of original and copy.

While one may doubt Poe's *intention* to have created precisely this kind of disruption, the intensity and breadth of public reaction, and the far reach of the figure of the juvenile for understanding what is inassimilable about Poe, are less easily dismissed.[12] The degree to which the trope of the juvenile was a threat to existing models of authorship is best indicated by its rapid conversion in the public sphere into the opposing forms of authorship it would deny. Appalled by his lack of respect for their commission of an original poem, Poe's enemies credited his performance to drunkenness or insanity, recasting the intrusion of the juvenile into the discourse of originality as the total surrender of authorial control (Thomas and Jackson 1987, 690; Walker 1986, 236–39). Seeking to regain authority over a situation that threatened to undo him, Poe shifted to the pole of absolute self-possession, insisting that he had intended all along to recite an obviously inferior poem. In Poe's account, it was the Boston audience's much vaunted powers of discrimination that had been thoroughly discredited by "the soft impeachment of the hoax" (Poe 1986, 299).

Poe's claim to have hoaxed the Bostonians has been regarded as self-aggrandizing and foolishly self-incriminating, a perverse confession of his own incompetence (Silverman 1991, 266–70). Yet in light of Poe's exemplary status within the discourse of literary nationalism, his attempt to shift attention from his performance to that of the Boston audience seems a remarkably clever retrenchment. Poe's revised account not only places him in complete control of the event, it also places him squarely back within the terms and aspirations of the literary nationalist project. According to Poe, his recitation of a juvenile poem did not display his own lack of originality; it exposed the Bostonians' lack of judgment. In effect, Poe claims to have been doing the work of the Young Americans all along.

While it is not surprising that Poe's explanation failed to satisfy the Bostonians, it is odd that critics and biographers continue to view the Boston Lyceum affair almost exclusively from their perspective. Poe's performance is most often cited as evidence of his psychic instability, with little or no mention of his circumvention of the cultural demand for originality, or his attempt to shift attention to the struggle over literary judgment that was bound up with this demand. The illegibility of the cultural significance of Poe's performance can be traced to the specific form of his transgression. Although Poe disclaims property in his poem by asserting that it is the work of a minor—a self who cannot own—this assertion is undeniably a proprietary gesture. At the Lyceum, Poe challenged his portrayal as a figure of instant maturity by insisting on placing his poem within a developmental narrative. He attempted to shatter his status as an exemplary subject by aggressively reasserting the contingent facts of his biography. While from Poe's perspective, such a fracture might look like reclamation, it represents an unforgivable breach of contract to anyone invested in the cultural fantasy of his autonomy. In a report that reads remarkably like the standard critical interpretation of this event, the board of the Lyceum described the impropriety of Poe's performance as the irruption of his person onto the field of its expectations. As the members of the board explained, they had invited Poe "on the strength of his literary reputation, and were not aware of his personal habits or the eccentricities of his character" (Thomas and Jackson 1987, 642). In this account, the difference between the cultural construction of Poe and his self-presentation is refigured as the product of ineradicable and inexplicable aspects of Poe's personality—his habits and eccentricities. Rather than a complex struggle over originality, authorial identity, and the standards of literary judgment, the Boston Lyceum disaster becomes the scandal of Poe's person.

What this critical dynamic regrettably obscures is the deeply equivocal nature of Poe's proprietary claims. Reciting "Al Aaraaf" may have released Poe from the impossible task of performing his exemplary originality, but this strategy stopped short of full flight: a juvenile poem is something Poe need not fully have owned, and yet it could not be fully disowned. Rather than an act of senseless self-sabotage, Poe's exposure of his poem as a juvenile one was an extraordinary attempt to claim legitimacy for his poem in the absence of a legitimating authorial subject. Poe's was an act of defiance that nevertheless sought approval. Ironically, this act of defiance recapitulated the structure of the literary standard it presumed to repudiate. In reading a juvenile poem rather than a work written for the occasion, Poe exploited the moral indeterminacy of self-plagiarism, which, while undoubtedly a borrowing, also stands as a parodic counterpart to the demand for self-creation. In attempting to circumvent and to challenge the terms of his invitation, Poe performed an all-too-literal fulfillment of the Lyceum's demands.

Even Poe's later claim to have hoaxed the Bostonians inscribes a comparable double movement of evasion and self-assertion. Lurking behind Poe's disparagement of his poem and his description of his performance as a "soft impeachment" of the Boston literati lies a powerful proprietary claim that, however brazen, cannot finally be pinned on Poe himself. For Poe's attempt to regain authority over his performance is cast in borrowed speech. His triumphant declaration of absolute self-possession is a partial and unacknowledged citation from Sheridan's *Rivals*: "I own the soft impeachment" (5.3.198–99). Simultaneously signifying proprietorship and confession, that which is held and that which is released from one's grasp, the unvoiced assertion "I own" resonates despite its detachment from any speaking subject. On the model of Poe's definition of true poetry, this is either empty possession or a full haunting.

NOTES

I am grateful to Stephen Engelmann, John Irwin, Neill Matheson, Margaret Russett, Robert Schreur, Susan Williams, and Larzer Ziff for their thoughtful readings of earlier drafts of this essay.

1. Poe had received biographical treatment once before, as part of the "Poets and Poetry of Philadelphia" series published in the *Philadelphia Saturday Museum* in 1843. However, that essay does not seem to have received much notice outside the Philadelphia

newspapers (Thomas and Jackson 1987, 398–402). As the title of the series suggests, it was intended primarily for local consumption.

2. Magazines did not routinely copyright their contents until late in the century, so even editors and proprietors regularly surrendered control over future publication of a text upon issue of the magazine. Poe's motivation for taking on the editorship of the *Broadway Journal*, however, was directly related to his desire to establish a different form of ownership over his writing, both in terms of his ability to profit from its success (rather than accepting a flat fee for his contribution, regardless of sales) and in terms of his ability to control the medium in which his writing appeared. His frustrating experience as an editor of *Graham's* hardened his resolve on both counts. While watching the circulation figures for this magazine climb—largely because of his own efforts—Poe had to remain content with his editor's salary. In addition, he had to suffer the indignity of watching Graham become wealthy and spend increasingly lavish amounts for illustrations and fashion plates, embellishments Poe felt cheapened his product. Unfortunately, the part-share arrangement Poe signed with Briggs, and his eventual full ownership of the *Broadway Journal*, failed to generate the profits he expected. For a detailed account of this agreement and the financial reasons for the *Journal*'s collapse, see Ehrlich 1986.

3. There is strong evidence to suggest that this is the way in which Poe desired his alliance with the literary nationalists to be perceived. In an important *Broadway Journal* editorial expressing "the most earnest sympathy in all the hopes, and the firmest faith in the capabilities of 'Young America,'" Poe stops short of explicitly endorsing their project, while at the same time claiming a stake in their success. Just as affirming "sympathy in *hopes*" and "faith in *capabilities*" dodges the question of support of present action, so Poe's most explicit declaration of solidarity is characterized by a signal evasion. Poe writes of Young America, "We look upon its interests as our own" (Poe 1986, 171), suggesting that his investment is not ideological, but economic. For Poe's later renunciation of Young America, see his unpublished manuscript "Living Writers of America" (ibid., 166–68).

4. Although early in his career Lowell had been an enthusiastic supporter of the Young Americans, the publication of the *Pioneer* marked a parting of their ways. While the journal demonstrated a strong Young American influence in design and sentiments, Lowell broke ranks in the first issue by calling for a "natural," not a "national," literature (1843, 1). Worse still, the second issue included as promotional material an anonymous review written by Poe praising all the journal's critical notices *except* that of Mathews's *Puffer Hopkins*, which Poe termed "one of the most trashy novels that ever emanated from an American press" (*Pioneer*, February 1843, back cover). Poe's comment instigated a quarrel between Lowell and Mathews, formalizing the split that had become apparent in their rhetoric.

Lowell's falling out with the Young Americans occurred just as Poe had taken on the young poet, engaging him in friendly correspondence, soliciting contributions for his proposed magazine, the *Stylus*, and publishing a flattering but admonitory review of his second book of poetry in *Graham's*. One might argue, then, that Lowell's essay succeeds in bridging the gap between Poe's aesthetics and the discourse of literary nationalism largely because Lowell set out to perform this kind of mediation in the first place, using the essay to reconcile the competing claims of two of his most formative influences.

5. The figure of the stillborn child is an extraordinarily important one for Lowell, and for his relation with Poe. See, for instance, Poe's praise of "The Legend of Brittany," a poem that centers on this figure (Poe 1984a, 809–14), and Lowell's 1849 essay "Nationality in Literature." In this essay Longfellow displaces Poe as the exemplar of Lowell's critical ideals. Likewise, the image of the stillborn child is displaced by the image of an enduring pregnancy. Self-consciously revising his position in his biography of Poe, Lowell refers in this essay to "the period of gestation which a country must go through, ere it bring forth a great poet," and urges, "Let us not be in any hurry to resort to a Caesarian operation" (1913, 13).

6. In his analysis of William Carlos Williams's essay "Edgar Allan Poe," Jonathan Elmer notes a similar anxiety about generation and the critical investment in Poe as a figure of autogenesis. Williams's account is almost certainly indebted to Lowell's essay, which was widely circulated as prefatory matter for Griswold's edition of Poe's works. What is striking about Williams's recasting of the terms of Lowell's essay, however, is the attenuation of its political content. What Williams characterizes as Poe's abstract impulse "to clear the GROUND" (Carlson 1966, 127) for the sake of authenticity is more clearly identified in the antebellum period with the cause of literary nationalism. This is apparent from Lowell's opening polemic, and from F. O. Darley's illustrations for a magazine satire, "A Mirror for Authors." Darley counterposes a silhouette of Poe as a tomahawk-wielding Indian with one of Longfellow depicted as a walking pair of scissors, contrasting Poe's barbarous but original literary practice with Longfellow's more genteel and derivative snipping (Phillips 1926, 2:1371).

7. Although many readers undoubtedly knew Poe to be the author of *Arthur Gordon Pym*, the poems that appeared in Griswold's *Poets and Poetry of America*, the tales collected in the *Tales of the Grotesque and Arabesque*, or those circulated in the *Southern Literary Messenger*, *Burton's*, or *Graham's*, there exist numerous testimonies to readers' ignorance of significant portions of Poe's work. Poe's reputation as an author was scattershot, disarticulated by both genre and region. For example, early in 1845 Charles Briggs mentioned in a letter to Lowell that he was unfamiliar with "The Gold Bug," a tale that had been a popular sensation in Philadelphia (Thomas and Jackson 1987, 494). Likewise, soon after the publication of Griswold's anthology, *Poet's Magazine* scornfully asked concerning Poe, "Who ever dreamed that the cynical critic, the hunter up of small things, journeyman editor of periodicals, and Apollo's man of all work . . . wrote *Poetry?*" (ibid., 368). Poe attributed this ignorance to the erratic nature of magazine readership. In a letter to Charles Anthon, he complained that "unless the journalist collects his various articles, he is liable to be grossly misconceived and misjudged by men . . . who see, perhaps, only a paper here and there, by accident—often only one of his mere extravaganzas, written to supply a particular demand" (Poe 1966, 1:270–71).

8. That Longfellow intended to play on the ambiguous property status of "fugitive" or uncollected magazine verse is clear from his epigraph to the volume, which is taken from book 4 of Spenser's *Faerie Queene:* "A waif the which by fortune came / Upon your seas, he claimed as property / And yet nor his, nor his in equity, but / Yours the waif by high prerogative" (4.12.33–36). In employing this context to justify the publication of his volume, Longfellow imagines a transaction among poet, editor, and reader that matches the complexity of the negotiation that concludes book 4. This is the voice of Cymodeche

imploring Neptune to release Florimell from her captivity at the hands of Proteus, who "claimed" her while she was drifting at sea. Casting the book itself in the role of Florimell, Longfellow tacitly disavows property in the volume, suggesting that his editorial appropriation of these poems is no more legitimate than Proteus's seizure. And yet Poe is right to question this gesture of renunciation. In invoking the romance context, Longfellow obscures the origin of these poems, refiguring authorship as accidental (and fortunate) dispossession. Moreover, in addressing the reader in the role of Neptune, Longfellow seeks to restore ownership not to the poems' authors, but to the sovereign reader. Longfellow's epigraph bears out Poe's offhand comments on the volume's manipulative tone and structure. Longfellow's overt disavowal of property rights conceals a powerful bid to act as the instrument of their rearticulation.

9. Critics are divided on the issue of the identity of Outis, many speculating that Outis was Poe himself, attempting to generate scandal in the form of an antagonistic exchange. The true identity of Outis, however, is less important than the idea that it is in dialogue with a personification of anonymity and impersonality that Poe conducts his most extensive treatment of the problem of plagiarism. Arguments over whether the entire episode was staged by Poe, or whether his response was a defensive overreaction to a legitimate outside challenge, drive accounts of the Longfellow War back to the extremes of authorial control and authorial surrender that Poe was troubling in this series of responses.

10. Like the Young Americans, Poe directs his attack at a split target, representing Outis's anonymity both as evidence of a gentlemanly conspiracy and as a form of mob violence. Poe claims that Outis has resorted to anonymity "with the view of decrying by sheer strength of lungs—of trampling down—of rioting down—of mobbing down any man with a soul that bids him come out from the general corruption of our public press" (Poe 1984a, 741). And yet hovering behind this characterization of anonymous publication as mob aggression is an image of Outis as an aristocrat who, like Longfellow, cleverly manipulates the technology of print. Outis is an "anonymous gentleman" who "manufactures" similarities between poems through the use of typography, "appealing from the ears to the eyes of the most uncultivated classes of the rabble" (ibid., 729). Print circulation may be a dangerous form of popular power, but Poe is deeply suspicious that this power is in the control of the elite.

11. The source of this report, Rufus Wilmot Griswold, is famously unreliable when it comes to the life of Poe, and so it seems safe to speculate that Poe's decision to read a juvenile poem may have been motivated by something more than sheer desperation. For an account of the Lyceum disaster that reads Poe's recitation of "Al Aaraaf" as a good faith gesture toward the interests of the Boston audience, see Casale 1973.

12. See, for example, T. S. Eliot's association of Poe with poetic adolescence (Carlson 1966, 205) and Henry James's famous assertion that "an enthusiasm for Poe is the mark of a decidedly primitive stage of reflection" (ibid., 66).

"Ut Pictura Poe"

Poetic Politics in "The Island of the Fay" and "Morning on the Wissahiccon"

LOUIS A. RENZA

There are few thinkers who will not be surprised to find, upon retrospect of the world of thought, how very frequently the first, or intuitive, impressions have been the true ones. —Edgar Allan Poe, "Chapter of Suggestions" (1845)

If it strikes one as strange to argue that "The Island of the Fay," a plate article accompanying an engraving by John Sartain in the June 1841 issue of *Graham's Magazine*, contains Edgar Allan Poe's political cache, it will no doubt appear even more strange to assert that this cache further conceals Poe's autobiographical fantasy about writing. Doing criticism in a community that leaves no text unturned for its political or ideological implications, how can we regard such a project, assuming it exists, except as perverse, and in the end as downright impossible?[1] And yet, fantasy or not, Poe's particular desire to have inscribed his own reading of his text *in* that text perforce exposes the limitations of the text's various political redactions.

"The Island of the Fay" suggestively stages this desire on its very surface, although paradoxically at the outset it requests quite conventional responses. First, Poe clearly conforms to the magazine "custom then prevailing of writing a poem or sketch to go with [and attach a moral to] a picture," in this case the Sartain engraving, itself depicted as deriving from "an original [picture] by [John] Martin," a popular English artist Sartain had personally known in England (Miller 1942, 135–36; Poe 1969–78, 2:597).[2] Second, the article serves to illustrate certain Romantic shibboleths.

Like a latter-day Rousseau, for example, the narrator states his preference for private reveries in nature over relations with people. He wants to regard nature "exclusively alone"; any sign "of life in any other form than that of the green things which grow upon the soil and are voiceless" is for him "a stain upon the landscape—is at war with the genius of the scene."[3] A Romantic pantheist as well, he advocates a kind of spiritual-materialistic vision of the universe: mathematics and telescopes demonstrate that all natural things, animate or inanimate, are "but the colossal members of one vast animate and sentient whole" (Poe 1969–78, 2:600); each thing constitutes a "cycle within cycle without end," or, in more vitalistic terms, a "life within life, the less within the greater, and all within the Spirit Divine." For the narrator, human beings thus err in supposing that their existence is "of more moment in the universe than that vast 'clod of the valley' . . . to which [they would deny] a soul" (ibid., 601).

The narrator's "fancies," as he himself calls them, prepare us for the single narrative event represented toward the end of "The Island of the Fay." Having "strayed through many a dim deep valley" completely "*alone*,"[4] he once "chanced upon a certain rivulet and island" at sunset in "a far distant region of mountain locked within mountain" (ibid., 602). The west side of the island "was all one radiant harem of garden beauties"; in stark contrast, its eastern side "was whelmed in the blackest shade," emphasized by trees "dark in color and mournful in form and attitude . . . spectral shapes, that conveyed ideas of mortal sorrow and untimely death" (ibid., 603). The narrator takes exceptional note of how the "little river" at once reflected and yet appeared to absorb the shadows issuing from the trees; as the light changed, "other shadows issued [forth] . . . taking the place of their predecessors thus entombed" (ibid., 602, 603).

Tired, he lies down; still entranced by this scene, he fancies it "the haunt of the few gentle Fays who remain from the wreck of the race" (ibid., 604). Like the shadows, such fays, he further muses, lose their existence "little by little . . . exhausting their substance unto dissolution." In a state of mind that "might have converted" any one object "into any thing [he] pleased," the narrator then turns the "large, dazzling, white flakes of the bark of the sycamore" circling "round and round the island" into "one of those very Fays about whom I had been pondering." Each time she circles the island "in a singularly fragile canoe," "she is a year nearer unto her Death" (ibid., 604). "At length, when the sun had utterly departed, the Fay, now the mere ghost of her former self, went disconsolately with her boat into the region of the ebony flood—and that she issued thence at all I cannot say,—for darkness fell over all things, and I beheld her magical figure no more" (ibid., 605).

This story of the doomed fay lends itself to a host of instantly recognizable Romantic motifs: as emphasized by the article's original epigraph

(Poe's own previously published "Sonnet—To Science"),[5] the inability, in the modern, scientific world, to sustain imaginative experience; or because of the apocalyptic "darkness" falling "over all things," the inescapable truth of "life's vicissitudes" (Pollin); or a variant of the former two motifs, the historical loss of (faith in) a pristine, pastoral "garden" (Furrow 1973, 23). Or, given the extremity of Poe's representation of these motifs, one could argue that he here actually exposes their egregious ineffectuality, at least as represented by the article's narrator.

Poe, after all, had notoriously criticized Joseph Rodman Drake's "forced" realistic depiction of fairies in *The Culprit Fay* (Poe 1984a, 519). This precedent alone suggests Poe's general "critical detachment from . . . world[s] of evanescent magic and unstable beauty," just as the narrator's obvious indulgence in the pathetic fallacy—"I love . . . to regard the dark valleys . . . that silently smile . . . the forests that sigh" (Poe 1969–78, 2:600)—indicates Poe's critical distance from the narrator's "sentimental endowment of natural objects with human significance" (Ljungquist 1983, 148, 151). Poe, in other words, ironically frames his narrator as a "Romantic true believer," his desire to regard nature utterly alone indicating his solipsistic tendencies, and his "intention to recover the lost land of fays" in a "world of mundane concerns" clearly "fated for destruction" (ibid., 150, 153, 149).

And yet one can see that these "for *and* against" Romantic readings of "The Island of the Fay" clearly constitute moral or philosophical truths of the kind Poe eschewed for his writing from the beginning of his career. He would allow "instruction" in poetic art only if as an "under-current" theme it resulted in "happiness" or "pleasure" for the reader (Poe 1984a, 7, 691, 685). This position serves to justify rather than to undercut the appearance of fays in Poe's plate article. Existing by definition as completely imaginary creatures, fays represent the one poetic topos free from "mundane" moral concerns or referential adjudication. Poe's "Drake-Halleck" review thus does not criticize this topos per se, but only how Drake forces his readers self-consciously to compare fairies with familiar natural objects and human "passions" only arbitrarily related to the poetic imagination (ibid., 518). In contrast, Shelley's *Queen Mab*, for Poe, represents a fairy who "is not a mere compound of incongruous natural objects . . . but a being" seeming to "spring immediately . . . from the brain of the poet" (ibid., 519, 520, 525).

More than once in his critical reviews, Poe goes out of his way to praise Baron de la Motte Fouqué's prose romance *Undine*, for example for its "exquisite *management of imagination,* which is so visible in the passages where the brooks are water-spirits, and the water-spirits brooks—neither distinctly either" (ibid., 258). This attitude clearly diminishes whatever irony one may wish to impute in "The Island of the Fay" to the narrator's blurring of natural with imaginary objects, such as in his fantasy *of* the fay. But more important, Poe also praises *Undine* for how it suffers "its morality to be *suggested*" rather than obtrusively presented (ibid., 812), and for the way it represents an essentially amoral "Undine" or fairy figure: "one of the race of water spirits—a race who differ . . . from mankind, only in a greater beauty, and in the circumstances of possessing no soul" (ibid., 253).

Poe, in fact, associates poetry itself precisely with "all that is airy and fairy-like" (ibid., 11)—in other words, with any verbal expression that escapes the truth-telling imperatives of the human "soul." If anything, then, the disappearing fay in "The Island of the Fay" must represent Poe's sense of the mortality of this kind of poetic activity before a recurring pressure for "instruction" that supersedes the finally unpersuasive for-and-against Romantic readings of the article.

II

Part and parcel of the 1841 plate article's topical setting are its inescapable cultural-political codifications. As many critics have noted, after the War of 1812 and through Poe's time, the American public's desire to secure a unique national identity perforce charged pictorial and literary references to American nature with an ideological significance (Charvat 1936, 140; Huth 1957, 124). Moreover, when comparing American with European natural scenery in order to effect this nationalist goal, American artists adapted the three eighteenth-century aesthetic conventions of the "sublime," "beautiful," and "picturesque."[6] Given the American landscape's vastness and "stunning variety," these artists in particular "turned to the sublime for emotional intensification of American scenery both to assert personal freedom as romantic artists and to assert their cultural independence of Europe as Americans" (Poenicke 1967, 273; Sanford 1961, 138).

One can easily find signs of such Burkean sublimity in "The Island of the Fay." John Martin, the artist whose "original" work somehow inspired Sartain's engraving, was known for his painting *Sadak in Search of Oblivion*, which depicts the sublime scene of a "little figure" virtually "lost in the wild landscape of gigantic rocks" (Miller 1942, 137). In the article itself, the narrator refers to his experience of "the fantastic" in his "meditations" on conventionally sublime scenery: "the mountains, and the forests . . . the rivers and the ocean" (Poe 1969–78, 2:601). He also thinks sublime thoughts, whether about cosmic "cycles," infinite space (ibid.), or the most extremely small natural objects: "the *animalculae* which infest the brain" (ibid., 600).

Beyond these testimonies to "the immense force and labour" of Creation (Burke 1900, 260), the specific island scene that the narrator discovers in some sublime "far-distant region of mountain locked within mountains" is riddled with "shadows." Like its synonyms in the tale ("sombre . . . gloom," "spectral shapes," and "shade"), "shadows" is virtually a code word in Poe's article for Burkean "obscurity," or the concept of the sublime itself (Ljungquist 1984, 23). Moreover, the narrator's desire to be exclusively alone in a remote, unspecified natural scene clearly invokes Burke's isolation of the most painful and thus sublime situation conceivable, namely "entire solitude, that is, the total and perpetual exclusion from all society" (Burke 1900, 229).

Yet *as* explicit markers of "sublime" landscapes, these allusions show us that the tale's would-be "American" narrator cannot clear his thinking or language from Burkean—English—or other European aesthetic-conceptual influences.[7] If anything, then, the island's western "garden" signifies an allegorical image of the frontier American West as "home of the new" (Fussell 1965, 164); but its ultimately dominant and "sombre" eastern side adumbrates the "old" ideological sensibilities identified with ("eastern") Europe or the northeastern United States. In short, the elegiac suggestion of the fays' inevitable deracination here constitutes a prediction about the eventual "Eastern assimilation" of untamed American nature (ibid., 165).

This fated because already occurring co-optation of American nature's sublimity by European and especially British cultural-aesthetic codes receives its clearest expression in a later plate article by Poe, "Morning on the Wissahiccon." Accompanied by a John G. Chapman engraving "showing an elk in romantic scenery" (Poe 1969–78, 3:860), this article first appeared in *The Opal*, an 1844 giftbook actually released at the end of 1843. Here again, the central narrative anecdote purports to illustrate the commissioned picture. And here again, a narrator first frames this anecdote with general remarks, this time about the comparative merits of Old World and American "natural scenes" (Poe 1969–78, 3:861).

In contrast to its less culturally quarrelsome precursor, an article written by Benjamin Matthias of Philadelphia for the December 1835 issue of the *Southern Literary Messenger*, "Morning on the Wissahiccon" self-evidently outlines a charged cultural project to prove the uniqueness of American scenery beyond those well-known "*lions* of the land—the Hudson, Niagara. . . ."[8] For Poe's narrator, tourists, especially foreign ones, miss "the real

Edens of the land," such as "the gorgeous interior scenery of" a Louisiana valley that realizes one's "wildest dreams of paradise" (Poe 1969–78, 3:862). At the same time, he asserts that the "sole character" of such scenery lies in its "*beauty*. . . . It has little, or rather nothing, of the sublime" (ibid.).

The narrator, in short, here rhetorically asserts "our" American cultural independence from European preferences for sublime landscapes. As if writing a political brief, the narrator advocates that Americans look primarily for native scenes to which one "must *walk* . . . leap ravines . . . risk [one's] neck among precipices," as opposed to scenes one can reach by the well-known routes favored by British tourists (ibid., 863). The Wissahiccon, "a brook" on the outskirts of Philadelphia, provides a prime example proving this thesis: "were it flowing in England . . . [it] would be the theme of every bard . . . if, indeed, its banks were not parcelled off in lots . . . as building-sites for the villas of the opulent." The narrator maintains that "the true beauty of the stream" in fact begins at a point where access to it by common roads ends, and where one can see "the most magnificent forest trees of America" surrounding the stream's "precipitous" banks (ibid., 864). Following the Wissahiccon's own "windings," one has the experience of "an endless succession of infinitely varied small lakes, or, more properly speaking, tarns" (ibid., 865).

Yet the narrator's references to "interior" American paradises and in particular to an "infinitely varied" brook already betray his inability to shed his attraction to the European *category* of the sublime landscape experience. In spite of his nationalist rhetoric, his sense of "beauty" is here synonymous with Burke's notion of the "sublime" (Dayan 1987, 106). For example, he argues that one can best see the Wissahiccon "amid the brightest glare of a noonday sun," for otherwise the "narrow gorge" and "foliage" through which it flows will "produce" a virtual *locus classicus* of sublime experience: "a gloominess, if not an absolute dreariness of effect, which, unless relieved by a bright general light, detracts from the mere beauty of the scene" (Poe 1969–78, 3:865). But since one Burkean source for sublime effects includes the extremity of light (Burke 1900, 263), the narrator's prescription for seeing this scenery in "the brightest glare of a noonday sun" concedes the very cultural ground he thinks to gain from his rhetorical resistance.

His final anecdote about a recent trip on the Wissahiccon equally fails to prove the uniqueness of American scenery. Drifting downstream in a boat, he drowsily fantasizes being in "ancient days . . . when the Demon of the Engine [the railroad] was not, when pic-nics were undreamed of, when 'water privileges' were neither bought nor sold, and when the red man trod alone, with the elk, upon the ridges that now towered above." Suddenly he indeed "saw, or dreamed that I saw," an elk standing on "a steep rocky cliff, abutting far into the stream," and still "half-slumberous [he] fancie[d]" that this elk was "one of the oldest and boldest of those identical elks which had been coupled with the red men of my vision" (Poe 1969–78, 3:865). The narrator, however, cannot sustain this vision of a pristine American nature. He soon imagines "the elk repining . . . at the manifest alterations for the worse, wrought upon the brook and its vicinage, even within the last few years, by the stern hand of the utilitarian"; he then spots "a negro" coming out of the woods, coaxing the elk to come to him until it "lay quietly down and was secured with a halter"—the elk actually being "a *pet* of great age and very domestic habits [that] belonged to an English family occupying a villa in the vicinity" (ibid., 866).

For the narrator, it is not only "the stern hand of the utilitarian" and the presence of "pic-nics" in the Wissahiccon area that haunt his dream of experiencing a pristine American nature. His rhetorical efforts to believe in a *native* American vision on the basis of *native* American scenery—as if seen by "the red men of my vision"—continually revert on all levels to Euro-centric aesthetic values. Like Poe's view of American critics being influenced by English criticism,[9] the narrator's discovery of a domesticated elk belong-ing "to an *English* family occupying a villa in the vicinity" (emphasis added) punctuates his failure to deny the pervasive influence of European cultural codes on American perceptions of American scenery. Just as the narrator of "The Island of the Fay" cannot quite avoid the fantasy aspect of his desire to witness American scenery "alone," so the narrator of "Morning on the Wissahiccon" cannot sustain his fantasy of "our" American cultural inde-pendence, *even as a desired ideal,* on the basis of some myth about this scenery's primordial ("red man") uniqueness.

In this sense, one could even regard the narrator as a "pious nationalist," his article a parody of what by Poe's time had become a "hackneyed" nationalist question about "the relative merits of Old World and New World scenery" (Ljungquist 1984, 126). Throughout his career Poe steadfastly re-sisted the cultural and literary nationalist sentiments of his critical contem-poraries.[10] If he argues against excessive subservience to British "critical dicta," he can also claim that American critics are now "becoming boister-ous and arrogant in the pride of a too speedily assumed literary freedom. . . . We forget . . . that *the world* is the true theatre of the biblical histrio" (Poe 1984a, 506). Indeed, the plate article's narrator seems to "puff" the "little" Wissahiccon in the same way in which American critics overvalue "the many disgraceful literary failures to which our own inordinate vanities and mis-applied patriotism have lately given birth" (ibid.).

In terms of his cultural-nationalist project, the word *morning* in the sketch's title—otherwise absent from the narrative itself—thus ironically confesses the narrator's "mourning" or loss of faith in an autonomous American identity. Yet if Poe would make "the world . . . the true theatre" of his own literary work, he could also regard as "the purest insanity" the British charge that American "utilitarian ability" undermines the "poetic sentiment" in Americans: "nor can any social, or political, or moral, or physical conditions do more than momentarily repress the impulses which glow in our own bosoms as fervently as in those of our progenitors" (Poe 1984a, 549). One could actually ascribe the conspicuous absence of the word *morning* in his article to Poe's more carefully imagined brand of cultural nationalism: "morning" light undercuts the narrator's faulty—because dis-cursively Burkean—nationalist recommendation that we see the stream "amid the brightest glare of a noonday sun." Poe, if not his narrator, can position himself in an American culture imaginatively conceived as still in its "morning" or historically infant stage.

Moreover, the very brevity of both "The Island of the Fay" and "Morning on the Wissahiccon" argues for Poe's *active* resistance to the sublime mode of literary representation. In accord with Burke's identification of the beautiful with small or fragile objects (Burke 1900, 292–95), Poe insisted on the affec-tive superiority of the short tale over the novel even before his well-known 1842 review of Hawthorne's *Twice-Told Tales*.[11] Poe's mere employment of the short tale could thus constitute a kind of generic-illocutionary act in which he would displace the sublime—or the landscape aesthetic privileged by "the Old World" (Poe 1969–78, 3:861)—with the beautiful "gorgeous" scenery of America. Indeed, Poe's short plate articles further focus our attention on brief descriptive episodes and emphasize diminutive or beauti-ful objects that double or advertise their generic settings as such: not "large rivers" (ibid., 863) but a "rivulet" (ibid., 864); or in "The Island of the Fay," such images as a circumscribed island, a surrounding "little river," "the dainty fay" (in the tale's original epigraph) and her "singularly fragile canoe."

Poe's subtle yet open semiotic maneuvers to resist European ideologies of the sublime help explain his distaste for its American artistic translations. James Fenimore Cooper's works, for example, accrued public approbation because they exploited the "intrinsic and universal interest" built into the topos of the American wilderness.[12] In this sense, Poe's textual strategies in "The Island of the Fay" and "Morning on the Wissahiccon" indicate his resistance to European (or specifically British) *and* American (or Cooper-like) visions of sublime American scenery and its ideological double, a unique American national character. But at the same time, Poe here only assumes the impossibility of realizing this cultural-national project by refer-ential means. Exploiting American scenery in a direct manner, as the narra-tor does in "Morning on the Wissahiccon," American writers paradoxically defeat the very nationalist project they otherwise intend to promulgate. But this project can take a dialectical form that, although by definition ineffec-tive in the public sphere, proves the attractive force—the beautiful truth, as it were—of a fantasy about a postpolitical form of American writing.

III

Poe's "nationalist" project becomes clearer when one considers the way the two articles internalize the "picturesque" mode of artistic representation. Derived from such British and Scottish aestheticians as William Gilpin, Uvedale Price, and Archibald Alison, the category of the picturesque offers an alternative to the overwhelming impressions of nature required by the sublime, and the merely pleasant ones that came to be associated with the beautiful. The picturesque scene stirs the viewer's "curiosity" by emphasiz-ing unexpected, irregular, various, or intricate visual aspects of scenery, sometimes also hinting at "concealment" and the transient temporality of things (Price 1810, 1:68–69, 83–85, 88, 279; Hipple 1957, 213). The pictur-esque, in short, adds point to the beautiful, even as it sets visually compre-hensible boundaries—as in the frame of a picture—to the sublime scene.

Poe's attraction to compositional originality as the result of "novel com-binations" (Poe 1984a, 319) shows his awareness of picturesque modes of representation. In "Morning on the Wissahiccon," the narrator explicitly designates the little stream "as an object of picturesque interest" (Poe 1969–78, 3:864). Picturesque fantasias characterize the Louisiana valley's "gentle undulations of soil, interweaved with fantastic crystallic streams" (ibid., 862), as well as the landscape in a tale like "The Domain of Arnheim."[13] Moreover, "The Island of the Fay" clearly refers to picturesque worlds inso-far as literary versions "of the picturesque" (Pope's *Rape of the Lock*, for example) often include "volatile" figures of "a secondary fairy world" (Flet-cher 1970, 261). Poe's article also refers to the picturesque effect of temporal decay: trees with "sad, solemn, and spectral shapes," and especially "the wreck of the race" of fays in the process of "dying" and "wast[ing] away mournfully" (Poe 1969–78, 2:603, 604).

But most important, "The Island of the Fay" virtually allegorizes the picturesque mode of writing itself, a chief characteristic of which is allegorical suggestiveness or concealment. Just as the picturesque favors natural scenes or art (like the sketch) "in which form emerges only with study or is at the point of dissolution" (Price 1965, 278), so the fay becomes more and more "the mere ghost of her former self" (Poe 1969–78, 2:605). In the same way, the narrator's own fantasy terminates, one could say, just at the point before sublime "darkness" overtakes the scene: "I beheld her magical figure no more."[14]

Like the American sublime, however, the picturesque influence refers both of Poe's plate articles to a European and especially a British aesthetic-ideological context.[15] One could argue that Poe here perhaps parodies or criticizes "the various theories of the 'picturesque,' " as he does in his major landscape tales (Rainwater 1984, 42). Does his narrator in "Morning on the Wissahiccon" not seek "the true beauty of the stream . . . far above the *route* of the Philadelphian picturesque-hunters" (Poe 1969–78, 3:864)? Yet how can Poe escape the picturesque aesthetic mode if simply the act of writing a plate article protests its influence? Pressured by the demands of contemporary American magazine practice for verbally illustrated pictures, how can he avoid construing his two articles in terms of their pictorial doubles—in other words, in terms of the picturesque, which originated precisely to isolate objects suitable for painting (Huth 1957, 197)? Poe's two plate articles thus not only engage but literally invoke this aesthetic mode: through the socioeconomic pressure to practice "ut pictura poesis"; and through the simple, phenomenological fact of the accompanying Sartain and Chapman engravings.

Poe largely accepts rather than rejects the principle of "ut pictura poesis." "The Island of the Fay" ostensibly illustrates an engraving that itself is based on an "original" pictorial sketch (for a water project) done by the artist John Martin, who at the time was well known for being a "poet's painter" (Pollin). Poe's critical statements throughout his career also tend to support this pictorialist poetic principle.[16] In his 1842 review of Hawthorne's *Twice-Told Tales*, he argues that through a tale's well-executed "design" "a picture is at length painted which leaves in the mind of him who contemplates it with a kindred art, a sense of the fullest satisfaction" (Poe 1984a, 572). At most, Poe would reverse but not eliminate the usual binary relationship between painting and text in magazine plate articles by having the picture embellish or illustrate the literary text (ibid., 1026).

But at the same time, Poe's notorious critical vigilance against mixing "the obstinate oils and waters of Poetry and Truth" (ibid., 685) actually devolves on an antipictorial aesthetic. If poetic works present "perceptible images," he argues that they should coterminously elicit "*in*definite sensations" akin to those we experience with music (ibid., 11). Even a well-integrated fictional plot can convey "an artificial effect, requiring, like music, not only a natural bias, but long cultivation of taste for its full appreciation" (ibid., 482). In other words, our sense of a text's artifice can interrupt our tendency to read words as transparently referring to determinate images or referents—the phenomenological category of "truth"—and instead lead us to focus on their "music" or semiotic indefiniteness.[17] Truth concerns whatever is "distinctly thought" or "distinctly expressed" (ibid., 119); truth-statements therefore have "no sympathy with the myrtles" (ibid., 684).

Poe's notion of truth as a distinct, determinate referent bears a metaphorical resemblance to his pictorialist notion of the short tale: "in pieces of less extent, the pleasure is *unique* . . . the understanding is employed, without difficulty, in the contemplation of the picture *as a whole*" (ibid., 691). Although "long cultivation" is required to grasp a work's more musical effects, any reader presumably can grasp "without difficulty" the "unique" pictorial effect of a short work. But it is precisely the immediate sociality of the pictorial object (and by extension, the picturesque conception of art and natural scenery) that Poe's "indefinite" thesis about the "beauty" of poetic works contests. As Lord Kames argued, beauty essentially pertains to "objects of sight," and perceiving them in works of art "attaches us to external objects and promotes society" (Hipple 1957, 108, 109). One could apply this position to sublime art as well. Sublime experiences remain private, an anxious matter of self-preservation, whereas sublime art, as Burke argued, implies a socially shareable distance from this experience. In Poe's words, one should never "confound" the "obscurity of expression" (the attempt to represent the sublime experience directly) "with the expression of obscurity" (the attempt to elicit this experience in readers) (Poe 1984a, 321).

But Burke also claimed that "words undoubtedly have no sort of resemblance to the ideas for which they stand"; that empirically, "no real picture is formed" when one uses words; and therefore that "the picturesque connection [in poetry] is not demanded" (Burke 1900, 347, 345). With regard to represented objects, words allow us to "make such combinations as we can not possibly do otherwise," and certainly not with pictorial images (ibid., 348), a position Poe clearly seems to endorse when he argues that one can endlessly create "original combinations of words" or "ideas" (Poe 1984a, 869). But since one can bring any number of verbal associations to a represented object, no determinate signified or "truth" exists at all in the realm of art. After Burke, associationist aestheticians such as Alison openly acknowledged the indeterminate and even accidental effects of art. For Alison, a painted or verbally described natural object can "awaken a train of associations additional to what [a] scene as a whole is calculated to excite" (Hipple 1957, 163–64). At the same time, he maintains "that the moral and aesthetic law operate[s] in individuals with marked uniformity, and that Association change[s] not with the individual but with society" (Charvat 1936, 49). Thus even in the case of musical sounds, privately determined associations entail social principles of taste and perception, so that "the pleasures of taste conduce to moral improvement" (Hipple 1957, 180).

On the one hand, Poe similarly maintains "that taste itself . . . is an arbitrary something, amenable to no law, and measurable by no definite rules" (Poe 1984a, 679). But on the other, for him "taste" solely concerns "Beauty," not morality or truth (ibid., 685). A poem should be *"written solely for the poem's sake,"* not to promulgate "certain dogmas or doctrines (questionable or unquestionable) about PROGRESS" or any other social theory (ibid., 295). Moreover, Poe's formalist view of art also exists in the context of an idiosyncratic Romantic agenda. A particular work's indefinite effect conduces to one's spiritual as opposed to social or moral improvement: "Inspired with a prescient ecstasy of the beauty beyond the grave, [poesy] struggles by multiform novelty of combination among the things and thoughts of Time, to anticipate some portion of that loveliness whose very elements, perhaps, appertain solely to Eternity" (ibid., 686).

Poe's formalist critical position, in short, tacitly constitutes an antisocial act. For him, "all high excitements are necessarily transient," and so "the immense force derivable from *totality*" in the (picture-oriented) short tale is limited to one specific sitting in which "the soul of the reader is at the writer's control" (ibid., 571, 572). In this sense, Poe regards the tale's putatively universal or social effect, the coincidence of vision between writer and reader, as a transitory and even illusory event. At worst, physical and intellectual distractions (such as being led to consider the tale's "truth" while reading it) can cancel this effect ahead of time. At best, a short literary work projects pictorial referents within a unified design that for readers momentarily instantiates a shareable aesthetic experience of "indefinitiveness" (ibid., 837). But as soon as one finishes reading the work, this experience becomes vulnerable to a host of disintegrating pressures—for example, to the contingent, extratextual associations of readers, or to determinate comparisons with "the things and thoughts of Time," which is the sphere of the picturesque mode.

For Poe, then, the act of reading a short tale exemplifies an immediate yet unsustainable social compact that requires a kind of master-slave scenario (the reader under the writer's control) for the compact to exist at all. The social compact invoked in reading already comprises, as it were, a dying, beautiful text. And here one begins to see the antipicturesque, antisocial significance of "The Island of the Fay." Poe's article seems virtually to stage the picturesque. An article illustrating an engraving, it in effect also illustrates itself: the fictional anecdote of the fay proves the tale's essayistic thesis about "cycle[s] within cycle[s] without end" (Poe 1969–78, 2:601).

But "The Island of the Fay" also inscribes an allegory of its own reading that in the end makes indefinite all the allegorical references we could theoretically attribute to it, including the article's own cancellation of allegory. The narrator initially positions himself as a reader-figure when he insists that Marmontel's observation about the composer's "pleasure derivable from sweet sounds" applies to the talented listener as well, for whom music also becomes "susceptible of complete enjoyment, where there is no second party to appreciate its exercise" (ibid., 600). Music bespeaks the ideal effect Poe would have his poetic works produce on their readers, for just as "the *indefinite* is an element in the true [poem]," so is it "an element . . . of the true musical expression. Give it any undue decision—imbue it with any very determinate tone—and you deprive it, at once, of its ethereal, its ideal, its intrinsic . . . character. You dispel its luxury of dream. . . . You exhaust it of its breath of fäery" (Poe 1984a, 1331).

But such decisions are what any tale constantly tempts its readers to make, especially since the tale often aims at *representing* the truth—in other words, the illusion of determinate references—as in the case with "tales of ratiocination" (ibid., 573). In the same way, one cannot help drawing determinate comparisons between text and engraving in the case of "The Island of the Fay." But Poe's plate article in fact proposes and negates this "truth" impulse in reading, thus converting one's actual reading of the tale into a transitory trope for an ideal, indefinite reading that would not "exhaust" the tale's spirit of "fäery." On the one hand, Sartain's engraving invokes the nationalistic fault lines discussed earlier. Derived from an "original" sketch by John Martin for a London water project, the engraving perforce alludes to an "English" source that Poe's "American" text either imitates or resists. But insofar as the tale allegorically refers to the ideal conditions for its own reading, it clearly resists thematic arrest by any kind of political frame. For what is the nature of a water-project sketch if not its determinate public or *social* significance?

Since Poe's particular resistance to "truth" in reading here also applies to the principle of "ut pictura poesis" associated with his use of Martin's sketch, "The Island of the Fay" becomes irreducible to Poe's ironic criticism *or* his support of cultural-nationalistic attitudes, or for that matter to some socioeconomic pique at contemporary magazine versions of "ut pictura poesis." Poe's tale, in short, resists the sheer sociality or public-use value (a water project) signified by its would-be pictorial double. In effect verbally dissolving Martin's public project, "The Island of the Fay" determines its own public uselessness, or what amounts to the same thing: the paradoxical necessity and impossibility of apprehending it outside any social influence or system of evaluation whatsoever.

And so the tale defines itself as a fantasy—the narrator all but acknowledges this possibility himself (Poe 1969–78, 2:604)—and thus as possessing at best minor literary value. Moreover, as the tale's *linguistic* images allegorically double themselves and come to exist "no more," the image of the "dainty" fay passes from picturelike smallness to utter invisibility. Overused and, as Poe's Drake-Halleck review suggests, presently abused, the topos of fairies now exists as a passing convention within literary history and as a useless referent vis-à-vis the socioliterary taste of an "antiromantic" American audience (Poe 1984a, 252). For a reader to suspend disbelief in the fay's imaginative reality, he or she must repress such criteria within the act of reading. But the fay *in* the article represents precisely this (im)possible reading *of* the article—that is, the fay stands as a figure totally devoid of "use" value except in the way it reflects back this uselessness. In this sense, the fay becomes the "magical figure" or nonpictorial representation of poetic beauty itself—Poe's dying, beautiful woman—which one can apprehend or read only "when we are exclusively alone" (Poe 1969–78, 2:600).

In this necessary misreading of the tale, the gradual and cyclical disappearance of the fay allegorically doubles the disappearing pictorial (or picturesque) aspect of the text and its accompanying engraving into indefinite self-reference. The first or essayistic portion of the tale stages the reader's wish to approach its "truth" or socially apprehensible meanings: cosmic pantheism, "life's vicissitudes," or politically specific allusions to such issues as American cultural nationalism. But the second or "beauty" portion of "The Island of the Fay" focuses precisely on a scene of reading, the fay disappearing into nonreference, defined entirely as a deictic experience of the tale's indefinite beauty or "the expression of obscurity": the "alone" experience of things once emptied of their sociopicturesque frames of reference. By definition, this experience constitutes for Poe a transitory and radically "novel" moment that the reader "enjoys . . . as absolutely original with the writer—*and* himself. They two, [the reader] fancies, have, alone of all men, thought thus. They two have, together, created this thing" (Poe 1984a, 581).

But this radically solitary yet paradoxically "social" experience clearly requires constant renewal. As the tale's essayistic introduction demonstrates, other readings precede and supersede this imaginary social moment. Inscribing a similar project of poetic politics, "Morning on the Wissahiccon" concerns the inescapable fate of such readings. On the one hand, it inscribes an ideal private reading of *its* "little" narrative's beauty with *its* "many and abrupt [windings]" or condensed allusions to American nature. On the other hand, it inscribes the inevitability of its public ("utilitarian") appropriations through readings defined according to its value as superficial entertainment ("pic-nics"), its economic value as a magazine piece with an engraving (bought and sold "water privileges"), its potential cultural value as travel information for American tourists, and not least, its value as a political manifesto or critique of American cultural nationalism. Indeed, Poe's sketch strays into further moral and political minefields with its unavoidably charged allusions to the white man's genocidal removals of the "red men" and enslavement of the "negro," both deeds introducing a "surprising snare in the bower of bliss" or the would-be American "Garden" traced in Poe's sketch (Dayan 1991, 103).

But since the "Garden" in Poe's sketch ironically refers to a nonreferential or indefinite (because desired) scene of reading, *any* public understanding of this tale would interfere with its "bliss" of reading. The tale allegorizes its readability in such a way as effectively to dissolve the specific referentiality (and hence moral force) of these racial or nationalist issues. They thus become metaphorically interchangeable with the tale's self-referential "literary" concerns. For example, one could argue that "the elk who is the Indian is also, not unimaginably, the too impressionable, the too easily tamed native writer" (Fussell 1965, 170). Or one could argue that the tale's allusion to the "negro" servant of an English master refers to the American writer's enslavement to British cultural or American commercial criteria.

Still, such interpretations merely shift the focus from political to literary-political readings of the sketch. Once released from the quest for an original, deictic apprehension of indefinite "beauty" in Poe's terms, a text's self-referential strategies also become no less public than definitive political allusions. If only to himself, Poe drives home this point by overexposing his article's public literary seams. In one sense—to others—Poe conceals his sketch's intertextual reference to Matthias's 1835 "Wissahiccon" article, the better to preserve its aura of originality in the marketplace. But in another sense—to himself—his intertextual allusion serves to place *both* sketches within the anonymous public domain of an impermanent periodical literature.[18] Indeed, "Morning on the Wissahiccon" explicitly refers to Matthias's "Wissahiccon" in ways that could not have escaped Poe: common references to the Wissahiccon's surrounding scenery; the use of similar verbal elements (the spelling of "pic-nic," for instance); both employing the same number of paragraphs (Pollin 1983, 259–60). By later changing his article's title to "The Elk," Poe also indicated his willingness to allow Chapman's accompanying picture to interpret "Morning on the Wissahiccon" in sublime terms. Chapman's picture, that is, shows an elk against the background not of a stream but of a river that resembles Chapman's favorite artistic topos, sublime Hudson River scenery (ibid., 261).

Deliberately associating it with periodical literature and popular landscape pictures, Poe thus defines and even projects his sketch within the public domain. At the tale's end, the narrator admits that his "romance of the elk" has "ended" (Poe 1969–78, 3:866). And at first glance, Poe's allegorically inscribed concessions to public readings warrant a similar elegiac mood. But more than any reader, he himself must register these intertextual and pictorial concessions. What possible purpose could this backstage knowledge serve unless to transform his text's determinate public meanings into figures of misreading—of others reading these two articles for their "truth" instead of their "breath of fäery"? In this way, Poe arrives at the point where, as it were, he has prepared himself to read his own sketch "exclusively alone."

Put another way, Poe writes to project himself at the beginning (or "morning") of a project that by definition no one else has ventured. Formulated in the context of a culturally charged question about uniquely American scenery, national character, and art, this project inevitably carries internalized "social" implications. As the first (and in a dialectical sense, the only) reader of his text, he can analogously imagine discovering the radical meaning of a truly original American literature—one of the "most unspeakable glories of the land"—a primordial "Wissahiccon" literature of the "red man" or "race" of "gentle Fays." This discovery frames such literature as itself a project always about to begin: not as an already lost (pre)historical opportunity; not as a matter of reference to what always ends up being an already culturally mediated American nature; but as "a longing for solitude—a scorn of all things present, in an earnest desire for the future" (Poe 1966, 22–23).[19]

IV

One can always argue that Poe's reactionary, antebellum political views undermine the force of his project to found the conditions for writing an original American literature. Little doubt exists about his antiabolitionist, even racist, sentiments, or his bias against the democratic "mob," which he especially associates with the northeastern section of the United States. In retrospect this political agenda also effectively transforms into sheer political rationalization—rhetorical denials of the abolitionist-alias-moral claims of northeastern intellectuals—Poe's formalist "poetic principle," his privileging of beauty over truth, and his often-expressed contempt for the "mass" of "uneducated" and intellectually "obtuse" readers.[20]

Indeed, the wish to escape unpleasant sociopolitical realities may define the subtext of the narrator's quest in "The Island of the Fay" for a socially isolated scene—"a far-distant region of mountain locked within mountain"—where he could imagine anything he pleased. At the very least, the fay's disappearance into fantasy suggests the limitations of any attempt to realize a "locked" or self-contained southernist imaginary. In a similar vein, when the "negro" secures the once wild elk "with a halter" at the end of "Morning on the Wissahiccon" (Poe 1969–78, 3:866), Poe in effect acknowledges how the slavery issue ultimately haunts his freedom to entertain fantasies of sectionalist-alias-aesthetic autonomy.[21]

First, Poe's actual commitment to a "Southern" political stance remains uncertain at best (Thompson 1988, 264). Second, in a *literary*-political context such a stance could at once reflect his resistance to northeastern literary cliques effectively controlling the means of American literary production and reception in his time and his desire "to establish conditions favorable" for literary work within the nation as a whole (Moss 1963, 3). More important, since for Poe such conditions *did not yet exist*, he could here again imaginatively position himself as if at the beginning of an as yet undefined and undetermined American literature. One could even argue that all of Poe's public political poses at once mask and serve this primary literary-historical motivation. For example, his elitist attitude toward the "uneducated" democratic "mob" does not prevent him from maintaining that the American public, not established critics, can and should choose the representative literary works for any prospective American literary canon, the beginnings of which one finds in literary anthologies: "The public has been desirous of obtaining a more distinct view of our poetical literature than the scattered effusions of our bards and the random criticisms of our periodicals, could afford. But, hitherto, nothing has been accomplished in the way of supplying the *desideratum*" (Poe 1984a, 550). Since an American literature presently exists only in the dispersed state of uncollected, "scattered" texts, it does not *yet* exist. The same situation obtains because of the "random" state of American critical opinion.

Above all, Poe here virtually concedes that literary objects, especially magazine pieces, belong wholly in the public domain, and primarily as marketplace commodities. Even before he joined the Democratic literary clique of Young America, Poe maintained that "the book of the author is the property of the public" (Poe 1984a, 1012). But for a writer fantasizing about founding an American literature, this "public" must have seemed anxiously synonymous with an alienated social sphere. Phenomenologically speaking, a writer producing texts as commodities for public consumption "loses control over his creations," or discovers "the identity he has invested in the writing dispersed and dislocated among the masses" (Auerbach 1989, 56).

In one sense, the inscribed resistance to public readings discernible in his two plate articles could indicate Poe's wish for a less alienated public sphere for his writing, for example one such as that assumed by the preceding generation of American Federalist critics.[22] Even early in his career, Poe could idealistically maintain that "a people is not a mob, nor a mob a people, nor a mob's idol the idol of a people—that in a nation's self is the only security for a nation" (Poe 1984a, 146). Poe here clearly postulates a "people" grounding the American "nation's self," and at least conditionally adopts a nationalist rather than a sectionalist political position.[23] At the same time, in accord with another Federalist shibboleth, Poe imagines that only a few "people" can read texts as private or intimate communications between writer and reader, rather than as impersonal public commodities.

Yet if Poe is, to say the least, no Jacksonian Democrat, neither is he a simple recidivist Federalist disguised as a contemporary Whig. First, whereas he consistently opposes the use of literature to edify society with "truth" of any kind, the previous generation of American Federalist critics were precisely "preoccupied with the social implications of literature," if only to preserve "the political, economic, and moral *status quo*" (Charvat 1936, 6, 7). Second, one could argue that both "The Island of the Fay" and "Morning on the Wissahiccon" trace Poe's vocational-autobiographical revision of a central Federalist ideological tenet: the protection of the few's private property in the face of disruptive political and economic demands by the democratic many (ibid., 5). Insofar as both narrators wish to witness natural scenes "alone"—that is, to treat these scenes in the mode of private property—Poe's plate articles initially appear to endorse rather than to revise this tenet. And given Poe's notorious sensitivity to literary plagiarisms, such property-alias-scenery probably includes the very status of these articles as private *literary* property. For him, plagiarisms occur when a writer's literary vision, "his most intangible, and therefore his least defensible and least reclaimable *property*, is purloined" by a later writer (Poe 1984a, 678; emphasis added).

Yet Poe's anxious sense of plagiarism also bespeaks his actual literary position as well as his economic situation. He himself essentially possesses no property to protect. He owns no magazine, despite his career-long ambition to do so. Given their commodified status, their vulnerability to criticism by literary cliques, and even idealistic civic-republican demands for their elicitation of social truths, his own literary works appear to him always in the process of becoming "the property of the public." Like the finally disappearing fay, the narrator in "The Island of the Fay" (as his very need to write this narrative may indicate) can only temporarily fantasize witnessing a scene utterly by himself, or as if it were his own private property. In similar fashion, the narrator of "Morning on the Wissahiccon" encounters what he at first assumes to be a private American scene; gradually senses the Wissahiccon's encroaching contamination by democratic "pic-nics" and demands for "water-privileges" (Poe 1969–78, 3:865); and ultimately recognizes its preoccupation by the cultural elite—"an English family occupying a villa in the vicinity."

But this recognition occurs in a conspicuously abrupt manner at the end of the sketch. The narrator records it, but one can ask whether he registers it or, as this abruptness suggests, represses its significance. It is as if Poe's text continues to wish itself free from its unavoidable sociopolitical—or indeed any of its possible public—appropriations or readings, so that these remain "in the vicinity," but do not determine his text's identity. In fact, both plate articles constitute perverse autobiographical revisions of their otherwise politically codifiable meanings. Poe ultimately uses the political codifications of his articles as pretexts for disclosing his own "intangible" autobiographical scene of writing: his reimagined spatial and temporal origins as a writer that occurred, as it were, before producing an "American literature" became for him subject to political or literary-political determinations.

Poe himself tends to read the serious, allegorical undercurrent of a poetic work in terms of its writer's withheld, conventionally understood auto-biographical situation. *Undine,* for example, provides him with evidence to surmise "that the author has deeply suffered from the ills of an ill-assorted marriage" (Poe 1984a, 256).[24] In a sense, one could argue for a similar autobiographical reference in "The Island of the Fay": that the fay's plight self-evidently refers to Virginia Poe's becoming a "mere ghost of her former self" due to a recently diagnosed case of tuberculosis (Pollin). But this autobiographical connection clearly depends on public *biographical* knowledge of his marital situation that Poe could safely assume most readers of "The Island of the Fay" would not possess. In other words, like the fay herself, this autobiographical direction in effect exists in the process of disappearing from public view, of becoming more private, or of referring Poe back to a possible experience of his text minus any kind of public mediation. For example, the tale's diminutive depiction of its diminutive topos—"the dainty fay" (in the first epigraph), or "the few gentle Fays" and other "little" references (Poe 1969–78, 2:604)—conceals throughout a pun affecting the tale's entire *mise-en-scène:* English words for the French "la fée-ette."

How does the tale refer us to Lafayette, the famous French general? In a sense compatible with American Federalist anxieties about unruly, demo-cratic mobs, "Lafayette" perhaps stands for a political-allegorical trope for a historical figure opposed to the excesses of the French Revolution. But this political association merely conceals one closer to Poe's literary desire to witness the founding of a genuine American literature. "Lafayette," that is, here constitutes a dreamlike allusion to a celebrated Revolutionary War hero, and in this sense effectively associates Poe's text with the country's founding political scene. But this association itself metamorphoses into an autobiographical reference to Poe's own genealogical origins: to his grand-father David Poe, also a Revolutionary War hero, whose grave Lafayette specifically honored in Poe's presence at Richmond, Virginia, when Lafa-yette revisited the country in 1824 (Phillips 1926, 1:17).

These allusions thus become less and less accessible to public and espe-cially political readings. Poe would even replace the tale's original epi-graph—which included his specific addition of "the dainty fay" to his "Son-net—To Science"—with a more conventional and so here politically latent epigraph referring to "spirit of place."[25] In an even less obvious vocational-autobiographical allusion, both plate articles point us back to the literal "vicinity" of Poe's literary beginnings. For example, the narrator's depiction of the fay in "The Island of the Fay" explicitly refers to certain lines from

"The Lake of the Dismal Swamp," a poem by one of the young Poe's favorite English poets, Thomas Moore, who had actually visited the Dismal Swamp area in Virginia in 1803:

> And she's gone to the Lake of the Dismal Swamp,
> Where, all night long, by a fire-fly lamp,
> She paddles her white canoe. . . .
> . . . .
> And I'll hide the maid in a cypress tree,
> When the footstep of death is near.

And just as the narrator in Poe's tale "beheld her magical figure no more," so in Moore's poem "Far, far he followed the meteor spark, / . . . the clouds were dark, / And the boat returned no more" (ibid., 63).

Connoting elegiac termination but in the present context also an auto-biographical limit to referential communication, this "no more" and its supplementary variants (e.g., "nevermore," "forevermore," "Lenore," per-haps, covertly, even "Moore") will identify Poe's literary signature, espe-cially as the poet he primarily wished to become. The tale thus invokes "Moore" not as a source of Poe's poetic anxiety or as a figure associated with American and English political-cultural opposition. Rather, "The Island of the Fay" refers to a poem written by a poet whom Poe recalls having wished to emulate. Poe's tale incorporates a past scene of influence that he now wishes to *repeat* rather than revise, in comparison with the kinds of politi-cal-alias-pictorial pressures that mitigate his relation to writing even this particular plate article.

This desired scene not only includes the topical and temporal locus of Moore's poem—a past, more unexplored America-alias-Virginia—but also an analogous *literary* locus specifically associated with Poe's first moments of literary-vocational possibility: the *Southern Literary Messenger*. One source of "The Island of the Fay" and its "cyclical" rendition of the fay seems to have been Margaret Mercer's "Fairy Tale," which appeared in the January 1836 issue of this journal (Poe 1969–78, 2:598). But "The Island of the Fay" also refers to one of Poe's own earlier tales. The passage where the narrator imagines shadows from the trees becoming "entombed" (ibid., 603) virtually duplicates a passage found in the 1835 tale "Hans Pfaall" (ibid., 598–99), which appeared in the *Southern Literary Messenger* right around the time Poe became its editor.[26]

Is this the reason why in "Morning on the Wissahiccon," Poe quite literally traces Matthias's 1835 "Wissahiccon" article—because it too happens to have appeared in the *Southern Literary Messenger*? Here again, one could argue that Poe in effect conceals his autobiographical investment in his article by subsequently changing its title to "The Elk." No doubt motivated by the foregrounded elk in John Chapman's accompanying engraving, this change *refers* to Chapman: himself originally a Virginian; himself an artist who, in a situation analogous to the Moore allusion in "The Island of the Fay," had done a "celebrated picture" of the Dismal Swamp, which Poe most certainly knew (Pollin 1983, 248, 252, 253). Also, given the "scattered" state of American literature at the time, changing his article's title redundantly served to disguise the allusion of "Morning on the Wissahiccon" to the earlier "Wissahiccon" article; and it does so not so much to preserve his article's appearance of originality in the public domain as to reinforce his private, imaginary recollection of a former noncoercive scene of writing literature.

Doubtless one can always consider Poe's inscribed strategies of return to a past scene of writing as politically motivated "southern" nostalgia vis-à-vis his more recent experience of northern commercialism and moral abolitionism. Yet these allusions to past associations of Lafayette, Moore, Chapman, the locus of Virginia, and not least, Poe's first optimistic moments on the literary stage with the *Southern Literary Messenger* signify a time in which he now imagines his literary career to have begun in a "morning"-like atmosphere, free from sociopolitical constraints—and indeed from his own subsequent capitulations to them. In 1835 the *Messenger* still maintained a certain distance from extreme sectionalist stances (Thompson 1988, 263), and so included articles like Matthias's on northern scenes or customs. It also included articles that could attribute the retardation of an indigenous American literature precisely to the American public's interest in "political pursuits" that can never develop the mind's "beauties and majesty" (H.J.G. 1835a, 220).

This earlier notion that American literature begins where politics ends defines the rhetorical-autobiographical direction of both "The Island of the Fay" and "Morning on the Wissahiccon." Both plate articles refer to Poe's literary beginnings. Both, as it were, sabotage their political readings, so as subliminally to locate themselves at the beginning of an imagined, postpolitical American literature. Poe converts the Revolutionary War or historical-political connotation of "Lafayette" in "The Island of the Fay" into a private figure for his—Poe's—founding or inwardly original relation to such literature. And one could claim that the same conversion occurs in "Morning on the Wissahiccon." Encountering the elk on "a steep rocky cliff" (Poe 1969–78, 3:864), the narrator actually happens on a site "known as 'Mom Rinker's Rock.'" Named "in honor of an American [Revolution-ary] spy who sat on it and dropped her letters over the brink, concealed in a ball of yarn, which found its way to Washington at Valley Forge" (Quinn 1941, 397), this "rock," left unnamed in the tale, represents the publicly forgotten site of an as yet unfinished revolution in American "letters."

Poe, of course, would later die in a charade of American politics. Earlier, as his accession to the pictorial illustrations for his two plate articles sug-gests, he had recognized the difficulty of separating politics from poetics, or of escaping the dominance of the public sphere in the act of reading. For Poe, the private literary moment becomes synonymous with a fantastic project to die from social-political consciousness, the imagined realization of which is "beauty" or literary work per se. But this project is impossible to express in the public sphere except as a fantasy continually discredited by a recurrent, socially vigilant criticism. And so only "when we are exclusively alone" can we at least imagine reading a text like "The Island of the Fay" in the way Poe wrote to read it himself.

NOTES

1. Cf. David A. Long's article "Poe's Political Identity" (1990), which makes a strong case for Poe's perverse distortion of the Whig politics to which he was otherwise at-tracted. My essay will seek to distort his relation to politics even further.

2. Poe's tale differs in certain respects from Sartain's engraving, for example by not distinguishing between the eastern and western sides of the island (Pollin). The picture also represents the fay as "making her way towards the shaded portion of its shore" instead of as circling the island (Miller 1942, 138).

3. Poe 1969–78, 2:600. For the connection of the narrator to Rousseau, see Phillips 1926, 1:87–88.

4. Emphasis in original. Except where noted, quotations throughout reflect Poe's emphasis.

5. Poe clearly revised his poem's final two lines for this tale: "The elfin from the grass?—the dainty *fay,* / The witch, the sprite, the goblin—where are they?" In the work's subsequent reprintings, Poe omitted this epigraph in favor of a putative quota-tion from Servius's commentary on Virgil's *Aeneid,* "No place without its genius" (Poe 1969–78, 2:605). This motto indeed accords with the tale's Romantic "genius loci" topos: a natural scene marked *as* unique by the "magical figure" of a fay.

6. Huth 1957, 32. In an 1835 issue of the *Southern Literary Messenger,* for which Poe soon after served as editor, a writer had argued that "every state [in the Union] ... has more of the interesting, the romantic and picturesque in incident and scenery than in Scotland" (H.J.G. 1835b, 392).

7. The narrator's desire for solitude could also reflect American impulses toward cultural (and commercial) isolationism. Charles Sanford depicts the United States' "na-

tional superiority complex" in the nineteenth century as alternating "between isolationism which would retreat behind . . . protecting oceans to a hermetically sealed paradise in the Mississippi Valley, and a messianic internationalism which would make the world over in the American image" (Sanford 1961, 134).

8. Poe 1969–78, 3:860, 862; Pollin 1983, 164. Wishing "to bury [himself] in the hidden recesses of nature," which for him *includes* the sublime "Niagara," Matthias finds that the "almost unknown" scenery around the stream at once bears "the undoubted impress of the hand of the God of nature," and already "the desolating depredations and officious interference of the onward march of civilization" such as "the unpoetic noise of a laboring mill," or a reserved area for "occasional pic-nic parties of young ladies and gentlemen from the city" (Matthias 1835, 25, 24). As the history of its criticism shows, responses to Poe's "Morning" sketch tend to frame it in general autobiographical or aesthetic contexts. See, for example, Quinn 1941, 397; Pollin 1983, 164.

9. For example: "as a nation, we seem merely to have adopted [certain critical procedures from] the British Quarterly Reviews, upon which our own Quarterlies have been slavishly . . . modelled" (Poe 1984a, 1028).

10. The exception was Poe's strange alliance with the "Young America" critics in 1845–46. For a general depiction of this movement and Poe's unexpected place in it, see Stafford 1952 and Miller 1956. For Poe's possibly "bad faith" motives in joining this group, see Richard 1968. I suggest that by a perverse kind of logic, Poe's tangential compatibility with the Young America movement is not so strange as it first appears. [See also Meredith L. McGill's closely related argument in this volume—Eds.]

11. See, for example, his "Dickens" review in Poe 1984a, 205.

12. "A man of genius," Poe argues, "will rarely, and should never, undertake" conventionally sublime themes having to do with wilderness or ocean (Poe 1984a, 479–80).

13. See Kehler 1975, 178, for a discussion of the picturesque "effect" in "The Domain of Arnheim."

14. In terms of genre, "The Island of the Fay" also exemplifies "the scene of fancy," a special kind of picturesque sketch that conventionally "begins not as an observed landscape but as a dream-like mood projected into an imagined landscape," and for this reason most often invites an "allegorical reading" (Conron 1974, 165).

15. Even if one argues that Poe deploys the picturesque to represent more realistically the increasing "development of the [American] frontier" (Ljungquist 1984, 43), both "concepts of the sublime and the picturesque in landscape . . . were European concepts rooted in European landscapes" (Conron 1974, 166).

16. For example, see Poe's 1836 review of "Peter Snook," in which he explicitly states that "the principle rules of the plastic arts . . . will apply in their fullest force to every species of literary composition" (1984a, 220). Critics have variously argued that Poe "thought the rules of the visual arts could be applied to literature," and that he uses pictorial images to represent "psychological journeys" (Furrow 1973, 16, 27), or to destroy his readers' conventional confidence in rational thought (Baym 1966, 47). Also cf. Jacobs (1969, 184), who argues that after 1831, Poe, along with other Romantic critics, abandoned the view that poetry resembles painting; and Carton (1985, 97), who maintains that the narrators of Poe's landscape tales maniacally "seek not only to make pictures in words but to conflate picture and word."

17. For analogous reasons, Poe argues that rhythm in poetry functions as a trope of artificiality, thus barring "the development of all points of thought or expression which have their basis in *Truth*" (Poe 1984a, 573).

18. Charvat argues that Poe's diverse tales derived from his situation as a magazine writer, and that he "perceived that by its very nature magazine writing encouraged ephemerality and courted oblivion. Only the book offered the possibility of recognition and a passport to posterity," although Poe (perhaps as a necessary rationalization) also envisaged a magazine that would possess "the physical dignity of well-printed books" (1968, 91).

19. Cf. Poe's comment from *Marginalia*, November 1844: "The theorizers on Government, who pretend always to 'begin with the beginning,' commence with Man in what they call his *natural* state—the savage. What right have they to suppose this his natural state. Man's chief idiosyncrasy being reason . . . not until he has stepped upon the highest pinnacle of civilisation—will his *natural* state be ultimately reached, or thoroughly determined" (1984a, 1313).

20. Hovey 1987, 343, 349–50; Stafford 1952, 49; Poe 1984a, 177. See Poe's criticism of Longfellow's abolitionist poems in ibid., 761–64; also Sidney Kaplan's thesis about Poe's biblical-fundamentalist-racist vision in *The Narrative of Arthur Gordon Pym* (Kaplan 1967, esp. 155–63). Kenneth Hovey maintains that Poe probably coauthored a proslavery article in his early career at the *Southern Literary Messenger*, and that his anti-"truth" poetic principle is motivated by his opposition to abolitionist Northern writers such as Longfellow, who "read in the [political-historical] decline of Virginia the proof that slavery was self-destructive" (Hovey 1987, 347). On the other hand, one could argue that Poe's work resists *any* form of "ethnocentrism that identifies discourse with place" (De Prospo 1988, 53).

21. Other possible readings come to mind when using this perspective. For example, instead of representing the American writer tamed by European cultural standards, the elk could represent Poe's or the southern writer's abject subservience to magazine practices defined and controlled by northeastern publishers, editors, and critics. In short, motivated by ideological guilt, Poe, the complicit southern victimizer, here tries to rationalize himself as the southern victim.

22. The Federalist critic Fisher Ames, for example, had argued for the unrestricted "public and . . . universalist" value of American literature. Defined neither as nationalistic events nor alienated public commodities, "all publications," for Ames, "belong to the public sphere . . . all literature is a dimension of civic virtue," and so "the actions of literacy are political actions" (Warner 1990, 149).

23. On the other hand, Poe is possibly seeking here to reclaim literary authority through association with the once politically ascendant Presidential Federalists of his native state, Virginia (Hovey 1987, 347).

24. To much the same effect, Poe argues for the "insinuated" autobiographical meaning of the protagonist's words and actions in Hawthorne's "Minister's Black Veil" (Poe 1984a, 575).

25. See note 5 above.

26. Poe excised this passage from "Hans Pfaall" after 1840.

The Poetics of Extinction

GILLIAN BROWN

Compensation for the brevity of human existence has since ancient times been found in the idea of the longevity of art. But in the nineteenth century, the solace provided by the sense that humans survive through their artifacts was disturbed by new understandings of time and the place of human life within time. The rise of the life sciences—the term *biology* was coined by Lamarck in 1802—both elongated the span of natural history and emphasized the profusion and variation of life forms.[1] Within the new schema, human existence appeared to be merely a temporary phenomenon in an infinite and vast natural order.

As the scope of natural history widened, not just humanity, but the very operations by which human and other life forms appear and disappear, suffered a diminution. In Charles Lyell's *Principles of Geology* (1830–33), change appears to be a process so continuous over so long a span of time that it is indecipherable.

We often behold, at one glance, the effects of causes which have acted at times incalculably remote, and yet there may be no striking circumstances to make the occurrence of a great chasm in the chronological series of Nature's archives. In the vast interval of time which may really have elapsed between the results of operations thus compared, the physical condition of the earth may, by slow and insensible modifications, have become entirely altered; one or more races of organic beings may have passed away, and yet have left behind, in the particular region under contemplation, no trace of their existence. (Lyell 1970, 1:81)[2]

Against the backdrop of the earth's story, the human story that composes history diminishes. Beings vanish without a trace of themselves or the causes of their vanishing. Neither artifacts nor the forces of their obliteration leave a mark. Whatever observable effects may remain in nature are so remote from their causes that they cannot even be understood as effects. In this geological narrative, nothing escapes extinction. Even the durability of art is only relative to the extreme shortness of life.

It is in this light that I want to consider Poe's "Fall of the House of Usher," an appropriately short story of the extinction of a family and its environment. To compensate for the minuteness of human history, Poe's persistent, obsessive contemplation of death in his poems, tales, essays, and sketches (as well as in his cosmology) aims to create and, above all, maintain what Lyell called the "striking circumstances" and "effects" of existence. His productions of terror, itself a reverberating state, revivify not only bodies and events but the very principle of *ars longa*.

Although "The Fall of the House of Usher" describes the end of a line, the degeneration and extinction of the Ushers, it does so through a style of proliferation: the story repeats the event it describes through the anticipation Poe creates of that event. In this story, the anticipation of some inevitable horror, imaged in both the narrator's initial "sense of insufferable gloom" and Roderick Usher's "peculiar gloom," propels events to the point where they resemble the presentiments of them. Madeline returns from her tomb to corroborate her brother's fear of (and desire for) this very event (Poe 1984b, 317, 323).

Roderick had prefigured Madeline's entombment in a painting that "presented the interior of an immensely long and rectangular vault or tunnel, with low walls, smooth, white, and without interruption or device" (ibid., 325). Before her return, the narrator discovers Roderick "in an attitude of the profoundest attention, as if listening to some imaginary sound" (ibid., 330). This prophetic attentiveness to an impending event proves contagious. "Terrified" and "infected" by Roderick's "fantastic yet impressive superstitions," the narrator also hearkens "to certain low and indefinite sounds" (ibid.). These build to a "harsh, protracted, and most unusual screaming or grating sound," coincident with the sounds described in the romance of the "Mad Trist" that the narrator now reads aloud to calm Roderick and himself. The "mighty great and terrible ringing sound" attributed to a falling shield at the climax of "Mad Trist" is echoed in a clangor identified by Roderick as the "rending of [Madeline's] coffin, and the grating of the iron hinges of her prison, and her struggles within the coppered archway of the vault" (ibid., 335). Madeline's return confirms as it reverberates with what her brother has heard for "many minutes, many hours, many days" since he and the narrator "put her living in the tomb!" (ibid., 334).

Such reverberations, repetitions, and resemblances abound in "The Fall of the House of Usher." The tale is so crowded with prefigurements or representational equivalents of the same event that the House of Usher appears to sink under their weight. Like Madeline's return, the final sinking of the house into the tarn resounds with forebodings earlier in the tale—for example, the narrator's "sorrowful impression" of the house's reflection in its adjoining "lurid tarn" (ibid., 318). All the analogues and omens for Madeline's death, and thus for Usher's as well, intensify the inexorability of extinction. Poe writes in "The Fall of the House of Usher" a kind of natural history of artifacts in which human creations—the aesthetic productions of music, painting, architecture, decoration, and poetry—both describe and share the fate of their creators. Like the Ushers, they seem headed for extinction. But if the lack of "collateral issue" (ibid., 319) in the Usher family has reduced it to one thin vanishing line, the collateral connections made through its aesthetic forms of issue and representation provide the possibility of a line of descent. While the Ushers wane and expire, all the sounds and images of extinction that the tale generates compose a monument to consciousness, a legacy of impressions. "The Fall of the House of Usher," this terminus in all its multiple forms, is thus the extension and indeed the perpetuity of mental states. Poe finds in the terror of demise the perpetuation of consciousness. There is no ultimate extinction in Poe's tale, for the aesthetics of terror preserve and transmit signs of intelligence.

Poe accordingly precedes the end of the House of Usher with a state of hyperacuity, inserting awareness if not agency into the portrait of an inevitable process. Roderick Usher's "morbid acuteness of the senses" (ibid., 322) operates to intensify not simply the consciousness of impending doom but the fact of consciousness registering sights and sounds. So long as there are images and their allusions, sounds and their reverberations (so strikingly and often monotonously present in Poe's poetry), there is human consciousness, and thus some mental registration of what passes when time passes. We see and hear in "The Fall of the House of Usher" the evidence of the Ushers' existence and extinction.

For Poe, mind survives over the matter of bodies and histories, and the horror tale, saturated with the effects of consciousness, charts that survival. Even in his cosmology *Eureka,* where he declares his belief in an inevitable apocalypse because of the earth's collision with a comet, Poe asserts his sense of the eternity of mind. There he posits that the universe is simply God's, or a Divine Being's, "present expansive existence" (ibid., 1358). All creatures, which are all "more or less conscious Intelligences," are really "infinite individualizations" of this being. Though the earth will at some point "instantaneously disappear," and matter will then be "Matter no more," "God will remain all in all." In the immortality of Divinity, whose operations Poe claims as "our own," we can hope that the processes of what we know as life and its dissolution will be "renewed forever, and forever, and forever." Consciousness will continue, though manifest in "a new and perhaps totally different series of conditions" (ibid., 1354–56). In the astronomical rather than geological vision of extinction that preoccupies Poe in *Eureka*, consciousness is imagined as so transcending the forces of oblivion that all existence is its effect and verification. Humanity remains at the center of the cosmos, whatever happens. Poe's cosmology presents a cosmos that mirrors humanity: an unlimited human legibility.

It is this indelible legibility that Poe assumes and tries to perpetuate as he plots and detects consciousness in his horror and mystery tales. From the perspective of what I take to be the anthropological imperative of Poe's exercises in terror, the premonitory dread of Roderick and the narrator is not simply a tactic of terror or an inversion of guilt (guilt for something Roderick may know he will do or has done), but a way of prefabricating an eventuality so as to amplify its traces. Matching anticipation with event, Poe multiplies the effects of the fate he depicts. He thus fills the short time left the Ushers before their annihilation with the effects of that event before it even happens. This precipitation of experience punctuates the finality of the Ushers' fate with the awareness of it.

The same structure of obsessive acceleration and prefabrication of a given fate can be traced in reverse in Poe's tales of detection, where the processes through which certain circumstances have come about are revealed and recapitulated. There Dupin solves mysteries by projecting himself into the movements or mental operations of the criminals: for example, retracing the exit and entry of the perpetrator in "The Murders in the Rue Morgue," or imitating the practice of the minister when he purloins the letter and substitutes his own in "The Purloined Letter." Imaginatively matching the manner of crimes, Dupin dispenses with police and press searches for evidence, concentrating instead on constructing a narrative from the available effects of the crime. In the case of "The Purloined Letter," both the crime and its trace are in plain sight: the minister openly steals, keeps, and hides the letter. The visibility of his actions confounds the police because in looking for hiding places for the letter they fail to see the narrative of the available trace.[3] Keyed to the stories registered in traces, Dupin requires no other evidence to grasp the occurrences that they signify. As both story and object, "The Purloined Letter" perfectly instances Poe's ideal of human legibility: the readability of events in effects.

In the case of "The Murders in the Rue Morgue," the effects of the crime signify animal rather than human actions. Only a creature like the orangutan (or, as Poe spells it, the Ourang-Outang) could easily enter and exit the locked room of Madame L'Espanaye and her daughter through its high window; only the strength of a large, agile animal could account for the violent disposal of the corpses of the two women—one thrust up the chimney and the other thrown out the window. Once Dupin realizes that the murders are the work of an animal with "prodigious strength and activity . . . wild ferocity, and . . . imitative propensities," he has only to identify the perpetrator by consulting Cuvier's zoological descriptions and placing a newspaper ad asking about a missing orangutan (Poe 1984b, 424).

But it is in the guise of human actions that the animal behavior leaves discernible traces. In keeping with Poe's anthropological project of discovering and preserving human consciousness, the murders in the Rue Morgue produce an anthropomorphic narrative. The tale presents a thoroughly legible world in which every event and its effects fit into a human grid. Dupin succeeds in detecting the criminal because he places the evidence of the crime in a human context, attending to the effects on witnesses of what they assume to be human behavior. What alerts Dupin to the inhuman nature of the criminal—besides the evidence of great violence, strength, and agility—is each witness identifying the sounds heard from the murderer as some form of unfamiliar foreign speech. The only consistency in the witnesses' accounts of what they heard is in each instance an ignorance of the language attributed to the killer. Dupin then knows that each witness heard an alien voice, and moreover, that the voice was unilaterally alien. Dupin reads in the readiness of the witnesses to name the alien sounds a rather xenophobic exercise of an anthropomorphic reflex operating in the presence of something nonhuman. Thus the attempt to identify human agency and human speech leads to the discovery of animal actions.

As in "The Purloined Letter," the effects of events reveal the whole story. Even a narrative of nonhuman acts can be traced through their effects because anthropomorphism translates all events into anthropological narratives. Poe makes "The Murders in the Rue Morgue" an ironic parable of manifest humanity. Not only is the criminal revealed through anthropomorphic thinking, but the criminal acts are recapitulated as horrific imitations of human acts. The orangutan, as Dupin reconstructs the crime, took the weapon, a razor, from its owner, and in an awful aping of shaving, slit the throat of Madame L'Espanaye. The murders thus reenact a familiar human practice, reflecting a man's hand. A human act properly occupies the center of this anthropomorphic narrative. Knowing this, Dupin knows not just to find the animal, but to find the man.

If Dupin displays the perfect form of anthropological intelligence, his expertise lies not in any remarkable powers of observation (such as those that Sherlock Holmes routinely displays) but in an acute sense of the ample evidence that actions routinely supply. The Parisian world of the tales of ratiocination is abundantly present—that is, teeming with human effects. Such a world must be constructed in the remote setting of the House of Usher. Poe often dramatizes the precariousness of human consciousness in his horror stories by unmooring persons from locales, stranding them in coffins (as in "The Premature Burial") or in their own mental landscapes (as in "The Tell-Tale Heart"). To project the durability of consciousness in "The Fall of the House of Usher," Poe fashions an environment that tallies with its inhabitants: "the perfect keeping of the character of the premises with the accredited character of the people" (ibid., 319). The "equivocal appellation of 'the House of Usher'" accordingly designates "both the family and the family mansion" (ibid.).

More than sharing an identity with the family, the Usher home, Roderick believes, exerts "a terrible influence which for centuries had moulded the destinies of his family, and which made *him* . . . what he was" (ibid., 328). The Ushers are the "result," the "discoverable" proof of their home's "sentience" (ibid.). Other "evidence of the sentience" of the house is discernible "in the gradual yet certain condensation of an atmosphere of their own about the waters and walls" (ibid., 327–28). Imagined as a physical and moral force, the House of Usher shapes its tenants. Though such a force would seem to exemplify environmental power over humanity, Poe's presentation of this force instead suggests its anthropomorphic character. The house that makes its inhabitants expressions of itself signifies its habitation. As sentience is accorded the house, the consciousness of the family is extended backward in time. Far from muting the Ushers, the sentient House of Usher makes them indelible, if self-extinguishing, traces of themselves.

In his evidentiary campaign for substantiating the Ushers, Poe discovers even in inanimate matter—which he calls, following the nineteenth-century naturalist vocabulary, "the kingdom of inorganization"—sentience and organization, an index of humanity. His anticipatory mode, producing phenomena in advance of their natural eventuality, thus works in an anthropomorphic fashion to identify temporal operations with aesthetic techniques.

In this identity, the progressions of time can appear human procedures. Read this way, "The Fall of the House of Usher" (along with "The Philosophy of Composition" and *Eureka*) composes a new statement of *ars longa* in response to nineteenth-century natural science.[4]

Yet if this response rails against the diminution of the human species in the life sciences' taxonomies, it also echoes an anthropomorphism that one can see at work in naturalists' attempts to map the natural order. Lamarck in fact undertook his classifications of life forms (plants and animals) in order to refute late-eighteenth-century theories of extinction. Unconvinced that the array of fossils discovered and studied by eighteenth-century naturalists and philosophers represented organisms no longer present in nature, he accepted and promulgated the transformist doctrine—the idea that species change into new and better-equipped forms rather than disappearing. Lamarck's famous, or infamous, contribution to transformism is his theory of acquired traits. This theory "assumes that by the influence of environment on habit, and thereafter by that of habit on the state of the parts and even on organisation, the structure and organisation of any animal may undergo modifications, possibly very great, and capable of accounting for the actual condition in which all animals are found" (Lamarck 1984, 127).[5] These modifications are then "preserved by reproduction to the new individuals which arise" (Lamarck 1984, 113). Citing the proverb "Habits form a second nature," Lamarck finds in human behavior the best examples for his theory that habit affects physique.

Compare two men of equal ages, one of whom has contracted the habit of eating very little, since his habitual studies and mental work have made digestion difficult, while the other habitually takes much exercise, is often out-of-doors, and eats well; the stomach of the first will have very little capacity left and will be filled up by very small quantity of food, while that of the second will have preserved and even increased its capacity. (Ibid., 119)

Leaving aside Lamarck's problematic accounts of human transmission and physiology, I want to consider the way that human habit persistently informs Lamarck's vision of the natural order. Habit appears to be the engine of change and perpetuation in Lamarckian natural history, and in keeping with his opposition to extinction scenarios, habit imprints and makes manifest the histories of individuals and species. The operations of agency and taste demonstrated in Lamarck's example of eating habits also appear in his descriptions of the long-legged waterside bird "which does not like swimming and yet is in need of going to the water's edge to secure its prey." He continues:

> Now this bird tries to act in such a way that its body should not be immersed in the liquid, and hence makes its best efforts to stretch and lengthen its legs. The long-established habit acquired by this bird and all its race of continually stretching and lengthening its legs, results in individuals of this race becoming raised as though on stilts, and gradually obtaining long, bare legs, denuded of feathers up to the thighs and often higher still. (Ibid., 119–20)[6]

As the bird exercises its preferences and efforts, it shapes itself into the effects of its habits. "We note again that this same bird wants to fish without wetting its body, and is thus obliged to make continual efforts to lengthen its neck. Now these habitual efforts in this individual and its race must have resulted in course of time in a remarkable lengthening as indeed we actually find in the long necks of all water-side birds" (ibid., 120). From dislike (of water) and desire (for food) follows the shape of the race. The actions of individuals form themselves and fashion the natural order we observe. Lamarck's natural history manifests the designs of individuals and races: each entry in the zoological cabinet is an effect of some habitual expression. Every organism bears witness to its successful negotiation with its environment; every body is a text on which we can read a history of effort and achievement.

Nature thus emerges as a graph of intentionality. Lamarck's naturalization of an organism's environmental encounters has figured notoriously in the history of race as a rationalization of the poor economic conditions of particular races. In Lamarck's own view of the history of race, however, the crucial point of linking environment, habit, and form is not to justify the states of races, but to make histories legible in races: to make races manifest their own histories. The acquisition and inheritance of traits imprint a record of individual agency in nature. The great appeal of Lamarckian explanations in matters other than racial differences lies in the reassuringly neat natural order of individual cause and effect that he maintains. You can become what you want and what you practice. More than this, you *are* what you have wanted and practiced. Individual agency matters and persists in Lamarckian nature.

Lamarck's investment in a transparently readable nature helps explain his peculiar reinstatement of the ancient belief in spontaneous generation. He proposes "that preparation for life may be made either by an organic act, or by the direct agency of nature without any such act; so that certain bodies, without possessing life, are yet made ready for its reception by an impression, which does no doubt trace out in these bodies the earliest outlines of organisation" (ibid., 241). The impressibility of certain organisms gives them a "special disposition" for life. "Sexual fertilisation is nothing else than an act for establishing" this disposition. And "nature under certain circumstances imitates what occurs in sexual fertilisation and herself endows with life isolated portions of matter which are in a condition to receive it" (ibid., 241, 244). Here a personified nature is imagined as performing an identical version of the natural process of fertilization. What is most striking in Lamarck's assertions is not his revival of a long-disputed, and, by the early nineteenth century, disreputable theory of origins, but his reformulation of that theory to denote a parallel and similar process to fertilization (which was the accepted narrative of generation in Lamarck's era).[7] His notion of spontaneous generation in no way differs from the structure of fertilization; he simply introduces "the direct agency of nature" into the process, thereby accelerating it. What first appears as the odd redundancy of Lamarck's insistence on spontaneous generation as an explanation for life beginnings—his recapitulation of both the ancient hypothesis and the modern fertilization concept—in fact establishes a personified and more immediate account of generation. In that account nature "imitates" nature and "endows" with life those organisms with a "special disposition." Even in the earliest moments of the animal kingdom, therefore, organisms displayed an agency in their existence. So Lamarck's rewriting of spontaneous generation hypotheses infuses the paradigm of fertilization with intentionality.

Furthermore, Lamarck's supplemental model of fertilization foregrounds the legibility of life forms. Positing impressibility as the precondition for life—as a readiness for its reception—Lamarck suggests that "the earliest outlines of organisation" (that is, of life) can be traced in those bodies that have received organizing impressions. Bodies thus bear the records of their experiences, and even the evidence of the initiation of their existences. From Lamarck's revision of spontaneous generation arises the historical and historicizing body, the same textual object that appears in his imagination of habit and trait acquisition.

Rather than thinking of Lamarck's theories of spontaneous generation and trait acquisition as the preeminent example of an erroneous conception of natural history, one might instead usefully reconsider them as part of the nineteenth-century preoccupation with retaining the concept of life histories. As the definitions of *life* and *history* were being recast by scientific discoveries, naturalists as well as writers focused on the preservation of history.[8] Whatever the rivalries and disputes among naturalists, they could all revere historical evidence. Though well known for his refutations of Lamarckian theories, Lyell shares his enthusiasm for the proofs of the past transmitted by the Egyptians through their embalmed animal bodies. He approvingly quotes the 1802 report on the value of the embalmed objects discovered by the French in Egypt, written by Lamarck, Cuvier (the most visible and successful anti-Lamarckian), and Lacepede, for the Musée National d'Histoire Naturelle in Paris:

> It seems, say they, as if the superstition of the ancient Egyptians had been inspired by nature, with a view of transmitting to after ages a monument of her history. That extraordinary and whimsical people, by embalming with so much care the brutes which were the objects of their stupid adoration, have left us, in their sacred grottoes, cabinets of zoology almost complete. The climate has conspired with the art of embalming to preserve the bodies from corruption, and we can now assure ourselves by our own eyes what was the state of a great number of species three thousand years ago. We can scarcely restrain the transports of our imagination, on beholding thus preserved with their minutest bones, with the smallest portions of their skin, and in every particular most perfectly recognizable, many an animal, which at Thebes or Memphis, two or three thousand years ago, had its own priests and altars. (Lyell 1970, 2:29–30)[9]

Here nature is seen as joining the naturalists in the making of natural history, inspiring the Egyptians to produce a lasting historical record. The Egyptian contribution to the nineteenth-century zoological cabinet is no less than a "monument" to natural history, a testimony to existence and its memorability.

The Egyptian preservationist achievement consists not simply in passing on evidence of themselves but in supplying the nineteenth century with zoological cabinets of the species present nearly three thousand years before. While Lyell, Lamarck, Cuvier, and Lacepede ethnocentrically dismiss the Egyptian worship of animals as "stupid adoration," they revere the evidentiary archive such worship produced. Lamarck's own vision of preserving history exceeds the Egyptian feat by obviating the necessity of preservation. If, as he posits, existent organisms embody the history of their species, naturalists need look no further than present life forms to see what animals existed previously, albeit in different shape.

Lamarck's optimistic vision of the perpetuation of individual agency through transformism runs counter to the nineteenth-century naturalist enterprise that culminated in Darwin's principle of natural selection. Inval-

idating Lamarck's narratives of individual mutation, Darwin's theory rein-
states the phenomenon of extinction that Lyell so elegiacally describes and
Lamarck so imaginatively dispels. Still, despite Lamarck's divergence from
the prevailing current of nineteenth-century science, his work held an enormous appeal throughout the century and long after, particularly for the
social sciences.[10] As natural science sought to discover the origins and spans
of species, Lamarck's attempt to stretch the limits of life forms, and of
agency, projected a reassuring portrait of longevity: a naturalist counter-
statement to naturalism.

In light of Lamarck's radically antiextinction zoological philosophy, Poe's
aim to maintain the principle of *ars longa* through the reverberations of
terror appears to be aligned with principles of preservation and vitality
instead of with necrophilia. More precisely, Lamarckian thought provides
the preservationist context for Poe's necrophilic interests. This is not to say
that Poe was a Lamarckian—he certainly was not—but to underscore the
anthropological and anthropomorphic imperatives shaping literary works
as well as zoological ones. In Poe's counterstatements to the event of extinction, a strikingly misanthropic accent characterizes his anthropological
commitment to retain the legibility of human consciousness. Poe imagines
not just perpetuation, but the perpetuation of specific isolated identities,
such as the Ushers. From this point of view, Lamarckian transformism,
carrying life forward in changed forms, is tantamount to death. Thus reproduction, the mechanism crucial to Lamarck's theory of how the signs of life
histories are transmitted—indeed, the medium through which nature's legibility appears—rarely occurs in Poe's tales. Poe focuses instead on the ex-
tinguishable body and ways of making it indelible.

Like the Egyptians, Poe would preserve bodies so as to prolong their
historical effects. Corpses, particularly female ones, are regularly revived in
Poe's tales: Ligeia, Morella, Berenice, and Eleanora all revisit the scenes of
their lives. Many readers of Poe have noted the prevalence of female deaths in
his work. His dictum that "the death . . . of a beautiful woman is, unquestionably, the most poetical topic in the world" has long suggested both a
personal obsession with lost women—stemming from the early loss of his
mother, a loss then recapitulated in the death of his young wife—and an
aesthetic misogyny working to delimit and destroy women (Poe 1984a, 19).[11]
Yet however much Poe's stories and poems seem to propel and be propelled
by the deaths of women, the morbidity of his treatment of women is
regularly accompanied by the imagination of their regeneration. The horror,
and sometimes solace, for the husbands, brothers, and lovers of these women

is that they cannot be extinguished: they return as indestructible forces to haunt their partners. At the same time, these resurrected women testify to the stories their partners tell; they verify the narratives about themselves. Their regenerate corpses thus embody a principle of preservation, safeguarding the consciousnesses in which they figure as memories and thus poetic subjects.

The misogyny in Poe's representations of women consists less in his death plots than in his revivification of women in service to the history of consciousness. Poe's necrophilic interest in women quite distinctively eschews their given generative power and their role in the perpetuation of the species. He fantasizes a self that is always and only self-transmitting. The only woman in Poe's tales to leave biological issue—Morella—returns to inhabit the body of her daughter (also named Morella), who then dies young, reenacting her mother's history. Continuance through generation is almost as much a threat as extinction to individual consciousness because it images the male individual's successors, the marks of his end. In *Eureka*, Poe mitigates this threat with the concept of the divinity and hence immortality of all individual intelligences. In the tales, he assuages the fear of termination with the notion of succession through regeneration, a regeneration of women's bodies to prolong not themselves but men's minds. The ghoulishness of Poe's portrayal of women lies in this single-minded prohibition of female generativity in order to produce evidence of a particular existence.

The anthropological and androcentric function of such figures as Ligeia, Morella, Berenice, and Eleanora is also to supply a legibility, albeit a problematic one, to death. Their returns, like Madeline's, suggest an uncertainty, both hopeful and horrific, about death. On the one hand, bodies somehow survive death, but on the other hand, bodies seem subject to many forms of death, or to conditions that seem indistinguishable from death.[12] Madeline suffers from catalepsy. The loss of consciousness and rigidification of the muscles caused by this disease make its sufferers likely candidates for premature burial. As Poe explains in "The Premature Burial," even "the most rigorous medical tests fail to establish any material distinction between the state of the sufferer and what we conceive of absolute death" (Poe 1984b, 673). Thus bodies in such states can be misread, and effectively murdered by misreading. Such fatal misreadings anticipate the eventuality of death, making it the result of human (mis)calculations. The horror of premature burial in "The Fall of the House of Usher" and other Poe tales ("Berenice," "The Cask of Amontillado," and "Loss of Breath") lies in the body's helplessness to govern interpretations of itself. Individual intention always exists

amidst other intentionalities, other agents. The consciousness that resurrected bodies signify is not just their own.[13] Corpses in Poe, then, are always
potential evidence of murder.

Murder narratives nicely serve Poe's anthropological purposes because
they highlight the presence of some form of agency. When Madeline emerges
from her premature interment, she reveals her brother's murderous mistake,
literally scaring him to death. In her "now final death-agonies," she bears
"him to the floor a corpse, and a victim to the terrors he had anticipated"
(Poe 1984b, 335). He dies in a "struggle with the grim phantasm, FEAR," just as
he had foreseen (ibid., 322). Since Roderick's anticipation produces both
deaths, the story of the extinction of his family reads as the record of his
sensibility. Anticipation thus operates as an engine of transmission, dis-
seminating the traces of human agency in death.

Not just any human agency: what survives is evidence of Roderick's consciousness, imprinted on his friend the narrator, who has shared his presentiments and aided Roderick in entombing Madeline. Unlike Lamarck's
rather happily indiscriminate conception of the legibility of natural history
in which nature bears the traces of many individualities, Poe's history ad-
heres to a single individual. For Poe ontogeny is never ontogenetic enough.
He must sever it from phylogeny so that the end of a family or race reads as an
individual achievement. The ultimate terror of Poe's tale may be the policy of
elimination implemented to guarantee the vitality of such a single consciousness.

NOTES

1. The term *biology* covers "all those studies that deal with the structure, nature, and
behavior of living beings"—as opposed to physics, which concerns the features and
operations of nonliving matter or of matter that does not emanate from living things
(*Encyclopedia Britannica*, s.v. "biology"). While Lamarck certainly popularized the term
in his *Hydrogeologie* (1802) and may have independently invented it, the term also
appeared simultaneously in Treviranus, *Biologie oder die Philosophie der libenden Natur*.
On the formation of, and prevailing theories and debates in, early-nineteenth-century
natural science, see Corsi 1988 and Burkhardt 1977.

2. This passage is also important to Gillian Beer's work on Victorian narrative and
evolutionary theories (Beer 1986, 70). Beer treats in greater detail the significance of
nineteenth-century natural science's reconfigurations of human history for the novel in
Darwin's Plots (1983). In what follows, I want to examine the narrative of extinction in
Poe's horror tales, particularly in "The Fall of the House of Usher." Unlike Beer's Victorian novelists, Poe does not specifically engage with contemporary naturalists in his
fiction. I am not, therefore, tracing a narrative of influence but exploring another

instance of the nineteenth-century preoccupation with beginnings, ends, durability, and perpetuity.

3. I would thus qualify Barbara Johnson's observation that the story seems to subvert "any possibility of a position of analytical mastery." Poe quite conspicuously endows Dupin with that mastery, and if it eludes the reader in whose path Poe throws one digression after another, we might understand this strategy of distancing as a tactic for concealing the legibility of the purloined letter—not because the letter is illegible (though the minister has attempted to disguise it by making it appear illegible) but because the legibility of human actions that the letter epitomizes is all too apparent. As an anthropological parable, the tale projects both the ease and the difficulty of recognizing traces, of seeing the obvious. See Johnson 1980, 110.

4. Examinations of Poe's relation to science have focused on physics and mathematics, the sciences Poe explicitly addressed in his work; see in particular Limon 1990 and Chai 1987. Rather than exploring Poe's actual encounters with scientific concepts, I am interested here in how his aesthetics and cosmology operate both against and within the nineteenth-century naturalist project to imagine the limits of human intelligence. A useful reading of *Eureka* in this context can be found in Hoffman 1972, 278–99.

5. The main sources for Lamarck's ideas in nineteenth-century America were Lyell's *Principles of Geology* (1830–33) (Lyell 1970) and an English translation of Georges Cuvier's *Elogie* (1836).

6. In keeping with this anthropomorphic characterization of animal behavior, Lamarck also writes of the "inner feeling" in organisms (1984, 332–42).

7. A useful history and discussion of the long and varied controversy concerning spontaneous generation can be found in Farley, *The Spontaneous Generation Controversy from Descartes to Oparin* 1974. Farley's treatment focuses on both the scientific details and the cultural contexts of the disputes. In my reading of Lamarck, I am not concerned with placing his work in the history of science, but with illuminating its participation in what might be called the construction of the history of consciousness. Lamarck's work is noteworthy in literary history for its persistent personifications of nature and for its vivid conceptualizations of nature's legibility. My understanding of the literary and cultural dimensions of nineteenth-century natural science has benefited from the work of Lee Rust Brown in "The Emersonian Museum" (Brown 1989).

8. So much has Lamarck figured as a buffoon in the history of science that the characterization "Lamarckian" immediately serves to discredit any position so described. Informative accounts of the reception of Lamarckian doctrine include Corsi 1988, and the introductory essays to *Zoological Philosophy* (Lamarck 1984): R. W. Burkhardt, "The Zoological Philosophy of J. B. Lamarck," and David L. Hull, "Lamarck among the Anglos."

9. Lyell devoted the first two chapters of this volume to refuting Lamarckian arguments on the transmutation of the species.

10. On the endurance of Lamarckian ideas, see Farley 1974 and Corsi 1988. The literature of neo-Lamarckianism in the social sciences is too vast to inventory here; the rise of the term in the late nineteenth century attests to the scope of Lamarck's appeal and influence.

11. The classic biographical reading of Poe's morbid attitude toward women is Bona-

parte's psychoanalytic study (Bonaparte 1949). More recently, feminist readings have emphasized the eradication of women in Poe's stories. As Jordan writes, "Poe was especially prolific in creating images of violently silenced women." Jordan, however, attributes a feminist function to these crimes against women: they represent a "second story" of female experience that can be detected in the stories. The stories thus represent not Poe's misogyny, but his attempt to expose and overturn misogyny. From this perspective, a tale like "The Fall of the House of Usher" in which a woman is effectively murdered "critiques male-authored interpretive paradigms that fail—forget—to do justice to women." See Jordan 1989, 134, 145. Neither the feminist readings that pathologize or vilify Poe nor those that seek to validate his work for feminism explore his proscription of generation, or fully explain the force of the incidence of regeneration that accompanies the deaths of women in Poe's tales.

12. Mesmerism also fascinates Poe as a production of deathlike states. In "The Facts in the Case of M. Valdemar," mesmerism not only approximates death but accelerates the total degeneration and final dissolution of the body. In "Mesmeric Revelation," mesmerism more benignly affords access to the experience of death as the metamorphosis from a present incarnation to a future, immortal one. See Poe 1984b, 717–27, 833–42.

13. Rosenheim similarly points out that "the central problem of Poe's fiction is the problem of the existence of other minds" (1989, 385).

Works Cited

Poe's Works

Poe, Edgar Allan. 1943. *Edgar Allan Poe's Contributions to Alexander's Weekly Messenger.* Edited by Clarence Brigham. Worcester, Mass.: American Antiquarian Society.

———. 1966. *The Letters of Edgar Allan Poe.* Edited by John Ward Ostrom. 2 vols. 1947. Reprint, New York: Gordian Press.

———. 1969–78. *Collected Works of Edgar Allan Poe.* Edited by Thomas Ollive Mabbott. 3 vols. Cambridge: Harvard University Press, Belknap Press.

———. 1973. *Eureka: A Prose Poem.* Edited by Richard P. Benton. Hartford: Transcendental Books.

———. 1979. *The Complete Works of Edgar Allan Poe.* Edited by James A. Harrison. 12 vols. New York: AMS Press.

———. 1981a. *The Annotated Tales of Edgar Allan Poe.* Edited by Stephen Peithman. New York: Schocken Books.

———. 1981b. *Marginalia.* Charlottesville: University Press of Virginia.

———. 1983. *The Unabridged Edgar Allan Poe.* Edited by Tam Mossman. Philadelphia: Running Press.

———. 1984a. *Edgar Allan Poe: Essays and Reviews.* Edited by G. R. Thompson. New York: Library of America.

———. 1984b. *Edgar Allan Poe: Poetry and Tales.* Edited by Patrick Quinn. New York: Library of America.

———. 1986. *Collected Writings of Edgar Allan Poe.* Vol. 3, parts 1 and 2, *Writings in the Broadway Journal.* Edited by Burton Pollin. New York: Gordian Press.

———. 1991. "*The Living Writers of America:* A Manuscript by Edgar Allan Poe." In *Studies in the American Renaissance,* edited by Burton Pollin, 151–211. Charlottesville: University Press of Virginia.

Secondary Sources

Abraham, Nicholas, and Maria Torok. 1986. *The Wolf Man's Magic Word: A Cryptonomy.* Foreword by Jacques Derrida. Minneapolis: University of Minnesota Press.

Allen, Hervey. 1927. *Israfel: The Life and Times of Edgar Allan Poe.* 2 vols. London: Bretano's.

Allen, Michael. 1969. *Poe and the British Magazine Tradition.* New York: Oxford University Press.

Anderson, Benedict. 1983. *Imagined Communities: Reflections on the Origins and Spread of Nationalism.* London: Verso.

Apollodorus. 1976. *The Library.* Edited by J. G. Frazier. 2 vols. Loeb Classical Library. Cambridge: Harvard University Press.

Auerbach, Jonathan. 1989. *The Romance of Failure: First-Person Fictions of Poe, Hawthorne, and James.* Oxford: Oxford University Press.

Barnes, James J. 1974. *Authors, Publishers, and Politicians.* Columbus: Ohio State University Press.

Barthes, Roland. 1973. *Le plaisir du texte.* Paris: Editions du Seuil.

——. 1981. *Camera Lucida: Reflections on Photography.* Translated by Richard Howard. New York: Farrar, Straus, and Giroux.

——. 1985. "Textual Analysis of a Tale of Poe." In *On Signs,* edited by Marshall Blonsky, 84–97. Oxford: Blackwell.

Baudelaire, Charles. 1972. *Selected Letters of Charles Baudelaire.* Edited and translated by Rosemary Lloyd. Chicago: University of Chicago Press.

Baym, Nina. 1966. "The Function of Poe's Pictorialism." *South Atlantic Quarterly* 65:46–54.

——. 1978. *Woman's Fiction: A Guide to Novels by and about Women in America, 1820–1870.* Ithaca: Cornell University Press.

——. 1984. *Novels, Readers, and Reviewers: Responses to Fiction in Antebellum America.* Ithaca: Cornell University Press.

Beckford, William, Jr. 1788. *Remarks upon the Situation of the Negroes in Jamaica.* Military Library. London: T. and J. Egerton.

Beer, Gillian. 1983. *Darwin's Plots: Evolutionary Narrative in Darwin, George Eliot, and Nineteenth-Century Fiction.* London: Routledge and Kegan Paul.

——. 1986. "Origins and Oblivion in Victorian Narrative." In *Sex, Politics, and Science in the Nineteenth-Century Novel: Selected Papers from the English Institute, 1983–84,* edited by Ruth Bernard Yeazell. Baltimore: Johns Hopkins University Press.

Bell, Michael Davitt. 1980. *The Development of American Romance: The Sacrifice of Relation.* Chicago: University of Chicago Press.

Benjamin, Walter. 1969. *Illuminations.* Edited by Hannah Arendt, translated by Harry Zohn. New York: Schocken Books.

——. 1973. *Charles Baudelaire: A Lyric Poet in the Era of High Capitalism.* Translated by Harry Zohn. London: Verso.

Benton, Richard. 1968. "Poe's 'Lionizing': A Quiz on Willis and Lady Blessington." *Studies in Short Fiction* 5:239–44.

Bloch, Ernst. 1988. *The Utopian Function of Art and Literature.* Cambridge: MIT Press.

Bloom, Harold. 1985. Introduction to *Edgar Allan Poe,* edited by Harold Bloom, 1–14. New York: Chelsea House.

Bonaparte, Marie. 1949. *The Life and Works of Edgar Allan Poe.* Translated by John Rodker. London: Hogarth Press. Originally published as *Edgar Poe: Étude psychanalytique* (Paris: Les Éditions Denoël et Steele, 1933).

Borges, Jorge Luis. 1948. "The Garden of Forking Paths." Translated by Anthony Boucherin. *Ellery Queen's Mystery Magazine* 12, no. 5:101–10.

——. 1978. *The Aleph and Other Studies, 1933–1969.* Translated and edited by Norman Thomas di Giovanni. New York: E. P. Dutton.

Bourdieu, Pierre. 1984. *Distinction: A Social Criticism of the Judgment of Taste.* Translated by Richard Nice. Cambridge: Harvard University Press.

——. 1991. *Language and Symbolic Power.* Translated by Gino Raymond and Matthew Adamson. Cambridge: Harvard University Press.

Bradley, Sculley, ed. 1947. *The Pioneer: A Literary Magazine.* New York: Scholars' Facsimiles.

Brand, Dana. 1985. " 'Reconstructing the Flâneur': Poe's Invention of the Detective Story." *Genre* 18 (Spring): 35–56.

——. 1991. *The Spectator and the City in Nineteenth-Century American Literature.* Cambridge: Cambridge University Press.

Breen, T. H. 1980. *Puritans and Adventurers: Change and Persistence in Early America.* Oxford: Oxford University Press.

Breitwieser, Mitchell Robert. 1990. *American Puritanism and the Defense of Mourning: Religion, Grief, and Ethnology in Mary White Rowlandson's Captivity Narrative.* Madison: University of Wisconsin Press.

Brissenden, R. F. 1974. *Virtue in Distress: Studies in the Novel of Sentiment from Richardson to Sade.* London: Macmillan.

Brodhead, Richard H. 1988. "Sparing the Rod: Discipline and Fiction in Antebellum America." *Representations* 21 (Winter): 67–96.

Brooks, Peter. 1985. *Reading for the Plot: Design and Intention in Narrative.* New York: Random House.

——. 1987. "The Idea of a Psychoanalytic Literary Criticism." In *Discourse in Psychoanalysis and Literature,* edited by Shlomith Rimmon-Kenan, 1–17. New York: Methuen.

Browder, Clifford. 1988. *The Wickedest Woman in New York: Madame Restell, the Abortionist.* Hamden, Conn.: Archon Books.

Brown, Herbert Ross. 1940. *The Sentimental Novel in America, 1789–1860.* Durham, N.C.: Duke University Press.

Brown, Lee Rust. 1989. "The Emersonian Museum." Manuscript.

Brown, William Hill. 1969. *The Power of Sympathy*. Edited by William S. Kable. Columbus: Ohio State University Press.

Buffon, George Louis Leclerc. 1831. *A Natural history of the globe, of man, of beasts, birds, fishes, reptiles, insects, and plants*. Edited by John Wright, translated by W. Kendrick. 3 vols. Boston: Gray and Brown.

Burke, Edmund. 1900. "On the Sublime and the Beautiful." In *Orations and Essays*, 198–350. New York: D. Appleton.

Burkhardt, R. W. 1977. *The Spirit of the System: Lamarck and Evolutionary Biology*. Cambridge: Harvard University Press.

Burnett, James, Lord Monboddo. 1974. *The Origin and Progress of Language*. 6 vols. New York: Olms.

Butler, Judith. 1990. *Gender Trouble: Feminism and the Subversion of Identity*. London: Routledge, Chapman, and Hall.

Byer, Robert H. 1986. "Mysteries of the City: A Reading of Poe's 'The Man of the Crowd.'" In *Ideology and Classic American Literature*, edited by Sacvan Bercovitch and Myra Jehlen, 221–46. Cambridge: Cambridge University Press.

Caldwell, Charles. 1982. *Facts in Mesmerism, and Thoughts on Its Causes and Uses*. 1842. Reprint, New York: Da Capo Press.

Calhoun, Craig, ed. 1992. *Habermas and the Public Sphere*. Cambridge: MIT Press.

Campbell, Killis. 1933. *The Mind of Poe and Other Studies*. Cambridge: Harvard University Press.

Carby, Hazel V. 1987. *Reconstructing Womanhood: The Emergence of the Afro-American Novelist*. Oxford: Oxford University Press.

Carlson, Eric W., ed. 1966. *The Recognition of Edgar Allan Poe*. Ann Arbor: University of Michigan Press.

Carton, Evan. 1985. *The Rhetoric of American Romance: Dialectic and Identity in Emerson, Dickinson, Poe, and Hawthorne*. Baltimore: Johns Hopkins University Press.

Casale, Ottavio M. 1973. "The Battle of Boston: A Revaluation of Poe's Lyceum Appearance." *American Literature* 45:423–28.

Cavell, Stanley. 1986. "In Quest of the Ordinary." In *Romanticism and Contemporary Criticism*, edited by Morris Eaves and Michael Fischer, 214–25. Ithaca: Cornell University Press.

——. 1988. *In Quest of the Ordinary: Lines of Skepticism and Romanticism*. Chicago: University of Chicago Press.

Chai, Leon. 1987. *The Romantic Foundations of the American Renaissance*. Ithaca: Cornell University Press.

Charvat, William. 1936. *The Origins of American Critical Thought: 1810–1835*. Philadelphia: University of Pennsylvania Press.

——. 1968. "Poe: Journalism and the Theory of Poetry." In *The Profession of Author-*

ship in America, 1800–1870: The Papers of Williams Charvat, edited by Matthew J. Bruccoli, 84–99. Columbus: Ohio State University Press.

Chielens, Edward, ed. 1986. *American Literary Magazines: The Eighteenth and Nineteenth Centuries.* New York: Greenwood Press.

Code noir, ou recueils de reglements, edits, declarations et arrêts . . . Concernant le Discipline et le Commerce des Esclaves Negres des Isles Francaises de l'Amerique (1685). 1745. Paris: Chez les libraires associés.

Coleman, William. 1964. *Georges Cuvier, Zoologist: A Study in the History of Evolution Theory.* Cambridge: Harvard University Press.

Conron, John. 1974. *The American Landscape: A Critical Anthology of Prose and Poetry.* New York: Oxford University Press.

Corsi, Pietro. 1988. *The Age of Lamarck: Evolutionary Theories in France, 1790–1830.* Berkeley: University of California Press.

Cox, James. 1968. "Edgar Poe: Style as Pose." *Virginia Quarterly Review* 44 (Winter): 67–89.

Cuvier, Georges. 1832. *The Animal Kingdom.* Translated and abridged by H. M'Murtrie. Philadelphia: n.p.

Dabney, Virginius. 1976. *Richmond: The Story of a City.* New York: Doubleday.

Davidson, Cathy. 1986. *Revolution and the Word: The Rise of the Novel in America.* Oxford: Oxford University Press.

Davis, Andrew Jackson. 1869. *Tales of a Physician; or, The Seeds and Fruits of Crime.* Boston: William White.

Dayan, Joan. 1987. *Fables of Mind: An Inquiry into Poe's Fiction.* Oxford: Oxford University Press.

——. 1991. "Romance and Race." In *The Columbia History of the American Novel,* edited by Emory Elliot, 89–109. New York: Columbia University Press.

——. 1994. *Haiti, History, and the Gods.* Berkeley: University of California Press.

De Prospo, R. C. 1988. "Deconstructive Poe(tics)." *Diacritics* 18, no. 3:43–64.

Derrida, Jacques. 1973. *Speech and Phenomena: On Husserl's Theory of Signs and Other Essays.* Translated by David B. Allison. Evanston: Northwestern University Press.

——. 1975. "The Purveyor of Truth." Translated by Willis Domingo et al. *Yale French Studies* 52:50–101.

——. 1988. "The Purveyor of Truth." Translated by Alan Bass. In *The Purloined Poe: Lacan, Derrida, and Psychoanalytic Reading,* edited by John P. Muller and William J. Richardson, 173–212. Baltimore: Johns Hopkins University Press.

de Saint-Méry, Moreau. 1913. *Voyage aux États-Unis de l'Amérique.* Edited by Stewart L. Mims. New Haven: Yale University Press.

Descartes, René. 1958. *Descartes' Philosophical Writings.* Translated by Norman Kemp Smith. New York: Random House.

Dickens, Charles. 1865. *Sketches by Boz.* London: Chapman and Hall.

Disraeli, Isaac. 1823. *Curiosities of Literature*. London: John Murray.

Dixon, George W. 1841. *Trial of Madame Restell, alias Ann Lohman for abortion and causing the death of Mrs. Purdy: being a full account of all the proceedings on the trial, together with the suppressed evidence and editorial remarks*. New York: n.p.

Dods, John Bovee. 1886. *The Philosophy of Mesmerism and Electrical Psychology, Comprised in Two Courses of Lectures (Eighteen in Number), Complete in One Volume*. Progressive Library. London: James Burns.

Domínguez, Virginia. 1988. *White by Definition: Social Classification in Creole Louisiana*. New Brunswick, N.J.: Rutgers University Press.

Douglas, Ann. 1975. "Heaven Our Home: Consolation Literature in the Northern United States, 1830–1880." In *Death in America*, edited by David E. Stannard. Philadelphia: University of Pennsylvania Press.

———. 1978. *The Feminization of American Culture*. New York: Avon Books.

Doyle, Mildred Davis. 1941. *Sentimentalism in American Periodicals, 1741–1800*. Ph.D. diss., New York University.

Duyckinck, Evert. 1840. "Bryant's American Poets." *Arcturus* 1, no. 1:24–29.

———. 1841. "Nathaniel Hawthorne." *Arcturus* (May): 330–37.

———. 1845. "The Literary Prospects of 1845." *American Review* (February): 146–51.

Duyckinck, Evert, and George Duyckinck. 1875. *Cyclopaedia of American Literature*. 2 vols. Philadelphia: William Rutter.

Eaton, Clement. 1964. *The Freedom of Thought Struggle in the Old South*. 1940. Reprint, New York: Harper and Row.

Ehrlich, Heyward. 1986. "Briggs's Dilemma and Poe's Strategy." In *Collected Writings of Edgar Allan Poe*, vol. 3, part 2, *Writings in the* Broadway Journal, edited by Burton Pollin, xii–xxxi. New York: Gordian Press.

Elbert, Monika M. 1991. " 'The Man of the Crowd' and the Man Outside the Crowd: Poe's Narrator and the Democratic Reader." *Modern Language Studies* 21 (Fall): 16–30.

Eliot, George. 1984. *Silas Marner*. Harmondsworth: Penguin.

Ellis, Jennifer. N.d. "Rereading Poe's Textual Body in 'Ligeia,' and Ligeia's Body as Text: Doubling and the Racial Unconscious." Manuscript.

Emerson, Ralph Waldo. 1904. "Emancipation in the British West Indies." In *The Complete Works of Ralph Waldo Emerson*, 2:97–147. Boston: Houghton Mifflin.

———. 1960. *Selections from Ralph Waldo Emerson*. Edited by Stephen E. Whicher. Boston: Houghton Mifflin.

———. 1982. *Emerson in His Journals*. Edited by Joel Porte. Cambridge: Harvard University Press.

Ermamesta, Erik. 1951. "A Study of the Word 'Sentimental' and of Other Linguistic Characteristics of Eighteenth-Century Sentimentalism in England." *Annales Academiae Scientiarum Fennicae*. Helsinki: Suomalainen Tiedeakatemia.

Fabian, Ann. 1992. "From the Mouths of Murderers." Manuscript. New Haven.

Farley, John. 1974. *The Spontaneous Generation Controversy from Descartes to Oparin.* Baltimore: Johns Hopkins University Press.

Faulkner, William. 1964. *Absalom, Absalom!* New York: Modern Library.

Faust, Drew Gilpin. 1977. *A Sacred Circle: The Dilemma of the Intellectual in the Old South, 1840–1860.* Philadelphia: University of Pennsylvania Press.

Felman, Shoshana. 1988. "On Reading Poetry: Reflections on the Limits and Possibilities of Psychoanalytical Approaches." In *The Purloined Poe: Lacan, Derrida, and Psychoanalytic Reading,* edited by John P. Muller and William J. Richardson, 133–56. Baltimore: Johns Hopkins University Press.

Ferguson, Frances. 1977. *Wordsworth: Language as Counter-Spirit.* New Haven: Yale University Press.

Fiering, Norman S. 1976. "Irresistible Compassion: An Aspect of Eighteenth-Century Sympathy and Humanitarianism." *Journal of the History of Ideas* 37, no. 2 (April–June): 195–218.

Fisher, Philip. 1985. *Hard Facts: Setting and Form in the American Novel.* Oxford: Oxford University Press.

———. 1986. "Appearing and Disappearing in Public: Social Space in Late-Nineteenth-Century Literature and Culture." In *Reconstructing American Literary History,* edited by Sacvan Bercovitch, 155–88. Cambridge: Harvard University Press.

Fletcher, Angus. 1970. *Allegory: The Theory of a Symbolic Mode.* Ithaca: Cornell University Press.

Fliegelman, Jay. 1982. *Prodigals and Pilgrims: The American Revolution against Patriarchal Authority, 1750–1800.* Cambridge: Cambridge University Press.

Foucault, Michel. 1973. *The Order of Things: An Archeology of the Human Sciences.* New York: Vintage.

———. 1984. "What Is an Author?" In *The Foucault Reader,* edited by Paul Rabinow, 101–20. New York: Pantheon.

Fox-Genovese, Elizabeth. 1988. *Within the Plantation Household: Black and White Women of the Old South.* Chapel Hill: University of North Carolina Press.

Franklin, Benjamin. 1987. *The Autobiography.* In *Writings,* edited by J. A. Leo Lemay. New York: Library of America.

Freehling, Alison Goodyear. 1982. *Drift toward Dissolution: The Virginia Slavery Debate of 1831–1832.* Baton Rouge: Louisiana State University Press.

Freud, Sigmund. 1953–. *The Standard Edition of the Complete Psychological Works of Sigmund Freud.* Translated and edited by James Strachey. New York: Macmillan.

———. 1963a. *Dora: An Analysis of a Case of Hysteria.* Edited by Philip Rieff. New York: Macmillan.

———. 1963b. *Freud: Therapy and Technique.* Edited by Philip Rieff. New York: Macmillan.

Fried, Michael. 1980. *Absorption and Theatricality: Painting and Beholder in the Age of Diderot.* Berkeley: University of California Press.

Friedberg, Anne. 1993. *Window Shopping: Cinema and the Postmodern.* Berkeley: University of California Press.

Fruman, Norman. 1971. *Coleridge: The Damaged Archangel.* New York: Braziller.

Fuller, Margaret. 1971. *Women in the Nineteenth Century.* New York: Norton.

Fuller, Robert C. 1982. *Mesmerism and the American Cure of Souls.* Philadelphia: University of Pennsylvania Press, 1982.

Furrow, Sharon. 1973. "Psyche and Setting: Poe's Picturesque Landscapes." *Criticism* 15:16–27.

Fussell, Edwin. 1965. *Frontier: American Literature and the American West.* Princeton: Princeton University Press.

G., H. J. 1835a. "American Literature—Its Impediments." *Southern Literary Messenger* 2 (January): 22–23.

——. 1835b. "Influence of Free Governments on the Mind." *Southern Literary Messenger* 1 (April): 398–93.

Gilman, Amy. 1993. "Edgar Allan Poe Detecting the City." In *The Mismaking Frame of Mind: Social Imagination and American Culture,* edited by James Gilbert, Amy Gilman, Donald M. Scott, and Joan W. Scott. Belmont, Calif.: Wadsworth.

Goodman, Lord. 1982. "Plagiarism: A Symposium." *Times Literary Supplement,* 9 April, 413.

Gray, Francine du Plessix. 1992. "Splendor and Miseries." *New York Review of Books,* 16 July, 31–35.

Gray, Richard. 1986. *Writing the South: Ideals of an American Region.* Cambridge: Cambridge University Press.

——. 1987. " 'I Am a Virginian': Edgar Allan Poe and the South." In *Edgar Allan Poe: The Design of Order,* edited by A. Robert Lee, 182–201. London: Vision Press.

Greenberg, Kenneth S. 1990. "The Nose, the Lie, and the Duel in the Antebellum South." *American Historical Review* 95 (February): 57–74.

Grubb, Gerald G. 1950. "The Personal and Literary Relationship of Dickens and Poe." *Nineteenth-Century Fiction* 5, no. 3:209–21.

Habermas, Jürgen. 1989. *The Structural Transformation of the Public Sphere: An Inquiry into a Category of Bourgeois Society.* Cambridge: MIT Press.

Haltunen, Karen. 1982. *Confidence Men and Painted Women: A Study of Middle-Class Culture in America, 1830–1870.* New Haven: Yale University Press.

Harrowitz, Nancy. 1983. "The Body of the Detective Model: Charles S. Peirce and Edgar Allan Poe." In *The Sign of Three,* edited by Umberto Eco and Thomas A. Sebeok, 179–97. Bloomington: Indiana University Press.

Hartman, Geoffrey. 1964. *Wordsworth's Poetry.* New Haven: Yale University Press.

——. 1975. "Literature High and Low: The Case of the Mystery Story." In *The Fate of Reading and Other Essays,* 203–22. Chicago: University of Chicago Press.

Hartwell, David G., ed. 1987. Introduction to *The Dark Descent,* 1–11. New York: Tor Books.

Hegel, G. W. F. 1970. *Phenomenology of Mind.* Translated by J. B. Baillie. New York: Macmillan.

——. 1971. *Hegel's Philosophy of Mind, Being Part Three of the Encyclopaedia.* Translated by William Wallace and A. V. Miller. Oxford: Clarendon Press.

Heidegger, Martin. 1962. *Being and Time.* Translated by John Macquarrie and Edward Robinson. New York: Harper and Row.

Hertz, Neil. 1982. "Two Extravagant Teachings." *Yale French Studies* 63:59–71.

Hipple, Walter. 1957. *The Beautiful, the Sublime, and the Picturesque in Eighteenth-Century British Aesthetic Theory.* Carbondale: Southern Illinois University Press.

Hoffman, Daniel. 1972. *Poe Poe Poe Poe Poe Poe Poe.* Garden City, N.Y.: Doubleday.

Holmes, George Frederick. 1852. "Uncle Tom's Cabin." *Southern Literary Messenger* 18 (December): 721–31.

Homans, Margaret. 1986. *Bearing the Word: Language and Female Experience in Nineteenth-Century Women's Writing.* Chicago: Chicago University Press.

Hovey, Kenneth Alan. 1987. "Critical Provincialism: Poe's Poetic Principle in Antebellum Context." *American Quarterly* 39, no. 3 (Fall): 341–54.

Howells, William Dean. 1902. "The Psychology of Plagiarism." In *Literature and Life.* New York: Harper and Brothers.

Hull, William Doyle. 1941. *A Canon of the Critical Reviews of Edgar Allan Poe in The Southern Literary Messenger and Burton's Gentleman's Magazine, with an Examination of His Relationships with the Proprietors.* Ph.D. diss., University of Virginia.

Huth, Hans. 1957. *Nature and the American: Three Centuries of Changing Attitudes.* Berkeley: University of California Press.

Irwin, John. 1980. *American Hieroglyphics: The Symbol of the Egyptian Hieroglyphics in the American Renaissance.* New Haven: Yale University Press.

——. 1991. "Journey to the South." *Virginia Quarterly Review* 67, no. 3 (Summer).

——. 1992. "Reading Poe's Mind: Politics, Mathematics, and the Association of Ideas in 'The Murders in the Rue Morgue.'" *American Literary History* 4 (Summer): 187–206.

Isaac, Rhys. 1982. *The Transformation of Virginia, 1740–1790.* Chapel Hill: University of North Carolina Press.

Jacobs, Robert. 1969. *Poe: Journalist and Critic.* Baton Rouge: Louisiana University Press.

Jacobus, Mary. 1990. "In Parenthesis: Immaculate Conceptions and Feminine Desire." In *Body/Politics: Women and the Discourses of Science,* edited by Mary Jacobus, Evelyn Fox-Keller, and Sally Shuttleworth, 11–28. New York: Routledge.

James, C. L. R. 1980. *The Black Jacobins: Toussaint L'ouverture and the San Domingo Revolution.* London: Allison and Busby.

Jefferson, Thomas. 1975. *Notes on the State of Virginia.* In *The Portable Thomas Jefferson,* edited by Merrill D. Peterson. New York: Viking.

Johnson, Barbara. 1980. "The Frame of Reference: Poe, Lacan, Derrida." In *The Critical Difference: Essays in the Contemporary Rhetoric of Reading*, 110–46. Baltimore: Johns Hopkins University Press.

Jordan, Cynthia S. 1989. *Second Stories: The Politics of Language, Form, and Gender in Early American Fictions*. Chapel Hill: University of North Carolina Press.

Jordan, Winthrop. 1968. *White over Black: American Attitudes toward the Negro, 1550–1812*. New York: Norton.

Kant, Immanuel. 1951. *The Critique of Judgment*. Translated by J. H. Bernard. New York: Hafner Press.

Kaplan, Sidney. 1967. "An Introduction to *Pym*." In *Poe: A Collection of Critical Essays*, edited by Robert Regan, 145–63. Englewood Cliffs, N.J.: Prentice-Hall.

Kasson, John F. 1990. *Rudeness and Civility: Manners in Nineteenth-Century Urban America*. New York: Hill and Wang.

Kehler, Joel. 1975. "New Light on the Genesis and Progress of Poe's Landscape Fiction." *American Literature* 47:173–83.

Kerber, Linda K. 1981. *Women in the Republic*. New York: Norton.

Knapp, Steven. 1985. *Personification and the Sublime*. Cambridge: Harvard University Press.

Krappe, Edith Smith. 1940. "A Possible Source for Poe's 'Tell-Tale Heart' and 'The Black Cat.'" *American Literature* 12, no. 1:84–88.

Kristeva, Julia. 1987. *Tales of Love*. New York: Columbia University Press.

Kulikoff, Allan. 1986. *Tobacco and Slaves: The Development of Southern Cultures in the Chesapeake, 1680–1800*. Chapel Hill: University of North Carolina Press.

Lacan, Jacques. 1977. *Écrits: A Selection*. Translated by Alan Sheridan. New York: Norton.

——. 1988a. *The Seminar of Jacques Lacan, Book II: The Ego in Freud's Theory and in the Technique of Psychoanalysis, 1954–55*. Edited by Jacques-Alain Miller, translated by Sylvana Tomaselli. New York: Norton.

——. 1988b. "Seminar on 'The Purloined Letter.'" Translated by Jeffrey Mehlman. In *The Purloined Poe: Lacan, Derrida, and Psychoanalytic Reading*, edited by John P. Muller and William J. Richardson, 28–54. Baltimore: Johns Hopkins University Press.

Lamarck, J. B. 1984. *Zoological Philosophy: An Exposition with Regard to the Natural History of Animals*. Translated by Hugh Elliot. Chicago: University of Chicago Press.

Laplanche, J., and J.-P. Pontalis. 1974. *The Language of Psycho-Analysis*. Translated by Donald Nicholson-Smith. New York: Norton.

Levin, Harry. 1958. *The Power of Blackness: Hawthorne, Poe, Melville*. New York: Vintage.

Levine, Stuart. 1990. Introduction to *The Short Fiction of Edgar Allan Poe: An Annotated Edition*, edited by Stuart Levine and Susan Levine. Urbana: University of Illinois Press.

Limon, John. 1990. *The Place of Fiction in the Time of Science: A Disciplinary History of American Writing.* Cambridge: Cambridge University Press.

Ljungquist, Kent. 1983. "Poe's 'The Island of the Fay': The Passing of Fairyland." In *The Naiad Voice: Essays on Poe's Satiric Hoaxing,* edited by Dennis Eddings, 148–54. Port Washington, N.Y.: Associated Faculty.

———. 1984. *The Grand and the Fair: Poe's Landscape Aesthetics and Pictorial Techniques.* Potomac, Md.: Scripta Humanistica.

Ljungquist, Kent, and Buford Jones. 1988. "The Identity of 'Outis': A Further Chapter in the Poe-Longfellow War." *American Literature* 60, no. 3:402–15.

Lloyd, David. 1989. "Kant's Examples." *Representations* 28 (Fall): 34–54.

Lockridge, Kenneth A. 1987. *The Diary, and Life, of William Byrd II of Virginia, 1674–1744.* Chapel Hill: University of North Carolina Press.

Long, David A. 1990. "Poe's Political Identity: A Mummy Unswathed." *Poe Studies* 23 (June): 1–22.

Long, Edward. 1774. *The History of Jamaica, or General Survey of the Antient and Modern State of that Island.* 3 vols. London: T. Lownades.

Longfellow, Henry Wadsworth. 1886. *Poems on Slavery.* In *The Poetical Works of Henry Wadsworth Longfellow,* vol. 1. Boston: Houghton Mifflin.

Lowell, James Russell. 1843. "Introduction." *Pioneer* (January): 1–3.

———. 1898. *Lowell's Complete Poems.* New York: Houghton, Mifflin.

———. 1913. "Nationality in Literature." In *The Round Table,* 9–39. Boston: Goreham Press.

———. 1943. "Our Contributors.—No. XVII: Edgar Allan Poe." In *The Shock of Recognition,* edited by Edmund Wilson, 5–20. New York: Doubleday, Doran.

Lyell, Sir Charles. 1970. *Principles of Geology; or, The Modern Changes of the Earth and Its Inhabitants.* Vol. 1, 1830. Vol. 2, 1832. Reprint, Lehre, Germany: J. Cramer.

Mabbott, Thomas Ollive. 1942. Introduction to *The Raven and Other Poems,* by Edgar Allan Poe. New York: Columbia University Press.

Mallon, Thomas. 1989. *Stolen Words: Forays into the Origins and Ravages of Plagiarism.* New York: Ticknor and Fields.

Malson, Lucie. 1972. *Enfants sauvages.* Translated by Edmund Fawcett, Peter Ayrton, and Joan White. New York: Monthly Review Press.

Mathews, Cornelius. 1842. "Appeal to American Authors and the American Press in Behalf of International Copyright." *Graham's Magazine* (September): 121–24.

Matthews, W. H. 1970. *Mazes and Labyrinths: Their History and Development.* New York: Dover.

Matthias, Benjamin. 1835. "The Wissahiccon." *Southern Literary Messenger* 2 (December): 24–27.

Matthiessen, F. O. 1941. *American Renaissance: Art and Expression in the Age of Emerson and Whitman.* London: Oxford University Press.

May, Henry F. 1976. *The Enlightenment in America.* Oxford: Oxford University Press.

McKeon, Michael. 1987. *The Origins of the English Novel, 1600–1740.* Baltimore: Johns Hopkins University Press.

McKitrick, Eric L., ed. 1963. *Slavery Defended: The Views of the Old South.* Englewood Cliffs, N.J.: Prentice-Hall.

Meier, Pauline. 1989. "Good Show: George Washington Plays George Washington." *Reviews in American History* 17 (June): 187–98.

Melville, Herman. 1929. *Pierre; or, The Ambiguities.* New York: E. P. Dutton.

Miller, Christopher. 1985. *Blank Darkness.* Chicago: University of Chicago Press.

Miller, F. DeWolfe. 1942. "The Basis for Poe's 'The Island of the Fay.'" *American Literature* 14 (May): 135–40.

Miller, Perry. 1956. *The Raven and the Whale: The War of Words and Wits in the Era of Poe and Melville.* New York: Harcourt, Brace, and World.

Mohr, James C. 1978. *Abortion in America: The Origin and Evolution of National Policy, 1800–1900.* Oxford: Oxford University Press.

Moretti, Franco. 1987. *The Way of the World: The Bildungsroman in European Culture.* London: Verso.

Morgan, Edmund. 1975. *American Slavery, American Freedom: The Ordeal of Colonial Virginia.* New York: Norton.

Morgan, Lady. 1821. *Italy.* New York: S. Van Winkle.

Morrison, Toni. 1989. "Unspeakable Things Unspoken: The Afro-American Presence in American Literature." *Michigan Quarterly Review* 28, no. 1 (Winter): 1–34.

Moss, Sidney P. 1963. *Poe's Literary Battles: The Critic in the Context of His Literary Milieu.* Durham, N.C.: Duke University Press.

Mott, Frank Luther. 1957. *A History of American Magazines, 1741–1850.* Cambridge: Harvard University Press, Belknap Press.

"Necessity for a National Literature." 1845. *Knickerbocker* (May): 415–23.

Nelson, Dana D. *The Word in Black and White.* New York: Oxford University Press, 1992.

Olasky, Marvin. 1986. "Advertising Abortion during the 1830s and 1840s: Madame Restell Builds a Business." *Journalism History* 13, no. 2 (Spring): 49–55.

Olmsted, Frederick Law. 1984. *The Cotton Kingdom: A Traveller's Observations on Cotton and Slavery in the American Slave States.* 1861. Reprint, edited by Arthur M. Schlesinger, Sr., New York: Modern Library.

O'Sullivan, John. 1837. "Introduction." *Democratic Review* (October): 1–15.

———. 1843. "The International Copyright Question." *Democratic Review* (February): 113–22.

Papke, David Ray. 1987. *Framing the Criminal: Crime, Cultural Work, and the Loss of Critical Perspective, 1830–1900.* Hamden, Conn.: Archon Books.

Parrington, Vernon. 1927. "Edgar Allan Poe: Romantic." In *Main Currents in American Thought: An Interpretation of American Literature from the Beginning to 1920,* 2:57–59. New York: Harcourt, Brace, and World.

Patterson, Orlando. 1982. *Slavery and Social Death: A Comparative Study.* Cambridge: Harvard University Press.

Paulding, James Kirke. 1836. *Slavery in the United States.* New York: Harper and Brothers.

Pease, Donald E. 1987. *Visionary Compacts: American Renaissance Writings in Cultural Context.* Madison: University of Wisconsin Press.

Person, Leland S., Jr. 1988. *Aesthetic Headaches: Women and a Masculine Poetics in Poe, Melville, and Hawthorne.* Athens: University of Georgia Press.

Philips, Edith. 1927. "The French of Edgar Allan Poe." *American Speech* 2 (March): 270–74.

Phillips, Elizabeth. 1979. *Edgar Allan Poe: An American Imagination.* Port Washington, N.Y.: Kennikat Press.

Phillips, Mary E. 1926. *Edgar Allan Poe: The Man.* 2 vols. Chicago: John C. Winston.

Poenicke, Klaus. 1967. "A View from the Piazza: Herman Melville and the Legacy of the European Sublime." *Contemporary Literature Studies* 4, no. 3:267–81.

Pollin, Burton R. 1983. "Edgar Allan Poe and John G. Chapman: Their Treatment of the Dismal Swamp and the Wissahickon." In *Studies in the American Renaissance,* edited by Joel Myerson, 245–74. Charlottesville: University Press of Virginia.

——. N.d. Letter. *Poe Studies Newsletter* 17, no. 2:6.

——. N.d. "Poe as Author of the 'Outis' Letter and 'The Bird of the Dream.'" *Poe Studies* 20, no. 1:10–15.

Porter, Katherine Anne. 1964. "Old Mortality." In *Pale Horse, Pale Rider,* 3–92. New York: Harcourt, Brace, and World.

Price, Burton R. 1972. "Poe's Illustration for 'The Island of the Fay': A Hoax Detected." In *Mystery and Detection Annual,* edited by Donald Adams, 33–45. Beverly Hills: Donald Adams.

Price, Martin. 1965. "The Picturesque Moment." In *From Sensibility to Romanticism,* edited by Frederick W. Hilles and Harold Bloom. New York: Oxford University Press.

Price, Uvedale. 1810. *Essays on the Picturesque.* 3 vols. London: J. G. Barnard.

Pückler-Muskau, Furst von. 1833. *Tour in England, Ireland, and France.* Translated by Sarah Austin. Philadelphia: Carey, Lea, and Blanchard.

Quinn, Arthur Hobson. 1941. *Edgar Allan Poe: A Critical Biography.* New York: D. Appleton–Century.

Quinn, Patrick. 1957. *The French Face of Edgar Poe.* Carbondale: Southern Illinois University Press.

Rainwater, Catherine. 1984. "Poe's Landscape Tales and the 'Picturesque' Tradition." *Southern Literary Journal* 16, no. 2:30–43.

"Recent American Novels." 1835. *Southern Literary Messenger* 1 (May): 478–79.

Regan, Robert. 1970. "Hawthorne's 'Plagiary'; Poe's Duplicity." *American Literature* 25, no. 3 (December): 281–98.

Renza, Louis A. 1985. "Poe's Secret Autobiography." In *The American Renaissance Reconsidered*, edited by Walter Michaels and Donald E. Pease, 58–89. Baltimore: Johns Hopkins University Press.

Review of *The Hand Phrenologically Considered*. 1851. *Littel's Living Age* 28 (March): 283–84.

Reynolds, David. 1988. *Beneath the American Renaissance: The Subversive Imagination in the Age of Emerson and Melville*. New York: Knopf.

Richard, Claude. 1968. "Poe and 'Young America.'" In *Papers of the Bibliographical Society of the University of Virginia*, edited by Fredson Bowers, 21:25–58. Charlottesville: University Press of Virginia.

Richardson, Samuel. 1985. *Clarissa; or, The History of a Young Lady*. Edited by Angus Ross. Harmondsworth: Penguin Books.

Riddel, Joseph. 1979. "The 'Crypt' of Edgar Allan Poe." *Boundary* 2 (Spring): 117–41.

Ridgely, J. V. 1992. "Review." *Poe Studies Association Newsletter* 20, no. 2 (Fall): 1–6.

Rose, Mark. 1988. "The Author as Proprietor: *Donaldson v. Becket* and the Genealogy of Modern Authorship." *Representations* 23:51–85.

Rosenheim, Shawn. 1989. "The King of 'Secret Readers': Edgar Allan Poe, Cryptography, and the Origins of the Detective Story." *ELH* 56:376–400.

Rosenthal, Bernard. N.d. "Poe, Slavery, and the *Southern Literary Messenger*: A Reexamination." *Poe Studies* 7, no. 2:29–38.

Rowson, Susanna Haswell. 1986. *Charlotte Temple*. Edited by Cathy Davidson. New York: Oxford University Press.

Rubin, Louis D., Jr. 1989. *The Edge of the Swamp: A Study in the Literature and Society of the Old South*. Baton Rouge: Louisiana State University Press.

Sanford, Charles. 1961. *Quest for Paradise*. Urbana: University of Illinois Press.

Schiller, Dan. 1981. *Objectivity and the News: The Public and the Rise of Commercial Journalism*. Philadelphia: University of Pennsylvania Press.

Schreiber, Carl. 1930. "Mr. Poe at His Conjurations Again." *Colophon* 2 (May): 1–11.

Schudson, Michael. 1978. *Discovering the News: A Social History of American Newspapers*. New York: Basic Books.

Sedgwick, Eve Kosofsky. 1985. *Between Men: English Literature and Male Homosocial Desire*. New York: Columbia University Press.

——. 1986. *The Coherence of Gothic Conventions*. New York: Methuen.

Shattuck, Roger. 1980. *The Forbidden Experiment: The Story of the Wild Boy of Aveyron*. New York: Farrar, Straus, and Giroux.

Shaw, Peter. 1982. "Plagiary." *American Scholar* 332–50.

Sheridan, Richard Brinsley. 1979. *The Rivals*. Edited by Elizabeth Duthie. New York: Norton.

Shore, Laurence. 1986. *Southern Capitalists: The Ideological Leadership of an Elite, 1832–1865*. Chapel Hill: University of North Carolina Press.

Siegel, Frederick F. 1987. *The Roots of Southern Distinctiveness: Tobacco and Society in Danville, Virginia, 1780–1865*. Chapel Hill: University of North Carolina Press.

Silverman, Kaja. 1988. *The Acoustic Mirror: The Female Voice in Psychoanalysis.* Bloomington: Indiana University Press.

Silverman, Kenneth. 1991. *Edgar Allan Poe: Mournful and Never-Ending Remembrance.* New York: HarperCollins.

Simpson, Lewis P. 1975. *The Dispossessed Garden: Pastoral and History in Southern Literature.* Athens: University of Georgia Press.

——. 1989. *Mind and the American Civil War: A Meditation on Lost Causes.* Baton Rouge: Louisiana State University Press.

Smith-Rosenberg, Carroll. 1985. "The Abortion Movement and the AMA, 1850–1880." In *Disorderly Conduct: Visions of Gender in Victorian America*, 217–44. Oxford: Oxford University Press.

Spenser, Edmund. 1977. *The Faerie Queene.* Edited by A. C. Hamilton. New York: Longman.

Stafford, John. 1952. *The Literary Criticism of "Young America": A Study of the Relationship of Politics and Literature, 1837–1850.* Berkeley: University of California Press.

Stansell, Christine. 1987. *City of Women: Sex and Class in New York, 1789–1860.* Chicago: Knopf.

Stovall, Floyd. 1925. "The Women of Poe's Poems and Tales." *Texas Studies in English* 5:187–204.

Stowe, Harriet Beecher. 1982. *Uncle Tom's Cabin; or, Life among the Lowly.* Edited by Ann Douglas. Harmondsworth: Penguin Books.

Stowe, Steven M. 1987. *Intimacy and Power in the Old South: Ritual in the Lives of the Planters.* Baltimore: Johns Hopkins University Press.

Taine, Hippolyte. 1875. *The Ancient Regime.* New York: Henry Holt.

Tanner, Tony. 1979. *Adultery in the Novel: Contract and Transgression.* Baltimore: Johns Hopkins University Press.

Tate, Allen. 1967. "Our Cousin, Mr. Poe." In *Poe, A Collection of Critical Essays*, edited by Robert Regan, 38–50. Englewood Cliffs, N.J.: Prentice-Hall.

Thomas, Dwight, and David K. Jackson. 1987. *The Poe Log.* Boston: G. K. Hall.

Thompson, G. R. 1988. "Edgar Allan Poe and the Writers of the Old South." In *Columbia Literary History of the United States*, edited by Emory Elliott, 262–77. New York: Columbia University Press.

Todd, Janet. 1986. *Sensibility: An Introduction.* London: Methuen.

Townshend, Chauncey Hare. 1982. *Facts in Mesmerism, with Reasons for a Dispassionate Inquiry into It.* 1841. Reprint, New York: Da Capo Press.

Trachtenberg, Alan. 1974. "Experiments in Another Country: Stephen Crane's City Sketches." *Southern Review* 10, no. 2:266.

Treviranus, G. R. 1802. *Biologie oder die Philosophie der libenden Natur.* Leipzig: n.p.

Tucker, Nathaniel Beverly. 1836. *George Balcombe: A Novel.* 2 vols. New York: Harper and Brothers.

Twain, Mark. 1980. *Life on the Mississippi.* New York: Signet.

——. 1985. *The Adventures of Huckleberry Finn.* Berkeley: University of California Press.

Wade, Richard C. 1964. *Slavery in the Cities, 1820–1860.* Oxford: Oxford University Press.

Walker, I. M., ed. 1986. *Edgar Allan Poe: The Critical Heritage.* New York: Routledge.

Walsh, John. 1968. *Poe the Detective: The Curious Circumstances behind "The Mystery of Marie Rogêt."* New Brunswick, N.J.: Rutgers University Press.

Warner, Michael. 1990. *The Letters of the Republic: Publication and the Public Sphere in Eighteenth-Century America.* Cambridge: Harvard University Press.

Warner, Samuel. 1971. "Authentic and Impartial Narrative of the Tragical Scene which Was Witnessed in Southampton Country (Virginia) on Monday the 22nd of August." In *Slave Revolt of 1831: A Compilation of Source Material,* edited by Henry Irving Tragle, 281–300. Amherst: University of Massachusetts Press.

Whalen, Terence. 1992. "Edgar Allan Poe and the Horrid Laws of Political Economy." *American Quarterly* 44, no. 3 (September): 381–417.

Wilbur, Richard. 1967. "Recent Studies of Edgar Allan Poe." *New York Review of Books* 9, no. 1:26–27.

Williams, Linda. 1989. *Hardcore: Power, Pleasure, and the "Frenzy of the Visible."* Berkeley: University of California Press.

Williams, Raymond. 1958. *Culture and Society, 1780–1950.* New York: Harper and Row.

Williams, William Carlos. 1956. *In the American Grain.* New York: New Directions.

Wimsatt, William Kurtz. 1941. "Poe and the Mystery of Mary Rogers." *PMLA* 56, no. 1 (March): 230–48.

——. 1949–50. "Mary Rogers, John Rogers, and Others." *American Literature* 21: 482–84.

Wolf, Bryan J. 1992. "How the West Was Hung, Or, When I Hear the Word 'Culture' I Take Out My Checkbook." *American Quarterly* 44, no. 3 (September): 418–38.

Wolff, Janet. 1985. "The Invisible *Flâneuse*: Women and the Literature of Modernity." *Theory, Culture, and Society* 2, no. 3:37–46.

Woodbury, George E. 1928. *The Life of Edgar Allan Poe.* 2 vols. New York: Biblo and Tannen.

Workers' Writers' Program of the Work Projects Administration in the State of Virginia. 1940. New York: Hastings House Publishers.

Wordsworth, William. 1974. *Wordsworth's Literary Criticism.* Edited by W. J. B. Owen. London: Routledge and Kegan Paul.

——. 1984. *William Wordsworth.* Edited by Stephen McGill. Oxford: Oxford University Press.

Worthen, Samuel Copp. 1948–49. "Poe and the Beautiful Cigar Girl." *American Literature* 20:305–12.

Wright, Richard. 1966. *Native Son.* New York: Harper and Row.

Wyatt-Brown, Bertram. 1982. *Southern Honor: Ethics and Behavior in the Old South.* Oxford: Oxford University Press.

——. 1988. "The Mask of Obedience: Male Slave Psychology in the Old South." *American Historical Review* 93 (December): 1228–52.

Zizek, Slavoj. 1989. *The Sublime Object of Ideology.* London: Verso.

Contributors

GILLIAN BROWN is associate professor of English at the University of Utah, and the author of *Domestic Individualism: Imagining Self in Nineteenth-Century America*. She is now working on a study of ideas of transmission in the nineteenth century.

STANLEY CAVELL is Walter M. Cabot Professor of Aesthetics and the General Theory of Value at Harvard University. One of America's leading philosophers, he is the author of a multitude of books, including *The World Viewed, The Senses of Walden, Pursuits of Happiness*, and *Must We Mean What We Say?*

EVA CHERNIAVSKY is assistant professor of English at Indiana University. Her essay is part of a manuscript entitled *"That Pale Mother Rising": Sentimental Discourses and the Imitation of Motherhood in Nineteenth-Century America*. Her work has appeared in *Arizona Quarterly* and *Qui Parle*.

JOAN DAYAN is professor of English at the University of Arizona. She is the author of *Fables of Mind: An Inquiry into Poe's Fiction*, and of a forthcoming book on Voudoun. Her essays on Haitian culture and French literature have appeared in *Raritan, Yale Review, Arizona Quarterly*, and *Yale French Studies*.

JONATHAN ELMER is assistant professor of English at Indiana University. He is the author of "The Exciting Conflict: The Rhetoric of Pornography and Anti-pornography" (*Cultural Critique*), and of a study of Roland Barthes in *Qui Parle*. His essay is drawn from a book-length project, *Poe and the Imagination of Mass Culture*.

JOHN T. IRWIN is professor of English and director of the Writing Seminars at Johns Hopkins University. His critical works include *Doubling and Repetition/Incest and Revenge, American Hieroglyphics*, and *The Mystery to the Solution*.

BARBARA JOHNSON is professor of Romance languages and literatures at Harvard University. She is the author of *The Critical Difference* and, most recently, *A World of Difference*.

DAVID LEVERENZ is professor of English at the University of Florida. His publications include *Manhood and the American Renaissance, The Language of Puritan Feeling, Mindful Pleasures: Essays on Thomas Pynchon*, coedited with George Levine, and various articles and essays.

MEREDITH L. MCGILL is assistant professor of English and of history and literature at Harvard University. She has published on Wallace Stevens and on American copyright law, and is now writing a book on antebellum American literature and reprint culture.

STEPHEN RACHMAN is assistant professor of English at Michigan State University. He is currently completing a manuscript entitled *Narrative Pathologies: Plagiarism, Exhaustion, and Obscenity in the American Renaissance*.

LOUIS A. RENZA, chair of the English Department at Dartmouth University, has written widely on American literature. His books include *A "White Heron" and the Question of a Minor Literature*.

SHAWN ROSENHEIM, associate professor of English and American Studies at Williams College, has published on Poe in *ELH* and *American Quarterly*. His essay is part of a manuscript entitled *The King of Secret Readers: Edgar Allan Poe and the Cryptographic Imagination*.

LAURA SALTZ teaches writing at Harvard University. She is completing a dissertation on women's bodies in American fiction and film between 1900 and 1920.